Managing and Using MySQL

SECOND EDITION

Managing and Using MySQL

George Reese, Randy Jay Yarger, and Tim King
with Hugh E. Williams

O'REILLY®

Beijing · Cambridge · Farnham · Köln · Paris · Sebastopol · Taipei · Tokyo

Managing and Using MySQL, Second Edition
by George Reese, Randy Jay Yarger, and Tim King
with Hugh E. Williams

Published by O'Reilly Media, Inc., 1005 Gravenstein Highway North, Sebastopol, CA 95472.

O'Reilly Media, Inc. books may be purchased for educational, business, or sales promotional use. Online editions are also available for most titles (*safari.oreilly.com*). For more information, contact our corporate/institutional sales department: (800) 998-9938 or *corporate@oreilly.com*.

Editors:	Andy Oram and Ellen Siever
Production Editor:	Linley Dolby
Cover Designer:	Edie Freedman
Interior Designer:	David Futato

Printing History:

July 1999:	First Edition (released under the title *MySQL & mSQL*).
April 2002:	Second Edition.

 This book uses RepKover™, a durable and flexible lay-flat binding.

ISBN: 0-596-00211-4
[M]

Table of Contents

Preface

Programmers have always put together software on their own time to "scratch their own itches." Until the 1990s, however, programmers lacked distribution mediums for mass marketing their creations. The Internet changed that and gave life to grass-roots software distribution philosophies that have challenged those of the software giants. These philosophies include the Free Software and Open Software movements.

Though significant differences cause endless debate between the Free Software and Open Software camps, they share a core belief in the freedom to access and modify the source code of any legally licensed software. Though neither philosophy revolves directly around price, both have had the ultimate effect of reducing the cost of some traditionally high-cost software. The most famous example of this effect is, of course, the Linux operating system.

Database software has always been notoriously overpriced. The entire fortune of Oracle is largely founded on a single product—the Oracle database engine. Consequently, only large corporations have had the financial resources to leverage the power of relational databases. While database vendors struggled with how to license their software on the Internet, however, several groups of people were busy developing free and low-cost database solutions based on Free and Open Software philosophies. Our focus is one of these databases: MySQL.

MySQL is powerful and flexible, while at the same time lightweight and efficient. It packs a large feature set into a very small, fast engine. While it does not have anywhere near the full feature set of expensive corporate databases, it easily offers enough to meet the needs of mid-range database management.

Audience

This book is primarily for two classes of readers. The most obvious is the reader interested in using MySQL from either a database administration perspective or from a database programmer perspective. In addition, anyone who wants to learn about relational database administration and programming without paying out the nose for a license from one of the big guys will find MySQL an excellent starting point.

From a database administrator's perspective, we cover the basic methods of creating and managing databases and tables in MySQL. We go beyond the simple tasks and provide performance tuning and troubleshooting tips to help you make sure your MySQL applications are running at their best. We assume no prior knowledge of SQL or relational databases.

Database programmers will find that we have covered all the major programming interfaces from the most popular client/server and web programming languages. When we cover the interface for a particular language, we assume the reader has a basic grasp of the language in question. For example, in the Java™ chapter, we assume the reader knows how to write basic Java applications, and we show how to make those Java applications talk to MySQL databases.

The immense popularity of MySQL on the Web has made it natural to provide a focus on CGI programming with *Managing and Using MySQL*. Web developers should therefore find this book useful in describing how to drive their web sites with a MySQL database. For these chapters, very little CGI knowledge is needed, but we still assume that the reader is familiar with the basics of the programming language in question.

Purpose

At first glance, the purpose of this book seems obvious: MySQL is one of the most popular open source applications of all time. One of the biggest complaints about open source projects is the lack of comprehensive and comprehensible documentation. In the case of MySQL, however, lack of online documentation is rarely a problem.

MySQL has a wonderfully complete and free online reference manual available from the web site, at *http://www.mysql.com*. This manual covers the full MySQL SQL syntax, installation, and its C API, as well as database administration and performance tuning.

To make matters even more complex, MySQL is a moving target because of rapid development. In fact, "moving target" is a euphemism. Thanks mainly to the efforts of Michael "Monty" Widenius, MySQL is moving about as fast as an SST. So be prepared; you may find that some of the information in this book is either ahead of older versions or behind newer versions.

Using This Book

We have divided this book into four sections. Part I introduces the world of relational databases and MySQL's place in that world. Part II supports database administrators by covering all the elements of MySQL database administration. Part III builds upon the basic understanding of MySQL from the first section by demonstrating how to build applications that use your MySQL database. Finally, in Part IV, we provide a reference section as a resource for quickly looking up APIs we cover in the first three sections.

Part I is naturally aimed at people new to relational databases and/or MySQL. It begins with a basic introduction to MySQL and relational databases and covers getting started with MySQL. You might want to skip Part I if you are an experienced MySQL user or simply skim it if you have experience with other database engines.

The job of the database administrator is to make certain that the database is up and running efficiently and supporting its applications. If this is your job, Part II is for you. We cover security, performance tuning, and database design. Proper database design is essential for database architects if the goal is to build database applications flexible enough to scale as their needs change. You also need a proper database design if you want your database to actually perform well.

Part III is aimed at database architects and programmers. It contains chapters devoted to programming in specific languages or using specific tools. Of particular interest to web programmers will be the chapters on Perl, Java, Python, and PHP.

The book closes with a reference section covering elements of MySQL and some APIs.

Conventions Used in This Book

The following conventions are used in this book:

Constant width

> Used to indicate anything that might appear in a program, including keywords, function names, SQL commands, and variable names. This font is also used for code examples, output displayed by commands, and system configuration files.

Constant width bold

> Used to indicate user input.

Constant width italic

> Used to indicate an element (e.g., a filename or variable) that you supply.

Italic

> Used to indicate directory names, filenames, program names, Unix commands, and URLs. This font is also used to introduce new terms and for emphasis.

 This icon is used to indicate a tip, suggestion, or general note.

 This icon is used to indicate a warning.

Comments and Questions

Please address comments and questions concerning this book to the publisher:

O'Reilly & Associates, Inc.
1005 Gravenstein Highway North
Sebastopol, CA 95472
(800) 998-9938 (in the U.S. or Canada)
(707) 829-0515 (international or local)
(707) 829-0104 (fax)

To ask technical questions or comment on the book, send email to:

bookquestions@oreilly.com

Before submitting a bug report concerning MySQL, please check the online manual (and particularly the list of problems and common errors) at:

http://www.mysql.com/Manual_chapter/manual_toc.html

You can search the MySQL mailing list at:

http://www.mysql.com/doc.html

and the MySQL web site at:

http://www.mysql.com/search.html

We have a web site for the book, where we'll list examples, errata, and any plans for future editions. You can access this page at:

http://www.oreilly.com/catalog/msql2/

For more information about this book and others, see the O'Reilly web site:

http://www.oreilly.com

Acknowledgments

The authors would first like to thank their editors, Andy Oram and Ellen Siever, for both their skill at making our work look more professional and for the less obvious and likely less enjoyable task of putting us back on focus when our minds would wander.

Hugh Williams contributed the two chapters on PHP.

We also owe a huge debt of gratitude to those who provided us with critical looks at both editions of the book. Anyone familiar with MySQL knows the name Michael Widenius, the head of the MySQL project. He and another member of the MySQL team, Paul DuBois, sent in many valuable comments. Brian Jepson, Glenn MacGregor, Michael Schecter, and Jeremy Zawodny provided useful comments on the book overall.

Tim Allwine intensively reviewed the Perl material in Chapter 9 and provided some new examples and ideas. Chris Brooks and Tim Bunce also made corrections to the Perl code.

From Randy Yarger

I would like to thank my fiancée, Stacie Sheldon, for the support and love that has kept me sane. I would also like to thank Andy Oram for encouraging a relatively unknown author. Finally, but definitely not lastly, I would like to thank those who made it possible for me to be here: my mother, my father, and my creator.

From George Reese

I would specifically like to thank my wife, Monique, for using her professional proof-reading abilities on each one of my chapters. Leigh Caldwell also provided some critical eleventh-hour feedback on the first edition of the MySQL chapters. Finally, I have to mention my cats, Misty, Gypsy, and Tia.

From Tim King

I wish to acknowledge Professor John Carlis, for getting me interested in database technology and data modeling in the first place; Mark Kale, for teaching me more about it than I ever learned in college; the lovely Ann Soter, for her moral support and patience; and my mother and father, for encouraging my interest in computers before it was cool to be a geek!

## PART I

Introduction

Getting started with MySQL requires you to install the database and configure it for use with your applications. In Part I, we will provide an introduction to relational databases and MySQL. By the end of this section, you should have MySQL installed and running and be ready to tackle system administration tasks.

## CHAPTER 1

MySQL

Anyone can relate to the gap in usefulness between piles of paper on a desktop and those same papers organized in a filing cabinet. The former is a mess. If you actually want a particular paper, you need to dig through the piles to find it. If you are lucky, you will just happen to start with the pile in which the desired paper is located. It could, however, require you to go through each piece of paper in each pile to find what you are seeking. With a filing cabinet, however, you know exactly where to look and will fumble through just a few papers to find your goal.

Relational databases have been acting as the electronic filing cabinets for the voluminous and complex data storage needs of large companies for over two decades. A relational database is simply the only tool capable of structuring most data so that it is actually usable—not just piles of bits on a hard drive. Until recently, you were simply out of luck if you wanted to build an application backed by a robust database on a small budget. Your choices were quite simple: shell out thousands—or even tens or hundreds of thousands—of dollars on Oracle or Sybase or build the application against "toy" databases such as Access and FileMakerPro. Thanks to such databases as mSQL, PostgreSQL, and MySQL, however, you now have a variety of choices that suit different needs. This book, of course, is the story of MySQL.[*]

Relational Databases

In the simplest terms, a database is a collection of data. An example of a nonelectronic database is the public library. The library stores books, periodicals, and other documents. When you need to locate some data at the library, you search through the card catalog or the periodicals index, or maybe you even ask the librarian. Those unsorted piles of papers on your desk also form a database. This database can potentially work, because the size of the database is incredibly small. A stack of papers certainly would not work with a larger set of data, such as the collections in the library.

---

[*] SQL is pronounced either "sequel" or "ess-que-ell," though the preferred form is "ess-que-ell."

The library would still be a database without the card catalog, periodicals index, and librarian; it would just be an unusable database. A database generally requires some sort of organization to be of value. The paper pile, for example, is of greater value when organized into filing cabinets. So, restating our definition, a database is an *organized* collection of data.

The library and the stack of papers have many similarities. They are both databases of documents. It makes no sense, however, to combine them because your papers are interesting only to you, and the library contains documents of general interest. Both databases have specific purposes and are organized according to those purposes. We will therefore amend our definition a bit further: a database is a collection of data that is organized and stored *according to some purpose*.

Traditional paper-based databases have many disadvantages. They require a tremendous amount of physical space. Libraries occupy entire buildings, and searching a library is relatively slow. Anyone who has spent time in a library knows that it can consume a nontrivial amount of time to find the information you seek. Libraries are also tedious to maintain, and an inordinate amount of time is spent keeping the catalogs and shelves consistent. Electronic storage of a database helps to address these issues.

MySQL is not a database, per se. It is computer software that enables you to create, maintain, and manage electronic databases. This category of software is known as a database management system (DBMS). A DBMS acts as a broker between the physical database and the users of that database.

When you began managing electronic information, you almost certainly used a flat file, such as a spreadsheet. The filesystem file is the electronic version of the pile of papers on your desk. You likely came to the conclusion that this sort of ad hoc electronic database did not meet your needs anymore. A DBMS is the logical next step for your database needs, and MySQL is the first stepping stone into the world of relational DBMSs.

A relational database is a special kind of database that organizes data into tables and represents relationships among those tables. These relationships enable you to combine data from multiple tables to provide different "views" of that data. Table 1-1 describes a table that might appear in a library's database.

Table 1-1. A table of books

ISBN	Title	Author
0-446-67424-9	L.A. Confidential	James Ellroy
0-201-54239-X	An Introduction to Database Systems	C.J. Date
0-87685-086-7	Post Office	Charles Bukowski
0-941423-38-7	The Man with the Golden Arm	Nelson Algren

Tables 1-2 and 1-3 are two tables that might appear in an NBA database.

Table 1-2. A table of NBA teams

Team #	Name	Coach
1	Sacramento Kings	Rick Adelman
2	Minnesota Timberwolves	Flip Saunders
3	L.A. Lakers	Phil Jackson
4	Portland Trailblazers	Mike Dunleavy

Table 1-3. A table of NBA players

Name	Position	Team #
Vlade Divac	Center	1
Kevin Garnett	Forward	2
Kobe Bryant	Guard	3
Rasheed Wallace	Forward	4
Damon Stoudamire	Guard	4
Shaquille O'Neal	Center	3

We will get into the specifics about tables later on, but you should note a few things about these examples. Each table has a name, several columns, and rows containing data for each of the columns. A relational database represents all of your data in tables just like this and provides you with retrieval operations that generate new tables from existing ones. Consequently, the user sees the entire database in the form of tables.

Also note that the "Team #" column appears in both tables. It encodes a relationship between a player and a team. By linking the "Team #" columns you can determine that Vlade Divac plays for the Sacramento Kings. You could also figure out all the players on the Portland Trailblazers. This linking of tables is called a *relational join*, or *join* for short.

A DBMS for a relational system is often called a relational database management system (RDBMS). MySQL is an RDBMS.

The History of MySQL

This story actually goes back to 1979 when MySQL's inventor, Michael Widenius (a.k.a. Monty) developed an in-house database tool called UNIREG for managing databases. UNIREG is a tty interface builder that uses a low-level connection to an ISAM storage with indexing. Since then, UNIREG has been rewritten in several different languages and extended to handle big databases. It is still available today, but is largely supplanted by MySQL.

The Swedish company TcX began developing web-based applications in 1994 and used UNIREG to support this effort.* Unfortunately, UNIREG created too much overhead to be successful in dynamically generating web pages. TcX thus began looking at alternatives.

TcX looked at SQL and mSQL.† mSQL was a cheap DBMS that gave away its source code with database licenses—almost open source. At the time, mSQL was still in its 1.x releases and had even fewer features than the currently available version. Most important to Monty, it did not support any indexes. mSQL's performance was therefore poor in comparison to UNIREG.

Monty contacted David Hughes, the author of mSQL, to see if Hughes would be interested in connecting mSQL to UNIREG's B+ ISAM handler to provide indexing to mSQL. Hughes was already well on his way to mSQL 2, however, and had his indexing infrastructure in place. TcX decided to create a database server that was more compatible with its requirements.

TcX was smart enough not to try to reinvent the wheel. It built upon UNIREG and capitalized on the growing number of third-party mSQL utilities by writing an API into its system that was, at least initially, practically identical to the mSQL API. Consequently, an mSQL user who wanted to move to TcX's more feature-rich database server would only have to make trivial changes to any existing code. The code supporting this new database, however, was completely original.

By May 1995, TcX had a database that met its internal needs: MySQL 3.11. A business partner, David Axmark at Detron HB, began pressing TcX to release this server on the Internet and follow a business model pioneered by Aladdin's L. Peter Deutsch. Specifically, this business model enabled TcX developers to work on projects of their own choosing and release the results as free software. Commercial support for the software generated enough income to create a comfortable lifestyle. The result is a very flexible copyright that makes MySQL "more free" than mSQL. Eventually, Monty released MySQL under the GPL so that MySQL is now "free as in speech" and "free as in beer."

As for the name MySQL, Monty says, "It is not perfectly clear where the name MySQL derives from. TcX's base directory and a large amount of their libraries and tools have had the prefix 'My' for well over ten years. However, my daughter (some years younger) is also named My. So which of the two gave its name to MySQL is still a mystery."

A few years ago, TcX evolved into the company MySQL AB, at *http://www.mysql. com*. This change better enabled its commercial control of the development and support of MySQL. MySQL AB, a Swedish company run by MySQL's core developers,

---

* For most of its existence, TcX had a single employee: Monty.
† mSQL is miniSQL, from Hughes Technologies.

owns the copyright to MySQL, as well as the trademark "MySQL." Since the initial Internet release of MySQL, it has been ported to a host of Unix operating systems (including Linux, FreeBSD, and Mac OS X), Win32, and OS/2. MySQL AB estimates that MySQL runs on about four million servers.

MySQL Design

Working from the legacy of mSQL, TcX decided MySQL had to be at least as fast as mSQL with a much greater feature set. At that time, mSQL defined good database performance, so TcX's goal was no small task. MySQL's specific design goals were speed, robustness, and ease of use. To get this sort of performance, TcX decided to make MySQL a multithreaded database engine. A multithreaded application performs many tasks at the same time as if multiple instances of that application were running simultaneously. Fortunately, multithreaded applications do not pay the very expensive cost of starting up new processes.

In being multithreaded, MySQL has many advantages. A separate thread handles each incoming connection with an extra thread that is always running to manage the connections. Multiple clients can perform read operations simultaneously without impacting one another. But write operations, to a degree that depends on the type of table in use, only hold up other clients that need access to the data being updated. While any thread is writing to a table, all other threads requesting access to that table simply wait until the table is free. Your client can perform any allowed operation without concern for other concurrent connections. The connection-managing thread prevents other threads from reading or writing to a table in the middle of an update.

Another advantage of this architecture is inherent to all multithreaded applications: even though the threads share the same process space, they execute individually. Because of this separation, multiprocessor machines can spread the threads across many CPUs as long as the host operating system supports multiple CPUs.

In addition to the performance gains introduced by multithreading, MySQL has a richer subset of SQL than mSQL. MySQL supports over a dozen data types and additionally supports SQL functions. Your application can access these functions through the American National Standards Institute (ANSI) SQL statements.

MySQL actually extends ANSI SQL with a few features. These features include new functions (ENCRYPT, WEEKDAY, IF, and others), the ability to increment fields (AUTO_INCREMENT and LAST_INSERT_ID), and case sensitivity.

Some SQL features found in the major database engines were omitted intentionally from MySQL. For the longest time, transaction support was the most notable omission. The latest releases of MySQL, however, provide support for transactions. Stored procedures, another notable omission, are scheduled for the 4.1 release that should be available at the same time as this book. Finally, MySQL does not support most additions to the SQL standard as of SQL3. The most important SQL3 feature missing from MySQL is support for object-oriented data types.

The Great Transaction Debate

Transactions are important for applications that support complex rules for concurrent updating of data. They prevent concurrent updates from putting the database in an inconsistent state at any point in the database's life.

Transactions are a relatively new feature of the MySQL database engine. In fact, the transaction features are not present unless you set up your tables to support them. Many people wondered what use MySQL was without transactions and why someone would set up a table without supporting them. The answer is one word: performance.

The minute you introduce transactions into the picture, the database takes a performance hit. Transactions add the overhead of complex locking and transaction logging. The complex locking includes support for transaction isolation levels, discussed in Chapter 8. Basically, however, increasing transaction isolation levels requires an increasing amount of work by the database to support the same functionality. The more work the database has to do for a task, the slower it performs that task.

Since 1996, MySQL AB has been using MySQL internally in an environment with more than 40 databases containing 10,000 tables. Of these 10,000 tables, more than 500 contain over 7 million records—about 100 GB of data.

MySQL Features

We have already mentioned multithreading as a key feature to support MySQL's performance design goals. It is the core feature around which MySQL is built. Other features include:

Openness
> MySQL is open in every sense of the term. Its SQL dialect uses ANSI SQL2 as its foundation. The database engine runs on countless platforms, including Windows 2000, Mac OS X, Linux, FreeBSD, and Solaris. If no binary is available for your platform, you have access to the source to compile to that platform.

Application support
> MySQL has an API for just about any programming language. Specifically, you can write database applications that access MySQL in C, C++, Eiffel, Java, Perl, PHP, Python, and Tcl. In this book, we cover C, Java, Python, Perl, and PHP.

Cross-database joins
> You can construct MySQL queries that can join tables from different databases.

Outer join support
> MySQL supports both left and right outer joins using both ANSI and ODBC syntax.

Internationalization

MySQL supports several different character sets, including ISO-8859-1, Big5, and Shift-JIS. It also supports sorting for different character sets and can be customized easily. Error messages can be provided in different languages as well.

Above all else, MySQL is cheap and fast. Other features of MySQL may attract you, but cost and performance are its greatest benefits. The other relational databases fall into two categories:

- Low-cost database engines such as mSQL, PostgreSQL, and InstantDB
- Commercial vendors such as Oracle, Microsoft, and Sybase

MySQL compares well with other free database engines. It blows them away, however, in terms of performance. In fact, mSQL does not compare with MySQL on any level. InstantDB compares reasonably on a feature level, but MySQL is still much faster. PostgreSQL has some cool SQL3 features, but it carries the bloat of commercial database engines. If you are looking at low-cost database engines and are using advanced SQL3 features, you probably want PostgresSQL; use MySQL if you are doing anything else.

Oddly enough, comparing MySQL with Oracle or some other commercial database is a lot like comparing MySQL with PostgreSQL. The commercial database engines support just about every feature you can think of, but all those features come at a performance cost. None of these database engines can compete with MySQL for read-heavy database applications. They certainly cannot compete on price. They really compete only in terms of SQL3 feature set and commercial support. MySQL AB is working to close the gap on both counts.

Like many applications, MySQL has a test suite that verifies that a newly compiled system does indeed support all the features it is supposed to support without breaking. The MySQL team calls its test suite "crash-me" because one of its features is to try to crash MySQL.

Somewhere along the way, someone noticed that crash-me was a portable program. Not only could it work on different operating systems, but you could use it to test different database engines. Since that discovery, crash-me has evolved from a simple test suite into a comparison program. The tests encompass all of standard SQL as well as extensions offered by many servers. In addition, the program tests the reliability of the server under stress. A complete test run gives a thorough picture of the capabilities of the database engine being tested.

You can use crash-me to compare two or more database engines online. The crash-me page is *http://www.mysql.com/information/crash-me.php*.

MySQL Applications

According to our definition, a database is an organized collection of data that serves some purpose. Simply having MySQL up and running is not sufficient to give your database a purpose. How you use the data you put in your MySQL database defines its purpose. Imagine a library where nobody ever reads the books. There would not be much point in storing and organizing all those books if they're never used. Now, imagine a library where you could not change or add to the collection. The utility of the library as a database would decrease over time since obsolete books could never be replaced and new books could never be added. In short, a library exists so that people may read the books and find the information they seek.

Databases exist so that people can interact with them. In the case of electronic databases, the interaction occurs not directly with the database, but indirectly through software applications. Before the emergence of the World Wide Web, databases typically were used by large corporations to support various business functions: accounting and finance, shipping and inventory control, manufacturing planning, human resources, and so on. The Web and more complex home computing tasks have helped move the need for database applications outside the realm of the large corporation.

Therefore, it is not surprising that the area in which databases have experienced the most explosive growth—an area where MySQL excels—is web application development. As the demand for more complex and robust web applications grows, so does the need for databases. A database backend can support many critical functions on the Web. Virtually any web content can be driven by a database.

Consider the example of a catalog retailer who wants to publish on the Web and accept orders online. If the contents of the catalog are entered directly into one or more HTML files, someone has to hand edit the files each time a new item is added to the catalog or a price is changed. If the catalog information is instead stored in a relational database, it is possible to publish real-time catalog updates simply by changing the product or price data in the database. It is also possible to integrate the online catalog with existing electronic order-processing systems. Using a database to drive such a web site has obvious advantages for both the retailer and the customer.

Here is how a simple web application typically interacts with a database. The database is on your web server or another machine to which your server can talk (a good DBMS makes this kind of distributed responsibility easy). You put a form on one web page that the user fills in with a query or data to submit. When the user submits the form to your server, the server runs a program that you've written to extract the data from the form. These programs are most often written as CGI scripts and Java servlets, but they can also be implemented by embedding programming commands directly inside the HTML page. We will look at all of these methods later in this book.

Now your program knows what the user is asking for or wishes to add to the database. The program issues an SQL query or update, and the database magically takes care of the rest. Any results obtained from the database can be formatted by your program into a new HTML page to send back to the user.

What You Get

MySQL is a relational database management system. It includes not only a server process to manage databases, but also tools for accessing the databases and building applications against those databases. Among these tools are:

mysql
> Executes SQL against MySQL, and can be used to execute SQL commands stored in a file

mysqlaccess
> Manages users

mysqladmin
> Enables you to manage the database server, including the creation and deletion of databases

mysqld
> The actual MySQL server process

mysqldump
> Dumps the definition and contents of a MySQL database or table to a file

mysqlhotcopy
> Performs a hot backup of a MySQL database

mysqlimport
> Imports data in different file formats into a MySQL table

mysqlshow
> Shows information about the MySQL server and any objects (such as databases and tables) in that server

safe_mysqld or *mysqld_safe*
> Safely starts up and manages the *mysqld* process on a Unix machine

Over the course of this book, we will go into the details of each of these tools. How you use these tools and this book will depend on how you want to use MySQL.

Are you a database administrator (DBA) responsible for the MySQL runtime environment? The chief concerns of a DBA are the installation, maintenance, security, and performance of MySQL. We tackle these issues in Part II.

Are you a database or application architect responsible for the design of solid database applications? We address the impact of MySQL on these issues in the first few chapters of Part III.

Are you a database application developer responsible for building applications that rely on a database? Database application developers need tools for providing their applications with data from MySQL. Most of Part III covers the various programming APIs that support application interaction with MySQL.

No matter who you are, you need to know the language spoken by MySQL: SQL. Like most database engines, MySQL supports the ANSI SQL2 standard with proprietary extensions. Chapter 3, is a comprehensive tutorial on MySQL's dialect of SQL. The details of the language are covered in Part IV.

## CHAPTER 2

Installation

This chapter describes how to download and install MySQL. MySQL is available for a wide variety of target operating systems. In this chapter, we provide an overview of how to install MySQL in binary and source formats for Solaris and Linux as well as binary installation for Windows 9x/NT/2000/XP. Though we specifically address only Solaris, Linux, and Win32, the Solaris/Linux instructions apply to most Unix-based operating systems, including Mac OS X, FreeBSD, and AIX.

Preparation

Before you begin installing MySQL, you must answer the following questions:

1. Which version will you install?

   This is typically a decision between the latest stable release and the latest development release. In general, we recommended that you go with the latest stable release, unless you need specific features in a development release that are not available in the stable release.

   The current stable versions are MySQL 3.23 and MySQL-Max 3.23. MySQL-Max is a beta release of the MySQL software with support for transactions (via BerkeleyDB and InnoDB tables). The standard MySQL binary does not include support for these types of tables.

   The current development versions are MySQL 4.0 and MySQL-Max 4.0. The installation instructions provided here will work with either Version 3.23 or 4.0.

2. Are you going to install MySQL as root or as another user?

   MySQL does not require root access to run, but installing it as root will enable you to make one copy available to everyone on your system. If you do not have root access, you must install it in your home directory. However, even if you install MySQL as root, it is a good idea to run it as a different user. In this way, all data in the database can be protected from all other users by setting the permissions on the datafiles to be readable by only the special MySQL user. In addition, if the security of the database becomes compromised, the attacker has access only to the special MySQL user account, which has no privileges beyond the database.

3. Do you want to install a source or binary distribution?

In general, we recommend that you install a binary distribution if one is available for your platform. In most cases, a binary distribution is easier to install than a source distribution and provides the fastest and most reliable way to get MySQL up and running. The MySQL team and contributors have gone to great lengths to ensure that the binary distributions on their site are built with the best possible options. However, you may encounter cases in which you need to build your MySQL distribution from scratch. For example, here are a few reasons why you would need to install a source distribution:

- You are unable to locate a binary distribution for your target system.
- You want to configure MySQL with some combination of options that is not available in any of the binary distributions.
- You want to compile in support for additional character sets.
- You want to optimize your MySQL installation by modifying compiler options or by using a different compiler.
- You need to apply a bug fix patch.

Having decided on a version and whether to use a binary or source distribution, you can complete the first step in installing MySQL: downloading it. The best place to obtain MySQL source or binary distributions is from the MySQL downloads page, at *http://www.mysql.com/downloads*. You can alternately find MySQL on one of the many mirror sites, at *http://www.mysql.com/downloads/mirrors.html*.

Unix Installation

MySQL is available for a wide variety of Unix platforms. In this chapter, we go over the steps necessary to install binary and source distributions on Solaris and Linux. These can also be used as a general guide to installation on other operating systems, which should be very similar to our examples.

Binary (Tarball) Distributions

To install a binary distribution, you need the *tar* utility and the GNU *gunzip* utility. These tools are now a part of the standard distribution of many Unix systems.

 Solaris *tar* is known to have problems with some of the long filenames in the MySQL binary distribution. To unpack the binary distribution successfully on a Solaris system, you may need to obtain GNU *gtar*. A binary distribution version of this is available from *http://www.mysql.com/downloads/os-solaris.html*.

The binary distributions are all named using the following convention: *mysql-version-os.tar.gz*. The *version* placeholder is the version number of the software contained in the distribution. The *os* placeholder is the operating system for which the binary distribution is built. Binary distributions named *mysql-max-version-os.tar.gz* contain a version of MySQL compiled with support for transaction-safe tables.

Assume, for example, that we have chosen to install MySQL 3.23.40 on a Sun Solaris server. Also assume the distribution file *mysql-3.23.40-sun-solaris2.7-sparc.tar.gz* has been downloaded into the */tmp* directory.

We recommend that you create a user and group for MySQL administration. This user should be used to run the *mysql* server and perform administrative tasks. It is possible to run the server as root, but this is not recommended.

The first step is to create a user to run the MySQL server. On Solaris and Linux, this can be done with the *useradd* and *groupadd* utilities. In our example, we create a user called *mysql*. In practice, you can choose any username you like. Typically, you will need to be the root user to successfully perform these tasks, so before anything else, use the *su* command to become root:

```
$ su - root
$ groupadd mysql
$ useradd -g mysql mysql
```

Select the desired location for the *mysql* software and change your current directory to that location. In this example, we install into */usr/local*, which is the standard install location assumed by the MySQL software. You can, of course, install it wherever you like. If you choose an install location other than */usr/local*, you will need to modify some of the scripts provided by MySQL. See the MySQL installation instructions at *http://www.mysql.com/documentation* for more details.

```
$ cd /usr/local
```

Now unpack the software:

```
$ gunzip -c /tmp/mysql-3.23.40-sun-solaris2.7-sparc.tar.gz | tar -xf -
```

Since we are installing on a Solaris server, the previous command may not work if GNU *tar* is installed as a separate version of *tar*. In this case, use the command:

```
$ gunzip -c /tmp/mysql-3.23.40-sun-solaris2.7-sparc.tar.gz | gtar -xf -
```

You should now see a new directory.

```
$ ls -ld mysql*
total 1
drwxr-xr-x  28 user  users  1024 Jul 18 14:29 mysql-3.23.40-sun-solaris2.7-sparc/
```

The next step is to create a symbolic link so that the installation can be referred to as */usr/local/mysql*:

```
$ ln -s mysql-3.23.40-sun-solaris2.7-sparc mysql
$ ls -ld mysql*
lrwxrwxrwx 1 user users 31  Jul 26 18:32 mysql -> mysql-3.23.40-sun-solaris2.7-sparc/
drwxr-xr-x 12 user users 1024 Jul 18 17:07 mysql-3.23.40-sun-solaris2.7-sparc/
```

Now, let's go into the *mysql* directory and have a look around:

```
$ cd mysql
$ ls -l
total 4476
-rw-r--r--   1 user      users        19076 Jul 18 14:21 COPYING
-rw-r--r--   1 user      users        28011 Jul 18 14:21 COPYING.LIB
-rw-r--r--   1 user      users       122213 Jul 18 14:19 ChangeLog
-rw-r--r--   1 user      users        14842 Jul 18 14:21 INSTALL-BINARY
-rw-r--r--   1 user      users         1976 Jul 18 14:19 README
drwxr-xr-x   2 user      users         1024 Jul 18 17:07 bin/
-rwxr-xr-x   1 user      users          773 Jul 18 17:07 configure*
drwxr-x---   4 user      users         1024 Jul 26 18:27 data/
drwxr-xr-x   2 user      users         1024 Jul 18 17:07 include/
drwxr-xr-x   2 user      users         1024 Jul 18 17:07 lib/
-rw-r--r--   1 user      users      2321255 Jul 18 14:21 manual.html
-rw-r--r--   1 user      users      1956858 Jul 18 14:21 manual.txt
-rw-r--r--   1 user      users        80487 Jul 18 14:21 manual_toc.html
drwxr-xr-x   6 user      users         1024 Jul 18 17:07 mysql-test/
drwxr-xr-x   2 user      users         1024 Jul 18 17:07 scripts/
drwxr-xr-x   3 user      users         1024 Jul 18 17:07 share/
drwxr-xr-x   7 user      users         1024 Jul 18 17:07 sql-bench/
drwxr-xr-x   2 user      users         1024 Jul 18 17:07 support-files/
drwxr-xr-x   2 user      users         1024 Jul 18 17:07 tests/
```

Although the software is now installed, we have a few set-up tasks left to do. Run *scripts/mysql_install_db* to create the MySQL grant tables:

```
$ scripts/mysql_install_db
Preparing db table
Preparing host table
Preparing user table
Preparing func table
Preparing tables_priv table
Preparing columns_priv table
Installing all prepared tables
010726 19:40:05  ./bin/mysqld: Shutdown Complete
```

Set up the ownership of the binaries so they are owned by root in the MySQL administrator group that you created earlier (in our case, *mysql*):

```
$ chown -R root /usr/local/mysql
$ chgrp -R mysql /usr/local/mysql
```

Set the ownership of the data directories to the MySQL administrative user you created earlier (for this example, *mysql*):

```
$ chown -R mysql /usr/local/mysql/data
```

MySQL is now installed and ready to go. To start the server, run *safe_mysqld*:

```
$ bin/safe_mysqld --user=mysql &
```

Typically, you will want to start up MySQL at server boot. To do this, you can copy *support-files/mysql.server* to the appropriate location on your system. This is covered in Chapter 5.

Binary (RPM) Distributions

The recommended way to install MySQL on an Intel Linux system is via RedHat Package Manager (RPM). Table 2-1 lists the files that comprise a full MySQL installation.

Table 2-1. The files in a full MySQL RPM distribution

Filename	Description
MySQL-version.i386.rpm	MySQL server software
MySQL-client-version.i386.rpm	MySQL client software
MySQL-bench-version.i386.rpm	MySQL tests and benchmarks; requires the Perl and *msql-mysql* RPMs
MySQL-devel-version.i386.rpm	Libraries and include files for compiling other MySQL clients
MySQL-shared-version.i386.rpm	MySQL client shared libraries

The procedure for installing an RPM distribution is simple. First, obtain the RPMs you wish to install. At a minimum, you should install the server and client software. Second, use the *rpm* utility to install the packages.

For this example, we assume that all the RPM packages for Version 3.23.40 on an Intel Linux system will be installed. Also, assume the following RPM files have been downloaded to */tmp*:

- *MySQL-3.23.40-1.i386.rpm*
- *MySQL-client-3.23.40-1.i386.rpm*
- *MySQL-devel-3.23.40-1.i386.rpm*
- *MySQL-bench-3.23.40-1.i386.rpm*
- *MySQL-shared-3.23.40-1.i386.rpm*

Execute this sequence of commands to install them:

```
$ rpm -i /tmp/MySQL-3.23.40-1.i386.rpm
$ rpm -i /tmp/MySQL-client-3.23.40-1.i386.rpm
$ rpm -i /tmp/MySQL-devel-3.23.40-1.i386.rpm
$ rpm -i /tmp/MySQL-bench-3.23.40-1.i386.rpm
$ rpm -i /tmp/MySQL-shared-3.23.40-1.i386.rpm
```

The RPM creates the appropriate entries in */etc/rc.d* to automatically start and stop the server at system boot and shutdown. The RPM also starts the *mysql* server, so after the RPM install is complete, you are ready to start using MySQL.

The RPM distributions place the files in different locations from the tarball distributions. To examine an RPM to determine where the files were placed, use the RPM query option:

```
$ rpm -qpl MySQL-version.i386.rpm
```

If you wish to determine the location but have discarded the RPM files already, you can query the RPM database:

```
$ rpm -ql MySQL-version
```

Also note that the RPM places data in */var/lib/data* instead of */usr/local/mysql/data*.

Source Distributions

Installing from a source distribution is different from installing a binary distribution. Since you will be building the software from source code, you will need a full set of tools, including:

- GNU *gunzip*
- *tar* or GNU *tar*
- An ANSI C++ compiler: GNU gcc 2.95.2 (or higher) is recommended; egcs 1.0.2/ egcs 2.91.66, SGI C++, and SunPro C++ are known to work (for the Mac OS X, gcc is part of the OS X Developers Tools at *http://www.apple.com/developer*)
- make (GNU make is recommended)

Compiling from source is an intricate process with many possible variations depending upon your operating system, your desired configuration, your toolset, etc. As a result, we provide an overview of the process to get you started. However, we assume that you are experienced with building software from source. If you encounter problems building or installing MySQL, please refer to the full MySQL install documentation set at *http://www.mysql.com/documentation*.

The source distributions are named using the following convention: *mysql-version. tar.gz*. There is no special MySQL-Max version of the MySQL source, because all versions are compiled from the same code base.

For our example, assume that *mysql-3.23.40.tar.gz* has been downloaded to */tmp*.

As with the binary install, the first step is to create a user who will run the MySQL server:

```
$ su - root
$ groupadd mysql
$ useradd -g mysql mysql
```

In your filesystem, move to the location where you would like to unpack the source. Unpack the bundle:

```
$ gunzip -c /tmp/mysql-3.23.40.tar.gz | tar -xf -
```

Move into the newly created *mysql* directory. You must configure and build MySQL from this location:

```
$ cd mysql-3.23.40
```

Now, use the *configure* script to configure your build. In this example, we use the *prefix* option to set the install location to */usr/local/mysql*:

```
$ ./configure --prefix=/usr/local/mysql
```

The *configure* utility offers a host of options that you can use to control how your build is set up. For more help on the available options, run:

```
$ ./configure --help
```

Also, check the full install documentation at *http://www.mysql.com/documentation* for a list of common *configure* options.

The *configure* utility may take a few minutes to complete. Once it is done, it is time to build the binaries:

```
$ make
```

If all goes well, you now have a binary version of MySQL. The last thing you need to do is install it:

```
$ make install
```

The software is now installed. We have a few set-up tasks left to do. Run *mysql_install_db* to create the MySQL grant tables:

```
$ cd /usr/local/mysql
$ scripts/mysql_install_db
Preparing db table
Preparing host table
Preparing user table
Preparing func table
Preparing tables_priv table
Preparing columns_priv table
Installing all prepared tables
010726 19:40:05  ./bin/mysqld: Shutdown Complete
```

Set up the ownership of the binaries so they are owned by root and in the MySQL adminstrator group that you created earlier (in this case, *mysql*):

```
$ chown -R root /usr/local/mysql
$ chgrp -R mysql /usr/local/mysql
```

Set the ownership of the data directories to the MySQL administrative user you created earlier (for this example, *mysql*):

```
$ chown -R mysql /usr/local/mysql/data
```

MySQL is now installed and ready to go. To start the server, run *safe_mysqld*:

```
$ bin/safe_mysqld --user=mysql &
```

Typically, you will want to start up MySQL at server boot. To do this, you can copy *support-files/mysql.server* to the appropriate location on your system. This is covered in greater detail in Chapter 5.

Windows Installation

The distributions for Windows can be found in the same place as the distributions for Unix: at *http://www.mysql.com/downloads* or at one of the mirror sites. Windows installation is simply a matter of downloading the *mysql-version.zip*, unzipping it, and running the set-up program.

The default install location for MySQL Windows is *c:\mysql*. The installer will allow you to change the location. However, if you choose to do so, you may need to modify some configuration files to get everything working correctly. Refer to the full MySQL installation documentation at *http://www.mysql.com/documentation* for more information.

The installer will give you the choice between a typical, compact, or custom install. You should use the typical install unless you wish to modify the list of components that are installed. In that case, use the custom install.

The Windows binary distribution contains several servers from which to choose. Table 2-2 lists these servers.

Table 2-2. Servers that come with the Windows distribution

Server name	Description
mysqld	Debug binary with memory allocation checking, symbolic link support, and transactional table support (InnoDB and DBD)
mysqld-opt	Optimized binary with no support for transactional tables
mysqld-nt	Optimized binary with support for NT named pipes
mysqld-max	Optimized binary with support for transactional tables
mysqld-max-nt	Optmized binary with support for NT named pipes and transactional tables

Once you have the software installed, the next step is to start the server. Though the binaries are the same, the procedure for running the server is different depending on whether you are using Windows 95/98 or Windows NT/2000. Each is covered separately.

Windows 9x Startup

To run MySQL on a Windows 9x system, you need TCP/IP support installed. This can be found on your Windows CD-ROM, if you have not installed it already. If your computer can connect to the Internet in any way, it already has TCP/IP support installed.

 If you are running Windows 95, make sure you have the right version of Winsock. MySQL requires Winsock 2. Obtain the latest version of Winsock from *http://www.microsoft.com*. This is not an issue for users of Windows 98 or Windows Me.

You will need to choose which server you would like to run from those described in Table 2-2. Note that you can run the '-nt' binaries, but you don't benefit from it, because named pipes are not supported on the Windows 9x platform. Assume for our example we have decided to run *mysql-opt*. To get the server started, open an MS-DOS window and type:

```
C:\> c:\mysql\bin\mysqld-opt
```

To stop the server, in an MS-DOS window type:

```
C:\> c:\mysql\bin\mysqladmin -u root shutdown
```

To get MySQL to start automatically with the operating system, stick a shortcut to the *winmysqladmin.exe* application in the *StartUp* folder. This will also have MySQL shut down automatically when you restart or shut down Windows.

Windows NT/2000 Startup

On Windows NT, you should have at least service pack 3 to get the right level of TCP/IP support for MySQL.

We recommend that you run the MySQL server as an NT service. The simplest way to install MySQL as a service is to use the *winmysqladmin.exe* utility that comes with a Windows installation of MySQL. You can use this tool to configure MySQL and install it as a service.

To install MySQL as a service by hand, open up an MS-DOS window and type:

```
C:\> c:\mysql\bin\mysqld-nt -install
```

This will create an NT service called *MySQL*. This service is now available from the Services control panel. To access this, open your control panel and double-click on the Services icon.* Figure 2-1 shows the Services control panel from a Windows NT box with MySQL installed as a service.

Now you can start MySQL by clicking on the Start button. If you would like to change the command-line options for the *MySql* service, you can type them in the Startup Parameters text box before starting the service. In Figure 2-2, after the service has started, the status shows as Started.

To stop the service, click on Stop. You can also start and stop the service from an MS-DOS prompt using the *net start* and *net stop* commands. To start it this way, open an MS-DOS window and type:

```
C:\> net start mysql
The MySql service is starting.
The MySql service was started successfully.
```

---

* On Windows 2000, click on the Administrative Tools icon in the control panel to open the Services control panel.

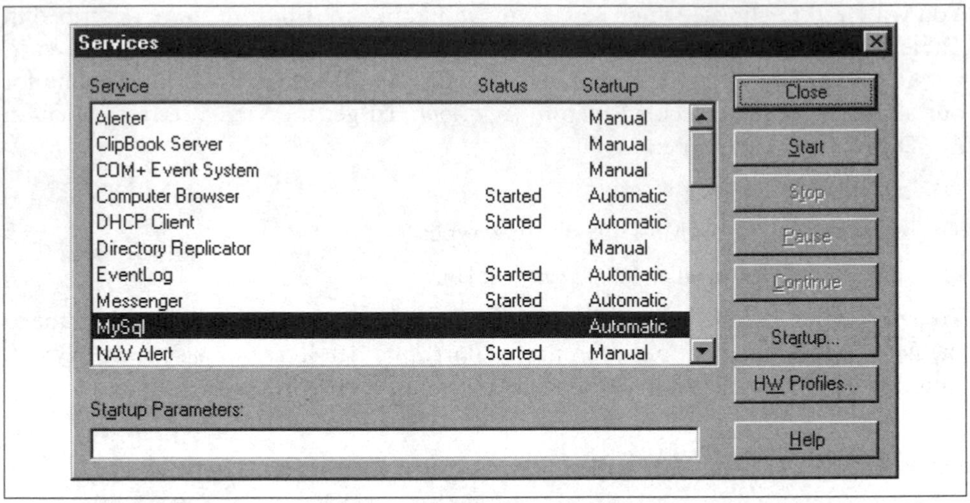

Figure 2-1. A Windows NT Services control panel with MySQL installed

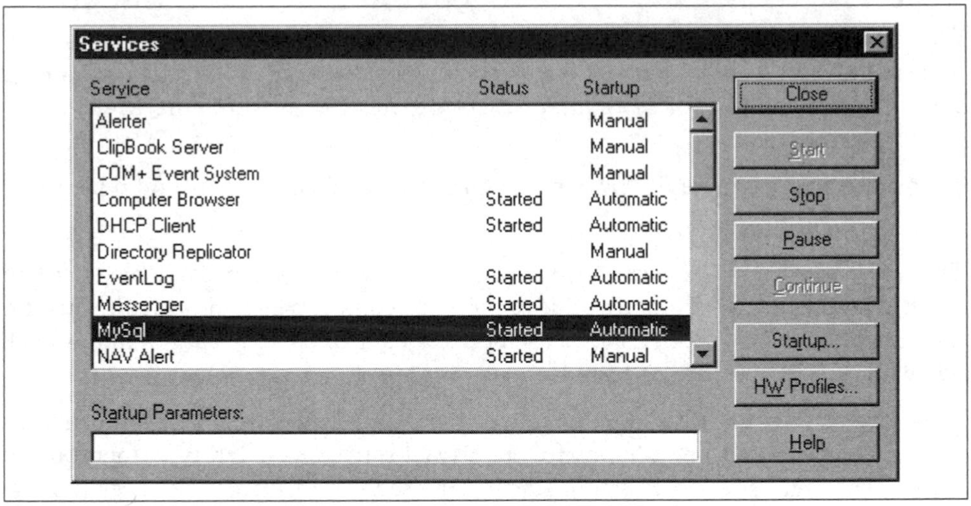

Figure 2-2. The Started MySQL service

To stop it again, type:

```
C:\> net stop mysql
The MySql service is stopping...........
The MySql service was stopped successfully.
```

## CHAPTER 3

SQL According to MySQL

The Structured Query Language (SQL) is used to read and write to MySQL databases. Using SQL, you can search for, enter, modify, or delete data. SQL is the most fundamental tool you will need for your interactions with MySQL. Even if you are using some application or graphical user interface to access the database, somewhere under the hood that application is generating SQL.

SQL is a sort of "natural" language. In other words, an SQL statement should read—at least on the surface—like a sentence of English text. This approach has both benefits and drawbacks, but the end result is a language unlike traditional programming languages such as C, Java, or Perl.

SQL Basics

SQL is "structured" in the sense that it follows a very specific set of rules. A computer program can parse a formulated SQL query easily. In fact, the O'Reilly book *lex & yacc* by John Levine, Tony Mason, and Doug Brown implements an SQL grammar to demonstrate the process of writing a program to interpret language! A *query* is a fully specified command sent to the database server, which then performs the requested action. Here's an example of an SQL query:

```
SELECT name FROM people WHERE name LIKE 'Stac%'
```

As you can see, this statement reads almost like a form of broken English: "Select names from a list of people where the names are like Stac." SQL uses few of the formatting and special characters that are typically associated with computer languages.

The SQL Story

IBM invented SQL in the 1970s shortly after Dr. E. F. Codd invented the concept of a relational database. From the beginning, SQL was an easy-to-learn, yet powerful language. It resembles a natural language such as English, so it is less daunting to a non-technical person. In the 1970s, even more than today, this advantage was important.

There were no casual hackers in the early 1970s. No one grew up learning BASIC or building web pages in HTML. The people programming computers were people who knew everything about how a computer worked. SQL was aimed at the army of non-technical accountants and business and administrative staff who would benefit from being able to access the power of a relational database.

SQL was so popular with its target audience, in fact, that in the 1980s, Oracle Corporation launched the world's first publicly available commercial SQL system. Oracle SQL was a huge hit and spawned an entire industry built around SQL. Sybase, Informix, Microsoft, and several other companies have since come forward with their implementations of SQL-based relational database management systems (RDBMSs).

When Oracle and its first competitors hit the scene, SQL was still relatively new and there was no standard. It was not until 1989 that the ANSI standards body issued the first public SQL standard. These days, the standard is referred to as SQL89. That new standard, unfortunately, did not go far enough into defining the technical structure of the language. Thus, even though the various commercial SQL languages were drawing closer together, differences in syntax still made it nontrivial to switch among implementations. It was not until 1992 that the ANSI SQL standard came into its own.

The 1992 standard is called both SQL92 and SQL2. The SQL2 standard expanded the language to accommodate as many of the proprietary extensions added by the commercial implementations as possible. Most cross-DBMS tools have standardized on SQL2 as the way in which they talk to relational databases. Due to the extensive nature of the SQL2 standard, however, relational databases that implement the full standard are very complex and resource intensive.

 SQL2 is not the last word on the SQL standard. With the growing popularity of object-oriented database management systems (OODBMS) and object-relational database management systems (ORDBMS), there has been increasing pressure to capture support for object-oriented database access in the SQL standard. The recent SQL3 standard is the answer to this problem.

When MySQL came along, it took a new approach to the business of database server development. Instead of manufacturing another giant RDBMS and risk having nothing more to offer than the big guys, Monty created a small, fast implementation of the most commonly used SQL functionality. Over the years, that basic functionality has grown to support just about anything you might want to do with most database applications.

The Design of SQL

As we mentioned earlier, SQL resembles a human language more than a computer language because it has a simple, defined imperative structure. Much like an English sentence, individual SQL commands, called "queries," can be broken down into language parts. Consider the following examples:

```
CREATE    TABLE              people (name CHAR(10))
verb      object             adjective phrase

INSERT    INTO people        VALUES ('me')
verb      indirect object    direct object

SELECT    name               FROM people          WHERE name LIKE '%e'
verb      direct object      indirect object      adjective phrase
```

Most implementations of SQL, including MySQL, are case insensitive. Specifically, it does not matter how you type SQL keywords as long as the spelling is correct. The previous CREATE example could just as well be:

```
cREatE TAblE people (name cHaR(10))
```

The case insensitivity extends only to SQL keywords.* In MySQL, names of databases, tables, and columns are case-sensitive. This case sensitivity is not necessarily true for all database engines. Thus, if you are writing an application that should work against all databases, you should assume that names are case sensitive.

This first element of an SQL query is always a verb. The verb expresses the action you wish the database engine to take. While the rest of the statement varies from verb to verb, they all follow the same general format: you name the object upon which you are acting and then describe the data you are using for the action. For example, the query CREATE TABLE people (name CHAR(10)) uses the verb CREATE, followed by the object TABLE. The rest of the query describes the table to be created.

An SQL query originates with a client (the application that provides the façade through which a user interacts with the database). The client constructs a query based on user actions and sends the query to the SQL server. The server must then process the query and perform the specified action. Once the server has done its job, it returns some value or set of values to the client.

Because the primary focus of SQL is to communicate actions to the database server, it does not have the flexibility of a general-purpose language. Most of the functionality of SQL concerns input to and output from the database: adding, changing, deleting, and reading data. SQL provides other functionality, but always with an eye towards how it can be used to manipulate the data within the database.

Sending SQL to MySQL

You can send SQL to MySQL using a variety of mechanisms. The most common way is through one of the programming APIs described in Part III. For the purposes of

---

* For the sake of readability, we capitalize all SQL keywords in this book. We recommend this convention as a solid "best practice" technique.

this chapter, however, we recommend you use the interactive command-line tool, *mysql*. When you run this program at the command line, it prompts you for SQL:

```
[09:04pm] carthage$ mysql -u root -p
Enter password:
Welcome to the MySQL monitor.  Commands end with ; or \g.
Your MySQL connection id is 3 to server version: 3.22.29

Type 'help' for help.

mysql>
```

The previous *mysql* command says to connect to the MySQL server on the local machine as the user root (the *-u* option) with the client prompting you for a password (the *-p* option). Another option, *-h*, enables you to connect to MySQL servers on remote machines:

```
[09:04pm] carthage$ mysql -u root -h db.imaginary.com -p
```

There is absolutely no relationship between operating-system usernames and MySQL usernames. In other words, MySQL keeps its own list of users, and a MySQL administrator needs to add new users to MySQL independently of the host on which they reside. No one, therefore, has an account on a clean MySQL installation except root. This root is not the same root as your Unix root account. As a general rule, you should never connect to MySQL as root except when performing database administration tasks. If you have a clean installation of MySQL that you can afford to throw away, it is useful to connect as root for the purposes of this chapter so you can create and drop databases. Otherwise, you will have to connect to MySQL as whatever username has been assigned to you.

Once *mysql* is running, you can enter your SQL commands all on a single line or split them across multiple lines. MySQL waits for a semicolon before executing the SQL:[*]

```
mysql> SELECT book_number
    -> FROM book
    -> ;
+-------------+
| book_number |
+-------------+
|           1 |
|           2 |
|           3 |
+-------------+
3 rows in set (0.00 sec)
```

With the *mysql* command line, you generally get a command history depending on how your client tools were compiled. If a command history is compiled into your *mysql* client, you can use the up and down arrows on your keyboard to navigate through previously executed SQL commands.

---

[*] MySQL also accepts \g at the end of an SQL statement to indicate that the SQL should be executed.

Database Creation

To get started using MySQL, you need to create a database. First, let's take a look at the databases that come with a clean MySQL installation using the SHOW DATABASES command. Upon installation of MySQL 3.23.40, the following tables already exist:

```
mysql> SHOW DATABASES;
+----------+
| Database |
+----------+
| mysql    |
| test     |
+----------+
2 rows in set (0.37 sec)
```

The first database, mysql, is MySQL's system database, which you will learn more about in Chapter 5. The second database, test, is a play database you can use to learn MySQL and run tests against. You may find other databases on your server if you are not dealing with a clean installation. For now, however, we want to create a new database to illustrate the use of the MySQL CREATE statement:

```
CREATE DATABASE TEMPDB;
```

and then to work with the new database TEMPDB:

```
USE TEMPDB;
```

Finally, you can delete that database by issuing the DROP DATABASE command:

```
DROP DATABASE TEMPDB;
```

You can create new objects using the CREATE statement and destroy things using the DROP statement, just as we used them here.

Table Management

You should now feel comfortable connecting to a database on a MySQL server. For the rest of the chapter, you can use either the test database that comes with MySQL or your own play database. Using the SHOW command, you can display a list of tables in the current database the same way you used it to show databases. In a brand new installation, the test database has no tables. The following shows the output of the SHOW TABLES command when connected to the mysql system database:

```
mysql> USE mysql;
Database changed
mysql> SHOW TABLES;
+-----------------+
| Tables_in_mysql |
+-----------------+
| columns_priv    |
| db              |
| func            |
| host            |
```

```
| tables_priv    |
| user           |
+----------------+
6 rows in set (0.00 sec)
```

These are the six system tables MySQL requires to do its work. To see what one of these tables looks like, you can use the DESCRIBE command:

```
mysql> DESCRIBE db;
+----------------+-----------------+------+-----+---------+-------+
| Field          | Type            | Null | Key | Default | Extra |
+----------------+-----------------+------+-----+---------+-------+
| Host           | char(60) binary |      | PRI |         |       |
| Db             | char(64) binary |      | PRI |         |       |
| User           | char(16) binary |      | PRI |         |       |
| Select_priv    | enum('N','Y')   |      |     | N       |       |
| Insert_priv    | enum('N','Y')   |      |     | N       |       |
| Update_priv    | enum('N','Y')   |      |     | N       |       |
| Delete_priv    | enum('N','Y')   |      |     | N       |       |
| Create_priv    | enum('N','Y')   |      |     | N       |       |
| Drop_priv      | enum('N','Y')   |      |     | N       |       |
| Grant_priv     | enum('N','Y')   |      |     | N       |       |
| References_priv| enum('N','Y')   |      |     | N       |       |
| Index_priv     | enum('N','Y')   |      |     | N       |       |
| Alter_priv     | enum('N','Y')   |      |     | N       |       |
+----------------+-----------------+------+-----+---------+-------+
13 rows in set (0.36 sec)
```

This output describes each column in the table showing its data type, whether it can contain null values, what kind of key it is, any default values, and extra information. If all this means nothing to you, don't worry. We will describe each of these elements as the chapter progresses.

You should now be ready to create your first table. First, connect back to the test database that comes with a clean MySQL install:

```
USE test;
```

Make sure you connect to the test database first, because you definitely do not want to add tables to the mysql database. The *table*, a structured container of data, is the most basic concept of a relational database. Before adding data to a table, you must define the table's structure. Consider the following layout:

```
+----------------------------------+
|            people                |
+--------------+-------------------+
| name         | char(10) not null |
| address      | text(100)         |
| id           | int               |
+--------------+-------------------+
```

Not only does the table contain the names of the columns, but it also contains the types of each field as well as any additional information the fields may have. A field's data type specifies what kind of data the field can hold. SQL data types are similar to data types in other programming languages. The full SQL standard allows for a large range of data types. MySQL implements most of them as well as a few MySQL-specific types.

The general syntax for table creation is:

```
CREATE TABLE table_name (
                    column_name1 type [modifiers]
                    [, column_name2 type [modifiers]]
)
```

 What constitutes a valid identifier (a name for a table or column) varies between DBMSs. MySQL allows up to 64 characters in an identifier, supports the character $ in identifiers, and lets identifiers start with a valid number. More importantly, however, MySQL considers any valid letter for your local character set to be a valid letter for identifiers.

A *column* is the individual unit of data for a row within a table. A table may have any number of columns, but too many columns can make a table inefficient. This is where good database design, discussed in Chapter 7, becomes important. By creating properly normalized tables, you can join tables to perform searches across data housed in more than one table. We discuss the mechanics of a join later in the chapter.

Consider the following CREATE statement:

```
CREATE TABLE USER (
    USER_ID     BIGINT UNSIGNED NOT NULL PRIMARY KEY,
    USER_NAME   CHAR(10)        NOT NULL,
    LAST_NAME   VARCHAR(30),
    FIRST_NAME  VARCHAR(30),
    OFFICE      CHAR(2)         NOT NULL DEFAULT 'NY');
```

This statement creates a table called USER with five columns: USER_ID, USER_NAME, LAST_NAME, FIRST_NAME, and OFFICE. After each column name comes the data type for that column, followed by any modifiers.

The NOT NULL modifier indicates that the column may not contain any null values. If you try to assign a null value to that column, SQL will generate an error. Actually, there are a couple of exceptions to this rule. First, if the column is defined as AUTO_ INCREMENT, a null value will cause a value to be generated automatically. (We cover auto-incrementing later in the chapter.) The second exception is when you specify a default value for a column, as we have for the OFFICE column in the previous example. In this case, the OFFICE column is assigned the default value of 'NY' when you assign a null value. (We will discuss data types and the PRIMARY KEY modifier later in this chapter.)

Like most things in life, destruction is much easier than creation. The command to drop a table from the database is:

```
DROP TABLE table_name
```

This command completely removes all traces of that table from the database. MySQL removes all data within the specified table from existence. If you have no backups of the table, you absolutely cannot recover from this action. The moral of this story is to always keep backups and be very careful about dropping tables. You will thank yourself for it someday.

With MySQL, you can specify more than one table to delete by separating the table names with commas. For example, DROP TABLE people, animals, plants would delete the three named tables. You can also use the IF EXISTS modifier to avoid an error, should the table not exist when you try to drop it. This modifier is useful for huge scripts designed to create a database and all its tables. Before creating the database, run a DROP TABLE IF EXISTS *table_name* command.

MySQL Data Types

In a table, each column has a type. As we mentioned earlier, an SQL data type is similar to a data type in traditional programming languages. While many languages define a bare-minimum set of types necessary for completeness, SQL goes out of its way to provide types such as DATE that will be useful to everyday users. You could store a DATE type in a more basic numeric type, but having a type specifically dedicated to the nuances of date processing adds to SQL's ease of use—one of SQL's primary goals.

Chapter 16 provides a full reference of SQL types supported by MySQL. Table 3-1 is an abbreviated listing of the most common types.

Table 3-1. Common MySQL data types (see Chapter 16 for a full list)

Data type	Description
INT	An integer value. MySQL allows an INT to be either signed or unsigned.
REAL	A floating-point value. This type offers a greater range and more precision than the INT type, but it does not have the exactness of an INT.
CHAR(*length*)	A fixed-length character value. No CHAR fields can hold strings greater in length than the specified value. Fields of lesser length are padded with spaces. This type is the most commonly used in any SQL implementation.
VARCHAR(*length*)	A variable-length character value.
TEXT(*length*)	A variable-length character value.
DATE	A standard date value. The DATE type stores arbitrary dates for the past, present, and future.
TIME	A standard time value. This type stores the time of day independent of a particular date. When used together with a date, a specific date and time can be stored. MySQL additionally supplies a DATETIME type that stores date and time together in one field.

MySQL supports the UNSIGNED attribute for all numeric types. This modifier forces the column to accept only positive (unsigned) numbers. Unsigned fields have an upper limit that is double that of their signed counterparts. For instance, an unsigned TINYINT—MySQL's single-byte numeric type—has a range of 0 to 255 instead of the −128 to 127 range of its signed counterpart.

MySQL provides more types than those mentioned in Table 3-1. In day-to-day programming, however, you will use these types most often. The size of the data you wish to store plays a large role in the design of your MySQL tables.

Numeric Types

Before you create a table, you should know what kind of data you wish to store in the table. Beyond obvious decisions about whether your data is character-based or numeric, you should know the approximate size of the data to be stored. If it is a numeric field, what is its maximum possible value? What is its minimum possible value? Could that change in the future? If the minimum is always positive or zero, you should consider an unsigned type. You should always choose the smallest numeric type that can support your largest conceivable value. If, for example, you have a field that represents the population of a state, use an unsigned INT field. No state can have a negative population. Furthermore, an unsigned INT field is certainly large enough to represent a state's population, unless that population grows to be roughly the current population of the entire Earth.

Character Types

Managing character types is a little more complicated. Not only do you have to worry about the minimum and maximum string lengths, but you also have to worry about the average size and the amount of variation. For our current purposes, an *index* is a field or combination of fields on which you plan to search—basically, the fields in your WHERE clause. Indexing is, however, much more complicated, so we will provide further details later in the chapter. What's important to note here is that indexing on character fields works best when the field is a fixed length. If there is little or, preferably, no variation in the length of your character-based fields, then a CHAR type is appropriate. An example of a good candidate for a CHAR field is a country code. The ISO provides a comprehensive list of standard two-character representations of country codes (US for the U.S., FR for France, etc.).* Because these codes are always exactly two characters, a CHAR(2) is the best way to maintain the country code based on the ISO representation

---

* States and provinces do not work the same way in internationalized applications. If you want to write an application that works in an international environment, make the columns for state and province codes CHAR(3), because Australia uses three-character state codes. Also note that there is a three-character ISO country-code standard.

A value does not need to be constant length to use a CHAR field. It should, however, have very little variance. Phone numbers, for example, can be stored safely in a CHAR(13) field even though phone number lengths vary from nation to nation. The variance is little enough that there is no point in making a phone number field variable in length. Keep in mind that with a CHAR field, no matter how big the actual string being stored is, the field always takes up exactly the number of characters specified as the field's size—no more, no less. Any difference between the length of the text being stored and the length of the field is made up by padding the value with spaces. While the few potential extra characters being wasted on a subset of the phone number data is not anything to worry about, you do not want to be wasting much more.

Variable-length text fields are appropriate for text fields with widely varying lengths. A good, common example of a field that demands a variable-length data type is a web URL. Most web addresses are relatively short (e.g., *http://www.ora.com*, *http://www.imaginary.com*, *http://www.mysql.com*) and consequentially do not pose problems. Occasionally, however, you will run into web addresses such as:

> *http://www.winespectator.com/Wine/Spectator/*
> *_notes|55272939268343232214804313547Xv11=&Xr5=&Xv1=&type-region-*
> *search-code=&Xa14=flora+springs&Xv4=*

If you construct a CHAR field large enough to hold this URL, you will be wasting a significant amount of space for almost every other URL being stored. A variable-length field lets you define a field length that can store the odd, long-length value while not wasting all that space for the common, short-length values.

Variable-length text fields in MySQL use only as much space as necessary to store an individual value into the field. A VARCHAR(255) field that holds the string "hello world," for example, takes up only 12 bytes (1 byte for each character plus an extra byte to store the length).

 MySQL varies from the ANSI standard by not padding VARCHAR fields. Any extra spaces are removed from a value before it is stored.

You cannot store strings with lengths greater than the field length you have specified. With a VARCHAR(4) field, you can store at most a string with four characters. If you attempt to store the string "happy birthday," MySQL will truncate the string to "happ." The downside is that there is no way to store the odd string that exceeds your designated field size. Table 3-2 shows the storage space required by the different text data types to store the 144-character Wine Spectator URL shown earlier, the space required to store an average-sized 30-character URL, and the maximum string size for that data type.

Table 3-2. *The storage space required by the different MySQL character types*

Data type	Storage for 144-char string	Storage for 30-char string	Maximum string size
CHAR(150)	150	150	255
VARCHAR(150)	145	31	255
TINYTEXT(150)	145	31	255
TEXT(150)	146	32	65535
MEDIUMTEXT(150)	147	33	16777215
LONGTEXT(150)	148	34	4294967295

In this table, note that storage requirements grow 1 byte at a time for the variable-length types of MEDIUMTEXT and LONGTEXT. This growth is due to the space required to store the size in variable-length fields. TEXT uses an extra byte to store the potentially greater length of the text it contains. Similarly, MEDIUMTEXT uses an extra 2 bytes over VARCHAR, and LONGTEXT uses an extra 3 bytes.

If after years of uptime with your database, you find that the world has changed and a field that once comfortably existed as a VARCHAR(25) must now hold strings as long as 30 characters, you are not out of luck. MySQL provides a command called ALTER TABLE that enables you to redefine a field type without losing any data:

```
ALTER TABLE mytable MODIFY mycolumn LONGTEXT
```

Binary Data Types

MySQL provides a set of binary data types that closely mirror their character counterparts. The MySQL binary types are CHAR BINARY, VARCHAR BINARY, TINYBLOB, BLOB, MEDIUMBLOB, and LONGBLOB. The practical distinction between character types and their binary counterparts is the concept of encoding. *Binary data* is basically a chunk of data that MySQL makes no effort to interpret. *Character data*, on the other hand, is assumed to represent textual data from human alphabets. It is thus encoded and sorted based on rules appropriate to the character set in question. On an ASCII system, MySQL sorts binary data in a case-sensitive, ASCII order.

Enumerations and Sets

MySQL provides two other special kinds of types. The ENUM type allows you specify (enumerate) at table creation a list of possible values that can be inserted into that field. For example, if you have a column named fruit into which you want to allow only the values apple, orange, kiwi, or banana, you would assign this column the type ENUM:

```
CREATE TABLE meal(meal_id INT NOT NULL PRIMARY KEY,
                  fruit ENUM('apple', 'orange', 'kiwi',
                        'banana'))
```

When you insert a value into that column, it must be one of the specified fruits. Because MySQL knows ahead of time which values are valid for the column, it can abstract them to some underlying numeric type. In other words, instead of storing apple in the column as a string, MySQL stores it internally as a single-byte number. However, you still refer to it as apple in a query or when you retrieve the value from MySQL. You also use apple when you call the table or view results from the table.

The MySQL ET type works in the same way, except it lets you store multiple values in a field at the same time and uses bits instead of bytes.

Other Kinds of Data

Every piece of data you will ever encounter can be stored using numeric or character types. Technically, you could even store numbers as character types. Just because you can do so, however, does not mean you should. Consider, for example, storing a date in the database. You could store that value as a Unix-style BIGINT or as a combination of several columns for the day, month, and year. How do you look for rows with a date value greater than two days after a specific date? Either you calculate the numeric representation of that date or employ a complex operation for a simple query mixing day, month, and year values.

Isn't all of that a major pain? Wouldn't it be nice if MySQL handled all of these issues for you? In fact, MySQL does. It provides several complex data types to help with abstract common concepts. It supports the concept of dates through the DATE data type. Other such data types include DATETIME and TIMESTAMP.

Indexing

While MySQL has better performance than any of the larger database servers, some problems still call for careful database design. For instance, if we had a table with millions of rows of data, a search for a specific row would take a long time. Most database engines allow indexes to aid in such searches.

Indexes help the database store data in a way that makes for quicker searches. Unfortunately, you sacrifice disk space and modification speed for the benefit of quicker searches. The most efficient use of indexes is to create an index for columns on which you tend to search the most. MySQL supports the following syntax for creating an index for a table:

```
CREATE INDEX index_name ON tablename (column1,
                                      column2,
                                      ...,
                                      columnN)
```

MySQL also lets you create an index at the same time you create a table using the following syntax:

```
CREATE TABLE material (id        INT      NOT NULL,
                       name      CHAR(50) NOT NULL,
                       resistance INT,
                       melting_pt REAL,
                       INDEX index1 (id, name),
                       UNIQUE INDEX index2 (name))
```

The previous example creates two indexes for the table. The first index—named index1—consists of both the id and name fields. The second index includes only the name field and specifies that values for the name field must always be unique. If you try to insert a field with a name held by a row already in the database, the insert will fail. Generally, you should declare all fields in a unique index as NOT NULL.

Even though we created an index for name by itself, we did not create an index for just id. If we did want such an index, we would not need to create it—it is already there. When an index contains more than one column (for example: name, rank, and serial_number), MySQL reads the columns in order from left to right. Because of the structure of the index MySQL uses, any subset of the columns from left to right are automatically created as indexes within the "main" index. For example, name by itself and name and rank together are both indexes created "for free" when you create the index name, rank, serial_number. An index of rank by itself or name and serial_number together, however, is not created unless you explicitly create it yourself.

MySQL also supports the ANSI SQL semantics of a special index called a primary key. In MySQL, a primary key is a unique key with the name PRIMARY. By calling a column a primary key at creation, you are naming it as a unique index that will support table joins. The following example creates a cities table with a primary key of id:

```
CREATE TABLE cities (id      INT  NOT NULL PRIMARY KEY,
                     name    VARCHAR(100),
                     pop     MEDIUMINT,
                     founded DATE)
```

Before you create a table, you should determine which fields, if any, should be keys. As we mentioned above, any fields that will support joins are good candidates for primary keys. See Chapter 7 for a detailed discussion on how to design your tables with good primary keys.

 ANSI SQL supports a special kind of key called a foreign key. Foreign keys help protect database integrity by enabling the database to manage things such as the deletion of rows with dependent relationships in other tables. Though MySQL supports the ANSI syntax for foreign keys, it does not actually use them to perform integrity checking in the database. This is a situation in which the introduction of a feature would cause a slowdown in performance with little real benefit. Applications themselves should generally worry about foreign key integrity.

Managing Data

The first thing you will probably want to do with a newly created table is add data to it. Once the data is in place, you need to maintain it—add to it, modify it, and perhaps even delete it.

Inserts

Adding a row to a table is one of the more straightforward concepts in SQL. You have already seen several examples of it in this book. MySQL supports the standard SQL INSERT syntax:

```
INSERT INTO table_name (column1, column2, ..., columnN)
VALUES (value1, value2, ..., valueN)
```

Under this syntax, you specify the columns followed by the values to populate those columns for the new row. When inserting data into numeric fields, you can insert the value as is; for all other fields, you must wrap them in single quotes. For example, to insert a row of data into a table of addresses, you might issue the following command:

```
INSERT INTO addresses (name, address, city, state, phone, age)
VALUES('Irving Forbush', '123 Mockingbird Lane', 'Corbin', 'KY',
       '(800) 555-1234', 26)
```

In addition, the escape character—\, by default—enables you to escape single quotes and other literal instances of the escape character:

```
# Insert info for the directory Stacie's Directory which
# is in c:\Personal\Stacie
INSERT INTO files (description, location)
VALUES ('Stacie\'s Directory', 'C:\\Personal\\Stacie')
```

MySQL allows you to leave out the column names as long as you specify a value for every column in the table in the order they were specified in the table's CREATE call. If you want to use the default values for a column, however, you must specify the names of the columns for which you intend to insert nondefault data. For example, if the earlier files table had contained a column called size, the default value would be used for *Stacie's Directory*. MySQL allows you to specify a custom default value in the table's CREATE call. If you do not have a default value set up for a column, and that column is NOT NULL, you must include that column in the INSERT statement with a non-NULL value.

Newer versions of MySQL support a nonstandard INSERT call for inserting multiple rows at once:

```
INSERT INTO foods VALUES (NULL, 'Oranges', 133, 0, 2, 39),
                         (NULL, 'Bananas', 122, 0, 4, 29),
                         (NULL, 'Liver', 232, 3, 15, 10)
```

While these nonstandard syntaxes supported by MySQL are useful for quick system administration tasks, you should not use them when writing database applications unless you really need the speed benefit they offer. As a general rule, you should stick as close to the ANSI SQL2 standard as MySQL will let you. By doing so, you make certain that your application can run against any other database in the future. Being flexible is especially critical for people with mid-range database needs because such users generally hope to become people with high-end database needs.

Another nonstandard syntax supported by MySQL enables you to specify the column name and value together:

```
INSERT INTO book SET title='The Vampire Lestat', author='Anne Rice';
```

Finally, you can insert data by using the data from some other table (or group of tables) to populate your new table. For example:

```
INSERT INTO foods (name, fat)
SELECT food_name, fat_grams FROM recipes
```

You should note that the number of columns in the INSERT call matches the number of columns in the SELECT call. In addition, the data types for the INSERT columns must match the data types for the corresponding SELECT columns. Finally, the SELECT clause in an INSERT statement cannot contain an ORDER BY modifier and cannot be selected from the same table where the INSERT occurs.

Sequence Generation

The best kind of primary key is one that has absolutely no meaning in the database except to act as a primary key. Primary keys are the tools used to identify rows uniquely in a relational database. When you use information such as a username or an email address as a primary key, you are in effect saying that the username or email address is somehow an intrinsic part of who that person is. If that person ever changes his username or email address, you will have to go to great lengths to ensure the integrity of the data in the database. Consequently, it is a better design principle to use meaningless numbers as primary keys.

To achieve this, simply make a numeric primary key that increments every time you insert a new row. Looking at the cities table shown earlier, the first city you insert would have an id of 1, the second 2, the third 3, and so on. To successfully manage this primary key sequencing, you need some way to guarantee that a number can be read and incremented by only one client at a time. You accomplish this task by making the primary key field AUTO_INCREMENT.

When you create a table in MySQL, you can specify at most one column as AUTO_
INCREMENT. When you do this, you can have this column automatically insert the
highest current value plus 1 for that column when you insert a row and specify NULL
or 0 for that row's value. The AUTO_INCREMENT columns must be indexed. The following command creates the cities table with an AUTO_INCREMENT id field:*

```
CREATE TABLE cities (id      INT  NOT NULL PRIMARY KEY AUTO_INCREMENT,
                     name    VARCHAR(100),
                     pop     INT,
                     founded DATE)
```

The first time you insert a row, the id field for your first row will be 1 as long as you
use NULL or 0 for that field in the INSERT statement. For example, this command takes
advantage of the AUTO_INCREMENT feature:

```
INSERT INTO cities (id, name, pop)
VALUES (NULL, 'Houston', 3000000)
```

If no other values are in that table when you issue this command, MySQL will set
this field to 1, not NULL (remember, it cannot be NULL). If other values are present in
the table, the value inserted will be one greater than the largest current value for id.

You can also implement sequences by referring to the value returned by the LAST_
INSERT_ID( ) function and doing your own incrementing:

```
UPDATE table_name SET id=LAST_INSERT_ID( id+1 );
```

The AUTO_INCREMENT attribute may be supplied for at most one column of an integer
type in a table. In addition to being an integer type, the column must be either a primary key or the sole column in a unique index. When you attempt an insert into a
table with such an integer field and fail to specify a value for that field (or specify a
NULL value), a value of one greater than the column's current maximum value will be
automatically inserted.

Chapter 17 contains reference material on the LAST_INSERT_ID( ) function.

Updates

The insertion of new rows into a database is just the start of data management.
Unless your database is read-only, you will probably also need to make periodic
changes to the data. The standard SQL modification statement looks like this:

```
UPDATE table_name
SET column1=value1, column2=value2, ..., columnN=valueN
[WHERE clause]
```

---

* You can seed AUTO_INCREMENT to start at any arbitrary number by specifying the seed value at the end of the
  CREATE statement. To start incrementing at 1025, for example, you would add AUTO_INCREMENT = 1025 after
  the closing parentheses of the CREATE TABLE statement.

You specifically name the table you want to update and the values you want to assign in the SET clause, and then identify the rows to be affected in the WHERE clause. If you fail to specify a WHERE clause, MySQL will update every row in the table.

In addition to assigning literal values to a column, you can also calculate the values. You can even calculate the value based on a value in another column:

```
UPDATE years
SET end_year = begin_year+5
```

This command sets the value in the end_year column equal to the value in the begin_year column plus 5 for each row in that table.

The WHERE Clause

The previous section introduced one of the most important SQL concepts, the WHERE clause. In SQL, a WHERE clause enables you to pick out specific rows in a table by specifying a value that must be matched by the column in question. For example:

```
UPDATE bands
SET lead_singer = 'Ian Anderson'
WHERE band_name = 'Jethro Tull'
```

This UPDATE specifies that you should change only the lead_singer column for the row where band_name is identical to Jethro Tull. If the band_name column is not a unique index, that WHERE clause may match multiple rows. Many SQL commands employ WHERE clauses to help pick out the rows on which you wish to operate. Because the columns in the WHERE clause are columns on which you search, you should generally have indexes created around whatever combinations you commonly use. We discuss the kinds of comparisons you can perform in the WHERE clause later in the chapter.

Deletes

Deleting data is a straightforward operation. You simply specify the table followed by a WHERE clause that identifies the rows you want to delete:

```
DELETE FROM table_name [WHERE clause]
```

As with other commands that accept a WHERE clause, the WHERE clause is optional. If you omit it, you will delete all of the records in the table! Of all the destructive commands in SQL, this is the easiest one to issue by mistake.

MySQL 4.0 has introduced a new, dangerous form of DELETE that supports the ability to delete from multiple tables with a single command:

```
DELETE table1, table2, ..., tablen
FROM table1, table2, ... tablen
[WHERE clause]
```

The FROM clause in this syntax does not mean the same thing as it does in the simpler form. In other words, it does not list the tables from which rows are deleted—it lists the tables referenced in the WHERE clause. If you are familiar with the SELECT statement, it works exactly the same as the FROM clause in SELECT statements. The tables you are deleting from are listed directly after the DELETE statement:

```
DELETE Author, Address
FROM Author, Book, Address
WHERE Author.author_id = Addess.address_id
AND Author.author_id = Book.author_id
AND Book.publish_date < 1980;
```

This statement deletes all the authors and any address information you have for those authors in the Address table for every author with books published before 1980. The old books will remain in the Book table, because Book was not named after the DELETE keyword. We further cover the complexities of the WHERE clause later in the chapter.

Queries

The last common SQL command, SELECT, enables you to view the data in the database. This action is by far the most common action performed in SQL. While data entry and modifications do happen on occasion, most databases spend the vast majority of their lives serving up data for reading. The general form of the SELECT statement is as follows:

```
SELECT column1, column2, ..., columnN
FROM table1, table2, ..., tableN
[WHERE clause]
```

This syntax is certainly the most common way to retrieve data from any SQL database. The SELECT statement enables you to identify the columns you want from one or more tables. The WHERE clause identifies the rows with the data you seek.

Of course, there are variations for performing complex and powerful queries. (We cover the full range of the SELECT syntax in Chapter 15.) The simplest form is:

```
SELECT 1;
```

This simple, though completely useless query returns a result set with a single row containing a single column with the value of 1. A more useful version of this query might be something like:

```
mysql> SELECT DATABASE();
+------------+
| DATABASE() |
+------------+
| test       |
+------------+
1 row in set (0.01 sec)
```

The expression DATABASE( ) is a MySQL function that returns the name of the current database. (We will cover functions in more detail later in the chapter.) Nevertheless, you can see how simple SQL can provide a quick-and-dirty way of finding out important information.

Most of the time, however, you should use slightly more complex queries that help you pull data from a table in the database. The first part of a SELECT statement enumerates the columns you wish to retrieve. You may specify a * to say that you want to select all columns. The FROM clause specifies which tables those columns come from. The WHERE clause identifies the specific rows to be used and enables you to specify how to join two tables.

Joins

Joins put the "relational" in relational databases by enabling you to relate the data in one table with data in other tables. The basic form of a join is sometimes described as an *inner join*. Joining tables is a matter of specifying equality in columns from two tables:

```
SELECT book.title, author.name
FROM author, book
WHERE book.author = author.id
```

This query pulls columns from two different tables where a relationship exists between rows in the two tables. Specifically, this query looks for situations in which the value of the author column in the book table matches the id value in the author table. Consider a database in which the book table looks like Table 3-3 and the author table looks like Table 3-4.

Table 3-3. A book table

ID	Title	Author	Pages
1	The Green Mile	4	894
2	Guards, Guards!	2	302
3	Imzadi	3	354
4	Gold	1	405
5	Howling Mad	3	294

Table 3-4. An author table

ID	Name	Citizen
1	Isaac Asimov	US
2	Terry Pratchett	UK
3	Peter David	US
4	Stephen King	US
5	Neil Gaiman	UK

An inner join creates a virtual table by combining the fields of both tables for rows that satisfy the query in both tables. In our example, the query specifies that the author field of the book table must be identical to the id field of the author table. The query's result would look like Table 3-5.

Table 3-5. Query results based on an inner join

Book title	Author name
The Green Mile	Stephen King
Guards, Guards!	Terry Pratchet
Imzadi	Peter David
Gold	Isaac Asimov
Howling Mad	Peter David

Neil Gaiman is nowhere to be found in these results. He is left out because there is no value for his author.id value found in the author column of the book table. In other words, he did not write any of the books in our database! An inner join contains only those rows that match the query exactly. We will discuss the concept of an outer join later in the chapter for situations in which we have an author in the database who does not have a book in the database.

Aliasing

When you use column names that are fully qualified with their table and column name, the names can grow to be quite unwieldy. In addition, when referencing SQL functions (which will be discussed later in the chapter), you will likely find it cumbersome to refer to the same function more than once within a statement. You can get around these issues by using aliases. An alias is usually a shorter and more descriptive way of referring to a cumbersome name. You can use it anywhere in the same SQL statement in place of the longer name. For example:

```
# A column alias
SELECT long_field_names_are_annoying AS myfield
FROM table_name
WHERE myfield = 'Joe'
# A table alias
SELECT people.names, tests.score
FROM tests, really_long_people_table_name AS people
```

Ordering and Grouping

The results from a SELECT are, by default, indeterminate in the order they will appear. Fortunately, SQL provides some tools for imposing discipline on this seemingly random list: ordering and grouping.

Basic ordering

You can tell a database to order any results you see by a certain column. For example, if you specify that a query should order the results by last_name, then the results will appear alphabetized according to the last_name value. Ordering is handled by the ORDER BY clause:

```
SELECT last_name, first_name, age
FROM people
ORDER BY last_name, first_name
```

In this situation, we are ordering by two columns. You can order by any number of columns. You can also use the special ORDER BY RAND( ) clause to return results in a random order.

If you want to see things in reverse order, add the DESC (descending) keyword:

```
ORDER BY last_name DESC
```

The DESC keyword applies only to the field that comes directly before it. If you are sorting on multiple fields, only the field directly before DESC is reversed; the others are sorted in ascending order.

Localized sorting

Sorting is actually a complex problem for applications that need to run on computers all over the world. The rules for sorting strings vary from alphabet to alphabet, even when two alphabets use mostly the same symbols. MySQL handles the problem of sorting by making it dependent on the character set used by the MySQL engine. Out of the box, the default character set is ISO-8859-1 (Latin-1). MySQL uses the sorting rules for Swedish and Finnish with ISO-8859-1.

To change the sorting rules, you change the character set. First, you need to make sure the correct character set was compiled into the server when you compiled and installed MySQL. With the proper character set compiled into the server, you can change the default character set by launching the server with the argument *--default-character-set=CHARSET*.

Because of the simplicity of the English alphabet, the use of a single set of sorting rules MySQL associates with ISO-8859-1 does not affect English sorting. This is not true, however, for languages such as Swedish and German, which both use the ISO-8859-1 character set. Swedish sorts ä after z, while German sorts ä before a. The default rules therefore fail German users.

MySQL lets you address this problem by creating custom character sets. When you compile the driver, you can compile in support for whatever character sets you desire as long as you have a configuration file for that character set. This file contains the characters that make up the character set and the rules for sorting them. You can write your own or use the ones that come with MySQL.

The real problem here is that MySQL incorrectly associates sorting rules with character sets. A character set is nothing more than a grouping of characters with a related purpose. Nothing about the ISO-8859-1 character set implies sorting for Swedes, Italians, Germans, or anyone else. When working with MySQL, however, you need to remember that sorting rules are directly tied to the character set.

Grouping

Grouping lets you group rows with matching values for a specific column into a single row in order to operate on them together. You usually do this to perform aggregate functions on the results. We will go into functions a little later in the chapter.

Consider the following:

```
mysql> SELECT name, rank, salary FROM people;
+--------------+----------+--------+
| name         | rank     | salary |
+--------------+----------+--------+
| Jack Smith   | Private  |  23000 |
| Jane Walker  | General  | 125000 |
| June Sanders | Private  |  22000 |
| John Barker  | Sergeant |  45000 |
| Jim Castle   | Sergeant |  38000 |
+--------------+----------+--------+
5 rows in set (0.01 sec)
```

If you want to get a list of different ranks, you can use the GROUP BY clause to get a full account of the ranks:

```
mysql> SELECT rank FROM people GROUP BY rank;
+----------+
| rank     |
+----------+
| General  |
| Private  |
| Sergeant |
+----------+
3 rows in set (0.01 sec)
```

You should not, however, think of these results as simply a listing of the different ranks. The GROUP BY clause actually groups all of the rows matching the WHERE clause (in this case, every row) based on the GROUP BY clause. The two privates are thus grouped together into a single row with the rank Private. The two sergeants are similarly aggregated. With the individuals grouped according to rank, you can find out the average salary for each rank. Again, we will further discuss the functions you see in this example later in the chapter.

```
mysql> SELECT rank, AVG(salary) FROM people GROUP BY rank;
+----------+-------------+
| rank     | AVG(salary) |
+----------+-------------+
| General  | 125000.0000 |
| Private  |  22500.0000 |
| Sergeant |  41500.0000 |
+----------+-------------+
3 rows in set (0.04 sec)
```

Here you see the true power of grouping. This query uses an aggregate function, AVG( ), to operate on all of the rows grouped together for each row. In this case, the salaries of the two privates (23000 and 22000) are grouped together in the same row, and the AVG( ) function is applied to them.

The power of ordering and grouping combined with the utility of SQL functions enables you to do a great deal of data manipulation even before you retrieve the data from the server. However, you should take great care not to rely too heavily on this power. While it may seem more efficient to place as much processing load as possible onto the database server, this is not really the case. Your client application is dedicated to the needs of a particular client, while the server is shared by many clients. Because of the greater amount of work a server already has to do, it is almost always more efficient to place as little load as possible on the database server. MySQL may be the fastest database around, but you do not want to waste that speed on processing that can be handled by client applications.

Limiting Results

A WHERE clause is not the only way to constrain the results you see from a query. MySQL provides two other common mechanisms: HAVING and LIMIT.

You will most commonly use HAVING with the GROUP BY clause we just described. Like a WHERE clause, it defines your result set based on some set of calculations. Unlike a WHERE clause, it performs these calculations after your results have been retrieved from the tables in which they are stored. A WHERE clause, for example, scans the table in the database and pulls all records matching the WHERE clause. A HAVING clause, on the other hand, looks only at rows that have been pulled from a database after they have been extracted. The following query goes one step beyond our previous search for the average salary of different ranks in getting the average salaries only for ranks with an average salary greater than $100,000.

```
mysql> SELECT rank, AVG(salary) FROM people
    > GROUP BY rank HAVING AVG(salary) > 100000.00;
+----------+-------------+
| rank     | AVG(salary) |
+----------+-------------+
| General  | 125000.0000 |
+----------+-------------+
1 row in set (0.04 sec)
```

Restricting the result set in a WHERE clause would make no sense. If it were to be valid SQL, it would work on the entire table! Instead, we first want to perform the select and then find only those groups in the result set whose average salary is greater than $100,000. The HAVING clause enables us to perform that further restriction. More importantly, consider a case with both a WHERE clause and a HAVING clause:

```
mysql> SELECT rank, AVG(salary) FROM people
    > WHERE rank <> 'Private'
    > GROUP BY rank HAVING AVG(salary) > 100000.00;
+----------+-------------+
| rank     | AVG(salary) |
+----------+-------------+
| General  | 125000.0000 |
+----------+-------------+
1 row in set (0.02 sec)
```

Because the HAVING clause executes on the results of the query, the average is calculated only for generals and sergeants—not the excluded privates.

Sometimes an application is looking for only the first few rows that match a query. Limiting queries can help prevent bogging down the network with unwanted results. MySQL enables an application to limit the number of results through a LIMIT clause in a query:

```
SELECT * FROM people ORDER BY name LIMIT 10;
```

To get the last 10 people from the table, you can use the DESC keyword. If you want people from the middle, however, you have to get a bit trickier; you need to specify the number of the first record you want to see (record 0 is the first record, 1 the second) and the number of rows you want to see:

```
SELECT * FROM people ORDER BY name LIMIT 19, 30;
```

This sample displays records 20 through 49. The 19 in the LIMIT clause tells MySQL to start with record 19, which is the twentieth record. The 30 then tells MySQL to return the next 30 records.

SQL Operators

So far, we have used the = operator for the obvious task of verifying that two values in a WHERE clause equal one another. Other fairly basic operations include <>, >, <, <=, and >=. Note that MySQL allows you to use either <> or != for "not equal." Table 3-6 contains a full set of simple SQL operators.

Table 3-6. The simple SQL operators supported by MySQL

Operator	Context	Description
+	Arithmetic	Addition
-	Arithmetic	Subtraction
*	Arithmetic	Multiplication

Table 3-6. The simple SQL operators supported by MySQL (continued)

Operator	Context	Description
/	Arithmetic	Division
=	Comparison	Equal
<> or !=	Comparison	Not equal
<	Comparison	Less than
>	Comparison	Greater than
<=	Comparison	Less than or equal to
>=	Comparison	Greater than or equal to
AND	Logical	And
OR	Logical	Or
NOT	Logical	Negation

MySQL operators have the following order of precedence:

1. `BINARY`
2. `NOT !`
3. `- (unary minus)`
4. `* / %`
5. `+ -`
6. `<< >>`
7. `&`
8. `|`
9. `< <= > >= = <=> <> IN IS LIKE REGEXP RLIKE`
10. `BETWEEN`
11. `AND &&`
12. `OR ||`

Logical Operators

SQL's logical operators—AND, OR, and NOT—let you build more dynamic WHERE clauses. The AND and OR operators specifically let you add multiple criteria to a query:

```
SELECT USER_NAME
FROM USER
WHERE AGE > 18 AND STATUS = 'RESIDENT';
```

This sample query provides a list of all users who are residents and are old enough to vote. In other words, it finds every resident 18 years or older.

You can build increasingly complex queries and override MySQL's order of precedence with parentheses. The parentheses tell MySQL which comparisons to evaluate first:

```
SELECT USER_NAME
FROM USER
WHERE (AGE > 18 AND STATUS = 'RESIDENT')
OR (AGE > 18 AND STATUS = 'APPLICANT');
```

In this more complex query, we are looking for anyone currently eligible to vote as well as people who might be eligible in the near future. Finally, you can use the NOT operator to negate an entire expression:

```
SELECT USER_NAME
FROM USER
WHERE NOT (AGE > 18 AND STATUS = 'RESIDENT');
```

In this case, negation provides all the users who are not eligible to vote.

Null's Idiosyncrasies

Null is a tricky concept for most people new to databases to understand. As in other programming languages, null is not a value, but the absence of a value. This concept is useful, for example, if you have a customer profiling database that gradually gathers information about your customers as they offer it. When you first create a record, for example, you may not know how many pets the customer has. You want that column to hold NULL instead of 0 so you can tell the difference between customers with no pets and customers whose pet ownership is unknown.

The concept of null gets a little funny when you use it in SQL calculations. Many programming languages use null as simply another kind of value. In Java, the following syntax evaluates to true when the variable is null and false when it is not:

```
str == null
```

The similar expression in SQL, COL = NULL, is neither true nor false—it is always NULL, no matter what the value of the COL column. The following query will therefore not act as you might expect:

```
SELECT title FROM book WHERE author = NULL;
```

Because the WHERE clause will never evaluate to true no matter what value is in the database for the author column, this query always provides an empty result set—even when you have author columns with NULL values. To test for "nullness," use the IS NULL and IS NOT NULL operators:

```
SELECT TITLE FROM BOOK WHERE AUTHOR IS NULL;
```

MySQL also provides a special operator called the null-safe operator <=>, which you can use when you are not sure if you are dealing with null values. It returns true if both sides are null or false if both sides are not null:

```
mysql> SELECT 1 <=> NULL, NULL <=> NULL, 1 <=> 1;
+------------+---------------+---------+
| 1 <=> NULL | NULL <=> NULL | 1 <=> 1 |
+------------+---------------+---------+
|          0 |             1 |       1 |
+------------+---------------+---------+
1 row in set (0.00 sec)
```

This simple query shows how the null-safe operator works with a variety of inputs.

Membership Tests

Sometimes applications need to check if a value is a member of a set of values or within a particular range. The IN operator helps with the former:

```
SELECT TITLE FROM BOOK WHERE AUTHOR IN ('Stephen King', 'Richard Bachman');
```

This query will return the titles of all books written by Stephen King.[*] Similarly, you can check for all books by authors other than Stephen King with the NOT IN operator.

To determine if a value is in a particular range, use the BETWEEN operator:

```
SELECT TITLE FROM BOOK WHERE BOOK_ID BETWEEN 1  AND 100;
```

Both of these simple examples could, of course, be replicated with the basic operators. The Stephen King check, for example, could have been done by using the = operator and an OR:

```
SELECT title
FROM book
WHERE author = 'Stephen King' OR author = 'Richard Bachman';
```

The check on book IDs could also have been done with an OR clause using the >= and <= or > and < operators. As your queries get more complex, however, membership tests can help you build both readable and better-performing queries than those you might create with the basic operators.

Pattern Matching

We provided a peek at ANSI SQL pattern matching earlier with the query:

```
SELECT name FROM people WHERE name LIKE 'Stac%'
```

Using the LIKE operator, we compared a column value (name) to an incomplete literal ('Stac%'). MySQL supports the ability to place special characters into string literals that match like wild cards. The % character, for example, matches any arbitrary number of characters, including no character at all. The above SELECT statement would therefore match Stacey, Stacie, Stacy, and even Stac. The character _ matches any single character. Stac_y would match only Stacey. Stac__ would match Stacie and Stacey, but not Stacy or Stac.

---

[*] Richard Bachman is a pseudonym used by Stephen King for some of his books.

Pattern-matching expressions should never be used with the basic comparison operators. Instead, they require the LIKE and NOT LIKE operators. It is also important to remember that these comparisons are case-insensitive except on binary columns.

MySQL supports a non-ANSI kind of pattern matching that is actually much more powerful using the same kind of expressions to which Perl programmers and *grep* users are accustomed. MySQL refers to these as extended regular expressions. Instead of LIKE and NOT LIKE, these operators must be used with the REGEXP and NOT REGEXP operators. MySQL provides synonyms for these: RLIKE and NOT RLIKE. Table 3-7 contains a list of the supported extended regular expression patterns.

Table 3-7. MySQL extended regular expressions

Pattern	Description	Examples
.	Matches any single character.	Stac.. matches any value containing the characters "Stac" followed by two characters of any value.
[]	Matches any character in the brackets. You can also match a range of characters.	[Ss]tacey matches values containing both "Stacey" and "stacey."
		[a-zA-Z] matches values containing one instance of any character in the English (unaccented) portion of the Roman alphabet.
*	Matches zero or more instances of the character that precedes it.	Ap*le matches values containing "Aple," "Apple," "Appple," etc.
		Los .*es matches values containing the strings "Los " and "es" with anything in between.
		[0-9]* matches values containing any arbitrary number.
^	What follows must come at the beginning of the value.	^Stacey matches values that start with "Stacey."
$	What precedes it must end the value.	cheese$ matches any value ending in the string "cheese."

You should note a couple of important facts about extended regular expressions. Unlike basic pattern matching, MySQL extended regular expressions are case sensitive. They also do not require a match for the entire string. The pattern simply needs to occur somewhere within the value. Consider the following example:

```
mysql> SELECT * FROM BOOK;
+---------+-----------------------------------------+---------------+
| BOOK_ID | TITLE                                   | AUTHOR        |
+---------+-----------------------------------------+---------------+
|       1 | Database Programming with JDBC and Java | George Reese  |
|       2 | JavaServer Pages                        | Hans Bergsten |
|       3 | Java Distributed Computing              | Jim Farley    |
+---------+-----------------------------------------+---------------+
3 rows in set (0.01 sec)
```

In this table, we have three books from O'Reilly's Java series. The interesting thing about the Java series is that all books begin with or end with the word "Java." The first sample query checks for any titles LIKE 'Java':

```
mysql> SELECT TITLE FROM BOOK WHERE TITLE LIKE 'Java';
Empty set (0.01 sec)
```

Because LIKE looks for an exact match of the pattern specified, no rows match—none of the titles are exactly 'Java'. To find out which books start with the word Java using simple patterns, we need to add a %:

```
mysql> SELECT TITLE FROM BOOK WHERE TITLE LIKE 'Java%';
+---------------------------+
| TITLE                     |
+---------------------------+
| JavaServer Pages          |
| Java Distributed Computing |
+---------------------------+
2 rows in set (0.00 sec)
```

This query had two matches because only two of the books had titles that matched Java% exactly. The extended regular expression matches, however, are not exact matches. They simply look for the expression anywhere within the compared value:

```
mysql> SELECT TITLE FROM BOOK WHERE TITLE REGEXP 'Java';
+---------------------------------------+
| TITLE                                 |
+---------------------------------------+
| Database Programming with JDBC and Java |
| JavaServer Pages                      |
| Java Distributed Computing            |
+---------------------------------------+
3 rows in set (0.06 sec)
```

By simply changing the operator from LIKE to REGEXP, we changed how it matches things. Java appears somewhere in each of the titles, so the query returns all the titles. To find only the titles that start with the word Java using extended regular expressions, we need to specify that we are interested in the start:

```
mysql> SELECT TITLE FROM BOOK WHERE TITLE REGEXP '^Java';
+---------------------------+
| TITLE                     |
+---------------------------+
| JavaServer Pages          |
| Java Distributed Computing |
+---------------------------+
2 rows in set (0.01 sec)
```

The same thing applies to finding titles with Java at the end:

```
mysql> SELECT TITLE FROM BOOK WHERE TITLE REGEXP 'Java$';
+---------------------------------------+
| TITLE                                 |
+---------------------------------------+
| Database Programming with JDBC and Java |
+---------------------------------------+
1 row in set (0.00 sec)
```

The extended regular expression syntax is definitely much more complex than the simple pattern matching of ANSI SQL. In addition to the burden of extra complexity, you should also consider the fact that MySQL extended regular expressions do not work in most other databases. When you need complex pattern matching, however, they provide you with power that is simply unsupportable by simple pattern matching.

Advanced Features

Using the SQL presented thus far in this chapter should handle 90% of your database programming needs. On occasion, however, you will need some extra power not available in the basic SQL functionality. We close out the chapter with a discussion of a few of these features.

Full Text Searching

MySQL introduced the ability to search on text elements within a text field in Version 3.23.23 through a special index called a FULLTEXT index. It specifically enables you to do something like:

```
INSERT INTO Document (url, page_text )
VALUES ('index.html', 'The page contents.');
SELECT url FROM Document WHERE MATCH ( page_text ) AGAINST ('page');
```

INSERT adds a row to a Document table containing the URL of a web page and its text content. SELECT then looks for the URLs of all documents with the word page embedded in their text.

The Basics

The magic behind full text searching lies in a FULLTEXT index. The CREATE statement for the Document table might look like this:

```
CREATE TABLE Document (
    url        VARCHAR(255) NOT NULL PRIMARY KEY,
    page_text TEXT          NOT NULL,
    FULLTEXT ( page_text )
);
```

The FULLTEXT index enables you to search the index using words or phrases that will not match exactly and then weigh the relevance of any matches. As with other indexes, you can create multicolumn FULLTEXT indexes:

```
CREATE TABLE Document (
    url        VARCHAR(255) NOT NULL PRIMARY KEY,
    title      VARCHAR(100) NOT NULL,
    page_text TEXT          NOT NULL,
    FULLTEXT ( title, page_text )
);
```

With this table structure, you can now search for documents that have the word MySQL anywhere in the title or body of the page. You must keep your searches structured against the index, not against the columns. In other words, you can match against `title` and `page_text` together with this table, but you cannot look for words that exist only in the title unless you create a separate FULLTEXT index on it alone. Your combined search will look like the following:

```
SELECT url FROM Document
WHERE MATCH ( title, page_text ) AGAINST ('MySQL');
```

Relevance values

The search that occurs here is a natural language search against the text in the specified columns. It is case insensitive. The result of the match is actually a relevance value that MySQL uses to rank the results. By default, MySQL shows the results with the most relevant results listed first and eliminates only those results with no relevance at all.

```
mysql> SELECT url FROM Document
    -> WHERE MATCH ( title, page_text ) AGAINST ('java');
+------------+
| url        |
+------------+
| java.html  |
+------------+
```

You can use the relevance to your advantage. To get a better picture of the relevance values, you can execute the following query:

```
mysql> SELECT url, WHERE MATCH ( title, page_text ) AGAINST ('java')
    -> FROM Document;
+------------+-------------------------------------------------+
| url        | MATCH ( title, page_text ) AGAINST ('java')     |
+------------+-------------------------------------------------+
| index.html |                                               0 |
| java.html  |                                  1.8016148151891 |
| perl.html  |                                               0 |
| c.html     |                                               0 |
+------------+-------------------------------------------------+
```

In this case, the *index.html* file is a web page about MySQL and *java.html* is about how MySQL and Java work together. As you might expect, the results show that *index.html* has no relevance to Java, while *java.html* has quite a bite of relevance.

 In the above example, you can include MATCH in both the SELECT clause and the WHERE clause without incurring any extra overhead. MySQL is smart enough to notice that the two matches are identical and thus execute them a single time. Using MATCH in both places is useful when you want to make use of relevance.

You might expect that a match against MySQL would turn up high relevance for both documents. In reality, however, it turns up zero relevance. Because the phrase MySQL is present in more than half the rows, it is considered a *stopword* and thus discounted. A stopword is simply a word with no value for text matching. Common stopwords are "the" and "but." They are critical to achieving meaningful results in a full text search. Unfortunately, our sample database has four rows about MySQL and thus MySQL itself is considered a stopword.

Boolean mode

MySQL 4.0.1 introduced the ability to perform more complex searches with MySQL full text searching using much the same syntax you would use in Internet search engines. These complex searches are called Boolean mode searches. To execute a Boolean mode search, you use the same syntax except:

- Add IN BOOLEAN MODE to your AGAINST clause.
- Add modifiers in the text you are searching with.

For example:

```
SELECT url, title FROM Document
WHERE MATCH ( title, page_text ) AGAINST ( '+MySQL -Java' IN BOOLEAN MODE );
```

This query enables you to look for all documents that include MySQL but exclude Java. Common words that might otherwise be used as stopwords can be used in Boolean mode searches. Without any modifiers, a term in a Boolean mode search is considered optional. You can modify your Boolean mode searches with the following operators:

+ The word must be in the matched index.

- The word must not be in the matched index.

~ The word's relevance is inverted. This operator is useful for removing words that MySQL is giving high relevance to, but you do not want in your hits. Unlike the - operator, returned rows can have the term in question.

< Decreases the word's contribution to the overall relevance of a match.

> Increases a word's contribution to the overall relevance of a match.

* This operator comes after the word it modifies. It works much like a wildcard, matching any words that start with the specified word.

() Groups words into subexpressions.

Now you can run complex queries such as:

```
SELECT url, title FROM Document
WHERE MATCH ( title, page_text ) AGAINST ( '+MySQL -optimiz* +(>Java <Perl)' IN
BOOLEAN MODE);
```

This query asks for all of the rows about MySQL and either Java or Perl that do not have words beginning with optimiz. It will then rank Java documents higher than Perl documents.

Tips

MySQL determines relevance based on several criteria. It ignores any stopwords as well as words of three characters or less. A match against an index that finds a single hit in the database will have a higher relevance than a match against an index with many hits. In other words, rare words have greater value than common words, and overly common words become stopwords that have no value at all. It is therefore important to the utility of MySQL's full text searching that you have a large set of data to search against. Small data sets such as the one above with only four rows will produce odd results—like no hits on the word MySQL!

When you are adding a lot of data at once, such as when you are indexing the web pages on your web site, you should drop the FULLTEXT index, insert your updated web pages, then recreate the index. Inserts on tables with FULLTEXT indexes are quite expensive and work better if you do the indexing all at once.

The MySQL team is working hard on this fairly recent addition to MySQL. In the near future, you can expect the ability to look for phrases instead of just words as well as the ability to define your own words that must always be indexed. In fact, by the time you read this book, some new features have probably already been added to MySQL full text searching.

Transactions

MySQL recently introduced transactions along with SQL for executing statements in a transactional context. By default, MySQL is in a state called autocommit. *Autocommit mode* means that any SQL you send to MySQL is executed immediately. In some cases, however, you may want to execute two or more SQL statements together as a single unit of work.

A transfer between two bank accounts is the perfect example of such a transaction. The banking system needs to make sure that the debit from the first account and the credit to the second account occur as a single unit of work. If they are treated separately, the server could in theory crash between the debit and the credit. The result would be that you would lose that money!

By making sure the two statements occur as a single unit of work, transactions ensure that the first statement can be "rolled back" in the event that the second statement fails. To use transactions in MySQL, you first need to create a table using a transactional table type such as BDB or InnoDB.[*] If your MySQL install was not compiled with support for these table types, you cannot use transactions unless you reinstall. The SQL to create a transactional table specifies one of the transactional types:

```
CREATE TABLE ACCOUNT (
    ACCOUNT_ID BIGINT UNSIGNED NOT NULL PRIMARY KEY AUTO_INCREMENT,
```

[*] Not all platforms support these table types.

```
    BALANCE    DOUBLE)
  TYPE = BDB;
```

For a transaction against a transactional table to work, you need to turn off autocommit. You can do this with the command:

```
SET AUTOCOMMIT=0;
```

Now you are ready to begin using MySQL transactions. Transactions start with the BEGIN command:

```
BEGIN;
```

Your *mysql* client is now in a transactional context with respect to the server. Any change you make to a transactional table will not be made permanent until you commit it. Changes to nontransactional tables, however, will take place immediately. In the case of the account transfer, we issue the following statements:

```
UPDATE ACCOUNT SET BALANCE = 50.25 WHERE ACCOUNT_ID = 1;
UPDATE ACCOUNT SET BALANCE = 100.25 WHERE ACCOUNT_ID = 2;
```

Once you're done with any changes, complete the transaction by using the COMMIT command:

```
COMMIT;
```

The true advantage of transactions, of course, comes into play should an error occur in executing the second statement. To abort the entire transaction before a commit, issue the ROLLBACK command:

```
ROLLBACK;
```

In reality, the logic behind such complex transactional operations, including commits and rollbacks, requires solid design and well-structured error handling. We will cover these programmatic elements of transaction management in Chapter 8.

Of course, it would be useful if MySQL performed the actual math. It can do just that as long as you store the values you want with a SELECT call:

```
SELECT @FIRST := BALANCE FROM ACCOUNT WHERE ACCOUNT_ID = 1;
SELECT @SECOND := BALANCE FROM ACCOUNT WHERE ACCOUNT_ID = 2;
UPDATE ACCOUNT SET BALANCE = @FIRST - 25.00 WHERE ACCOUNT_ID = 1;
UPDATE ACCOUNT SET BALANCE = @SECOND + 25.00 WHERE ACCOUNT_ID = 2;
```

In addition to the COMMIT command, a handful of other commands will automatically end any current transaction as if a COMMIT had been issued. These commands are:

- ALTER TABLE
- BEGIN
- CREATE INDEX
- DROP DATABASE
- DROP TABLE

- LOCK TABLES
- RENAME TABLE
- TRUNCATE
- UNLOCK TABLES

Chapter 8 covers some of the more intricate details of using transactions in database applications.

Table Locking

Table locking is the poor man's transaction. In short, MySQL lets you lock down a group of tables so that only a single client can use it. Unlike transactions, you are not limited by the type of table. You cannot, however, roll back any actions taken against a locked table.

Locking has two basic functions:

- Enables multiple statements to execute against a group of tables as one unit of work
- Enables multiple updates to occur faster under some circumstances

MySQL supports three kinds of locks: read, read local, and write. Both kinds of read locks lock the table for reading by a client and all other clients. As long as the lock is in place, no one can write to the locked tables. Read and read local locks differ in that read local allows a client to execute nonconflicting INSERT statements as long as no changes to the MySQL files from outside of MySQL occur while the lock is held. If changes might occur by agents outside of MySQL, a read lock is required.

A write lock locks the specified tables against all access—read or write—by any other client. To lock a table, use the following command:

```
LOCK TABLES ACCOUNT WRITE;
```

Now that the ACCOUNT table is locked, you can read from it and modify the data behind it and be certain that no one else will change the data you read between your read and write operations:

```
SELECT @BAL:=BALANCE FROM ACCOUNT WHERE ACCOUNT_ID = 1;
UPDATE ACCOUNT SET BALANCE = @BAL * 0.03 WHERE ACCOUNT_ID = 1;
```

Finally, you need to release the locks:

```
UNLOCK TABLES;
```

It is really important that you unlock the tables! Failing to do so can result in preventing further access to those tables. Finally, any table locking should be short lived. Long-lived locks seriously degrade database performance.

Functions

Functions in SQL are similar to functions in other programming languages such as C and Perl. The function takes zero or more arguments and returns some value. For example, the function SQRT(16) returns 4. Within a MySQL SELECT statement, functions may be used in one of two ways:

As a value to be retrieved

This form involves a function in the place of a column in the list of columns to be retrieved. The return value of the function, evaluated for each selected row, is part of the returned result set as if it were a column in the database.* For example:

```
SELECT name, FROM_UnixTIME(date)
FROM events
WHERE time > 90534323
```

This query selects the name of each event and the date of the event formatted in human-readable form for all events more recent than the given time. FROM_ UnixTIME( ) transforms a standard Unix time value into a human-readable form.†

```
# The LENGTH( ) function returns the character length of
# a given string.
SELECT title, text, LENGTH(text)
FROM papers
WHERE author = 'Stacie Sheldon'
```

This query selects the title of a paper, the full text of the paper, and the length of the text in bytes for all of the papers authored by Stacie Sheldon. The LENGTH( ) function returns the character length of a given string.

As part of a WHERE clause

This form involves a function used in place of a constant when evaluating a WHERE clause. The value of the function is used for comparison for each row of the table. For example:

```
SELECT name
FROM entries
WHERE id = ROUND( (RAND( )*34) + 1 )
```

This query randomly selects the name of an entry from a pool of 35 entries. The RAND( ) function generates a random number between 0 and 1. This random value is then multiplied by 34 to turn the value into a number between 0 and 34. Incrementing the value by 1 provides a number between 1 and 35. The ROUND( ) function rounds the result to the nearest integer. The result is a whole number between 1 and 35 and will therefore match one of the ID numbers in the table.

```
SELECT name, FROM_UnixTIME(date)
FROM events
WHERE time > (Unix_TIMESTAMP( ) - (60 * 60 * 24) )
```

---

* You can use aliasing, covered earlier in the chapter, to give the resulting columns "friendly" names.

† Remember that SQL is case insensitive. This particular function is simply written FROM_UnixTIME( ) by convention. You can use FROM_UNIXTIME( ) or From_UnixTime( ) if they feel more natural to you.

You may use functions in both the value list and the WHERE clause. This query selects the name and date of each event less than a day old. With no arguments, the UNIX_TIMESTAMP( ) function returns the current time in Unix format.

```
SELECT name
FROM people
WHERE password = ENCRYPT(name, LEFT(name, 2))
```

You may also use the value of a table field within a function. This example returns the names of people who used their names as passwords. The ENCRYPT( ) function returns a Unix password–style encryption of the specified string using the supplied two-character salt. The LEFT( ) function returns the left-most *n* characters of the specified string.

Date functions

The most common functions you use will likely be the MySQL functions that enable you to manipulate dates. You already saw some of these functions earlier for translating a Unix-style date into a human-readable form of the date. MySQL, of course, provides more powerful functions for doing things such as calculating the time between two dates:

```
SELECT TO_DAYS(NOW( )) - TO_DAYS('2000-12-31');
```

This example provides the number of days that have passed in this millennium. The NOW( ) function returns the DATETIME representing the moment in time when the command was executed. Less obviously, the TO_DAYS( ) function returns the number of days since the year 1 B.C., represented by the specified DATE or DATETIME.[*]

Not everyone likes to see dates formatted the way MySQL provides them by default. Fortunately, MySQL lets you format dates to your own liking using the DATE_FORMAT function. It takes a DATE or DATETIME and a format string indicating how you want the date formatted:

```
mysql> SELECT DATE_FORMAT('1969-02-17', '%W, %M %D, %Y');
+----------------------------------------------+
| DATE_FORMAT('1969-02-17', '%W, %M %D, %Y') |
+----------------------------------------------+
| Monday, February 17th, 1969                  |
+----------------------------------------------+
1 row in set (0.39 sec)
```

Chapter 15 contains a full list of valid tokens for the DATE_FORMAT( ) function.

---

[*] MySQL is actually incapable of representing this date. Valid date ranges in MySQL are from January 1, 1000, to December 31, 9999. There is also no support in MySQL for alternative calendar systems such as the Hebrew, Chinese, or Muslim calendars.

String functions

In addition to date functions, you are likely to use string functions. We saw one such function above: the LENGTH( ) function. This function provides the number of characters in the specified string. The most common string function you are likely to use, however, is the TRIM( ) function, which removes extra spaces from columns.

One interesting function is the SOUNDEX( ) function. It translates a word into its soundex representation. The soundex representation is a way of representing the sound of a string so that you can compare two strings to see if one is misspelled:

```
mysql> SELECT SOUNDEX('too');
+----------------+
| SOUNDEX('too') |
+----------------+
| T000           |
+----------------+
1 row in set (0.42 sec)

mysql> SELECT SOUNDEX('two');
+----------------+
| soundex('two') |
+----------------+
| T000           |
+----------------+
1 row in set (0.00 sec)
```

For these two homonyms, the SOUNDEX( ) function provided the same value. Consequently, an application can leverage this function to check spelling variations.

Outer Joins

MySQL supports a more powerful joining than the simple inner joins we saw earlier. Specifically, MySQL supports something called a *left outer join* (also known as simply an *outer join*), which you specify with the keywords LEFT JOIN. This type of join is similar to an inner join, except that it includes data in the first table named that does not match any in the second table. If you remember our author and book tables from earlier in the chapter, you will remember that our join would not list any authors who did not have books in our database. You may want to show entries from one table that have no corresponding data in the table to which you are joining. That is where an outer join comes into play:

```
SELECT book.title, author.name
FROM author
LEFT JOIN book ON book.author = author.id
```

This query is similar to the inner join that you already understand:

```
SELECT book.title, author.name
FROM author, book
WHERE book.author = author.id
```

Note that an outer join uses the keyword `ON` instead of `WHERE`. The key difference in results is that the new syntax of the outer join will include authors such as Neil Gaiman, for whom no book is in our database. The results of the outer join would therefore look like this:

```
+----------------+----------------+
| book.title     | author.name    |
+----------------+----------------+
| The Green Mile | Stephen King   |
| Guards, Guards!| Terry Pratchett|
| Imzadi         | Peter David    |
| Gold           | Isaac Asimov   |
| Howling Mad    | Peter David    |
| NULL           | Neil Gaiman    |
+----------------+----------------+
```

MySQL takes this concept one step further by using a natural outer join. A natural outer join will combine the rows from two tables that have identical column names with identical types and identical values:

```
SELECT my_prod.name
FROM my_prod
NATURAL LEFT JOIN their_prod
```

This natural join will list all product names with identical entries in the `my_prod` and `their_prod` tables.

Unions

One of the newest MySQL features as of MySQL 4.0 is the support for SQL unions. A *union* is simply a tool for combining the results from multiple selects into a single result set listing. A MySQL union looks like this:

```
SELECT first_name, last_name
FROM Author
UNION
    SELECT fname, lname
    FROM Editor;
```

This query will provide a list of all authors and editors in the database. The list will include in the first column the values of the `first_name` column for authors and the values of the `fname` column for editors. The second column will include the `last_name` values for authors and `lname` values for editors.

If one person is an author and an editor, he will appear a single time in the list. You can, however, get MySQL to show the person twice in the results by using the `ALL` keyword:

```
SELECT first_name, last_name
FROM Author
UNION ALL
    SELECT fname, lname
    FROM Editor;
```

Batch Processing

Batch loading is the act of loading a lot of data into or pulling a lot of data out of MySQL all at once. MySQL supports two types of batch loading.

Command-line loads

In the simplest kind of batch load, you stick all your SQL commands in a file and send the contents of that file to MySQL:

```
mysql -h somehost -u uid -p < filename
```

In other words, you are using the command line to pipe the SQL commands into the *mysql* command-line utility. The examples on this book's web site contain several SQL command files that you can load into MySQL in this manner before you run the examples.

The LOAD command

The LOAD command enables you to load data from a file containing only data (no SQL commands). For example, if you had a file containing the names of all the books in your collection with one book on each line and the title and author separated by a tab, you could use the following command to load that data into your book table:

```
LOAD DATA LOCAL INFILE 'books.dat' INTO TABLE BOOK;
```

This command assumes that the file *books.dat* has one line for each database record to be inserted. It further assumes that there is a value for every column in the table or \N for null values. So, if the BOOK table has three columns, each line of *books.dat* should have three tab-separated values.

The LOCAL keyword tells the *mysql* command line to look for the file on the same machine as the client.* Without it, MySQL looks for the file on the server. Of course, if you are trying to load something on the server, you need to have been granted the special FILE privilege. Finally, keep in mind that nonlocal loads refer to files relative to the installation directory of MySQL.

If you have a comma-separated value file such as an Excel file, you can change the delimiter of the LOAD command:

```
LOAD DATA LOCAL INFILE 'books.dat'
INTO TABLE BOOK
FIELDS TERMINATED BY ',';
```

If a file contains values that would cause duplicate records in the database, you can use the REPLACE and IGNORE keywords to dictate the correct behavior. REPLACE will cause the values from the file to replace the ones in the database, where the IGNORE keyword will cause the duplicate values to be ignored. The default behavior is to ignore duplicates.

---

* Reading from files local to the client is available only on MySQL 3.22.15 and later.

Pulling data from MySQL

Finally, MySQL provides a tool for copying the results of a SELECT from the database into a file:

```
SELECT * INTO OUTFILE 'books.dat'
FIELDS TERMINATED BY ','
FROM BOOK;
```

This query copies all rows in the BOOK table into the file *books.dat*. You could then use this file to load into an Excel spreadsheet or another database. Because this file is created on the server, it is created relative to the base directory for the database in use. On a Mac OS X basic installation, for example, this file is created as */usr/local/ var/test/test.dat*.

A more complex version of this command enables you to put quotes (or any other characters) around fields:

```
SELECT * INTO OUTFILE 'books.dat'
FIELDS ENCLOSED BY '"' TERMINATED BY ','
FROM BOOK;
```

Of course, you probably want only the string fields (CHAR, VARCHAR, etc.) enclosed in quotes. You can accomplish this by adding the OPTIONALLY keyword:

```
SELECT * INTO OUTFILE 'books.dat'
FIELDS OPTIONALLY ENCLOSED BY '"' TERMINATED BY ','
FROM BOOK;
```

Chapter 15 contains a full range of options for loading and extracting data from MySQL.

CHAPTER 4
Database Administration

For the most part, MySQL is low-maintenance software. Once you have installed MySQL, it does not place heavy administrative demands on you. It is not, however, maintenance free. Typical MySQL administration tasks include:

- Installation
- Configuration and tuning
- Access control
- Logging
- Backup and recovery
- Table maintenance

We cover some of these topics in detail in other chapters—installation in Chapter 2, performance tuning in Chapter 5, and access control in Chapter 6.

You may find this chapter helpful even if you are not the one responsible for the administration of your MySQL server. Knowing about database administration can help you diagnose problems before you have to approach your database administrator.

To perform many administrative tasks, you must have administrative access to MySQL. (We describe access privileges and how to set yourself up as the MySQL database administrator in detail in Chapter 6.) You will additionally require administrative access to your operating system—root on Unix systems, Administrator on Windows NT/2000/XP—to perform a number of tasks.[*]

Configuration

MySQL requires the configuration of the MySQL server process, *mysqld*, and its several client processes such as the *mysql* command-line utility. MySQL exposes its

---

[*] On Mac OS X, you must enable the root user to gain root access. As of now, there is no way to manage the MySQL operating system needs by supplying the password of a user with administrative privileges.

Unix roots in how you configure it. Specifically, you configure it using a combination of command-line options, configuration files, and environment variables. Just about any configurable item can be managed using these three mechanisms.

Because you can define options in multiple ways, MySQL has a built-in order of preference that defines how it resolves conflicts:

1. Command-line options
2. Configuration options
3. Environment variable options

In other words, if you have three different values specified for the password option, MySQL client tools will use the one you specified on the command line.

The simplest, most common way to handle your MySQL options is with a configuration file. A configuration file enables you to stick all your options in a file so you do not have to specify them each time you run a command or log into a machine.

File Locations

On Unix systems, MySQL looks in the following locations—in order—for configuration files:

1. In the */etc/my.cnf* file. The first place MySQL looks is the global options file. In general, you will want to place the default options to be used by all users and all servers in this file.

2. In the *DATADIR/my.cnf* file. *DATADIR* is the directory where a MySQL server instance keeps its datafiles. This configuration file exists specifically for configuration parameters specific to a given server instance.

3. In the location specified through the *--defaults-extra-file=filename* command-line option. This command-line option enables the MySQL server or client utilities to look in an arbitrary location for a configuration file.

4. In the *$HOME/.my.cnf* file. *$HOME* is the Unix environment variable that holds the home directory of the current user. This configuration file in a user's home directory is where individual users can keep their user-specific options. This location is where most client options are specified.

Windows has an extra global configuration file and no user-specific configuration file:

1. *My.ini* in the Windows system folder—generally *C:\WINNT\System32*
2. *C:\my.cnf*
3. *C:\mysql\data\my.cnf*
4. *--defaults-extra-file=filename*

If any option appears in multiple files, the last one read overrides the others. In other words, the user-defined options in *C:\my.cnf* override any values read from *My.ini*. This behavior makes it possible for a database administrator to provide default values for the client tools in *My.ini* and allow users to override specific options as their needs dictate.

File Content

All the configuration files share the same format. Example 4-1 is a sample configuration file. Much of it should be fairly straightforward, but we will take a moment to dissect the file.

Example 4-1. A sample MySQL configuration file

```
# Example mysql options file.
#
# These options go to all clients
[client]
password     = my_password
port         = 3306
socket       = /var/lib/mysql/mysql.sock


# These options go to the mysqld server
[mysqld]
port         = 3306
socket       = /var/lib/mysql/mysql.sock
skip-locking
set-variable = max_allowed_packet=1M
```

The first three lines beginning with # are comments. The MySQL configuration file format supports two kinds of comments: # and ;. MySQL ignores any data appearing after a pound sign or a semicolon until the end of the line on which it appears.

The next line indicates the start of a section:

```
[client]
```

This format is actually one you may be familiar with if you have played with Samba or Windows INI configuration. A MySQL configuration file contains sections with configuration options that apply only to that section. MySQL configuration files contain two sections: client and mysqld.

The lines appearing after a section marker support the named section until the end of the file is reached or another group is encountered. This client section contains three configuration items for the client tools. The first specifies the default password:

```
password     = my_password
```

This option is equivalent to using the command-line option *--password=my_password*. As a general rule, any command-line option specified as *--option=value* appears in the MySQL configuration files as *option=value*.

Specifying the password in the configuration file is a convenient way of connecting to MySQL without specifying a password all the time. It is, however, generally a bad idea to specify a password in a configuration file or on the command line. You should instead require your client utility to prompt you for a password.* If you do specify the password in a configuration file, you should definitely make sure no one else can read that file.

The next two lines after the password option configure the port and socket file that a client tool can use to connect to the server. After them, we encounter a new section:

```
[mysqld]
```

This section contains options that configure the MySQL server process. It contains options similar to the client section as well as two new ways of specifying options. The first is an option without a value:

```
skip-locking
```

This Boolean option tells the MySQL server to disable system locking. If the option is not defined, system locking is enabled. The command-line form of this option is *--skip-locking*.

The final format for MySQL options enables you to specify *mysqld* variables:

```
set-variable = max_allowed_packet=1M
```

This option is the same as specifying *--set-variable max_allowed_packet=1M* on the command line. Variables are additional settings used to control the runtime behavior of the server and clients.

Server Startup and Shutdown

Because the MySQL server is a server process, it should start up automatically when the machine starts up. It should also shut down cleanly when the computer shuts down. How you achieve these goals depends heavily on your operating system.

 You can start the server directly from the command line using the *mysqld* command. It is recommended, however, that you use *safe_ mysqld* when starting MySQL by hand under all operating systems.

Unix/Linux

On Unix and Unix-like systems such as Linux (but not on Mac OS X), there are a couple of different ways of starting and stopping MySQL depending on whether you are dealing with a SVR4 or another flavor of Unix. The *mysql.server* script exists for

---

* Using the MySQL client utilities, you can pass the *-p* parameter to force the utility to prompt you for a password. The command-line utilities will not echo the password to the screen.

SVR4 systems, and *safe_mysqld* works for any other Unix system.* We describe general "rules of thumb" for using these scripts. One of the maddening things about Unix systems, however, is in how they differ slightly from system to system in the details of service startup and shutdown.

SVR4

The *mysql.server* script supports the startup and shutdown of MySQL on SVR4 systems.† You can find this script in the *support-files* directory of your installation, usually */usr/local/mysql/support-files*. The SVR4 startup/shutdown mechanism relies on a set of scripts in the */etc* folder to start and stop services when the system enters different run levels.

 If you installed MySQL on Linux using the RPM packages, *mysql.server* was probably installed on your system. The RPM installer renames *mysql.server* to *mysql* when it copies the file to */etc/rc.d/init.d*. If the file */etc/rc.d/init.d/mysql* exists, you are already set up to have MySQL automatically start up and shut down.

The procedure for installing *mysql.server* on a RedHat Linux system is:

```
$ cp mysql.server /etc/rc.d/init.d
$ ln -s /etc/rc.d/init.d/mysql.server /etc/rc.d/rc3.d/S99mysql
$ ln -s /etc/rc.d/init.d/mysql.server /etc/rc.d/rc0.d/S01mysql
```

The first line installs the script into the initialization scripts directory, */etc/rc.d/init.d*. The second command creates a link to this script that causes Linux to execute the script when the system enters run-level 3. For a simple explanation, Linux executes the scripts in */etc/rc.d/rc3.d* when the system enters run-level 3. Run-level 3 typically means that an SVR4 system has entered multiuser mode. If your Unix flavor uses a different run level to represent multiuser mode, you should install the link in that directory.

The final line creates a link to the *mysql.server* script for run-level 0. Run-level 0 executes a system halt. The scripts in */etc/rc.d/rc0.d* execute when the system shuts down.

Other Unix

On non-SVR4 systems, the script *safe_mysqld* starts MySQL. You can find it in the */bin* directory of your MySQL install, usually */usr/local/mysql/bin*.

To use *safe_mysqld*, you need to know how your flavor of Unix starts services at boot and kills them at shutdown. On some BSD systems, there is a file called */etc/rc.local* that you modify to call *safe_mysqld*. Newer BSD systems such as FreeBSD, however, may have an *rc.local* file that you should not modify. FreeBSD, for example, expects you to place scripts such as *mysql.server* in */usr/local/etc/rc.d*.

---

* In the MySQL 4.0 alpha versions, this script has been renamed *mysqld_safe*.

† The *mysql.server* script is actually a specially designed script to call *safe_mysqld* on SVR4 systems.

Mac OS X

Mac OS X has introduced yet another way of automatically starting services on a Unix system. It specifically has three different startup directories:

- */System/Library/StartupItems*
- */Library/StartupItems*
- *$HOME/Library/StartupItems*

The */System/Library/StartupItems* directory is for operating system services, and the *$HOME/Library/StartupItems* is for user-owned services. MySQL should start up from */Library/StartupItems*, the directory for general services that should be started at system boot time.

The *StartupItems* directories expect each service to have its own directory, so your first step for MySQL is to create the directory */Library/StartupItems/MySQL*. It actually does not matter what you call this directory. Whatever you call it, in it you will place two files:

- A Unix script to start MySQL
- A startup parameters file called *StartupParameters.plist*

The Unix script is a simple script that calls the *safe_mysqld* command to start MySQL. It should have the same name as the directory in which you placed it (in this case, *MySQL*). It should look something like this:

```
#!/bin/sh

. /etc/rc.common

if [ "${MYSQLSERVER:=-NO-}" = "-YES
    cd /usr/local/mysql
    bin/mysqld_safe --user=mysql &
fi
```

The check on the value of $MYSQLSERVER enables you to turn off MySQL in your Mac OS X *hostconfig* file without having to delete the *MySQL* directory from your *Startup-Items*. To enable MySQL, you need to add the following line to */etc/hostconfig*:

```
MYSQLSERVER=-YES-
```

Similarly, you can stop MySQL from starting at boot time simply by changing -YES-to -NO-.

Once you have the script installed, you need to add the file *StartupParameters.plist*:

```
{
    Description     = "MySQL Database Server";
    Provides        = ("MySQL");
    Requires        = ("Resolver");
    OrderPreference = "None";
    Messages =
    {
```

```
        start = "Starting MySQL Server";
        stop  = "Stopping MySQL Server";
    };
}
```

This file tells Mac OS X about the service in this directory and any dependencies it has on other services. When you reboot, you should see the message "Starting MySQL Server" on your startup screen along with other service startup messages.

Windows NT/2000

Windows NT systems automatically start up and shut down any applications installed as NT services. In Chapter 2, we covered the details of installing MySQL as a server in Windows systems.

Logging

The MySQL server is capable of producing a number of useful log files:*

- Error
- Query
- Binary
- Slow query

MySQL produces the error log if you use *mysql.server* or *safe_mysqld* to start MySQL. You can enable any or all of the others if you wish. By default, MySQL writes the log files to the data directory.

The Error Log

The error log contains the redirected output from the *safe_mysqld* script. On Unix, it is a file called *hostname.err*. On Windows, it is called *mysql.err*. This file contains an entry for each startup and shutdown of the server, including an entry for every time the server restarted because it died. Critical errors and warnings about tables that need to be checked or repaired also appear here.

The Binary Log

The binary log contains all SQL commands that update data. MySQL logs only statements that actually change data. For example, a delete that fails to affect any rows is not logged. Updates that set column values to their current values are also not logged. MySQL logs updates in execution order.

---

* Old versions of MySQL support another kind of log, the update log. This log has been made obsolete by the binary log. If you are still using the update log, we recommend that you switch to the binary log.

The binary log is useful for journaling all update operations since the last backup. For example, if you back up your database once a day, and your database crashes in the middle of the day, you can restore the database up to the last completed transaction by:

1. Restoring the database (see the "Backup" and "Recovery" sections in this chapter for more information on this task)
2. Applying the transactions from all binary logs since the last backup

Enable the binary log through the *--log-bin=file* option. If you specify no filename, MySQL uses the file *hostname-bin*. If you specify a relative path, the path is assumed to be relative to the data directory. MySQL appends a numeric index to the filename so that the file ends up being *filename.number*; e.g., *hostname-bin.2*. MySQL uses the index for rotating the files and rotates to the next index under the following conditions:

- The server is restarted.
- The server is refreshed.
- The log reaches the maximum log size.
- The logs are flushed.

MySQL also creates an index file that contains a list of all used binary log files. By default, this file is called *hostname-bin.index*. You may change the name and/or location of the index with the *--log-bin-index=file* option.

The *mysqlbinlog* utility enables you to read the binary log. The example below illustrates how the binary log works. This example assumes we have started MySQL on a host called *odin* and specified *log-bin* in the global configuration file, */etc/my.cnf*. MySQL places the following files in the data directory:

```
$ cd /usr/local/mysql/data
$ ls -l
.
.
.
-rw-rw----   1  mysql       mysql       73 Aug  5  17:06 odin-bin.001
-rw-rw----   1  mysql       mysql       15 Aug  5  17:06 odin-bin.index
.
.
.
```

Inspecting *odin-bin.index*, we see:

```
$ cat odin-bin.index
./odin-bin.001
$
```

The index tells us there is one binary log file named *odin-bin.001* in the same directory as the index. The *mysqlbinlog* utility lets us read the actual log:

```
$ mysqlbinlog odin-bin.001
# at 4
#010805 17:06:00 server id 1    Start: binlog v 1, server 3.23.40-log created 010805
17:06:00
$
```

As clients perform updates on the database, the binary log grows. At the *mysql* command prompt, for example, suppose you issue the following command:

```
$ mysql
mysql> USE test;
mysql> INSERT INTO test ( object_id, object_title ) VALUES (1, 'test');
Query OK, 1 row affected (0.02 sec)
mysql> QUIT;
Bye
$
```

The binary log now looks like this:

```
$ mysqlbinlog odin-bin.001
# at 4
#010805  17:06:00 server id 1   Start: binlog v 1, server 3.23.40-log created 010805
17:06:00
# at 73
#010805  17:39:38 server id 1   Query   thread_id=2    exec_time=0    error_code=0
USE test;
SET TIMESTAMP=997058378;
INSERT INTO test ( object_id, object_title ) VALUES (1, 'test');
$
```

After the SQL update, the binary log contains the equivalent update. You can flush the log to start a new binary log:

```
$ mysqladmin -u root -ppassword flush-logs
```

The result is a new file called *odin-bin.002* where all new updates are logged. The *odin-bin.index* file is also updated to reflect the new log.

You can reexecute the commands in a binary log by piping the output from *mysqlbinlog* to the *mysql* client tool:

```
$ mysqlbinlog odin-bin.001 | mysql
```

MySQL provides a few options to help you control the binary logs. The option *--binlog-do-db=dbname* tells MySQL to log updates for only the specified database. The option *--binlog-ignore-db=dbname* tells MySQL to ignore the specified database for the purpose of binary logging.

The Slow Query Log

The slow query log contains a record of all SQL commands that took longer than the time specified in the system variable long_query_time. This log can help identify problem queries and expose parts of your database or application that need tuning.

You can enable the slow query log with the *--log-slow-queries=filename* option. If no filename is provided, it defaults to *hostname-slow.log*. If no directory is given, the directory defaults to the data directory. The long_query_time variable can be set using the *--set-variable long_query_time=time* command-line option (in which *time* is specified in seconds).

Log Rotation

No matter which log files you choose to enable, you need to maintain them so they do not fill up a filesystem.

Unfortunately, none of the techniques we discuss here work for the error log. Since it is written from the *safe_mysqld* script, it is not controlled by the MySQL server and the *flush-logs* command does not flush it. Also note that *safe_mysqld* will continue to append to it on successive restarts. You may want to modify the startup or shutdown scripts for your MySQL server to maintain the error log.

If you are running RedHat Linux, you can use *mysql-log-rotate* to rotate logs. It can be found in the *support-files* directory of your MySQL installation. It uses the *logrotate* utility to automatically rotate your error log for you. To install *mysql-log-rotate* on RedHat Linux, simply copy it to */etc/logrotate.d*. You may wish to edit the script to rotate other logs that you have enabled as well. By default, it rotates only the query log. For more information on *logrotate*, read the manpage or refer to your RedHat documentation.

If you installed MySQL on Linux using the RPM package, *mysql-log-rotate* may have already been installed on your system. The RPM installer renames *mysql-log-rotate* to *mysql* when it copies it to */etc/logrotate.d*. If the file */etc/logrotate.d/mysql* is already there, it has already been installed.

On systems other than RedHat, you will have to devise your own scripts for rotating the logs. Depending on which logs you have enabled and how you want them located, the scripts could range from very simple to very complex. In general, the procedure is to copy the log files out of the way and use *mysqladmin flush-logs* to reinitialize the logs.

Backup

A good backup strategy is by far the most important thing you can develop as an administrator. In particular, you will be really glad you have good backups if you ever have a system crash and need to restore your databases with as little data loss as possible. Also, if you ever accidentally delete a table or destroy a database, those backups will come in very handy.

Every site is different, so it is difficult to give specific recommendations on what you should do. You need to think about your installation and your needs. In this section, we present some general backup principles that you can adopt and cover the technical details of performing backups. With the information provided in this section, you should be able to devise a coherent strategy for your installation.

In general, there are a number of key backup considerations:

- Store your backups on a device other than the database (either on another disk or perhaps a tape device), if possible. If your disk crashes, you'll be really happy to have the backups in a different place. If you are doing binary logging, store the binary logs on the same device as the backups.
- Make sure you have enough disk space for the backups to complete.
- Use binary logging in addition to backups, if appropriate, so you can restore your database with minimal data loss. If you choose not to use binary logging, you will only be able to recover your database to the point of your last backup. Depending on your application, a backup without binary logs might be useless.
- Keep an adequate number of archived backups.
- Test your backups before an emergency occurs.

The next sections describe two MySQL utilities for taking backups.

mysqldump

mysqldump is the MySQL utility provided for dumping databases. It basically generates an SQL script containing the commands (CREATE TABLE, INSERT, etc.) necessary to rebuild the database from scratch. The main advantage of this approach over the direct copy (*mysqlhotcopy*) is that output is in a portable ASCII format that can be used across hardware and operating systems to rebuild a database. Also, because the output is an SQL script, it is possible to recover individual tables.

To use *mysqldump* to back up your database, we recommend that you use the *-opt* option. This turns on *-quick*, *--add-drop-table*, *--add-locks*, *--extended-insert*, and *--lock-tables*. This option should give you the fastest possible dump of your database. The option *--lock-tables* locks all the tables in the database, so the database will essentially be offline while you are doing this.

Your command will look something like this:

```
$ mysqldump --opt test > /usr/backups/testdb
```

This command dumps the test database into the file */usr/backups/testdb*. If you are using binary logging, you will also want to specify *--flush-logs*, so the binary logs get checkpointed at the time of the backup:

```
$ mysqldump --flush-logs --opt test > /usr/backups/testdb
```

mysqldump has a number of other options for customizing your backup. For a list of all the available options for *mysqldump*, type *mysqldump --help*.

mysqlhotcopy

mysqlhotcopy is a Perl script that uses a combination of LOCK TABLES, FLUSH TABLES, and Unix *cp* to perform a fast backup of the database. It simply copies the raw database files to another location. Because it does only a file copy, it is much faster than *mysqldump*. And because the copy is in native format, the backup is not portable to other hardware or operating systems, except for MyISAM tables, which are portable. Also, *mysqlhotcopy* can be run only on the same host as the database, whereas *mysqldump* can be executed remotely.

To run *mysqlhotcopy*, type:

```
$ mysqlhotcopy test /usr/backups
```

This command creates a new directory in the */usr/backups* directory that has a copy of all the data files in the test database.

If you are using binary logging, you will also want to specify *--flushlog*, so the binary logs get checkpointed at the time of the backup.

Recovery

Individual recovery scenarios vary widely, ranging from disk hardware failures to corrupted data files to accidentally dropped tables, and many points in between. In this section, we provide an overview of recovery procedures.

In general, you need two things to perform a database recovery: your backup files and your binary logs. Performing a recovery consists of:

- Restoring the database from the last backup
- Applying the binary logs to bring the system completely up to date

If you do not have binary logging enabled, the best you can do is restore the system to the last full backup.

mysqldump Recovery

This example assumes we are recovering the database named test that we dumped earlier.

The following command reloads the database:

```
$ cat test.dump | mysql
```

The command runs the SQL commands produced by *mysqldump* and brings the database back to the state it was at the last backup.

Once the system is back to its state at the time of the last backup, it is time to rerun the transactions that have taken place since the last backup using the binary log. If your log includes entries from multiple databases, and you want to recover only one of them, use the *--one-database mysql* option to filter out SQL commands that apply to other databases. You should then rerun only the binary logs that were created since your last backup. For each binary log file, type:

```
$ mysqlbinlog host-bin.xxx | mysql --one-database=testdb
```

Sometimes you will need to massage the log output from the *mysqlbinlog* program before sending it to MySQL. If you are recovering from a mistaken `DROP TABLE` statement, for example, you will need to remove this command from the output of *mysqlbinlog*; otherwise, you will drop the table again! If such intervention is necessary, you need send the output from *mysqlbinlog* to a text file and edit it before sending it to MySQL.

mysqlhotcopy Recovery

To recover from a *mysqlhotcopy* backup, reload the database by copying the database files from the backup location to the *mysql* data location *while the server is not running*. Assuming the database is backed up in */var/backup/test* and the *mysql* data location is */usr/local/mysql/data*:

```
$ cp -R /var/backup/test /usr/local/mysql/data
```

This command brings the database back to the state of the last backup.

It is now safe to restart the *mysql* server and apply the binary logs as described in the previous section to bring the system up to date.

Table Maintenance and Crash Recovery

Database tables can get out of whack when a write to the data file is not complete. This can happen due to a variety of reasons, such as a power failure or a non-graceful shutdown of the MySQL server.

MySQL provides two mechanisms for detecting and repairing table errors: *myisamchk/isamchk* and *mysqlcheck*. It is a wise practice to perform these checks regularly. Early detection may increase your chances of recovering from errors successfully.

mysqlcheck is new with Version 3.23.38 of MySQL. The main difference between *myisamchk/isamchk* and *mysqlcheck* is that *mysqlcheck* enables you to check or repair tables while the server is running. *myisamchk/isamchk* require that the server not be running.

myisamchk and *isamchk* are quite similar. They provide the same functions. The only difference is that *myisamchk* is used on MyISAM tables, and *isamchk* is used on ISAM tables. *mysqlcheck* can be used only with MyISAM tables.

Checking a Table

If you suspect errors on a table, the first thing you should do is use one of the utilities to check it out. You can tell what kind of table you are dealing with by looking at the extension of the data file. An extension of *.MYI* tells you it is a MyISAM table, and *.ISM* indicates an ISAM table. As we said earlier, *myisamchk* and *mysqlcheck* are used only with *.MYI* files, and *isamchk* with *.ISM* files.

Assume we have a database called test with two tables: table1, which is an ISAM table, and table2, which is a MyISAM table. First, check your table, using the appropriate utility. If you use *myisamchk* or *isamchk*, make sure your MySQL server is not running to prevent the server from writing to the file while you are reading it.

```
$ myisamchk table2.MYI
Data records:        0   Deleted blocks:       0
- check file-size
- check key delete-chain
- check record delete-chain
- check index reference
$ isamchk table1.ISM
Checking ISAM file: table1.ISM
Data records:        0   Deleted blocks:       0
- check file-size
- check delete-chain
- check index reference
$ mysqlcheck test table2
test.table2                                 OK
```

This output shows that there are no errors in either of the tables.

The default method is usually adequate for detecting errors. However, if no errors are reported but you still suspect damage, you can perform an extended check using the *--extend-check* option with *myisamchk/isamchk* or the *--extend* option with *mysqlcheck*. This will take a long time, but is very thorough. If the extended check does not report any errors, you are in good shape.

Repairing a Table

If the check reported errors on a table, you can try to repair them.

If you are using *myisamchk* or *isamchk*, make sure your MySQL server is not running when you attempt the repair. Also, it is a good idea to back up the data files before attempting a repair operation in case something goes haywire.

With *myisamchk/isamchk*, you should first try the *--recover* option:

```
$ isamchk --recover table1.ISM
- recovering ISAM-table 'table1.ISM'
Data records: 3
$ myisamchk --recover table2.MYI
- recovering (with keycache) MyISAM-table 'table2.MYI'
Data records: 2
```

If this fails for some reason, you can try *--safe-recover*, a slower recovery method that can fix some errors *--recover* cannot.

```
$ isamchk --safe-recover table1.ISM
- recovering ISAM-table 'table1.ISM'
Data records: 3
$ myisamchk --safe-recover table2.MYI
- recovering (with keycache) MyISAM-table 'table2.MYI'
Data records: 2
```

With *mysqlcheck*, your only recovery option is *--repair*.

```
$ mysqlcheck --repair test table2
test.table2                                        OK
```

If these operations fail, your only remaining option is to restore the table from your backups and binary logs. See the "Backup" and "Recovery" sections for more information.

Scheduled Table Checking

We recommend that you take steps to perform regularly scheduled table checks on your database files. This can be done by wrapping *isamchk/myisamchk/mysqlcheck* commands into a script that is executed periodically from *cron* or some other scheduling software.

You may also want to modify your system boot procedure to check tables at boot time. This is especially useful when you reboot the system after a system crash.

MySQL Administration

Now that you have MySQL installed and understand the basics of MySQL's dialect of SQL, it is time to turn towards administrative issues. In Part II, we tackle the tasks you will need to understand as someone in charge of a MySQL installation. Using this knowledge, you will be able to support the applications we will build in Part III.

## CHAPTER 5

Performance Tuning

MySQL is known for its speed. A number of factors out of MySQL's control, however, can impact application and database performance. Application architects control some of these factors, but database administrators control others. In this chapter, we will introduce you to some of the principles of performance tuning and discuss some of the tools you have at your disposal.

The key to good database performance is solid application and database design. Performance tuning cannot make up for poor design because it is too late in the application development process. Chapter 7 covers the elements of good database design. This chapter handles those things you can do after an application is deployed to help the system run its fastest.

An Approach to Performance Tuning

When performance tuning a MySQL application, there are five main things to consider:

1. Application tuning
2. SQL query tuning
3. Database server tuning
4. Operating system
5. Hardware

These are ranked in terms of "bang for the buck." For example, adding memory or upgrading your processor will usually improve the performance of your applications, but you should be able to achieve greater gains for lower cost if you tune your application code and database server first. In addition, any performance tuning on the MySQL server will apply to all applications using that server. Characteristics that are advantageous for one particular application may not improve the performance of another. Based on these factors, as a general methodology, we recommend that you look at tuning issues in the order listed above.

Application Tuning

Application performance tuning actually consists of two parts:

- Host application tuning (e.g., C/C++, Java, Perl, etc.)
- SQL query tuning

Host Application Tuning

Good application design and programming practices are crucial to getting good performance from your MySQL application. No amount of query tuning can make up for inefficient code. We cover many of the details of database application design in Chapter 8, but you can follow these general guidelines for designing your applications to optimize performance:

Normalize your database
> Elimination of redundancy from your database is critical for performance.

Denormalize your database where appropriate
> On the other hand, sometimes performance demands require that you denormalize your database. A classic example of this is a nightly report that summarizes basic information. These types of reports often require sifting through large quantities of data to produce summaries. In this situation, you can create a "redundant" table that is updated with the latest summary information on a periodic basis. This summary table can then be used as a basis for your report.

Let the MySQL server do what it does well
> This point may seem obvious, but it is frequently overlooked. For example, if you need to retrieve a set of rows from a table, you could write a loop in your host application to retrieve the rows:
>
> ```
> for (int i = 0; i++; i< keymax) {
>  select * from foobar where key=i;
>  process the row
>  }
> ```

The problem with this approach is that MySQL has the overhead of parsing, optimizing, and executing the same query for every iteration of the loop. If you let MySQL retrieve all the rows at once, you eliminate the excess overhead. For example:

```
select * from foobar where key < keymax;
for each row {
 process the row
 }
```

Cache data when appropriate

Caching some data in the application often provides performance improvements. As an example, assume you have a customer order application that accepts a state abbreviation as input and expands it to the full state name based on a lookup in the database.

```
Accept input from user into $state_abbr
Select state_name into $state_name from state where state_abbr = $state_abbr;
Set display field = $state_name
```

However, we know that the state lookup table does not change frequently, so, caching the state table can provide a performance gain. For example:

```
# at application startup
select state_name, state_abbr from state;
for each row {
 load state name into state_name
 hash table indexed by state_abbr
 }
accept input from user into $state_abbr
set display field = state_name[$state_abbr]
```

Here we save a query on the database every time the user enters an order. The lookup is done once at application startup.

Caching data works well with relatively static information. You don't want to cache data that will become stale quickly, because keeping the local cache updated will likely be greater work than any savings you get from the cache.

Use persistent connections or connection pooling if possible

Connecting and disconnecting from the database has an overhead associated with it. (We cover the concepts of connecting and disconnecting in detail in Chapter 8, as well as in each of the language-specific chapters for Perl, Python, PHP, C, and Java/JDBC.) Without going into too much detail, the idea is that you want to reduce the number of connections and disconnections to a minimum. In particular, this can be a problem with web applications in which each time a page is requested, the CGI or PHP script connects to the database to retrieve the relevant information. By using persistent connections or a connection pool, you bypass connect/disconnect overhead, and your application performs better. However, if you maintain too many pooled/persistent connections, you may bog down your MySQL server by consuming too many resources.

Connection pooling and persistent connections are handled differently in each host language. For example, PHP provides persistent connections to MySQL via the `mysql_pconnect( )` function. Java provides connection pooling via the JDBC driver. You should refer to the relevant chapters in this book to find out more about connection pooling or persistent connections in your chosen host language.

SQL Query Tuning

The data in your database is stored on your disk. Retrieving and updating the data is ultimately a series of disk input/output operations (I/Os). The goal of SQL query tuning is to minimize the number of I/Os. Your main weapon for tuning your queries is the index.

In the absence of indexes on your database tables, each retrieval would require that all the data in all of the involved tables be scanned. To illustrate this problem, consider the following example:

```
SELECT name FROM Employee WHERE ssnum = 999999999
```

In this example, we select the name of an employee from the Employee table for the employee with 999-99-9999 as a social security number (ssnum). We know the social security number should be unique. In other words, for each record in the table, ssnum will have a unique value. We thus expect a single row from the above query since only one row can have the social security number of 999-99-9999.

Because the Employee table in our example has no indexes, MySQL does not know that the query will return a single record. When it executes the query, it has to scan the entire table to find all the records that match the WHERE clause—a scan of the entire table for the one record with a social security number of 999-99-9999. If the Employee table has a thousand rows, MySQL will read each and every one of those rows to compare the ssnum value to the constant 999999999. This operation is linear with the number of rows in the table.

An index is a tool for telling MySQL critical information about the table. If, for example, we add an index on the ssnum column of the Employee table, MySQL can consult the index first to find matching ssnum values. In this case, the index sorts rows by ssnum and organizes them into a tree structure that helps MySQL find the records quickly. After it finds the matching records, it simply has to read the name data for each match. This operation is logarithmic with respect to the number of rows in the table—a significant improvement over the linear performance of an unindexed table.

Just as in this example, most MySQL query tuning boils down to a process of ensuring that you have the right indexes on your tables and that they are being used correctly by MySQL.

Index guidelines

We have established that the proper indexing of your tables is crucial to the performance of your application. The knee-jerk reaction might be to index every column in each table of your database. After all, indexing improves performance, right?

Unfortunately, indexes also have costs associated with them. Each time you write to a table—i.e., INSERT, UPDATE, or DELETE—with one or more indexes, MySQL also has to update each index. Each index thus adds overhead to all write operations on that

---

table. In addition, each index adds to the size of your database. You will gain a performance benefit from an index only if its columns are referenced in a WHERE clause. If an index is never used, it is not worth incurring the cost of maintaining it.

If an index is used infrequently, it may or may not be worth maintaining. If, for example, you have a query that is run monthly that takes two minutes to complete without indexes, you may decide that, because the query is run so infrequently, it is not worth the index maintenance costs. On the other hand, if the monthly query takes several hours to complete, you would probably decide that maintaining the indexes is worth it. These kinds of decisions have to be made to balance the needs of your application.

With these trade-offs in mind, here are some guidelines for index creation:

Try to index all columns referenced in a WHERE clause
As a general goal, you want any column that is referenced in a WHERE clause to be indexed. There are, however, exceptions. If columns are compared or joined using the <, <=, =, >=, >, and BETWEEN operators, the index is used. But use of a function on a column in a WHERE clause defeats an index on that column. So, for example:

```
SELECT * FROM Employee WHERE LEFT(name, 6) = 'FOOBAR'
```

would not take advantage of an index on the name column.

The LIKE operator, on the other hand, will use an index if there is a literal prefix in the pattern. For example:

```
SELECT * FROM Employee WHERE name LIKE 'FOOBAR%'
```

would use an index, but the following would not:

```
SELECT * FROM Employee WHERE name LIKE '%FOOBAR'
```

Also, as discussed earlier, it is important to note that you should not blindly index every column that is referenced in a WHERE clause. The cost of maintaining the index should be balanced by the performance benefits.

Use unique indexes where possible
If you know the data in an index is unique, such as a primary key or an alternate key, use a unique index. Unique indexes are even more beneficial for performance than regular indexes. MySQL is able to leverage its knowledge that the value is unique to make more optimization assumptions.

Take advantage of multicolumn indexes
Well-designed multicolumn indexes can reduce the total number of indexes needed. MySQL will use a left prefix of a multicolumn index if applicable. Say, for example, you have an Employee table with the columns first_name and last_name. If you know that last_name is always used in queries while first_name is used only occasionally, you can create a multicolumn index with last_name as the first column and first_name as the second column. With this index design, all queries with last_name or queries with last_name and first_name in the WHERE clause will use the index.

Poorly designed multicolumn indexes may end up either not being used at all or being used infrequently. From the example above, queries with only first_name in the WHERE clause will *not* use the index.

Having a strong understanding of your application and probable query scenarios is invaluable in determining the right set of multicolumn indexes. Always verify your results with the EXPLAIN SELECT tool (described later in the chapter).

Consider not indexing some columns

Sometimes performing a full table scan is faster than having to read the index and the data table. This is especially true for cases in which the indexed column contains a small set of evenly distributed data. The classic example of this is gender, which has two values (male and female) that are evenly split. Selecting by gender requires you to read roughly half of the rows. It might be faster to do a full table scan in this case. As always, test your application to see what works best for you.

EXPLAIN SELECT

MySQL provides a critical performance-tuning tool in the form of the EXPLAIN SELECT command. As a general rule, you should never deploy an application without running its queries through this utility to verify that they are executing as expected. This tool specifically tells you:

- How queries are using (or are failing to use) indexes
- The order in which tables are being joined

It shows you exactly how MySQL is executing your query and gives you clues about how the query performance can be improved.

Before going into the details of EXPLAIN SELECT, it is important to understand how MySQL compiles and executes SQL queries. The processing of a query can be broken up into several phases, as described in Figure 5-1.

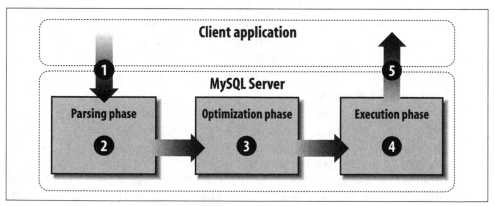

Figure 5-1. Phases of query processing

This model is a simplification of what really goes on in the MySQL server when it processes a query. Nonetheless, it is useful when discussing the process of query optimization to understand at a high level what is happening. Now, on to the phases:

1. The query is sent to the server. All query processing is initiated by the client sending a query to the server.

2. The parsing phase. During this phase, MySQL parses the SQL query for syntax correctness. In addition, it ensures that all referenced tables and columns are valid.

3. The optimization phase. During this phase, MySQL takes the information gathered during the parsing phase and generates an execution plan to satisfy the query. It considers all the information it knows about the relevant tables and columns and applies its internal optimization rules to generate an execution plan that should satisfy the query the fastest. Note that none of the tables or indexes are actually accessed here. Phases 2 and 3 are commonly called compilation.

4. The execution phase. In the execution phase, MySQL takes the query plan generated in the optimization phase and executes it. An important thing to note is that during the execution phase, MySQL will not adjust the query plan. So even if the optimization phase produces a flawed plan, it will be executed anyway.

5. The results are sent to the client. After the query has completed, the results are sent back to the client.

The execution of any query therefore hinges on the plan generated during the optimization phase. The key to improving the performance of any query is to understand the query plan that MySQL is using to satisfy that query. The query optimization is performed by a piece of very sophisticated software. Like any other software, it uses internal rules and assumptions to do its job. Usually it does a great job, but sometimes the plans it generates can be improved.

EXPLAIN SELECT helps us see the query plan so that we can improve it. It gives us a way to see the query plan so that we can see where the plan might be flawed.

For example, consider a database with a State table and a query to retrieve the state_name based on the code, state_cd.

```
mysql> SELECT state_name FROM State WHERE state_cd = 'CA';
+------------+
| state_name |
+------------+
| California |
+------------+
1 row in set (0.00 sec)
```

To use EXPLAIN SELECT, we simply prepend the EXPLAIN keyword to the query. MySQL won't execute the query; instead, it will produce output describing the plan for executing the query. For example:

```
mysql> EXPLAIN SELECT state_name FROM State WHERE state_cd = 'CA';
+-------+------+---------------+------+---------+------+------+------------+
| table | type | possible_keys | key  | key_len | ref  | rows | Extra      |
```

```
+-------+------+----------------+------+----------+------+------+------------+
| State | ALL  | NULL           | NULL |    NULL  | NULL |   50 | where used |
+-------+------+----------------+------+----------+------+------+------------+
1 row in set (0.00 sec)
```

This output is simply a set of steps to be performed in order during the execution phase. In our simple example, there is only one step. We will look at some more complicated query plans later. First, we should look at the columns returned by EXPLAIN SELECT and what they mean:

table
> The table to which the row of output refers. In queries with multiple tables, EXPLAIN SELECT will return a row for each table.

type
> The join type. Possible join types are listed below, ranked fastest to slowest:

> system
>> The table is a system table with only one row. This is a special case of the const join type.

> const
>> The table has at most one matching row, can be read once, and is treated as a constant for the remainder of query optimization. A const query is fast because the table is read only once.

> eq_ref
>> No more than one row will be read from this table for each combination of rows from previous tables. This type is used when all columns of an index are used in the query, and the index is UNIQUE or a PRIMARY KEY.

> ref
>> All matching rows will be read from this table for each combination of rows from previous tables. This is used when an index is neither UNIQUE nor a PRIMARY KEY, or if a left subset of index columns is used in the query.

> range
>> Only rows in a given range will be retrieved from this table, using an index to select the rows.

> index
>> A full scan of the index will be performed for each combination of rows from previous tables. This is the same as an ALL join type except only the index is scanned.

> ALL
>> A full scan of the table will be performed for each combination of rows from previous tables. ALL joins should be avoided by adding an index.

possible_keys
> possible_keys lists which indexes MySQL could use to find the rows in this table. When there are no relevant indexes, possible_keys is NULL. This indicates that you can improve the performance of your query by adding an index.

key

key lists the actual index that MySQL chose. It is NULL if no index was chosen.

key_len

key_len lists the length, in bytes, of the index that MySQL chose. This can be used to determine how many parts of a multicolumn index MySQL chose to use.

ref

ref lists which columns or constants are used to select rows from this table.

rows

rows lists the number of rows that MySQL thinks it will have to examine from this table to execute the query.

Extra

Extra lists more information about how a query is resolved. Possible values are:

distinct

After MySQL has found the first matching row, it will stop searching in this table.

not exists

MySQL was able to do a left join optimization of the query.

range checked for each record (index map: #)

MySQL was not able to identify a suitable index to use. For each combination of rows from the previous tables, it will look for an index to use. This is not ideal, but should be faster than using no index at all.

using filesort

MySQL has to sort the rows before retrieving the data.

using index

All needed information is available in the index, so MySQL doesn't need to read any data from the table.

using temporary

MySQL has to create a temporary table to resolve the query. This occurs if you use ORDER BY and GROUP BY on different sets of columns.

where used

The WHERE clause will be used to restrict the rows returned from this table.

A detailed example will help illustrate how to use EXPLAIN SELECT to optimize a query. Even though SELECT queries are referred to in this section, these guidelines apply to UPDATE and DELETE statements as well. INSERT statements do not need to be optimized unless they are INSERT...SELECT statements. Even in the case of INSERT... SELECT statements, it is still the SELECT statement that you are optimizing.

For this example, we use a State table, which includes data about all 50 U.S. states.

```
mysql> DESCRIBE State;
+------------+----------+------+-----+---------+-------+
| Field      | Type     | Null | Key | Default | Extra |
+------------+----------+------+-----+---------+-------+
```

```
| state_id   | int(11)  |     |   | 0        |       |
| state_cd   | char(2)  |     |   |          |       |
| state_name | char(30) |     |   |          |       |
+------------+----------+-----+---+----------+-------+
3 rows in set (0.00 sec)
```

To get the name for the state of California (the state matching the code CA):

```
SELECT state_name FROM State WHERE state_cd = 'CA';
```

Running EXPLAIN SELECT, we can discover how the query will be executed:

```
mysql> EXPLAIN SELECT state_name FROM State where state_cd = 'CA';
+-------+------+---------------+------+---------+------+------+------------+
| table | type | possible_keys | key  | key_len | ref  | rows | Extra      |
+-------+------+---------------+------+---------+------+------+------------+
| State | ALL  | NULL          | NULL |    NULL | NULL |   50 | where used |
+-------+------+---------------+------+---------+------+------+------------+
1 row in set (0.00 sec)
```

The join type ALL tells us that MySQL will scan all rows in the State table to satisfy the query. In other words, MySQL will read each of the rows in the table and compare it to the WHERE clause criteria (state_cd = 'CA'). The rows column tells us that MySQL estimates it will have to read 50 rows to satisfy the query, which is what we would expect since there are 50 states.

We can definitely improve on this performance. Because state_cd is being used in a WHERE clause, we can put an index on it and rerun the EXPLAIN SELECT to check its impact on performance:

```
mysql> CREATE INDEX st_idx ON State ( state_cd );
.
.
.
mysql> EXPLAIN SELECT state_name FROM State WHERE state_cd = 'CA';
+-------+------+---------------+--------+---------+-------+------+------------+
| table | type | possible_keys | key    | key_len | ref   | rows | Extra      |
+-------+------+---------------+--------+---------+-------+------+------------+
| State | ref  | st_idx        | st_idx |       2 | const |    1 | where used |
+-------+------+---------------+--------+---------+-------+------+------------+
```

The key column indicates that MySQL has decided to use the new index. Consequently, the processing of our query has been reduced from 50 rows to one.

The index on the state_cd column provided MySQL some more information to be used during the optimization phase. MySQL uses the st_idx index to find the rows that match the WHERE clause criteria. Because the index is sorted, MySQL can quickly locate the matching row. Each row in the index provides a pointer back to its corresponding row in the table. Once MySQL locates the rows in the index, it knows exactly which rows to read from the table to satisfy the query.

In the first (non-indexed) case, MySQL had to read each row in the table and compare it to the criteria to find the matching row. In the second (indexed) case, MySQL exploits the sorted index to locate the matching records, then read the matching row from the table—a much faster operation.

For a more complex operation, suppose we have the following City table:

```
mysql> DESCRIBE City;
+-----------+----------+------+-----+---------+-------+
| Field     | Type     | Null | Key | Default | Extra |
+-----------+----------+------+-----+---------+-------+
| city_id   | int(11)  |      |     | 0       |       |
| city_name | char(30) |      |     |         |       |
| state_cd  | char(2)  |      |     |         |       |
+-----------+----------+------+-----+---------+-------+
```

For the sake of this example, our database is populated with 50 cities for each state for a total of 2,500. We will also go back to the original State table with no indexes. The following query looks for the state in which San Francisco is located:

```
mysql> SELECT state_name FROM State, City
    -> WHERE city_name = "San Francisco"
    -> AND State.state_cd = City.state_cd;
```

The EXPLAIN SELECT command tells us about this query:

```
mysql> EXPLAIN SELECT state_name FROM State, City WHERE city_name =
    -> "San Francisco" AND State.state_cd = City.state_cd;
+-------+------+---------------+------+---------+------+------+------------+
| table | type | possible_keys | key  | key_len | ref  | rows | Extra      |
+-------+------+---------------+------+---------+------+------+------------+
| State | ALL  | NULL          | NULL | NULL    | NULL | 50   |            |
| City  | ALL  | NULL          | NULL | NULL    | NULL | 2500 | where used |
+-------+------+---------------+------+---------+------+------+------------+
```

This query plan now has two steps. The first step indicates that MySQL will read each row in the State table. This is indicated by the query type of ALL. It also tells us that MySQL estimates that it will read 50 rows. The second step indicates that for each of those 50 rows, MySQL will then read each of the 2,500 rows in the City table and look for a city named "San Francisco." This means that it will read a total of 125,000 (50 × 2,500) rows and compare each of them to the criteria before it can satisfy the query. This situation is obviously not ideal! Because we have some columns in the WHERE clause that are not indexed, we should be able to improve it. The first index is, of course, the original state code index we created earlier in the chapter:

```
mysql> CREATE UNIQUE INDEX st_cd ON State (state_cd);
```

The query now has a better query plan:

```
mysql> EXPLAIN SELECT state_name FROM State, City WHERE city_name =
    -> "San Francisco" AND State.state_cd = City.state_cd;
+-------+--------+---------------+-------+---------+---------------+------+-----
| table | type   | possible_keys | key   | key_len | ref           | rows | Extr
+-------+--------+---------------+-------+---------+---------------+------+-----
| City  | ALL    | NULL          | NULL  | NULL    | NULL          | 2500 | wher
| State | eq_ref | st_idx        | st_idx|       2 | city.state_cd |    1 | wher
+-------+--------+---------------+-------+---------+---------------+------+-----
```

We still have two steps, but now MySQL is reading each row in the City table and comparing it to the WHERE clause criteria. Once it finds the matching rows, it performs step two to join it with the State table based on the state code.

This one index has greatly improved the situation. MySQL will now read only one state for each city. If we add an index on the city_name column, that should do away with the ALL join type for the City table.

```
mysql> CREATE INDEX city_idx ON City ( city_name );
    .
    .
mysql> EXPLAIN SELECT state_name FROM State, City WHERE city_name =
    -> "San Francisco" AND State.state_cd = City.state_cd;
```

table	type	possible_keys	key	key_len	ref	rows	Extra
City	ref	city_idx	city_idx	30	const	1	where
State	ref	st_idx	st_idx	2	City.state_cd	1	where

By adding two indexes, we have gone from 125,000 rows read to two. This example illustrates the dramatic difference that indexes can make.

A query for all the cities in California shows extra complexity:

```
mysql> EXPLAIN SELECT city_name FROM City, State WHERE City.state_cd
    -> = State.state_cd and State.state_cd = 'CA';
```

table	type	possible_keys	key	key_len	ref	rows	Extra
state	ref	st_idx	st_idx	2	const	1	where used; Using index
city	ALL	NULL	NULL	NULL	NULL	2500	where used

We have a new problem because MySQL plans to scan all 2,500 cities. It takes this action because it cannot properly join on the state_cd column without an index in the City table. So let's add it.

```
mysql> CREATE INDEX city_st_idx ON City (state_cd);
    .
    .
mysql> EXPLAIN SELECT city_name FROM City, State where City.state_cd
    -> = State.state_cd and State.state_cd = 'CA';
```

table	type	possible_keys	key	key_len	ref	rows	Extra
State	ref	st_idx	st_idx	2	const	1	where u Using i
City	ref	city_st_idx	city_st_idx	2	const	49	where u

With that index, MySQL has to read only roughly 50 rows to satisfy the query. Remember that the numbers reported here are estimates. As you analyze the query plan, you should check these estimates against what you know about the database. In this case, roughly 50 rows are exactly what we would expect, since California has 50 cities in this database.

Other options

MySQL is not always perfect when optimizing a query. Sometimes it just will not choose the index that it should. The *isamchk/myisamchk* tools can help in this situation. MySQL assumes that values in an index are distributed evenly. *isamchk --analyze* or *myisamchk --analyze* reads a table and generates a histogram of data distribution for each column. This data provides some information that MySQL can use during the query optimization phase to make a more intelligent query plan. Note that *--analyze* is an independent operation that must be executed prior to execution of the query.

Another option is to use USE INDEX/IGNORE INDEX in your query. This trick will give MySQL specific instructions about which indexes to use or not use. Chapter 15 contains more information about this option.

Database Server Tuning

There are a number of settings you can tweak at the MySQL server level to influence application performance. One thing to keep in mind when tuning a server is that server behavior will affect all the applications using that server. An improvement for one application may have a detrimental effect for other applications on the same server.

There are a number of variables that can be modified in the MySQL server that may improve your performance. A full reference to these parameters can be found by typing `mysqld -help`.

In general, when tuning MySQL, the two most important variables are:

table_cache
: table_cache controls the size of the MySQL table cache. Increasing this parameter allows MySQL to have more tables open simultaneously without opening and closing files.

key_buffer_size
: key_buffer_size controls the size of the buffer used to hold indexes. Increasing this will improve index creation and modification and will allow MySQL to hold more index values in memory.

Operating System/Hardware Tuning

A full discussion of hardware and/or OS tuning is beyond the scope of this book. However, here are a few things to consider:

- Many of the traditional hardware upgrades can help MySQL perform better. For example, adding memory to your system gives you more memory to allocate to MySQL caches and buffers. Upgrading to faster disks will improve I/O speed.

- Intelligently distributing your databases across multiple physical devices can also help. For example, placing your data files and index files on different disks can improve performance.

- Static binaries are faster than dynamic binaries. You can configure MySQL to link statically instead of dynamically when you build it.

In general, you should do optimizations and upgrades based on an understanding of how your database is most frequently used.

## CHAPTER 6

Security

Among the many tasks of database administrators and architects is the critical one of making sure only the proper users can access data stored in the database. Ensuring proper data access (security) comes in many forms. For example:

- Database administrators (DBAs) manage access to the database engine itself. They provide access to individual databases for specific applications and developers. They also make sure that a poorly designed application cannot be used as a tunnel into the data of another application.

- System administrators manage the security of the operating system and hardware on which MySQL runs. Their job is to ensure that only MySQL DBAs have access to the physical files used by MySQL on a given machine. In many MySQL environments, the DBA and system administrator are the same person.

- Database architects design the access to the applications to which the DBAs have granted access. A DBA, for example, may have given a web site full `CREATE`, `INSERT`, `UPDATE`, and `DELETE` privileges to its database, but it is up to the database architect to ensure that only valid application users are taking advantage of those privileges.

A security failure at any one of these points can compromise the integrity of all the data in the database engine. In this chapter, we examine how to secure MySQL at all levels.

Database Security

Database security controls access to MySQL data via the MySQL database engine. It does not address access to that data through direct access to the database files; system security is responsible for protecting the files.

To MySQL, a user is any connection authenticated to the database engine. In a development environment, MySQL users will likely correspond to developers. In other words, each developer has a personal user ID and password for MySQL authentication during development. This MySQL user has no inherent relationship to the host system user. In other words, MySQL does not use your Unix ID; it uses its own internal user list.*

In a production environment, a user is likely to be an application. The DBA creates a user ID and password to support the application, and database security controls how that application is allowed to interact with MySQL. The application can then pass on its rights to individual users of the application by acting on their behalves to access MySQL.

For example, you might have a database storing the family CD library with a web interface. A single MySQL user—the application—has access to the read, add, delete, and update records in that database. The application may have its own internal security structure for differentiating family members who can make changes and friends who can just read. It cannot, however, give users powers it does not have, such as creating new tables. MySQL knows nothing about these application-specific users—they exist in the realm of application security.

As the DBA, your job is to create new users and assign them access rights. MySQL has an access hierarchy that controls privileges at certain levels of MySQL operations. You can control the ability to connect to a server, to use a particular database, to make changes to the structure of that database, or to modify the data inside the database.

User Management

The security responsibilities of the DBA basically amount to managing MySQL users and their privileges. Just as operating systems offer an administrative or "root" user for managing other users, MySQL offers a special user called *root* who can create other MySQL user accounts and grant them privileges. When you use administrative commands such as *mysql* or *mysqladmin* to manage users, make yourself the MySQL root user through the *-u* option:

```
$ mysql -u root
```

There is no relationship between the Unix system's root and MySQL's root. Anyone can issue the preceding command—and for that reason, it's critical for you to assign a password to the MySQL root user as soon as you install MySQL. The following command assigns the string P?:2002:My? as the root password:

```
$ mysqladmin -u root password 'P?:2002:My?'
```

---

* Some MySQL tools, such as the *mysql* command-line tool, do use your operating system user ID by default if you fail to specify one. If your Unix user ID is not the same as your user ID in MySQL, however, MySQL will deny you access.

After you execute this command, anyone who attempts to administer MySQL as the root user has to use a -p option and enter the password:

```
$ mysql -u root -p
Enter password: P?:2002:My?
```

Later in the chapter, we show you how to create other MySQL users through SQL GRANT commands. Always assign passwords to these users when you issue the GRANT commands.

While the bulk of your time will revolve around managing privileges, you will still need to put some thought into how you manage your users. In general, you will need to support three kinds of users:

- Individuals
- Applications
- Roles

Individual users are people who use MySQL to develop against it and support it. You should never have MySQL manage the users of the applications run against it; this is the job of the applications themselves. If, for example, you have a MySQL installation supporting several applications in which MySQL must manage the users, you would have a user namespace nightmare; each username would have to be unique across all applications. Furthermore, security issues with one application could potentially compromise the entire MySQL installation. We cover application security in more detail later in the chapter.

Application users are MySQL users that represent specific applications to MySQL. If, for example, you had two web sites using the same MySQL installation to store their data, you might create two separate users to represent those applications. You can use these two separate user IDs to protect each application from the other.

Many database engines support *roles*. A person who sometimes does DBA work, sometimes does development work, and sometimes migrates applications between environments could have a single user ID with three different roles. When that person connects to the database, she logs in using that single user ID and password, and additionally, specifies a role. As long as that user is connected under the specified role, she can act using only the permissions assigned to that role.

MySQL, however, has no concept of role. Each user has individualized permissions. You therefore have three choices for managing users who play multiple roles on a MySQL server:

1. Give them single user IDs and assign those user IDs the permissions associated with all of their roles.
2. Create role-based users, and have different people share the same user ID for a given role.
3. Create multiple user IDs for each role played by each user; e.g., Andy might have *andy-arch* for work as an architect and *andy-dev* for work as a developer.

The advantage of the first approach is that it is the only single sign on solution. In other words, no matter what work you do in a MySQL environment, you need to remember only a single user ID/password combination. Unfortunately, it leaves open too much risk of wreaking havoc accidentally. An innocent `DELETE FROM MYTABLE` executed in one context could, for example, end up deleting data from a table in a different context simply because you got your contexts confused.

The second approach stinks on all levels, but it is to some degree the default for MySQL. Your clean install comes with a default DBA user called "root." If you simply share this one user with all DBAs on a system, you run several security risks. First, if you want to take DBA access away from one of the DBAs, you need to change the password and communicate that change to all the other DBAs. Second, you have very few ways of tracking which DBA performed which action. Finally, you still have to remember different passwords for each role. The one advantage of this approach is you need to connect as a DBA only when doing DBA work. When doing development work, you can connect as a developer and not risk accidentally executing a statement in a developer context that should be run only in a DBA context.

The third approach marries many of the advantages of the first and second approaches. Each user role you create for an individual can share the same password. The user specifies the same username plus his role whenever he connects to the database. Users cannot accidentally perform actions outside the contexts in which they connected. You can then perform operations on all users with a specific role or all roles belonging to a specific user using wildcards:

```
UPDATE db SET Select_priv = 'Y'
WHERE Db = 'Library' AND User = 'dvl\_%'
```

The approach you choose really depends on the particulars of your environment. If you are the only one managing your MySQL server, it may work just fine if you have the default "root" user plus a "developer" user. In a complex environment with many different users and normal turnover, the third approach probably makes the most sense. Table 6-1 lists roles common to MySQL installations. We will cover what the different privileges mean later in the chapter.

Table 6-1. Common database user roles

Role	Environments	Privileges	Description
Developer	Development	DELETE, INSERT, SELECT, UPDATE	Developers write the application code. Their privileges should apply only to the applications they are developing.
Architect	Development	ALTER, CREATE, DELETE, DROP, INDEX, INSERT, SELECT, UPDATE	Architects design the database structure for specific applications. Their privileges should apply only to the applications they are designing.
QA	Testing	DELETE, INSERT, SELECT, UPDATE	QAs are responsible for testing whether an application behaves properly. They need the same privileges as the application user that will support the application in the production environment.

Table 6-1. Common database user roles (continued)

Role	Environments	Privileges	Description
Emigrator	Development, Testing, Staging	SELECT	Emigrators pull the database schema from one environment so that it may be migrated to another environment.
Immigrator	Testing, Staging, Production	ALTER, CREATE, DELETE, DROP, INDEX, INSERT, SELECT, UPDATE	Immigrators update the structure of the database to reflect changes made during development.
DBA	All	All	DBAs manage the running of the MySQL installation. Technically, DBAs should not modify the data in application databases; you could therefore get by without granting them the rights to modify the data in application databases. It would, however, be very difficult to explain this to a DBA.

Table 6-1 talks about different environments. A proper software development process includes the separation of software into separate environments. The number of environments generally depends on the number of developers, the number of applications, and the uptime requirements of the applications. Though cost often causes project teams using Oracle or Sybase to compromise on this issue by forcing teams to reduce the number of environments to save on licensing costs, an advantage of MySQL is that cost should never be a factor.

To ensure a smooth path from development through deployment, a project team needs the following environments and processes to support the migration of code through these environments:

Development
> Development is where all coding happens. MySQL is actually well suited to giving developers their own private development environments on their desktops. By having development separate from all other environments, developers never accidentally cause applications to become unusable or create phantom trouble tickets for the QA team.*

Testing
> Once the development team reaches the point where they are ready to test an application, they move the entire application state to a separate testing environment.

Staging
> Staging exists solely for validating that the full application is correctly configured from end to end with the proper data. It ensures that any configuration issues are discovered prior to moving the application into production.

---

* A phantom trouble ticket is a bug reported by QA that does not really exist. It signifies that, in executing the test, the QA analyst encountered an error simply because a developer was in the middle of changing something.

Production

Only code and data serving end users run in the production environment. No developers, testers, or architects should have access to this environment. No changes should ever be made in this environment.

Privilege Management

MySQL stores information about who has which privileges in special tables in the system database *mysql*. It then consults these tables when determining whether to allow certain operations. Because MySQL privilege information is stored as regular database data, you can manage privileges using the SQL you already know. We will cover the structure of these tables later in the chapter. First, however, we will go into the preferred method of managing privileges: ANSI SQL's GRANT and REVOKE statements.

GRANT and REVOKE

Privilege management includes granting privileges to users and taking them away. ANSI SQL provides two database-independent statements that support these operations. By learning these two statements, you can manage access privileges for MySQL and any other database without knowing the details of how the database actually stores privilege information.

The GRANT statement is the preferred method for adding new users and granting them access to MySQL objects. It has the following syntax:

```
GRANT privilege [(column)] [, privilege [(columns)], ...]
ON table1, table2, ..., tablen
TO user [IDENTIFIED BY 'password'] [, user [IDENTIFIED BY 'password'], ...]
[WITH GRANT OPTION]
```

The simplest form of this statement looks like the following SQL statement:

```
GRANT SELECT ON Book to andy;
```

This statement gives the user andy the ability to read data from the table Book. The GRANT statement has three basic components: the privilege, the object, and the user.

The privilege is a keyword that describes the operation the user is being granted. MySQL supports the following privileges:

ALTER

This provides the ability to alter the structure of an existing table. In particular, it enables the user with this privilege to execute SQL's ALTER statement as long as that statement does not affect indexes.

CREATE

This allows users to create new tables and databases. In particular, it enables a user to execute the CREATE statement as long as the user is not creating new indexes.

DELETE

This enables the user to delete rows from a table. It does not grant the ability to drop tables or databases.

DROP

This provides the ability to drop tables and databases, but not indexes. Though this privilege does not specifically enable a user to delete data from a table, a user with this privilege can simply drop the entire table and thus delete all table data.

FILE

This enables a user to access files on the server machine with the same privileges as the MySQL server process. This privilege is useful for executing the LOAD DATA INFILE and SELECT INTO OUTFILE statements that read from and write to server-side files. This privilege, however, can be abused as a backdoor around operating system security and thus should be granted sparingly.

INDEX

This enables a user to manage table indexes. With it, a user can create, alter, and drop indexes.

INSERT

This enables a user to insert new rows into tables. In particular, it grants a user the ability to execute the INSERT statement.

PROCESS

Like FILE, this is a privilege that a user may use to circumvent operating system security. It specifically grants a user access to the MySQL process threads, including the ability to kill them. In particular, it provides the ability to execute the SHOW PROCESSLIST and KILL SQL statements.

REFERENCES

This does nothing under MySQL. It does, however, provide compatibility with ANSI SQL scripts written for servers such as Oracle that support foreign keys.

RELOAD

This enables a user to force MySQL to reload data it usually keeps cached, such as user permissions. In particular, it enables a user to execute the FLUSH statement.

SELECT

This allows a user to read data from a table using the SELECT statement.

SHUTDOWN

This enables a user to shut down the MySQL server. A user with PROCESS privileges but not SHUTDOWN privileges can accomplish the same thing, however, by killing the MySQL server thread.

UPDATE

This enables a user to modify existing data in a table using the UPDATE statement. It does not grant the ability to delete data or add new data.

USAGE

    This enables a user to simply connect to the MySQL server. A user with only USAGE privileges can do nothing except establish a connection.

There is also a special privilege: ALL PRIVILEGES. ALL PRIVILEGES does not, however, grant all privileges. Though it does grant full control over all the databases and tables running on the server, it does not automatically grant the more dangerous FILE, PROCESS, RELOAD, and SHUTDOWN privileges. You must grant those privileges explicitly. You can use the synonym ALL in place of ALL PRIVILEGES.

A DBA may further grant the ability to a user to extend his privileges to other users. The optional WITH GRANT OPTION empowers the targeted user with this ability. The ability to grant privileges should be given only to trusted users, generally other DBAs. Their ability to grant is not limited to the privileges in the GRANT statement, but to any privileges they are granted at any time.

The object of GRANT is the database object—column, table, database, etc.—to which the privilege applies. Certain privileges, however, make sense only when applied to particular objects. For example, it makes no sense to grant SHUTDOWN privileges on a column. Table 6-2 identifies the objects to which different privileges may apply.

Table 6-2. Privileges and the objects to which they apply

Privilege	Column	Table	Database	Server
ALTER	X	X		
CREATE		X	X	
DELETE	X	X		
DROP		X	X	
FILE				X
INDEX		X		
INSERT	X	X		
PROCESS				X
RELOAD				X
SELECT	X	X		
SHUTDOWN				X
UPDATE	X	X		

For table, database, and server privileges, you specify the object in the ON clause of the GRANT statement. MySQL provides several different ways of naming tables in the ON clause:

table name

    The simplest way to specify a table is to name it. You may grant access to any table outside the current database—the database to which you are connected— by fully qualifying the table name using the *database.table_name* notation.

`*`

This syntax names every table in the current database. You can also reference all tables in a database other than the current database using *database*.*. You will find yourself using this syntax the most often.

`*.*`

This syntax references every table in every database. You should generally reserve the use of this syntax when granting server-wide privileges such as `SHUTDOWN`.

The `ON` clause does not address privileges targeting columns. When applying a privilege to a column, you still specify the table in the `ON` clause, but you specify the column right after the name of the privilege:

```
GRANT SELECT ( title, authorID ) ON Library.Book TO andy;
```

In this case, we have granted andy the ability to execute queries limited to the `title` and `authorID` from the `Book` table in the database `Library`.

The final component of the `GRANT` statement specifies who is being granted the privilege. The simplest form identifies users without indicating where they are connecting from:

```
GRANT ALL ON Library.* TO andy, tim, randy, george;
```

In reality, however, identifying users to MySQL is a little more complex than specifying usernames. MySQL identifies a user by both name and client host. In other words, when I connect from *www.imaginary.com*, I am a different user in the eyes of MySQL from when I connect from *www.mysql.com*. So far, we have not specified a location in any of our examples. When that happens, MySQL assumes you mean any andy, `tim`, `randy`, or george—without respect to the client hostname.

Specify the a specific user with a username and a hostname separated by the @ symbol:

```
george@www.imaginary.com
```

A valid MySQL username is any 16 characters or less. These characters do not need to be ASCII characters, but we recommend ASCII characters since some clients are not able to handle alternative character sets. If a username does consist of characters other than ASCII alphanumeric characters, you must enclose it in either single or double quotes. Usernames are case insensitive. In other words, MySQL treats `fred`, `Fred`, and `fReD` as the same user.

A location is a DNS host name (*www.imaginary.com*) or an IP address (192.168.2. 5). You may also use the SQL wildcards '`%`' and '`_`' to specify a range of addresses.[*] "`%.imaginary.com`", for example, matches all hosts in the *imaginary.com* domain while "`192.168.2.%`" matches all hosts in the 192.168.2.0/24 subnet.

---

[*] You must use quotes when using wildcards or any other nonalphanumeric characters.

You can alternatively specify that same subnet using a netmask: "192.168.2.0/255. 255.255.0". Failure to specify a location is the same as specifying user @"%". If you specify a host name, you should make sure it resolves via your host's configuration file or DNS.

Any user that does not exist when you issue the GRANT statement will be created for you. The user will have a blank password unless you specify one through the IDENTIFIED BY clause. IDENTIFIED BY names the password that identifies the user as authentic. The password may be up to 16 characters of any kind. MySQL will encrypt this password before storing it in the database. If you specify an IDENTIFIED BY clause for an existing user, you will change their password.

As a general rule, you should always provide passwords for new users. Blank passwords are huge security holes for the database.

In addition to the default DBA user root, a clean MySQL installation defines default privileges for any user on the *localhost*. These default privileges are limited to USAGE. In other words, any person with shell access to the machine on which the server is running can connect to the server, but they cannot access any database or data. Remote users cannot even connect unless granted a user ID in MySQL.

The default root user has complete control over every aspect of MySQL. Because a clean MySQL installation provides a root user with no password set, the very first thing you should do once you have installed MySQL is change the root password! As an added layer of security, you can go into the MySQL security tables described later in this chapter and change the name of the DBA user from root to something else.

The opposite of GRANT is REVOKE. It has a structure that is virtually identical to GRANT:

```
REVOKE privilege [(columns)] [, privilege [(columns)] ...]
ON table1, table2, ..., tablen
FROM user1, user2, ..., usern
```

Only a few elements of the REVOKE statement differ from the GRANT statement:

- Revoking the GRANT option is more straightforward—you simply specify GRANT as the privilege name.
- The ALL privilege actually means all privileges possessed by the specified users. All the user will have left is USAGE privileges.
- REVOKE does not have an IDENTIFIED BY clause.

The security tables

The GRANT and REVOKE statements provide complete access to the MySQL security infrastructure without you having to know the details about how that infrastructure works. At times, however, you may find it necessary to fine-tune security settings by going directly to the security tables that store user privileges.

MySQL uses five tables to store privilege information:

user
> This table is the main privilege table that contains the user ID, location, and global privileges. In addition, MySQL stores all metadata rights (including the ability to start and stop the server and grant rights to others) in this table.

db
> This table houses privileges relevant to individual databases.

host
> This table enables you to manage privileges based on location.

tables_priv
> This table contains the table-level privileges for the tables in MySQL's databases.

columns_priv
> This table manages the column-level privileges for specific columns.

MySQL consults these tables for two distinct events: the initial connection and the execution of any statement. During the initial connection, MySQL consults the user table described in Table 6-3.

Table 6-3. The schema for the user table

Field name	Data type	Default
Host (PK)	VARCHAR(60) BINARY	
User (PK)	VARCHAR(16) BINARY	
Password	VARCHAR(16) BINARY	
Select_priv	ENUM('N','Y')	'N'
Insert_priv	ENUM('N','Y')	'N'
Update_priv	ENUM('N','Y')	'N'
Delete_priv	ENUM('N','Y')	'N'
Create_priv	ENUM('N','Y')	'N'
Drop_priv	ENUM('N','Y')	'N'
Reload_priv	ENUM('N','Y')	'N'
Shutdown_priv	ENUM('N','Y')	'N'
Process_priv	ENUM('N','Y')	'N'
File_priv	ENUM('N','Y')	'N'
Grant_priv	ENUM('N','Y')	'N'

Table 6-3. The schema for the user table (continued)

Field name	Data type	Default
References_priv	ENUM('N','Y')	'N'
Index_priv	ENUM('N','Y')	'N'
Alter_priv	ENUM('N','Y')	'N'
ssl_type	ENUM('NONE', 'ANY', 'X509', 'SPECIFIED')	'NONE'
ssl_cipher	BLOB	
x509_issuer	BLOB	
x509_subject	BLOB	

The primary key of the user table is a joint key of the Host and User fields. In other words, MySQL uniquely identifies a user by the username used to connect to MySQL and the name of the host from which the connection comes. The user randy connecting from the local machine is different from the user randy connecting from *www.mysql.com*. The Host field may contain wildcards to indicate multiple hosts.

The user table is also the place where MySQL stores the passwords that authenticate users. MySQL expects the passwords in the Password column to be scrambled using the PASSWORD( ) function. When you create a user with the GRANT command, MySQL automatically scrambles the password you specify in the required fashion.* The most basic way to add a user to MySQL is:

```
INSERT INTO user ( User, Host, Password )
VALUES ( 'randy', 'www.mysql.com', PASSWORD('randyspass') );
```

This new user will not be able to do anything with MySQL since you have not provided the user with any privileges. The *xxx*_priv columns contain the privileges assigned to individual users. The values of these columns can be either 'Y' or 'N'.

The final four columns are new to MySQL 4.0. They exist to support SSL and X.509 certificates.

Whenever a client attempts to connect to a MySQL server, it sends MySQL a username and password. The client can grab the username and password by prompting a user or pulling the information from a configuration file. MySQL then consults the user table to determine whether the user can connect. The connecting user must specifically have matching User and Host values. Because both the User and Host tables may contain wildcards, it is possible that more than one row will match a connected user. For example, when andy connects to the server from *www.mysql.com*, the row with andy and "%" for User and Host as well as the row with "%" and "www.mysql.com" match his connection. MySQL, however, will use only one of those rows to determine the user's access rights using the following algorithm:

---

* A determined attacker can easily defeat this encryption mechanism if given read access to the user table. Access to this table should therefore be restricted to DBAs.

---

1. MySQL considers more-specific Host values before less-specific values. In other words, MySQL first considers values with no wildcards followed by mixed values and, finally, pure wildcards. MySQL views subnets to be less specific than individual hosts. MySQL considers the value "%" last.

2. MySQL examines rows with the same Host value according to the specificity of their User values. MySQL considers blank User values last. A blank User value therefore defines the default access rights for a given host. MySQL ships with default access rights for the *localhost*.

Consider the following User/Host values from the user table:

1. root/*localhost*
2. andy/*localhost*
3. [blank]/*localhost*
4. andy/"%"
5. tim/"%.imaginary.com"
6. randy/"%"

Table 6-4 shows how MySQL matches different user connections to these values.

Table 6-4. Resolution of various User/Host combinations

User ID	Hostname	Row matched	Explanation
root	localhost	1	Both User and Host are specific matches.
andy	localhost	2	Both User and Host are specific matches.
george	localhost	3	george has no entry, so the default values for localhost are used.
andy	www.imaginary.com	4	No specific host matches with the user andy, but the unspecific "%" does have andy as a user.
randy	localhost	3	Both 3 and 6 match, but 3 has the more specific host. One of the most common mistakes with MySQL security is to think that this one matches 6 because of the specific user match.
root	www.imaginary.com	NONE	No Host value matches *www.imaginary.com* for the user root. The connection is denied.

When MySQL finds no match in the User table for a connection, it rejects the connection. When it does find a match, it checks the password provided by the connection against the value in the Password column. If there is a match, the connection is allowed. Otherwise, the connection is denied.

Once a client connection is allowed, MySQL performs security checks for every SQL statement executed by the query. These security checks require all the security tables.

During query execution, MySQL first consults the user table using the row matched when the user connected. This row contains the user's global rights. In other words, if a user has a 'Y' value for a given privilege in this table, no further security checks are made—the operation is allowed. You should therefore be extremely cautious when setting privileges in the user table.

Should the user table not provide access to a specific resource, MySQL consults the database-level privileges in the db table with the schema described in Table 6-5.

Table 6-5. The schema for the db table

Field name	Data type	Default
Host (PK)	CHAR(60) BINARY	
Db (PK)	CHAR(64) BINARY	
User (PK)	CHAR(16) BINARY	
Select_priv	ENUM('N','Y')	'N'
Insert_priv	ENUM('N','Y')	'N'
Update_priv	ENUM('N','Y')	'N'
Delete_priv	ENUM('N','Y')	'N'
Create_priv	ENUM('N','Y')	'N'
Drop_priv	ENUM('N','Y')	'N'
Grant_priv	ENUM('N','Y')	'N'
References_priv	ENUM('N','Y')	'N'
Index_priv	ENUM('N','Y')	'N'
Alter_priv	ENUM('N','Y')	'N'

The primary key of the db table includes not only the Host and User columns, but also the Db column. Both the Host and Db columns can contain wildcards. The privilege columns in this table have the same semantics as the privilege columns in the user table. It has, however, fewer privileges than the user table to reflect the fact that some privileges make no sense when applied to a database.

MySQL performs matches in this table using rules similar to those used for the user table. Specifically, MySQL looks for an exact match on User, Host, and Db. If it finds no exact match, it searches for a row with a User and Db match but a "%" for Host. If it finds such a row, it looks in the host table for a match. The host table has the schema described in Table 6-6.

Table 6-6. The schema for the host table

Field name	Data type	Default
Host (PK)	CHAR(60) BINARY	
Db (PK)	CHAR(64) BINARY	
Select_priv	ENUM('N','Y')	'N'

Table 6-6. The schema for the host table (continued)

Field name	Data type	Default
Insert_priv	ENUM('N','Y')	'N'
Update_priv	ENUM('N','Y')	'N'
Delete_priv	ENUM('N','Y')	'N'
Create_priv	ENUM('N','Y')	'N'
Drop_priv	ENUM('N','Y')	'N'
Grant_priv	ENUM('N','Y')	'N'
References_priv	ENUM('N','Y')	'N'
Index_priv	ENUM('N','Y')	'N'
Alter_priv	ENUM('N','Y')	'N'

The primary key of this table is the combination of the Host and Db columns—the username is not involved. The privileges again share the same semantics as the user and db tables

This table is basically an extension of the db table. It provides default database access privileges for specific hosts where requests originate. MySQL checks the host table for matching Host and Db values. When it finds such a row, it uses the privileges defined in that row combined with the values from the matching row in the db table to determine whether to allow the user's statement to execute. The fact that the privilege must be positive in both tables is critical. This feature enables you to define a privilege granted to most people but selectively denied for specific hosts.

If MySQL still has not found positive permissions, and the object of the statement is the database, or the operation is a DROP, MySQL denies the operation. If the target of the query is a table or a column, then MySQL checks with the tables_priv table. It has the schema described in Table 6-7.

Table 6-7. The schema of the tables_priv table

Field name	Data type	Default
Host (PK)	CHAR(60) BINARY	
Db (PK)	CHAR(64) BINARY	
User (PK)	CHAR(16) BINARY	
Table_name (PK)	CHAR(60) BINARY	
Grantor	CHAR(77)	
Timestamp	TIMESTAMP(14)	NULL
Table_priv	SET('Select', 'Insert', 'Update', 'Delete', 'Create', 'Drop', 'Grant', 'References', 'Index', 'Alter')	
Column_priv	SET('Select', 'Insert', 'Update', 'References')	

The primary key of this table is a combination of four columns: Host, Db, User, and Table_name. As with other privilege tables, the Host and Db columns may contain SQL wildcards. The Table_name column may contain the special character "*" to indicate all tables in the database.

The remaining fields are new to this table. The Grantor field stores the name of the user who granted the particular privilege, and the Timestamp field indicates when the privilege was granted or modified. The final two columns, Table_priv and Column_priv, contain set values. For the Table_priv column, the values indicate the privileges that apply to the table as a whole. The Column_priv values, on the other hand, indicate the privileges applicable to individual columns.

MySQL again uses the "most-specific first" rule to match the statement to a specific row. If it finds a match, and a positive value exists for the privilege in question, the operation is allowed. If the privilege is negative, MySQL checks with the Column_priv value. If that value is negative, the operation is denied. If it is positive, MySQL moves on to the columns_priv table with the schema described in Table 6-8.

Table 6-8. The schema of the columns_priv table

Field name	Data type	Default
Host (PK)	CHAR(60) BINARY	
Db (PK)	CHAR(64) BINARY	
User (PK)	CHAR(16) BINARY	
Table_name (PK)	CHAR(64) BINARY	
Column_name (PK)	CHAR(64) BINARY	
Timestamp	TIMESTAMP(14)	NULL
Column_priv	SET('Select', 'Insert', 'Update', 'References')	

The primary key of this table is a joint key containing the Host, Db, User, Table_name, and Column_name columns. The Host and Db columns may contain wildcards, and the Table_name field may contain the "*" character to indicate all tables.

When MySQL consults the columns_priv table, it checks against each of the columns accessed by the statement. This table must have a match for each column, and the permission must be positive for the privilege for each of the columns.

Recovering from Password and Permission Problems

If you garble your GRANT commands or forget passwords and find that you don't have access to the critical mysql table—even as the root user—don't panic. Become the superuser on the operating system (we're talking now about the Unix root, not the MySQL root) and kill the MySQL process. On a RedHat Linux or other SVR4-type systems, you might be able to end MySQL through the command:

```
/etc/rc.d/init.d/mysql stop
```

Otherwise, find all MySQL processes and kill them explicitly as root:

```
$ ps ax | grep mysql
  2498 pts/1     S       0:00 /bin/sh bin/safe_mysqld
  2514 pts/1     S       0:00 /usr/local/src/mysql/bin/mysqld --defaults-extra-file
  2516 pts/1     S       0:00 /usr/local/src/mysql/bin/mysqld --defaults-extra-file
  2517 pts/1     S       0:00 /usr/local/src/mysql/bin/mysqld --defaults-extra-file
$ kill 2498 2514 2516 2517
```

Now start up MySQL again, bypassing the grant tables:

```
$ safe_mysqld --skip-grant-tables
```

Make sure you can now get access to the mysql database:

```
$ mysql mysql
mysql> quit
```

Assign a password once again to the MySQL root user:

```
$ mysqladmin -u root password 'new_password'
```

Terminate the MySQL server and restart it in the usual way. Make any necessary changes to the privileges through GRANT commands, running mysql as the root user.

System Security

System security applies to the environment in which MySQL is installed—the hardware, network topology, and operating system. For example, if your MySQL database is installed on a machine where dozens of people have root access, they can bypass your excellent database security through direct manipulation of the MySQL database and executable files.

A user in the system security context differs from a user in the MySQL database security context. Specifically, a user in a system security context is any individual with access to operating system processes—via either direct access or across the network.

Operating System Security

The job of the operating system is to protect the MySQL installation and its files from illegal external access. In short, this means that only the MySQL processes and authenticated database administrators should ever be able to touch the MySQL installation. However, certain files such as client configuration files do need to be readable by other users to enable them to connect to the server and perform valid operations. You therefore need to pay special attention to how you enable access to MySQL files.

Place data files in a separate directory.
> Whatever directory structure you choose for the rest of your MySQL installation, you must keep the MySQL data files in their own directory. By default, a MySQL Unix installation places these files in */usr/local/mysql/data*, */usr/var/ mysql*, or some other separate directory.

The MySQL server should run as a special user and group.

Because any user with read access to the MySQL data files or write access to the configuration and executable files has the potential to cause trouble, you should run the MySQL server under a special, dedicated user ID. The default MySQL installation expects a *mysql* user and group. You can customize this user/group pair to suit your own needs. This user and group should have full access to the MySQL data and should never be used for any purpose other than running MySQL.

The permissions on the data directory should be properly set.

If the previous two precautions have been addressed, you have a special directory for the MySQL data files and a special user and group under which the MySQL process runs. You therefore need to make sure that only this special user and group can access the data directory. You accomplish this task by setting the proper filesystem permissions on this directory. On a Unix system, the data directory and all its contents should be owned by your *mysql* user and group with 770 permissions for directories and 660 permissions for files.* Windows systems are not quite as simple. If your operating system (Windows 9x/ME) does not support NTFS, there is no way to protect the files. If you are using an NT-based Windows, you must have MySQL installed on an NTFS volume. You can then right-click on the MySQL data directory and set its permissions.

Protect other files from unauthorized writes.

Your configuration files and executables should be readable, but not writable by anyone. The executables, of course, should also be executable.

Hardware Security

Which is a bigger threat to your employee salary database?

- A script-kiddie with a password cracking script
- A disgruntled employee with a big hammer

The answer is the disgruntled employee with the big hammer. As a general rule, it is easier to take down a web site through brute force against the server hardware than it is to hack the site. People rarely spend enough effort on the relatively simple effort of securing the hardware.

The degree of hardware security you need is proportional to how badly outsiders wish to access or destroy the data it houses. If you have a machine hosting your personal home page, locking the door to your house is probably good enough. If, on the other hand, your MySQL database stores the salary data for your entire company, that machine better be locked behind a door whose access is monitored.

---

* 770 permissions means owner read/write/execute, group read/write/execute, and no permissions for the world. You can set this value using the command *chmod -R 770 datadir*.

Network Security

Because you almost always leverage MySQL across a network, you need to protect the 1s and 0s the database is exchanging with other applications. The simplest form of network security is, of course, to disable network access to the MySQL server. In general, this solution is impractical; it means all applications that need to talk to MySQL have to run on the same box as the database. Such an architecture is impossible for client/server applications in which the client is almost always running on some desktop machine. Though in a multitier application, you can stick in the middle tier on the same server as the database, you give up scalability and accomplish nothing more than shifting the security burden from the database to the middle tier.

To fully appreciate the network security needs of MySQL, it is helpful to know how different applications talk to it. All applications talk to MySQL in one of two ways:

- Using the MySQL C libraries
- Using the MySQL network protocol

Your application may use one of the many meta-APIs such as ODBC, JDBC, DB-API, etc. Under the hood, however, these APIs all use one of the two methods listed above. As a matter of fact, even the MySQL C library technically uses the network protocol. In situations where the client and server are on the same machine, however, it uses Unix sockets or Windows pipes instead of TCP/IP sockets.

Until MySQL 4.0, no support existed to encrypt this network protocol. In other words, all data exchanged between a client and MySQL—including user authentication—went across the network in plain text. MySQL has introduced support for SSL encryption on top of its network protocol with MySQL 4.0.

The network security tasks of a network administrator boil down to the following:

- Securing network paths so that each network service (i.e., the MySQL server process) can be accessed only by valid clients
- Verifying that no application is transmitting sensitive information across the network
- Ensuring that compromises of individual services on the network do not compromise all services on the network

Network topology

The network topology (how machines are connected to each other and other networks) determines who can access which services. As a general rule, no MySQL server should ever be accessible from the Internet. If your application requires a MySQL server to be directly accessible over the Internet, you have a serious application architecture problem. Instead, your MySQL installation should be hidden behind a firewall, preferably on a network segment in which only the client applications such as the web server or application server can route to it.

Encryption

Using software readily available on the Internet, it is simple for anyone to sniff network traffic and eavesdrop on data being transmitted between two applications. Therefore, no sensitive data should ever pass across a network—even protected networks—without encryption. No matter what you have in your database, you are always transmitting at least user IDs and passwords across a MySQL connection. Until MySQL 4.0, there was no way to implement this rule.

MySQL 4.0 introduced SSL support. Using SSL, the data is encrypted during its transmission across the network. Consequently, sniffers pick up only nonsense when they eavesdrop on your communications. To leverage SSL support, you need SSL libraries on both client and server machines, and you must compile MySQL and client components with SSL support. When compiled with SSL support, MySQL always attempts to use SSL before falling back to an unencrypted session.

Direct compromise

The network administrator needs to understand the privileges granted to services on the network and how a direct compromise may impact those services. With respect to MySQL, this task requires you to make sure that a flaw in one of your applications or the MySQL server itself cannot compromise the rest of the system. Flaws in service applications generally enable remote attackers to use a service to execute arbitrary code on a server using the privileges of that service. These flaws result from programming errors in the service itself. Though MySQL has a remarkable security record on this count, it has never been put through a formal security audit such as the one OpenBSD puts its services through.

First of all, you should never, *never* run MySQL as root. If you install MySQL using a special MySQL user and group and use them to support only MySQL, a compromise of a MySQL service can affect only your MySQL database. Of course, if your MySQL service is protected from the open Internet by a firewall, it becomes extremely difficult—but never impossible—for an attacker to manage a direct compromise of the MySQL service.

The second—and probably more vulnerable—thing to watch for is the quality of your own code. You need to audit it for two common security errors:

- Buffer overflow
- Execution of arbitrary code

The first error is the kind of error seen over and over again in Sendmail. A buffer overflow occurs when a programmer fails to verify that the data she is placing into memory fits the memory allocated for that data. The most common form of this error is copying a string where the target buffer is allocated to a size smaller than the actual string. The security problem occurs when the source string is sent from arbitrary data set across the network. An attacker can use this overflow to overwrite critical application memory space and access resources using the privileges of the compromised service. In short, you always need to check the size of any data you are copying before you copy it!

Execution of arbitrary code was a terribly common problem in the early days of CGI programing. Programmers would write their CGI scripts to execute applications on the server using data input from HTML form data. Clever attackers could use this mistake to coerce a CGI script to execute programs under the server using the privileges of the web server.*

Application Security

Earlier in the chapter, we noted how it is the responsibility of individual applications to manage their own users. This user management is a small part of the larger problem of database application security. As an application architect, you are responsible for designing your application to protect its data and ensure that a compromise against it cannot impact other applications.

How you approach application security is heavily dependent on the architecture of your application. Chapter 8 goes into the details of database application architecture. For the purposes of this chapter, however, we will talk about two common components under many architectures: application servers and clients.

The Application Server

For the purposes of this chapter, an application server is any middleware through which clients go to get data. The application server can be as complex as an Enterprise JavaBeans application server or as simple as a web server pulling dynamic content from MySQL. The application server is generally the piece of your application that will perform user management. It is also the final arbiter of who can access what system resources available to the application.

User management

User management is a very complex topic on its own. Not only does it cover how you store users, but it covers such topics as biometric authentication and digital certificates. All of that is well beyond the scope of a book on MySQL. We will take a look at simple user management as an example of how an application server can manage its users without making MySQL handle users in its security scheme.

To manage users, you need a place to store them. There are two common choices:

- A directory server
- A database

---

* In the early days of the Internet, it was common for web servers to run as root!

Some applications even store their user information in files on a server. The flat file approach, however, is very risky and hard to maintain.

A directory server is a database that stores its data hierarchically. Instead of structuring data in tables with foreign key relationships such as a relational database, a directory service stores data in a tree. This structure is useful for data that naturally fits into a hierarchical structure. User data often, but not always, fits well into this paradigm. Applications most commonly use LDAP-compliant directory services to store their user information.

If you have anything but the simplest user-management needs, you should probably use a directory service for user storage. This book, however, is about the relational database MySQL. We will therefore focus on MySQL-based user management.

As we covered earlier in this chapter, MySQL itself uses MySQL to store users. We will therefore use that as a model for simple user management. Specifically, in your application database, you should create a table to manage your user profile. It should contain at least the following information:

A user-friendly unique identifier
> A user-friendly unique identifier is any information a user can provide you that will uniquely identify the user to MySQL. This unique identifier can be an email address or a handle. It should not be some hard-to-remember system identifier. You may want to add a unique system identifier to make for quick joins and to enable users to change their user-friendly identifiers.

An authentication token
> In general, the authentication token will be a password. It could alternatively be a signed public key if you are using digital certificates. If you are using passwords, you must encrypt them. The PASSWORD( ) function provides a convenient way to encrypt passwords, but it is not terribly secure. It should be secure enough, however, if the table is readable only by your application server.

You will also want to store other basic profile information in this table such as the user's email address, password hints, etc. Unless you have a very well-defined set of resources and privileges as MySQL does, it is probably not a good idea to store permissions in this table. For complex permissions, you should create a separate table.

Resource protection

The first rule of the application server architect is always to assume that every client is malicious and out to cause trouble. This rule implies that you should:

- Never trust that the client is who it claims to be. The application server should perform its own authentication.
- Never send passwords to the client. Make the client send authentication information to you.

- Verify all attempts by a client to access application server resources. Specifically, be sure that the client is accessing things that it is allowed to access.

Luckily, some languages—notably Java—provide security libraries that make it easier to do all these things robustly. You also need to protect the application server against direct compromise. In the previous section, we discussed two critical aspects of protecting against direct compromise: avoiding buffer overflow errors and preventing the arbitrary execution of code. Another related design choice is to avoid keeping passwords in memory on your application server.

If your application crashes and dumps its core, any data in memory is available to anyone who can read the core file. Furthermore, another way to exploit poor memory management is to gain read access to an application's memory. If you have a password stored in memory, your application is potentially vulnerable to such exploits.

The first way to avoid keeping passwords in memory is never to pull them from the database. The following code authenticates a user against an AppUser table without selecting the actual password:

```
SELECT userID FROM AppUser
WHERE name = 'tim' and password = PASSWORD('clientpass');
```

This query looks for a userID value from the AppUser table where the username and password equal values the client passed the application server. If the query returns a row, the password was valid. Otherwise, the client gave the application server a bogus password and should be denied access. In short, you are letting the database do the authentication for you.

In the above example, you unfortunately need to store the password the client gives you to read it from the network and to construct your query. You can mitigate this necessary evil through two simple steps:

- Avoid copying the password among different storage buffers. Pass the password by reference instead.
- Write junk into the password buffer when you are done with it.

These two rules of thumb are simple enough in languages such as C, in which you have direct control over your memory management. In languages such as Java, however, you have to pay more attention to how you handle password strings. Java sometimes implicitly copies String objects, and you cannot overwrite the data in String objects. To get around the special way in which Java and other languages deal with strings, you should instead handle passwords using character arrays. This approach is not generally problematic since you should never need to perform odd string operations on passwords.

Client Applications

Client applications (e.g., Swing GUIs, CGI forms, ASPs, and command-line tools) generally have no inherent access to different resources. In a multitier architecture, they gain access to resources through an application server. In a client/server architecture, they gain access through the database engine. Thus, the key to this security is to avoid compromising the user authentication credentials and to make sure there is a finite time of inactivity during which a client is considered authenticated by the application server or database.

To protect passwords, take the following steps:

- Never store passwords in the MySQL client configuration files—or any other client configuration files.
- Never echo users' passwords to the screen when they type them in. Many languages even provide a password-safe text box that enables you to avoid storing passwords in memory for too long, as we described earlier in the chapter.

## CHAPTER 7

Database Design

Once you have installed the DBMS software on your computer, it can be very tempting to just jump right into creating a database without much thought or planning. As with any software development, this kind of ad hoc approach works only with the simplest of problems. If you expect your database to support any kind of complexity, some planning and design will definitely save you time in the long run. In this chapter, we'll take a look at what constitutes good database design.

Database Design Primer

Suppose you have a large collection of compact discs and you want to create a database to track them. The first step is to determine what data you are going to store. One good way to start is to think about why you want to store the data in the first place. In our case, we will most likely want to look up CDs by artist, title, and song. Since we want to look up those items, we know they must be included in the database. In addition, it is often useful to simply list items that should be tracked. One possible list might include: CD title, record label, band name, song title. As a starting point, we will store the data shown in Table 7-1.

Table 7-1. A CD database made up of a single table

Band name	CD title	Record label	Songs
Stevie Wonder	Talking Book	Motown	You Are the Sunshine of My Life, Maybe Your Baby, Superstition, ...
Miles Davis Quintet	Miles Smiles	Columbia	Orbits, Circle, ...
Wayne Shorter	Speak No Evil	Blue Note	Witch Hunt, Fee-Fi-Fo-Fum
Herbie Hancock	Headhunters	Columbia	Chameleon, Watermelon Man, ...
Herbie Hancock	Maiden Voyage	Blue Note	Maiden Voyage

For brevity's sake, we have left out most of the songs. At first glance, this table seems to meet our needs since we are storing all the data we need. Upon closer inspection, however, we find several problems. Take the band named Herbie Hancock, for example. "Band name" appears twice: once for each CD. This repetition is a problem for several reasons. First, when entering data in the database, we end up typing the same name over and over. Second, and more important, if any of the data changes, we have to update it in multiple places. For example, what if "Herbie" were misspelled? We would have to update the data in each of the two rows. The same problem would occur if the name Herbie Hancock changes in the future (like Jefferson Airplane changed to Jefferson Starship). As we add more Herbie Hancock CDs to our collection, we add to the effort required to maintain data consistency.

Another problem with the single CD table lies in the way it stores songs. We are storing them in the CD table as a list of songs in a single column. We will run into all sorts of problems if we want to use this data meaningfully. Imagine having to enter and maintain that list. And what if we want to store the length of the songs as well? What if we want to perform a search by song title? It quickly becomes clear that storing the songs in this fashion is undesirable.

This is where database design comes into play. One of the main purposes of database design is to eliminate redundancy from the database. To accomplish this task, we use a technique called *normalization*. Before we discuss normalization, let's start with some fundamental relational database concepts: entities, attributes, and data models.

Database Entities

An *entity* is a thing or object of importance about which data must be captured. Not all "things" are entities, only those things about which you need to capture information. Information about an entity is captured in the form of attributes and/or relationships. If something is a candidate for being an entity and it has no attributes or relationships, it is not really an entity. A database entity appears in a data model as a box with a title that is the name of the entity.

Entity Attributes

An *attribute* describes information about an entity that must be captured. Each entity has zero or more attributes that describe it, and each attribute describes exactly one entity. Each entity instance (row in the table) has exactly one value, possibly NULL, for each of its attributes. An attribute value can be numeric, a character string, a date, a time, or some other basic data value type. In the first step of designing a database, logical data modeling, we do not worry about how the attributes will be stored.

NULL provides the basis for dealing with missing information. It is specifically used for cases in which you lack a certain piece of information. As an example, consider a CD that does not list the song lengths of each of its tracks. Each song has a length, but you cannot tell from the case what that length is. You do not want to store the length as zero, since that would be incorrect. Instead, you store the length as NULL. If you are thinking you could store it as zero and use zero to mean "unknown," you are falling into one of the same traps that led to one of the Y2K problems. Not only did old systems store years as two digits, but they often gave a special meaning to 9-9-99, assuming it was safe to do that in the expectation that the system would be rewritten long before that date was ever reached.

Our example database refers to a number of things: CD titles, band names, songs, and record labels. Which of these are entities and which are attributes?

Data Model

A data model is a diagram of our database design. It documents and communicates how the database is structured.

Notice that we capture several pieces of data (CD title, band name, etc.) about each CD, and we absolutely cannot describe a CD without those items. CD is therefore one of those things we want to capture data about and is likely to be an entity. To start a data model, we will diagram CD as an entity. Figure 7-1 shows our sole entity as a data model.

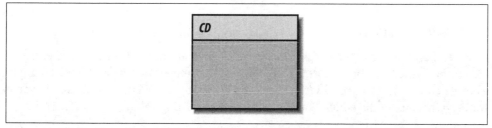

Figure 7-1. The CD entity in a data model

By common entity naming conventions, an entity name must be singular. We therefore call the table where we store CDs CD and not CDs. We use this convention because each entity names an instance. For example, "San Francisco 49ers" is an instance of "Football Team," not "Football Teams."

At first glance, it appears that the rest of the database describes a CD. This would seem to indicate that they are attributes of CD. Figure 7-2 adds them to the CD entity in Figure 7-1. In a data model, attributes appear as names listed in their entity's box.

Figure 7-2. The CD entity with its attributes

This diagram is simple, but we are not done yet. In fact, we have only just begun. Earlier, we discussed how the purpose of data modeling is to eliminate redundancy using a technique called normalization. We have a nice diagram for our database, but we have not gotten rid of the redundancy as we set out to do. It is now time to normalize our database.

Normalization

E. F. Codd, then a researcher for IBM, first presented the concept of database normalization in several important papers written in the 1970s. The aim of normalization remains the same today: to eradicate certain undesirable characteristics from a database design. Specifically, the goal is to remove certain kinds of data redundancy and therefore avoid update anomalies. Update anomalies are difficulties with the insert, update, and delete operations on a database due to the data structure. Normalization additionally aids in the production of a design that is a high-quality representation of the real world; thus, normalization increases the clarity of the data model.

First Normal Form

The general concept of normalization includes several "normal forms." An entity is said to be in the first normal form (1NF) when all attributes are single valued. To apply 1NF to an entity, we have to verify that each attribute in the entity has a single value for each instance of the entity. If any attribute has repeating values, it is not in 1NF.

A quick look back at our database reveals that we have repeating values in the Songs attribute, so the CD is clearly not in 1NF. An entity with repeating values indicates that we have missed at least one other entity. One way to discover missing entities is to look at each attribute and ask the question "What thing does this describe?"

What does Songs describe? It lists the songs on the CD. So a song is another "thing" that we capture data about and is probably an entity. We will add it to our diagram and give it a Song Name attribute. To complete the Song entity, we need to ask if there is more about a Song that we would like to capture. Earlier, we identified song length as something we might want to capture, so let's add it. Figure 7-3 shows the new data model.

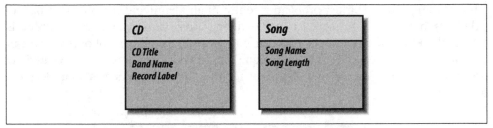

Figure 7-3. A data model with CD and Song entities

Now that Song Name and Song Length are attributes in a Song entity, we have a data model with two entities in 1NF. None of their attributes contain multiple values. Unfortunately, we have not shown any way of relating a CD to a Song.

The Unique Identifier

Before discussing relationships, we need to impose one more rule on entities. Each entity must have a unique identifier—we'll call it the ID. An *ID* is an attribute of an entity that meets the following rules:

- It is unique across all instances of the entity.
- It has a non-NULL value for each instance of the entity for the entire lifetime of the instance.
- It has a value that never changes for the entire lifetime of the instance.

Identifier selection is critical because the identifier is also used to model relationships. If, after you've selected an ID for an entity, you find that it doesn't meet one of the above rules, this could affect your entire data model.

Novice data modelers often make the mistake of choosing attributes that should not be identifiers and making them identifiers. If, for example, you have a Person entity, it might be tempting to use the Name attribute as the identifier because all people have a name and that name never changes. But names do change. What if the person marries? What if the person decides to legally change his name? What if you misspelled the name when you first entered it? If any of these events causes a name change, the third rule of identifiers is violated. Worse, is a name really ever unique? Unless you can guarantee with 100% certainty that the Name is unique, you will be violating the first rule. Finally, you do know that all Person instances have non-NULL names. But are you certain that you will always know the name of a Person when you first enter information about that person in the database? Depending on your application processes, you may not know the name of a Person when a record is first created. There are many problems with taking a non-identifying attribute and making it an identifier.

The solution to the identifier problem is to invent an identifying attribute that has no other meaning except to serve as an identifying attribute. Because this attribute is invented and completely unrelated to the entity, we have full control over it and can guarantee that it meets the rules of unique identifiers. Figure 7-4 adds invented ID attributes to each of our entities. A unique identifier is diagrammed as an underlined attribute.

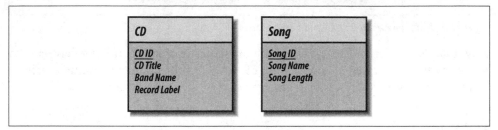

Figure 7-4. The CD and Song entities with their unique identifiers

Relationships

The identifiers in our entities enable us to model their relationships. A relationship describes a binary association between two entities. A relationship may also exist between an entity and itself. Such a relationship is called a *recursive relationship*. Each entity within a relationship describes and is described by the other entity. Each side of the relationship has two components: a name and a degree.

Each side of the relationship has a name that describes the relationship. Take two hypothetical entities, an Employee and a Department. One possible relationship between the two is that an Employee is "assigned to" a Department. That Department is "responsible for" an Employee. The Employee side of the relationship is thus named "assigned to" and the Department side "responsible for."

Degree, also referred to as cardinality, states how many instances of the describing entity must describe one instance of the described entity. Degree is expressed using two different values: "one and only one" (1) and "one or many" (M). An employee is assigned to one department at a time, so Employee has a one-and-only-one relationship with Department. In the other direction, a department is responsible for many employees. We therefore say Department has a "one-or-many" relationship with Employee. As a result, a Department could have exactly one Employee.

It is sometimes helpful to express a relationship verbally. One way of doing this is to plug the various components of the relationship into this formula:

entity1 has [one and only one | one or many] *entity2*

Note that this formula must be applied in both directions to fully describe the relationship between two entities. Using this formula, Employee and Department would be expressed like so:

Each Employee must be assigned to one and only one Department.
Each Department may be responsible for one or many Employees.

We can use this formula to describe the entities in our data model. A CD contains one or many Songs, and a Song is contained on one and only one CD. In reality, a Song can be contained on many CDs, but we ignore this for the purposes of this example. In our data model, this relationship can be shown by drawing a line between the two entities. Degree is expressed with a straight line for "one and only one" relationships or a "crow's foot" for "one or many" relationships. Figure 7-5 illustrates these conventions.

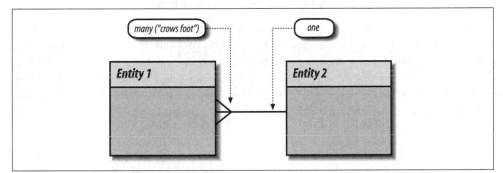

Figure 7-5. Anatomy of a relationship

How does this apply to the relationship between Song and CD? Figure 7-6 shows the data model with the relationships in place.

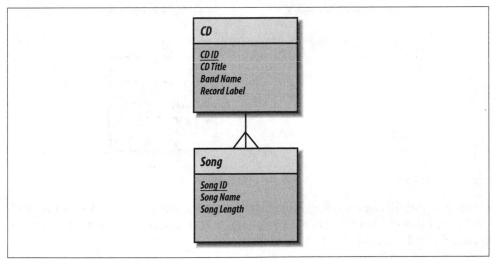

Figure 7-6. CD/Song relationship

With these relationships firmly in place, we can go back to the normalization process and improve upon the design. So far, we have normalized repeating song values into a new entity, Song, and modeled the relationship between it and the CD entity.

Second Normal Form

An entity is said to be in the second normal form (2NF) if it is already in 1NF and all non-identifying attributes are dependent on the entity's entire unique identifier. If any attribute is not dependent entirely on the entity's unique identifier, that attribute has been misplaced and must be removed. For example, "Herbie Hancock" is the band name for two different CDs, and therefore Band Name is not entirely dependent on CD ID. To normalize a misplaced attribute, either find the entity where the attribute belongs or create an additional entity for the attribute.

In our example, we have a sign that Band Name should be part of a new entity with some relationship to CD. As before, we resolve this problem by asking the question: "What does a band name describe"? It describes a band, or more generally, an artist. Artist is yet another thing we are capturing data about and is therefore probably an entity. We will add it to our diagram with Band Name as an attribute. Since not all artists are bands, we will rename the attribute Artist Name. Figure 7-7 shows the new state of the model.

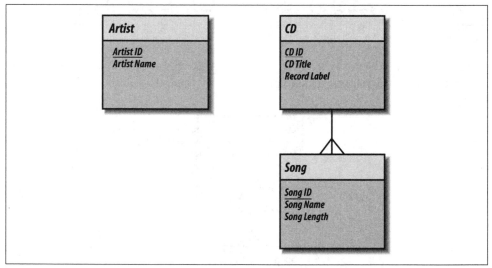

Figure 7-7. The data model with the new Artist entity

Of course, the relationships for the new Artist table are missing. We know that each Artist has one or many CD rows. Each CD could have one or many Artist rows. We model this in Figure 7-8.

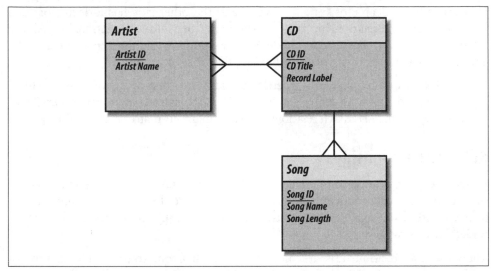

Figure 7-8. The Artist relationships in the data model

We originally had the Band Name attribute in the CD entity. It thus seemed natural to make Artist directly related to CD. But is this really correct? On closer inspection, it would seem that there should be a direct relationship between an Artist and a Song. Each Artist has one or more Song rows. Each Song is performed by one and only one Artist. The true relationship appears in Figure 7-9.

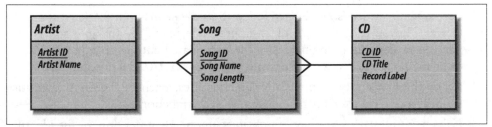

Figure 7-9. The real relationship between Artist and the rest of our data model

Not only does this make more sense than a relationship between Artist and CD, but it also addresses the issue of compilation CDs.

Kinds of Relationships

When modeling a relationship between entities, it is important to determine both directions of the relationship. After both sides of the relationship have been determined, we end up with three main kinds of relationships. If both sides of the relationship have a degree of one and only one, it is called a "one-to-one" or "1-to-1" relationship. As we will find out later, one-to-one relationships are rare. We do not have one in our data model.

If one side has a degree of "one or many," and the other side has a degree of "one and only one," the relationship is a "one-to-many" or "1-to-M" relationship. All the relationships in our current data model are one-to-many relationships. This is to be expected since one-to-many relationships are the most common.

The final kind of relationship is where both sides are "one or many" relationships. These are called "many-to-many" or "M-to-M" relationships. In an earlier version of our data model, the Artist/CD relationship was a many-to-many relationship.

Refining Relationships

As we noted earlier, one-to-one relationships are quite rare. In fact, if you encounter one during your data modeling, you should take a closer look at your design. A one-to-one relationship may imply that two entities are really the same and should be folded into a single entity.

Many-to-many relationships are more common than one-to-one relationships. In these relationships, there is often some data we want to capture about the relationship. For example, take a look at the earlier version of our data model in Figure 7-8 that had the many-to-many relationship between Artist and CD. What data might we want to capture about that relationship? An Artist has a relationship with a CD because an artist has one or more songs on that CD. The data model in Figure 7-9 is actually another representation of this many-to-many relationship.

All many-to-many relationships should be resolved using the following technique:

1. Create a new entity (sometimes referred to as a *junction entity*). Name it appropriately. If you cannot think of an appropriate name for the junction entity, name it by combining the names of the two related entities (e.g., ArtistCD). In our data model, Song is a junction entity for the Artist/CD relationship.

2. Relate the new entity to the two original entities. Each of the original entities should have a one-to-many relationship with the junction entity.

3. If the new entity does not have an obvious unique identifier, inherit the identifying attributes from the original entities into the junction entity and use them together as the unique identifier for the new entity.

In almost all cases, you will find additional attributes that belong in the new junction entity. In any case, the many-to-many relationship needs to be resolved; otherwise, you will have a problem translating your data model into a physical schema.

More 2NF

Our data model is still not in 2NF. The Record Label attribute has only one value for each CD, but we see the same Record Label in multiple CD rows. As we saw with Band Name, this duplication indicates that Record Label should be part of its own entity. Each Record Label releases one or many CD rows. Each CD is released by only one Record Label. Figure 7-10 shows this relationship with the data model in 2NF.

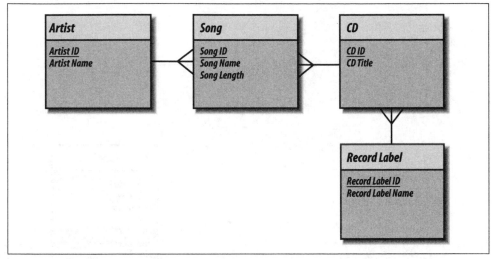

Figure 7-10. Our data model in second normal form

Third Normal Form

An entity is said to be in the third normal form (3NF) if it is already in 2NF and no non-identifying attributes are dependent on any other non-identifying attributes. A non-identifying attribute is any attribute that is not a part of the identifier for the entity. Attributes that are dependent on other non-identifying attributes are normalized by moving both the dependent attribute and the attribute on which it is dependent into a new entity.

If we wanted to track Record Label address information, we would have a problem putting it in 3NF. The Record Label entity with address data would have State Name and State Abbreviation attributes. Though we really do not need this information to track CD data, we will add it to our data model for the sake of our example. Figure 7-11 shows address data in the Record Label entity.

The values of State Name and State Abbreviation would conform to 1NF because they have only one value per record in the Record Label entity. The problem here is that State Name and State Abbreviation are dependent on each other. In other words, if we change the State Abbreviation for a particular Record Label—from MN to CA— we also have to change the State Name—from Minnesota to California. We would normalize this by creating a State entity with State Name and State Abbreviation attributes. Figure 7-12 shows how to relate this new entity to the Record Label entity.

Now our data model is in 3NF, and we can say that it is normalized. There are other normal forms that have some value from a database design standpoint, but these are beyond the scope of this book. For most design purposes, 3NF is sufficient to guarantee a proper design.

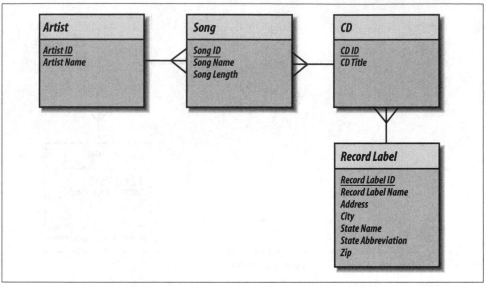

Figure 7-11. Record Label address information in our CD database

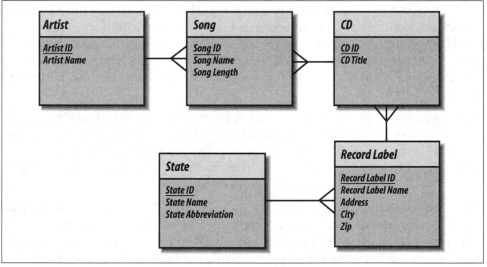

Figure 7-12. Our data model in third normal form

A Logical Data-Modeling Methodology

We now have a completed logical data model. Let's review the process we went through to get here.

1. Identify and model the entities.
2. Identify and model the relationships between the entities.
3. Identify and model the attributes.
4. Identify unique identifiers for each entity.
5. Normalize.

In practice, the process is rarely so linear. As shown in the example, it is often tempting and appropriate to jump around between entities, relationships, attributes, and unique identifiers. It is not as important that you follow a strict process as it is that you discover and capture all the information necessary to correctly model the system.

The data model we created in this chapter is quite simple. We created a model representative of the type and complexity of databases you are likely to encounter in developing MySQL databases. We did not cover a whole host of design techniques and concepts that are less important to small-scale database design, but these can be found in any text dedicated to database design.

Physical Database Design

What was the point in creating the logical data model? You want to create a database to store data about CDs. The data model is only an intermediate step along the way. Ultimately, you would like to end up with a MySQL database in which you can store data. How do you get there? Physical database design translates your logical data model into a set of SQL statements that define your MySQL database.

Since MySQL is a relational database system, it is relatively easy to translate from a logical data model, such as the one we described earlier, into a physical MySQL database. Here are the rules for translation:

- Entities become tables in the physical database.
- Attributes become columns in the physical database. Choose an appropriate data type for each column.
- Unique identifiers become columns that are not allowed to have NULL values. These are called *primary keys* in the physical database. You may also choose to create a unique index on the identifiers to enforce uniqueness.
- Relationships are modeled as *foreign keys*.

Tables and Columns

If we apply the first three rules to our data model—minus the Record Label address information—we will end up with the physical database described in Table 7-2.

Table 7-2. Physical table definitions for the CD database

Table	Column	Data type	Notes
CD	CD_ID	INT	Primary key
	CD_TITLE	VARCHAR(50)	
ARTIST	ARTIST_ID	INT	Primary key
	ARTIST_NAME	VARCHAR(50)	
SONG	SONG_ID	INT	Primary key
	SONG_NAME	VARCHAR(50)	
	SONG_LENGTH	TIME	
RECORD_LABEL	RECORD_LABEL_ID	INT	Primary key
	RECORD_LABEL_NAME	VARCHAR(50)	

Note that all of the spaces are gone from the entity names in our physical schema. This is because these names need to translate into SQL calls to create these tables. Table names should thus conform to SQL naming rules. Another thing to notice is we made all primary keys type INT. Because these attributes are complete inventions on our part, they can be of any indexible data type.* The fact that they are of type INT here is almost purely arbitrary—or rather, almost arbitrary, because it is actually faster to search on numeric fields in many database engines; hence, numeric fields make good primary keys. However, we could have chosen CHAR as the type for the primary key fields, and everything would work just fine. The bottom line is that this choice should be driven by your criteria for choosing identifiers.

CD_TITLE, ARTIST_NAME, SONG_NAME, and RECORD_LABEL_NAME are VARCHAR with a length of 50. The length has been chosen arbitrarily for the sake of this example. In reality, you should do some analysis of sample data to determine the length of text fields. If you set them too short, you may end up with a database that cannot capture all the data you need to store.

SONG_LENGTH is set to type TIME, which can store elapsed time.

Foreign Keys

We now have a starting point for a physical schema. We have not yet translated the relationships into the physical data model. As we discussed earlier, once you have refined your data model, you should have all 1-to-1 and 1-to-M relationships—the M-to-M relationships were resolved via junction tables. We model relationships by adding a foreign key to one of the tables involved in the relationship. A foreign key is the unique identifier, or primary key, of the table on the other side of the relationship.

---

* We covered the MySQL data types in Chapter 3, and a full reference is in Chapter 16.

The most common relationship is the 1-to-M relationship. This relationship is mapped by placing the primary key from the "one" side of the relationship into the table on the "many" side. In our example, this rule means we need to do the following:

- Place a RECORD_LABEL_ID column in the CD table.
- Place a CD_ID column in the SONG table.
- Place an ARTIST_ID column in the SONG table.

Table 7-3 shows the new schema.

Table 7-3. The physical data model for the CD database

Table	Column	Data type	Notes
CD	CD_ID	INT	Primary key
	CD_TITLE	VARCHAR(50)	
	RECORD_LABEL_ID	INT	Foreign key
ARTIST	ARTIST_ID	INT	Primary key
	ARTIST_NAME	VARCHAR(50)	
SONG	SONG_ID	INT	Primary key
	SONG_NAME	VARCHAR(50)	
	SONG_LENGTH	TIME	
	CD_ID	INT	Foreign key
	ARTIST_ID	INT	Foreign key
RECORD_LABEL	RECORD_LABEL_ID	INT	Primary key
	RECORD_LABEL_NAME	VARCHAR(50)	

We do not have any 1-to-1 relationships in this data model. If we did have such a relationship, we would map it by picking one of the tables and giving it a foreign key column that matches the primary key from the other table. In theory, it does not matter which table you choose, but practical considerations may dictate which column makes the most sense as a foreign key. Another way to handle a 1-to-1 relationship is to simply combine both entities into a single table. In that case, you have to pick a primary key from one of the tables to be the primary key of the combined table.

We now have a complete physical database schema. The last remaining task is to translate that schema into SQL. For each table in the schema, you write one CREATE TABLE statement. Typically, you should create unique indexes on the primary keys to enforce uniqueness.

Example 7-1 is an example SQL script for creating the example database in MySQL.

Example 7-1. An example script for creating the CD database in MySQL

```
CREATE TABLE cd (cd_id           INT NOT NULL PRIMARY KEY,
                 record_label    INT,
                 cd_title        VARCHAR(50));

CREATE TABLE artist (artist_id   INT NOT NULL PRIMARY KEY,
                     artist_name VARCHAR(50));

CREATE TABLE song (song_id       INT NOT NULL PRIMARY KEY,
                   song_name     VARCHAR(50),
                   song_length   TIME,
                   cd_id         INT,
                   artist_id     INT);

CREATE TABLE record_label (record_label_id   INT NOT NULL PRIMARY KEY,
                           record_label_name VARCHAR(50));
```

Note that no FOREIGN KEY reference is used in the script. This is because MySQL does not support FOREIGN KEY constraints in its default data type. MySQL will allow you to embed them in your CREATE TABLE statements, but they will not be enforced. The InnoDB table type, which was recently stabilized and is documented on the MySQL web site, supports foreign keys.

Data models are meant to be database independent. You can therefore take the techniques and the data model we have generated in this chapter and apply them not only to MySQL, but to Oracle, Sybase, or any other relational database engine. In the following chapters, we will discuss the details of how you can use your new database design knowledge to build applications.

## PART III

MySQL Programming

The power of a database is realized in the tools that use it. In Part III, we talk about how you build those tools using a variety of today's popular programming languages. From web-based programming to business application development, we will discuss the APIs and tools necessary for using MySQL to its fullest potential. Part III starts with a high-level chapter on database application design. The meat of Part III, however, deals with programming in various programming languages with MySQL as your backend database.

## CHAPTER 8

Database Applications

We have spent the entire book so far discussing the database as if it exists in some sort of vacuum. But it serves its purpose only when being used by other applications. We should therefore take a look at how the database relates to the other elements of a database application before exploring the details of database application development in various languages. This detour examines conceptual issues important not only to programming with MySQL, but to programming with any relational database engine. Our look at database programming covers such complex issues as understanding the basic architectures common to web-oriented database applications and how to map complex programming models into a relational database.

Architecture

Architecture describes how the different components of a complex application relate to one another. A simple web application using Perl to generate dynamic content has the architecture shown in Figure 8-1. This architecture describes four components: the web browser, the web server, the Perl CGI engine, and the MySQL database.

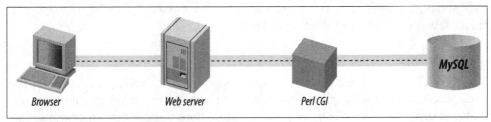

Figure 8-1. The architecture of a simple web application

Architecture is the starting point for the design of any application. It helps identify at a high level all of the relevant technologies and the standards those technologies will use to integrate. In the web architecture, for example, the web browser talks to the server using HTTP.

As we will cover in the later chapters of this section, MySQL exposes itself through a variety of APIs tailored to specific programming languages. Java applications access MySQL through JDBC, Python applications through the Python DB-API, etc.

There are numerous architectures used in database applications. In this chapter, we will cover the three most common architectures: client/server, distributed, and web. Though one could argue that they are all variations on a theme, they do represent three very different philosophical approaches to building database applications.

Client/Server Architecture

At its simplest, the client/server architecture is about dividing up application processing into two or more logically distinct pieces. The database makes up half of the client/server architecture. The database is the "server"; any application that uses that data is a "client." In many cases, the client and server reside on separate machines; in most cases, the client application is some sort of user-friendly interface to the database. Figure 8-2 provides a graphical representation of a simple client/server system.

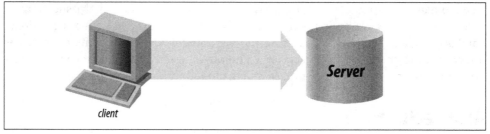

Figure 8-2. The client/server architecture

You have probably seen this sort of architecture all over the Internet. The Web, for example, is a giant client/server application in which the web browser is the client and the web server is the server. In this scenario, the server is not a relational database server, but instead a specialized file server. The essential quality of a server is that it serves data in some format to a client.

Application logic

Because a client/server architecture specifically separates out components for UI and data processing, actual application processing is left up to the programmer to integrate. In other words, a client/server architecture does not provide an obvious place for a banking application to do interest calculations. Some client/server applications place this kind of processing in the database in the form of stored procedures; others put it in the client with the UI controls. There is no general solution.

Under MySQL, the current method is to put the processing in the client because of the lack of stored procedure support in MySQL. Stored procedures are on the

MySQL to-do list, and—perhaps even by the time you read this book—stored procedures will eventually be a viable place for application logic in a client/server configuration. Whether or not MySQL has stored procedures, however, MySQL is rarely used in a client/server environment. It is instead much more likely to be used with the web architecture we will describe later in this chapter.

Fat and thin clients

There used to be two kinds of clients: fat clients and thin clients. A fat client included application processing; a thin client simply had user interface (UI) logic. With the advent of web applications, we now have the term ultra-thin to add to the list. An ultra-thin client has only display logic. Controller logic (what happens when you press "Submit") happens elsewhere. In short, an ultra-thin client might be a web form.

The advantage of an ultra-thin client is it makes real the concept of a ubiquitous client. As long as you can describe the application layout to a client using some sort of markup language, the client can paint the UI for a user without the programmer needing to know the details of the underlying platform. When the UI needs to respond to a user action, it sends information about the action to another component in the architecture to respond to the action. Client/server architecture, of course, has no such component.

Distributed Application Architecture

The distributed application architecture provides a place where application logic is supposed to occur. Figure 8-3 shows the layout of an application under the distributed application architecture.

As you can see, this architecture is basically the client/server architecture with a special place for application logic—the middle tier. This small difference, however, represents a major philosophical shift from the client/server design. It says, in short, that it is important to separate application logic from other kinds of logic.

In fact, placing application logic in the database or in the UI hinders your application's ability to grow with changing demands. If, for example, you need a simple change to your data model, you will have to make significant changes to your stored procedures if your application logic is in the database. A change to application logic in the UI, on the other hand, forces you to touch the UI code as well and thus risk adding bugs to systems that have nothing to do with the changes you are introducing.

The distributed application architecture does two things. It provides a home for application processing so that it does not get mixed in with database or UI code. However, it also makes the UI independent of the underlying data model. Under this architecture, changes to the data model affect only how the middle tier gets data from and puts data into the database. The client has no knowledge of this logic and thus does not care about such changes.

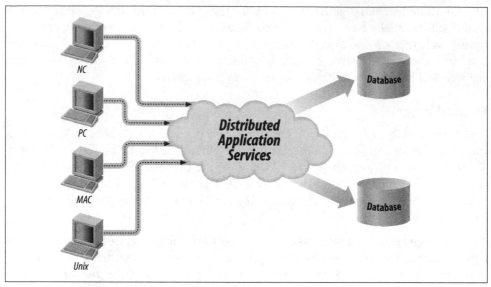

Figure 8-3. The distributed application architecture

The distributed application architecture introduces two truly critical elements. First of all, the application logic tier enables the reuse of application logic by multiple clients. Specifically, by abstracting out the application logic with well-defined integration points, it is possible to reuse that logic with UIs not conceived when the application logic was written.

The second, not so obvious thing this architecture offers applications is the ability to provide easy support for failover and scalability. The components in this architecture are logical components, meaning that they can be spread out across multiple actual instances. When a database or an application server introduces clustering, it can act and behave as a single tier while spreading processing across multiple physical machines. If one of those machines goes down, the middle tier itself is still up and running.

Web Architecture

The web architecture is another step in evolution that appears to be only slightly different from the distributed application architecture. It makes a true ultra-thin client possible by providing only display information in the form of HTML to a client. All controller logic occurs in a new component, the web server. Figure 8-4 illustrates the web architecture.

The controller comes in many different forms, depending on the technologies you are using. PHP, CGI, JSP, ASP, ColdFusion, and WebObjects are all examples of technologies for processing user events. Some of these technologies even divide

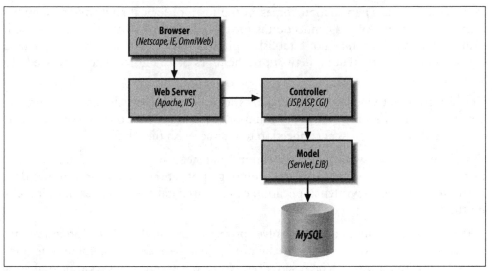

Figure 8-4. The web application architecture

things further into content creation and controller logic. If you use a content management system such as OpenMarket, for example, your JSP is nothing more than a tool for dynamically building your HTML. The actual controller logic is passed off to a servlet action handler that performs any application server interaction.

The focus of this book will be the web architecture since it is the most common architecture in which MySQL is used. We will use both the vision of the web architecture shown in Figure 8-4 and a simpler one in which the application logic is embedded with controller logic in the web server. The simpler architecture is mostly relevant to MySQL applications since MySQL performs best for heavy read applications—applications without complex application logic.

Connections and Transactions

Whatever architecture you use, the focus of this book lies at the point where your application talks to the database. As a database programmer, you need to worry about how to get data from and send it to your database. As we mentioned earlier, the tool to do that is generally some sort of database API. Any API, however, requires a basic understanding of managing a connection, the transactions under that connection, and the processing of the data associated with those transactions.

Connections

The starting point of your database interaction is in making a connection. The details behind what exactly constitutes a connection vary from API to API. Nevertheless, making a connection is basically establishing some sort of link between your code and the database. The variation comes in the form of logical and physical connections. Under some APIs, a connection is physical; i.e., a network link is established. Other APIs, however, may not establish a physical link until long after you make a connection, to ensure that no network traffic takes place until you actually need the connection.

The details about whether a connection is logical or physical should not generally concern a database programmer. The important thing is that once a connection is established, you can use that connection to interact with the database.

Once you are done with your connection, you need to close it and free up any resources it may have used. In a long-running application such as an Internet daemon process, a badly written application can eat up database resources until it locks up the system.

Part of cleaning up after yourself involves proper error handling. Some programming languages make it easy for you to remember to handle exceptional conditions (network failure, duplicate keys on insert, SQL syntax errors, etc.); but regardless of your language of choice, you must be aware of the error conditions that can arise from a given API call and act appropriately for each exceptional situation.

Transactions

You talk to the database in the form of transactions.* A database transaction is one or more database statements that must be executed together, or not at all. A bank account transfer is a good example of a complex transaction. In short, an account transfer is actually two separate events: a debit of one account and a credit to another. Should the database crash after the debit but before the credit, the application should be able to back out of the debit. A database transaction enables a programmer to mark when a transaction begins, when it ends, and what should happen if one of the pieces of the transaction fails.

Until recently, MySQL had no support for transactions. In other words, when you executed an SQL statement under old versions of MySQL, it took effect immediately. This behavior is still the default for MySQL. Newer versions of MySQL, however, support the ability to use transactions with certain tables in the database. Specifically, the table must use a transaction-safe table format. Currently, MySQL supports two transaction-safe table types: BDB (Berkeley DB) and InnoDB. Instructions for configuring MySQL to use these databases can be found on the MySQL web site.

---

* Even if you are using a version of MySQL without support for transactions, each statement you send to the database can, in a sense, be thought of as an individual transaction. You simply have no option to abort or package multiple statements together in a complex transaction.

In Chapter 3, we described the MySQL syntax for managing transactions from the MySQL client command line. Managing transactions from within applications is often very different. In general, each API will provide a mechanism for beginning, committing, and rolling back transactions. If it does not, you can likely follow the command-line SQL syntax to get the desired effect.

Transaction isolation levels

Managing transactions may seem simple, but there are many issues you need to consider when using transactions in a multiuser environment. First of all, transactions come with a heavy price in terms of performance. MySQL did not originally support transactions because MySQL's goal was to provide a fast database engine. Transactions seriously impact database performance. To understand how this works, you need to have a basic understanding of transaction isolation levels.

A transaction isolation level basically determines what other people see when you are in the middle of a transaction. To understand transaction isolation levels, however, you first need to understand a few common terms:

Dirty read

A dirty read occurs when one transaction views the uncommitted changes of another transaction. If the original transaction rolls back its changes, the one that read the data is said to have "dirty" data.

Repeatable read

A repeatable read occurs when one transaction always reads the same data from the same query no matter how many times the query is made or how many changes other transactions make to the rows read by the first transaction. In other words, a transaction that mandates repeatable reads will not see the committed changes made by another transaction. An application needs to start a new transaction to see those changes.

Phantom read

A phantom read deals with changes occurring in other transactions that would result in the new rows matching your transaction's WHERE clause. Consider, for example, a situation in which you have a transaction that reads all accounts with a balance of less than $100. Your transaction performs two reads of that data. Between the two reads, another transaction adds a new account to the database with no balance. That account will now match your query. If your transaction isolation allows phantom reads, you will see the new "phantom" row. If it does not allow phantom reads, you will see the same set of rows each time.

MySQL supports the following transaction isolation levels:

READ UNCOMMITTED
> The transaction allows dirty, nonrepeatable, and phantom reads.

READ COMMITTED
> The transaction does not allow dirty reads, but allows nonrepeatable and phantom reads.

REPEATABLE READ
> The transaction allows committed, repeatable reads and phantom reads. Nonrepeatable reads are not allowed.

SERIALIZABLE
> The transaction allows only committed, repeatable reads. Phantom reads are specifically not allowed.

As you climb the transaction isolation chain, from no transactions to serializable transactions, you decrease the performance of your application. You therefore need to balance your data integrity needs with your performance needs. In general, READ COMMITTED is as high as an application wants to go, except in a few cases.

Using READ UNCOMMITTED

One mechanism of getting the performance of READ UNCOMMITTED and the data integrity of READ COMMITTED is to make a row's primary key the normal primary key plus a timestamp reflecting the time in milliseconds when the row was last updated. When an application performs an update on the underlying row in the database, it updates that timestamp but uses the old one in the WHERE clause:

```
UPDATE ACCOUNT
SET BALANCE = 5.00, LAST_UPDATE_TIME = 996432238000
WHERE ACCOUNT_ID = 5 AND LAST_UPDATE_TIME = 996432191119
```

If this transaction has dirty data, the update will fail and throw an error. The application can then requery the database for the new data.

Object/Relational Modeling

Accessing a relational database from an object-oriented environment exposes a special paradox: the relational world manipulates data directly while the object world encapsulates data behind a set of behaviors. In an object-oriented application, the database serves as a tool for saving objects across application instances. Instead of seeing the query data as a rowset, an object-oriented application sees query data as a collection of objects.

The most basic question facing the object-oriented developer using a relational database is how to map relational data into objects. Your immediate thought might be to simply map object attributes to fields in a table. Unfortunately, this approach does not create the perfect mapping for two reasons:

- Objects do not store only simple data in their attributes. They may store collections or relationships with other objects.

- Most relational databases—including MySQL—have no way of modeling inheritance.

An application should manipulate data only through the objects. Most traditional programming methods, including most development in C, PowerBuilder, and Visual-Basic, require the developer to pull the data from the database and then process that data. Thus, the first task of an object-oriented application is to grab the data from the database and instantiate objects, through which all further application processing takes place.

Think about an address book application. You would probably have something like the address and person tables shown in Figure 8-5.

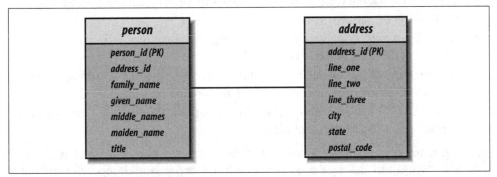

Figure 8-5. The data model for a simple address book application

Figure 8-6 shows the object model that maps to the data model from Figure 8-5. Each row from the database turns into a program object. Your application therefore takes each row from a result set and instantiates a new Address or Person instance. The hardest thing to deal with here is the issue mentioned earlier: how do you capture the relationship between a person and her address in the database application? The Person object, of course, carries a reference to that person's Address object. But you cannot save the Address object within the person table of a relational database. As the data model suggests, you store object relationships through foreign keys. In this case, we carry the address_id in the person table.

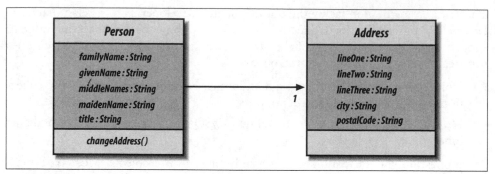

Figure 8-6. The object model supporting a simple address book application

Often, you need to add an extra layer to your object model to permit the flexibility provided by object-oriented programming and inheritance. For instance, you could create a base class called Entity and let both Person and Company inherit from it. Thus, the rules of thumb for object/relational modeling include:

- Each persistent class has a corresponding database table.
- Each row from a database table corresponds to an instance of its associated persistent class.
- Object fields with primitive data types (integers, characters, strings, etc.) map to columns in the associated database table.
- Each many-to-many object relationship requires a join table just as database entities with many-to-many relationships require join tables.
- Inheritance is modeled through a one-to-one relationship between the two tables corresponding to the class and subclass.

In some instances, the base class is purely abstract and subsequently has no data associated with it in the database. In that call, no entity would appear in the database for that class.

## CHAPTER 9

Perl

The Perl programming language has grown from a scruffy tool exploited by Unix systems administrators for informal scripting to the most widely used development platform for the World Wide Web. Perl was not designed for the Web or for databases, but its ease of use and powerful text-handling abilities have made it a natural for application development in these areas. A few of the libraries developed for Perl—called *modules*—have made it even more attractive for web and database applications.

Perl accesses databases through the DataBase Driver/DataBase Interface (DBD/DBI). The name arises from its two-layer implementation. At the bottom is the database driver layer. There, modules exist for each type of database accessible from Perl: MySQL, Oracle, and so on. On top of these database-dependent driver modules lies a database-independent interface layer, which is the interface you use.

The advantage of this scheme is that the programmer has to learn only one API: the database interface layer. Every time a new database comes along, someone needs only to write a DBD module for it, and it will be accessible to all DBD/DBI programmers. If you change databases, you can run your Perl program on the new database after changing only a couple lines of code.

This chapter is in three parts:

1. An introduction to DBI, which shows you the basic statements you need to manipulate MySQL from Perl.

2. A Common Gateway Interface (CGI) program that displays information from the database.

3. For readers of stout heart, already comfortable with Perl, a general model that can be applied to a wide range of applications and that makes maintenance easier.

Introduction to DBI

The Perl DBI interface is fully described in *Programming the Perl DBI* by Alligator Descartes and Tim Bunce (O'Reilly). The manpage for DBI is also a very informative reference. This chapter should make you competent, though not expert.

Before launching into a CGI application, let's try a couple trivial Perl programs you can run from the command line. These were tested on Unix and Linux systems, but should work the same way on other operating systems as well. After looking at the code, we'll show you how to provide the actual database and discuss some optimizations.

Basic Perl Example

Our first program is about as simple as Perl DBI can get. Example 9-1 is a program you can run at the command line to query a database and display the results. We'll describe how it works in this section, but you won't actually be able to run it until you've done the setup described in the next section.

Example 9-1. Submitting a query to MySQL using Perl DBI

```perl
#!/usr/bin/perl -w

use strict;
use DBI;

my $server = 'localhost'
my $db = 'Books';
my $username = 'andy' ;
my $password = 'ALpswd' ;

my $dbh = DBI->connect("dbi:mysql:$db:$server", $username, $password);

my $query = "SELECT * FROM Titles";
my $sth = $dbh->prepare($query);
$sth->execute( );

while (my $row = $sth->fetchrow_arrayref) {
    print join("\t", @$row),"\n";
}

$dbh->disconnect;
```

The basic sequence of events (which will be the same for nearly any Perl DBI application) is:

1. Connect to your database.
2. Build a query.
3. Build a statement handle.
4. Execute the statement handle.
5. Retrieve and process the results.

Now for a look at the code, line by line.

As with all Perl modules, you must issue a use statement to get access to the DBI module:

```
use DBI;
```

All interactions between Perl and MySQL are conducted through what is known as a *database handle*. This is an object that implements all the methods used to communicate with the database. You may have as many database handles open at once as you wish, limited only by your system resources.

The first DBI method you invoke, therefore, is a connect( ) method that creates the database handle. It takes three arguments, the first of which consists of several parts.

1. A data source, containing information that varies depending on the database engine you use. For MySQL, this argument includes the following information, separated by colons:

    a. The string dbi.

    b. The driver name, mysql.

    c. The database name, which is Books in our example.

    d. The host, which is localhost in our example. The local host is the most common choice, because most sites put the client application (such as a CGI program on a web server) on the same system as the MySQL server.

2. A username, which is andy in our example. This is actually an abbreviation of andy@localhost. MySQL assumes localhost as the hostname if you don't specify one.

3. A password, which is ALpswd in our example.

The call allows a fourth optional argument that can be used to change the default attributes of the connection. We'll show a bit of its use later.

The $dbh variable is returned by the DBI module and forms our handle into the MySQL server. The variable can be named anything you want, but $dbh is traditional. The handle can be used to to issue queries, updates, or any SQL statements we want. However, the SQL must be wrapped in Perl code.

Our example reads all the titles from the Titles table. We create the SQL query in the $query variable, wrapped up as a string in Perl. Then we prepare a *statement handle* $sth from the query. Finally, we execute the statement.

Note that prepare( ) is a method provided by $dbh, the database or connection handle, while execute( ) is a method provided by $sth, the statement handle. In other words, the database handle prepares a statement, which then executes itself.

The prepare( ) method takes an SQL query and stores it (either locally or on the database server) until execution. On database servers that store the query on the database server itself, one can perform operations on the query before executing it. However, MySQL does not support that ability yet; it simply stores prepared queries within the database driver until execution. The execute( ) method causes the query to be sent to the database server and executed.

The result of executing a query depends on the type of query. If the query is a non-SELECT query that returns no data (such as INSERT, UPDATE, or DELETE), the execute() method returns the number of rows that were affected by the query. That is, for an INSERT query that inserts one row of data, the execute( ) method will return 1 if the query is successful.

For SELECT queries, the execute( ) method simply returns a true value if the query is successful and a false value if there is an error. The data returned from the query is then available using various methods provided by the statement handle.

So we can now retrieve all the results of our query by issuing calls to the statement handle. We are finished with SQL and with our database, in this sample program. We use DBI methods and Perl arrays to manipulate the data from now on.

Most applications retrieve rows from a statement handle one at a time. The statement handle provides a fetchrow_arrayref( ) method to do this. A typical application issues fetchrow_arrayref( ) in a loop and processes each row in the body of the loop. For our first, simple program, we'll just display the data returned.

The fetchrow_arrayref( ) method graciously acts like a typical Perl function, returning undef when there are no more rows to fetch. Therefore, we can write a while loop that terminates at an undefined return value.

Because each row consists of multiple fields, the fetchrow_arrayref( ) method returns its results as a reference to an array. Each element of the array is a field in the row. We use @$row syntax to retrieve the array of fields from the reference $row.

Now that all the data has been printed, we can close the database handle. For our trivial program, this is not necessary, because Perl will automatically destroy the handle when the application exits. However, since cleaning up one's resources is necessarily in some environments (such as when using the Apache *mod_perl* module), it is a good habit to get into.

Before we run the program, we have to set up the andy user account and the database itself, which we'll do in the next section.

Setting Up the Database and Program

As raw material for our Perl programs, we'll create a simple database of information about O'Reilly & Associates. It's a very flat database with all its information in a single table, but it's sufficient to convey all the concepts you need for accessing MySQL with Perl.

First, you need a file of SQL commands that create the table and insert some data. The file is available on the O'Reilly online example site under the name *books.sql*, and it starts out with the commands in Example 9-2. We can save some room by declaring large VARCHAR fields for most text; only the isbn field has a known, fixed length.

Example 9-2. Beginning of SQL commands to load database

```
DROP TABLE IF EXISTS Titles;

CREATE TABLE Titles (
   isbn char(10) NOT NULL default '',
   title varchar(255) default NULL,
   publisher varchar(255) default NULL,
   author varchar(255) default NULL,
   pages int(11) default NULL,
   pubdate int(11) default NULL,
   PRIMARY KEY  (isbn)
) TYPE=MyISAM;

INSERT INTO Titles VALUES ('0596000448','Designing Active Server Pages','O\'Reilly &
Associates','Scott Mitchell',376,967795200);
INSERT INTO Titles VALUES ('1565924460','Developing Asp Components','O\'Reilly &
Associates','Shelley Powers',490,930816000);
INSERT INTO Titles VALUES ('156592567X','Writing Apache Modules with Perl and C: The
Apache API and mod_perl (O\'Reilly Nutshell)','O\'Reilly & Associates','Lincoln Stein,
Doug MacEachern, Linda Mui (Editor)',746,920275200);
INSERT INTO Titles VALUES ('1565927060','Apache : Pocket Reference','O\'Reilly &
Associates','Andrew Ford, Gigi Estabrook',107,959846400);
...
```

Once you have the file, make sure you have been granted CREATE and INSERT privileges by MySQL, as described in Chapter 6. The MySQL root user can create an account for andy, assign him a password, and grant him the privileges he needs all at once in the following command:

```
mysql> GRANT ALL on Books.* TO andy@localhost identified by 'ALpaswd';
```

Andy (or any user knowing the password) can now execute the following commands at the shell:

```
$ mysqladmin -u andy -p create Books
$ mysql -u andy Books -p < books.sql
```

The -*p* option prompts for the password ALpswd we assigned when granting privileges. After you successfully execute these commands, the database will be loaded with data and ready for some Perl applications.

Before running the program, you must make sure that Perl is installed on your system (virtually every modern Unix system has it) and that the DBI module is installed. You can check whether a module is installed through a Perl one-liner such as:

```
$ perl -MDBI -e 1;
```

If you see no output, the module is loaded and can be used in your programs. If Perl prints the message Can't locate DBI.pm in @INC..., it means the module has to be downloaded and installed. Instructions on downloading and installing Perl modules are beyond the scope of this book, but all the modules described in this chapter (and most other useful, stable Perl modules) are available from the Comprehensive Perl Archive Network (CPAN) at *http://www.cpan.org* or one of its many mirrors that have sprung up all over the world.

The MySQL username and password for andy are included in our sample program, so it can be run by anybody on the local system once the database is created. The output follows. We have broken some lines and inserted backslashes to fit the page.

```
$ perl perl1.pl
0596000448      Designing Active Server Pages    O'Reilly & Associates \
  Scott Mitchell  376     967795200
1565924460      Developing Asp Components         O'Reilly & Associates \
  Shelley Powers  490     930816000
156592567X      Writing Apache Modules with Perl and C: \
  The Apache API and mod_perl (O'Reilly Nutshell) O'Reilly & Associates \
  Lincoln Stein, Doug MacEachern, Linda Mui (Editor)    746     920275200
1565927060      Apache : Pocket Reference         O'Reilly & Associates \
  Andrew Ford, Gigi Estabrook     107     959846400
...
```

Error Handling and Attributes

Because of typos in their programs or problems in setting up their databases, most programmers turn up errors when they first run an example. We'll look at some ways to deal with errors here. Luckily, the DBI module provides useful diagnostic messages by default.

The connect() method offers an optional argument that controls the attributes of the database handle. Attributes include whether the statement prints an error message in case of failure, whether it throws a potentially fatal exception in case of failure, and many other things. We will not delve into the many subtleties here, such as the varied places where attributes can be set or the ones that statement handles inherit from the database handle. Instead, we will show a couple uses of attributes for error handling.

Suppose you want DBI to terminate your program if it cannot make a connection or if any later DBI method fails. You can put this behavior in your connect() command by adding a fourth argument that sets the RaiseError attribute, as follows:

```
my $dbh = DBI->connect("dbi:mysql:$db:$server", $username, $password,
                       { RaiseError => 1 } );
```

If you want to do something fancier with attributes, such as set them at runtime, here is the syntax for specifying the attribute argument (it is a reference to a hash):

```
my %attr = ( RaiseError => 1 );
my $dbh = DBI->connect("dbi:mysql:$db:$server", $username, $password,
                       \%attr);
```

In either case, running a program with an incorrect password produces the following output (we inserted a line break so the message would fit on the page):

```
$ perl perl_raise.pl
DBI->connect(Books:localhost) failed: Access denied for user: \
  'andy@localhost' (Using password: YES) at perl_raise.pl line 11
$
```

The program terminates automatically.

In production environments (and particularly CGI programs) you don't want the program to terminate. If RaiseError is set, you could run your statement within a Perl eval block—a traditional way to trap an error. But by default, the RaiseError attribute is 0 (turned off) and another attribute, PrintError, is 1 (turned on). This attribute makes DBI print an error message and continue. Internally, RaiseError calls the Perl die statement while PrintError calls the warn statement.

Let's look at an alternative way to handle errors. Suppose you want to trap the connection error in your application gracefully and try another course of action. We'll turn off both error attributes and catch the error in typical Perl fashion.

```
my %attr = ( PrintError => 0, RaiseError => 0 );
my $dbh = DBI->connect("dbi:mysql:$db:$server", $username, $password,
                        \%attr)
or do {
  warn "Cannot connect to dbi:mysql:$db:$server;
        trying another method" ;
  ...
  }
```

The connect method returns undef in case of error. So we use an or clause to run some recovery code. Running the program with incorrect connection arguments produces the following output:

```
$ perl perl_check.pl
Cannot connect to dbi:mysql:Books:localhost; trying another method \
at perl_check.pl line 13.
```

And the program continues within the do loop.

Introducing Bind Variables and Optimizations

As we indicated in the section "Basic Perl Example," creating a statement in DBI is a two-step process: first you create a query, then you create a statement handle from the query. One reason for this division is a complication in SQL called *bind variables*, which are a kind of placeholder. Instead of specifying every field and value literally in a query, such as:

```
SELECT author FROM Titles WHERE ISBN = '156592567X'
```

you can create a generalized query with a question mark as a bind variable:

```
SELECT author FROM Titles WHERE ISBN = ?
```

and plug in 156592567X or any other ISBN you want before executing the statement.

Databases operate much more efficiently if you create a general statement containing bind variables and issue repeated queries or updates with different values for the bind variables. This is because the database compiles the SQL statement into an internal format when you create the statement and reuses the internal version on each query or update. This compilation is shown as the second and third of the three phases, parsing and optimization, in Figure 5-1. Perl DBI performs compilation in the prepare( ) statement. If you use bind variables, you must plug in the values between the prepare( ) and the execute( ) statements.

We'll show a trivial example using a bind variable in this section. More sophisticated examples appear later in the chapter.

The new example alters the previous example to use a WHERE clause in the SELECT statement so that we can limit results to a particular publication date. Additionally, we request just two columns (ISBN and title) instead of all columns.

```
my $query = q{
    SELECT isbn,title FROM Titles
        where author like ?
};
```

The q{} syntax is an alternative to using single quotes. The string ends with a question mark, which holds a place for a bind variable. We can plug in the actual value as an argument when we execute the statement:

```
$sth->execute('%Tim Bunce%'); #just books published in 2001
```

As Chapter 3 explained, the percent signs are used by SQL to match any text before or after the specified text.

Assume you had to issue the same query many times using different values for bind variables (during the generation of a daily report, for instance, which retrieves values for many different books or authors). You would prepare the statement with prepare( ), then run a loop that executes the statement repeatedly with different values.

Our amended program is shown in Example 9-3.

Example 9-3. Submitting a query to MySQL using Perl DBI and bind variables

```
#!/usr/bin/perl -w

use strict;
use DBI;

my $server = 'localhost';
my $db = 'Books';
my $username = 'andy' ;
my $password = 'ALpswd' ;

my $dbh = DBI->connect("dbi:mysql:$db:$server", $username, $password);

# The SQL contains a question mark to indicate a bind variable.
my $query = q{
    SELECT isbn,title FROM Titles
```

Example 9-3. Submitting a query to MySQL using Perl DBI and bind variables (continued)

```
        where author like ?
};

my $sth = $dbh->prepare($query);

# We pass an argument to bind the value
# '%Tim Bunce%' to our bind variable.
$sth->execute('%Tim Bunce%'); #just books where Tim Bunce is an author

while (my $row = $sth->fetchrow_arrayref) {
    print join("\t",@$row),"\n";
}

$dbh->disconnect;
```

When run, the output is:

```
$ perl perl2.pl
1565926994      Programming the Perl DBI
```

Another way to use bind variables is to put bind_param( ) calls between the prepare( ) and execute( ) calls:

```
my $sth = $dbh->prepare($query);
$sth->bind_param (1, '%Tim Bunce%');
$sth->execute( );
```

This bind_param( ) call sets the first parameter (our only one) to '%Tim Bunce%'. A third, optional argument allows you to specify the SQL type of the parameter, and we'll see that argument in use later in the chapter.

Another small optimization we could make to our program is to retrieve all the rows from the statement handle at once, instead of one at a time. The selectall_ arrayref( ) retrieves the results as a reference to an array. Each element of the array is a single row, also packaged in a reference to an array. You can unpack the rows in a foreach loop as follows:

```
my $row;
my $result = $dbh->selectall_arrayref($sth);
foreach $row (@$result) {
    print join("\t", @$row),"\n";
}
```

The performance advantage is that your loop operates on a simple array, rather than having to call fetchrow_arrayref( ) on the statement handle on each iteration. You have to be careful when using this retrieval method, though, because if your data is enormous, it could put a strain on your program's memory use and even cause a crash. Make sure the results will fit into available memory.

If you choose to retrieve one row at a time, the fetchrow_arrayref( ) method is fastest. You can also use fetchrow_array( ) to return a simple array (instead of a reference to an array) or fetchrow_hash( ) to return a hash. The latter presents interesting possibilities, because you can then retrieve values by specifying the column name as a key. It is slow, however; if you want a hash, it is better to build it yourself from the results of `fetchrow_arrayref( )`.

DBI and CGI

In this section, we'll show Perl DBI and MySQL in what is probably the most popular context for their use: combined with the popular Perl CGI module to serve dynamic web pages.

As a protocol, CGI is the universal method by which web servers accept input from users and generate results on the fly. The CGI module in Perl makes it easy for programmers to retrieve user input and create output. In order to dispel any sense of magic surrounding CGI, let's look at how data travels from web form to Perl program.

An HTML form may contain a text field such as:

```
<input type="text" name="titleword" />
```

If a user enters the word `Linux` into the field and presses the Submit button, the field is sent to the web server. So if the form containing the input field started out like this:

```
<form method="post" action="/cgi-bin/book_view.cgi"
      enctype="application/x-www-form-urlencoded">
```

the user's browser would request the URL:

```
/cgi-bin/book_view.cgi?titleword=Linux
```

In other words, the browser requests the URL specified in the form's action field, with the field name and the field value tacked on at the end. The server invokes the *book_view.cgi* program, using a special protocol to pass the field name and field value. So now we have to shift our attention to the Perl program.

Introduction to Perl CGI

Having been passed the `titleword` field by the web server, the Perl CGI module extracts it through a `param( )` call:

```
my $titleword = $cgi->param('titleword');
```

Now the local variable `$titleword` contains the string `Linux`. The program can do whatever it wants with this information, but typically it makes a connection to a database and formulates an SQL query, as we did in the earlier DBI examples.

The CGI program is responsible both for handling user input and creating output. Since the server sends its output (more or less) directly to the browser, a Perl program can use simple `print` statements to create HTML. The program also has to create part or all of the HTTP header, but luckily the CGI module hides that activity behind the simple call:

```
print $cgi->header( );
```

Other CGI calls are also fairly intuitive to people who know HTML. For instance, the statement:

```
print $cgi->h2("Please enter a word in the box above.");
```

outputs the string:

```
<h2>Please enter a word in the box above.</h2>
```

which is, of course, an H2 header element in HTML. Sometimes you have to specify arguments as hash keys and values. The following call, for instance, sets two of the many parameters accepted by the start_html( ) call: one parameter to set the background color and another to set the web page's title:

```
$cgi->start_html(
                -bgcolor => '#ffffff',
                -title => 'MySQL CGI Example');
```

Parameters passed from the browser can easily be placed into SQL calls, and results retrieved from database calls can just as easily be placed into CGI calls and sent to the browser. The CGI module is described in great detail in *CGI Programming with Perl*, by Scott Guelich, Shishir Gundavaram, and Gunther Birznieks (O'Reilly).

In Chapter 5, we described a three-tier application model. It may have seemed rather abstract there, but if you use a database with a web server to generate dynamic web pages, you are implementing a three-tier model. The top tier is the browser, the middle tier is the web server and CGI program, and the bottom tier is the database server. We are going to implement a three-tier model twice more during the course of this chapter, so we'll take a moment to talk about it theoretically.

The Model/View/Controller Methodology

One of the best-known and most common structures that produce maintainable programs is called Model/View/Controller (MVC). There are plenty of other good methodologies, but we'll use MVC in this chapter because it's particularly well-suited to database applications. It's a very typical three-tier methodology.

MVC splits an application into the Model, the View, and the Controller. Each layer is an independent unit that performs a specific function. If you design the program correctly, you can—at least in theory—completely strip out one layer and replace it with something different without having to change the code in the other two layers.

Model
> The body of the application. Here, all objects that represent real-world "things" within the application are modeled. For example, a book, publisher, and author are represented in code on this layer. The Model is also responsible for making these objects persistent; that is, storing them so they can be retrieved after the program finishes. Therefore, all database interaction is performed by the Model.

View

The eyes, ears, and hands of the application. The View is responsible for presenting information to the user and collecting any user feedback. In a traditional desktop application, the View draws the screens and reads input from the keyboard and mouse. In a web-based application, the View generates the HTML viewed by the user's browser and passes down any form data submitted by the user. All I/O that involves the user of the system is done in the View. Any input by the user is passed to the Controller for processing.

Controller

The brains of the application. Any software logic performed by the application, such as the job discussed in Chapter 6 of authenticating users, is done within the Controller. The Controller is also the communication center of the application. It processes all user input from the View and all data retrieved from the Model.

It's fairly easy to fit CGI into the MVC methodology. The database maintains the Model, the CGI program (and the web server with which it interacts) is the Controller, and the browser acts as the View. The complete CGI program we'll show in the following section is also based on the MVC methodology in another way.

A Sample CGI/DBI Program

In this section, we present—once again—a program that queries a MySQL database and prints results from the query. This time, however, we will format the results into a CGI page. Instead of generating HTML directly, like the $cgi->h2( ) call in the previous section, we're going to separate the Model from the view in classic MVC fashion. We'll use a popular Perl module called the Template Toolkit.

In this program, we store all the data we want to print in a set of Perl hashes. There is a headers hash used to generate the headers of a table (TH elements in HTML) and a records hash used to store information on each row retrieved from the database. We even use a hash element to store the title of the web page. This hash is the Model in our methodology, because it indicates the data and their relationships without making any presuppositions about how they are displayed.

Then we invoke the Perl Template module to turn our hash into HTML. The module uses our hash and a template we develop and store in a file called *book_view.tt*. Here's the beginning of the file:

```
<html>
 <head>
     <title>[% title %]</title>
 </head>
```

It's HTML, but has a placeholder for the title. We can therefore use the template over and over with pages that have different titles. There are placeholders for the other elements of our hash as well, and a lot of logic to do looping and other runtime choices. For instance, Example 9-4 shows a loop in the *book_view.tt* template file that causes odd-numbered and even-numbered rows to print in different colors, in order to let the user distinguish different rows.

Example 9-4. Excerpt from Template Toolkit template file

```
[% FOREACH record = records -%]
  [%- IF loop.count MOD 2 -%]
    <tr bgcolor="#cccccc">
  [%- ELSE -%]
    <tr bgcolor="#ffccffcc">
  [%- END -%]
...
```

The format used by the Template module is beyond the scope of this book. But it is a much more robust way to develop web pages that you intend to change and maintain over time. Consequently, it is popular and highly regarded in the Perl community.

The advantage of developing web pages this way is that web designers can alter the template as much as they like without forcing the programmers to change their code (and possibly introduce errors into the logic of the program). Similarly, programmers can change the database and the program logic without worrying about the final look of the web page. The Template module represents a successful application of the MVC methodology, with the template file as the Model, the final HTML (designed by web designers) as the View, and the Template module as the Controller.

Since we've described the basic CGI calls and operations, we'll list the entire program in Example 9-5 and then describe a few interesting details. To run this code, you need not only the DBI and CGI modules, but the Template module and a module called AppConfig that Template depends on. You also need the *book_view.tt* file. Both Example 9-5 (under the name *book_view.cgi*) and *book_view.tt* are on the O'Reilly web page for this book. Finally, you probably want to select a special username and password for CGI programs, instead of using the andy user we defined earlier.

If you use the Apache web server, it is easy to get this CGI application working simply by copying the Perl program and template file to Apache's *cgi-bin* directory. Some configuration may be required, however, on Apache and on other web servers.

Example 9-5. CGI program

```
#!/usr/bin/perl -w
use strict;
use DBI;
use CGI;
use Template;
use URI::Escape;

# This code prints a small amount of HTML.
# Mostly, it creates data structures to plug into the template file,
# book_view.tt.
```

Example 9-5. CGI program (continued)

```perl
my $cgi = CGI->new();
my $tt = Template->new();

# The HTPP header must always be printed.
print 'Content-Type: text/html', "\n\n";

my $Records; # a container for our data
$Records->{title} = 'MySQL CGI Example with The Template Took Kit';
$Records->{vlink} = '#0000ff';
$Records->{bgcolor} = '#ffffff';

# If we have parameters, the user clicked on something.
# Otherwise, we just exit.

if($cgi->param) {
# Remove spaces from around the parameter that was passed in.
    my $titleword = $cgi->param('titleword');
    $titleword =~ s/^\s+//;
    $titleword =~ s/\s+$//;
# If the user typed in more the one word, use just the first.
    $titleword =~ s/\s+.*//;
    $Records->{esc_titleword} = uri_escape($titleword);
    $Records->{titleword} = $titleword;

# The following block of code runs when the program is first
# invoked or when the user has not typed in a word for the
# title search.

    unless ($titleword) {
        $Records->{no_word} = 1;
        $tt->process('book_view.tt',$Records)
            or print $tt->error();
        exit;
    }

    my @rows;
    my $url = $cgi->url ;

    # Find out which column, if any, the user clicked on.
    # The form passes that information in the 'col' parameter.
    my $order = $cgi->param('col');

    my $t = $cgi->param('t');

    # Fill in the headers. The information for each header
    # is an element of an array.
    # The array is stored in a hash element with the key $headers.
    # The $Records variable points to the whole hash.

    push(@{$Records->{headers}} , { col => 1,name => 'ISBN',toggle => 1});
    push(@{$Records->{headers}} , { col => 2,name => 'Title',toggle => 1});
    push(@{$Records->{headers}} , { col => 3,name => 'PubDate',toggle => 0});
    push(@{$Records->{headers}} , { col => 4,name => 'Author',toggle => 1});
```

Example 9-5. CGI program (continued)

```
# Check each column to see whether the user clicked on it.
# If so, we toggle the sorting order for that column.
# If the toggle was 1, we change it to 0 (that is, 1 - 1).
# If the toggle was 0, we change it to 1 (that is, 1 - 0).

    for my $hash ( @{$Records->{headers}}) {
        if($hash->{col} == $order) {
                $hash->{toggle} = 1 - $t;
        }
    }

    my $attr = ($t == 1)? 'asc':'desc';

    # Call getPat function, shown later, to transform the user's
    # word into a regular expression for searching.
    my $pat = getPat($titleword);

######### Start of interaction with the database #########

    # First invocation of a DBI method.
    # Connect to the database.
    # Set the RaiseError flag to catch all DBI errors in $@.

    # A row counter, used to mark alternating rows with different colors.
    my $c = 0;

    my $dbh;

    eval {
        $dbh = DBI->connect('dbi:mysql:Books:localhost','andy','ALpswd',
                {PrintError => 0 ,RaiseError => 1});

    # Create the query. Get the four fields for which we set up
    # headers in the $Records array earlier.
    # The 'rlike' clause requests a regular expression search,
    # a bit of nonstandard SQL supported by MySQL.
    # $attr is either undefined or 'desc' for a descending sort.

        my $sql = qq{
            select isbn,title,pubdate,author
                from Titles where title rlike ?
                and pubdate is not null
                order by $order $attr
        };

        my $sth = $dbh->prepare($sql);
        $sth->execute($pat);

######### End of interaction with the database #########

    # Fetch the data and add it to $Records as part of its
    # 'records' hash element.
        while (my $row = $sth->fetchrow_arrayref) {
```

Example 9-5. CGI program (continued)

```
            ++$c;
            my $hash = {
                isbn => {
                    value => $row->[0],
                },
                title => {
                    value => $row->[1],
                },
                pubdate => {
                    value => $row->[2],
                },
                author => {
                    value => $row->[3],
                }
            };
            push(@{$Records->{records}},$hash);
        }
        $dbh->disconnect;
    };
    if($@) {
        $Records->{error} = $@;
        $tt->process('book_view.tt',$Records)
            or print $tt->error();
        exit;
    }

    unless ($c) {
        $Records->{no_rows} = 1;
        $tt->process('book_view.tt',$Records)
            or print $tt->error();
        exit;
    }
}

# Now run $Records through the template processor

$tt->process('book_view.tt',$Records)
    or print $tt->error();

exit(0);

######### getPat Function ############################

# getPat accepts a word and returns a regular expression that
# MySQL will use to find titles. Knowing our data, we perform
# some sneaky tricks on certain input so that a search for 'Java'
# finds JavaBeans and words beginning with J2, while a search for
# .NET finds C and C# titles.

sub getPat {
    my $titleword = shift;
    my $_what = quotemeta $titleword;
    my $pat;
```

Example 9-5. CGI program (continued)

```
    if($titleword =~ /^[Jj][Aa][Vv][Aa]$/) {
        $_what .= '|j2[a-z][a-z]|javabean(s)?';
        $pat = "(^|[^a-zA-Z])($_what)([^a-zA-Z]|\$)";
    } elsif($titleword =~ /\.[nN][eE][tT]/) {
        $_what .= '|[cC]\#';
        $pat = "(^|[^a-zA-Z]+)?($_what)([^a-zA-Z]|\$)";
    } elsif($titleword =~ /\.\*/) {
        $pat = ".*";
    } else {
        $pat = "(^|[^a-zA-Z])($_what)([^a-zA-Z]|\$)";
    }
    return $pat;
}
```

The user's title word is escaped to make it work in an SQL query and then plugged back into the form so it is displayed along with results of the query. Even more importantly, the template file makes the title word the default value for the `titleword` field in the new form.

The program retrieves four columns from the database and reserves four entries for them in the `headers` hash that `$Records` points to: `ISBN`, `Title`, `PubDate`, and `Author`. It also plays a bit with the sort order. After the query is satisfied, books are displayed in descending order by `PubDate` (that is, the most recent book first). The user can choose an column to sort by, however, and reverse the order of the sort, by clicking on a header.

The database interaction should be familiar from the examples we showed earlier in the chapter. The code uses one interesting advanced feature of MySQL: it creates a regular expression and searches for that expression instead of for a plain string. The `getPat()` function turns the user's string into a regular expression. Among other tricks, it wraps the word in regular expression verbiage to make MySQL search for the string as a complete word. Thus, a search for `Java` will not turn up JavaScript titles. MySQL does not support the `\b` or `\w` metacharacters known to Perl programmers, so we have to use ungainly constructs such as `(^|[^a-zA-Z])` in our regular expression.

The `SELECT` call sets up the query to use the regular expression through an `RLIKE` clause, which specifies a regular expression search:

```
select isbn, title, pubdate, author
    from Titles where title rlike ?
```

There is no particular advantage to using the `?` and the bind variable in a CGI program. The whole program has to be rerun each time and rebuild the statement handle, so you cannot achieve any greater speed through the use of a bind variable. But doing so helps to make the program's operation clear and is a good habit.

The following lines process the $Records array through the *book_view.tt* template file:

```perl
my $tt = Template->new();

$tt->process('book_view.tt', $Records);
```

These statements come at the end of the program, because the Template module and web server take care of sending the resulting HTML to the browser.

In case you want to try out CGI and DBI without the extra trouble of using the Template module, another version of this program, called *book_view_simple.cgi*, is included on the O'Reilly web site. It does all its own processing using CGI module calls.

A General Model for Maintainable Perl Programs

Set aside all the wisecracks about Perl being unmaintainable or useful only for small scripts. Also be prepared to renounce the widely held assumption that it's not a truly object-oriented language. In this section we will develop a general Perl framework that will let you quickly add new features to applications and adapt applications to changing database structures.

The code that follows is complex and requires an in-depth knowledge of Perl. Among the features of Perl we exploit are references, recursion, variable type checking, function argument manipulation (the $_[0] syntax), dynamic array building through push statements, and multidimensional hashes—and of course, lots of object-oriented techniques. These features are amply explained in other Perl books, notably *Programming Perl* by Larry Wall, Tom Christiansen, and Jon Orwant (O'Reilly).

A Model for Relational Data

Because the topic of this book is database interaction, the rest of this chapter focuses on the Model layer of the MVC methodology. We will show you how to design abstract methods that can be used and reused in a variety of applications. We'll also show how to weave persistence into your Model with minimal duplication of code, and—for good measure—speed up access by implementation a caching layer.

The Model contains abstractions of all concrete things used within the application. Therefore, a solid Model is an important foundation for the rest of the application.

Luckily for us, designing a Model for a database-driven application is straightforward. That is because the work of discovering the relevant abstractions in a system is done when the database scheme is created, as we described in Chapter 7.

Usually, each table in the database corresponds to one class in the Model. The fields of the tables correspond to the attributes of the class. Relationships between tables can usually be expressed in the following manner:

One to One

If two tables have a one-to-one relationship, their relationship can involve either *containment* or *aggregation*, concepts that are familiar to object-oriented programmers. If one contains the other, the contained object should be defined as an attribute of the container class. For instance, if every ISBN corresponds to one and only one title, one of them can be an attribute of the other. If the relationship is one of aggregation, the more specific class should be a subclass of the less-specific class.

One to Many

If two tables have a one-to-many relationship, the "One" class should contain an array of "Many" objects. Thus, a corporation object could contain an array of objects representing products, because most corporations sell multiple products.

Many to Many

If two tables have a many-to-many relationship, each class can contain an array of objects from the other class. That is, a `Person` table can exist in a many-to-many relationship with an `Employer` table (with a many-to-many join table in the middle), because a `Person` usually has had more than one `Employer` and each `Employer` has more than one `Person`. In the Model, the `Person` class contains an array of `Employer` objects, and the `Employer` class contains an array of `Person` objects. This type of construct can be very challenging to implement, because of the complexities of recursion. When you create a `Person`, you create all his `Employers`, each of which then contains the `Person`, which contains the `Employers`, etc. Because of this, many designers avoid many-to-many relationships when possible. If they are necessary, however, it is possible to pull off with careful implementation.

Like all classes, a Model class is comprised of attributes and methods. An attribute is simply a variable that describes something about the class. As mentioned above, the attributes of a Model class represent the fields of the underlying table and objects from related tables. But what about the methods?

In object-oriented programming, classes have two kinds of methods: *instance* and *static*. Instance methods are only called on actual objects created from the class. Because of this, they have access to the attribute data within the object. Static methods (also known as class methods) are called on the class itself. They have no knowledge of individual objects of that class. For instance, in the first section of this chapter, we saw a static DBI method called `connect( )`.

Persistence requires each Model class to implement three instance methods, which we'll call update, remove, and create. These methods parallel the SQL UPDATE, DELETE, and INSERT statements that, along with SELECT, make up the vast majority of SQL statements.

update

> This method issues an UPDATE statement to save the current state of the object to the database. When an attribute of a Model object is altered somewhere in the application, the application issues its update method so that the change is reflected in the database and is visible to other applications.

remove

> This method issues a DELETE statement to remove the row representing the object from the database. Whenever an object is destroyed by the program, it must make sure to call this method. Destruction can occur through garbage collection or at the termination of the program, as well as through explicit requests. Unfortunately, delete is a keyword in Perl, so we can't use it is as the method name. We'll use remove in this chapter. Other common names include destroy, Delete, and deleteObject.

create

> This method issues an INSERT statement to create a new row of data in the database. Not all objects in the Model need to be in the database, but anything that you want to have persist beyond a single run of the application needs to be saved through a create method. We chose the name create because "creating" an object is a more logical term than "inserting" an object.

While these methods are the only required ones for a Model class, a common object-oriented practice is to use *accessor* or *getter/setter* methods to retrieve and change the values of attributes. If you do this, each attribute of the object should have two instance methods: a get method that retrieves the value of the attribute and a set method that sets the attribute to a new value. They can be named anything, but a common practice is to simply prepend "get" and "set" to the name of the attribute. So an attribute called firstName would have the methods getFirstName and setFirstName.

The instance methods described above cover three of the four basic SQL commands. This leaves SELECT unimplemented. To implement it, we turn to static methods. Unlike the others, the SELECT command does not operate on existing objects. The point of a SELECT query is to retrieve data from the database. In an object-oriented application, you must create new objects to represent data selected from the database. Therefore, it is necessary to use static methods that do not rely on instance data.

Therefore, we'll write a static method that sends SELECT queries to a database and creates new Model objects from the data returned. Unlike the other methods considered so far, there are often several methods within a Model class that need to select data. This is because there are usually different contexts in which to create new objects. We'll implement the two methods that almost every application needs: Generic Where and Primary Key. For better reuse of code, we'll implement Primary Key in terms of Generic Where. Only the latter needs to issue SQL.

Generic Where

> This is the most versatile and common select method. An SQL WHERE clause is passed into it as a parameter (or generated from other parameters) and it sends a

SELECT query to the database containing this WHERE. Out of the resulting data, an array of Model objects is created. Because of the flexibility of the WHERE clause, this method can be leveraged by more specialized select methods, such as the Primary Key select that follows.

Primary Key

Well-designed relational tables almost always have a primary key. If you know a primary key value, you can retrieve a single row of data from the table. A Model class uses the method to create a single object corresponding to a row of data. We implement this method by creating an SQL WHERE clause containing the value of the primary key and then calling the Generic Where select, previously described, to execute the query. Since we are sending in the value of the primary key, we know we will get an array containing a single row in return. This method then returns this single object.

You might consider Primary Key to be a utility or convenience function built on top of Generic Where.

Implementing the Model

In the rest of this chapter, we'll lay out the code that implements a robust Model for a class we'll call Publisher. For the sake of simplicity, each publisher has just two attributes: an ID and a name. The id field is the primary key and uniquely identifies each row of the table. The Name field is the name of the publisher.

In this class, you will recognize all the methods we discussed in the previous section. Of the 13 methods, 4 correspond directly to SQL activities:

create( )

An instance method that inserts a new row into the table to hold the data from this object. The primary key for this table is a MySQL AUTO_INCREMENT field that automatically creates a new value for that field. Therefore, this method inserts only the value of the name field. The id field is passed in by this method as NULL, set in the database by MySQL, and then retrieved and assigned to the object's id attribute by this method.

get( )

A static method that creates an SQL SELECT statement based on WHERE parameters passed to the function. For each row of the result set, a new object is created and an array of these objects is returned. This method represents the Generic Where method described in the previous section.

remove( )

An instance method that removes the row of data corresponding to this object in the database. It issues an SQL DELETE command to accomplish the removal. After this method is called, the program should destroy the object, because its underlying data is gone.

update( )

> An instance method that updates the data in the database with the attribute data in the object. In effect, this method "saves" the current state of the object into the database. For this method to work, the object must already have a row in the database, because the method uses the SQL UPDATE statement.

Some of these calls invoke lower-level functions to handle SQL WHERE clauses. These WHERE clauses can be very complex, especially when multiple tables are involved. Clauses may even be nested. The information stored within an SQL WHERE clause can also be stored in a Perl multilevel hash without losing any information. We allow a WHERE clause of any complexity by encapsulating the processing of the clause in the following two functions:

make_where( )

> A method that flattens the multilevel hash into a regular SQL WHERE clause that can be used in a SQL query.

bind_where( )

> A method that inserts the WHERE clause into a statement handle. While the make_ where( )method creates the actual SQL WHERE clause, the values of the parameters still need to be bound to the statement once the statement is prepared. This method calls the bind_param( ) method shown earlier in this chapter to insert each parameter value into the statement handle. After this method is called, the SELECT statement can be executed.

The following functions get and set the two attributes:

getId( )

> An accessor method that retrieves the current value of the id attribute.

setId( )

> An accessor method that sets the value of the id attribute. Because the id field of the table is the primary key, this method will rarely be called.

getName( )

> An accessor method that retrieves the current value of the name attribute.

setName( )

> An accessor method that sets the value of the name attribute.

The following is the Primary Key select function described in the previous section:

getByPrimaryKey( )

> A static method that creates a single object based on a primary key. This method calls the generic get method to perform the actual query.

The following are constructors:

new( )

> A generic constructor that simply creates an empty object.

```
populate_publisher( )
```
> A static method that creates a new Publisher object based on data from a result set. This is a utility method used by get. The advantage of making it a separate method is that it can be used externally by other Model classes that need to create new Publisher objects.

This *Publisher.pm* module must be located in a directory we've called *CBDB*. In addition to this class, which you can generalize and apply to other applications, we use three helper classes. These are entirely generic and can be reused in any application empoying our Model.

DB
> This class handles the creation of the connection and a couple of other low-level operations on the database that are required by some Publisher methods. The code must be placed in a module named *DB.pm* in the *CBDB* directory.

mysql
> This class implements other low-level functions that must be implemented by functions specific to MySQL. These functions are isolated here so that you can easily port the Model code to another database and just replace this class. The *mysql.pm* module must be placed in a directory named *BM* that is a sibling of the *CBDB* directory.

Cache
> This class provides a very simple mechanism for storing objects in memory and retrieving them later, to minimize the amount of traffic to and from the database. The *Cache.pm* module must be placed in the *CBDB* directory.

If you like to learn code from the bottom up, read the sections on the helper classes, then return to read the code for the Publisher class.

Finally, you may understand the wealth of functions better by seeing them organized into a hierarchy and seeing which functions are called by others. Figure 9-1 shows the main ways functions are called during major database operations.

The Publisher class

In the following subsections, we'll introduce each method of this class in the order in which we've previously described it. The file begins with the following initializations.

```perl
package CBDB::Publisher;

our $VERSION = '1.0';

use strict;
use DBI qw(:sql_types);
use CBDB::DB;
use CBDB::Cache;

our @ISA = qw( CBDB::DB );
```

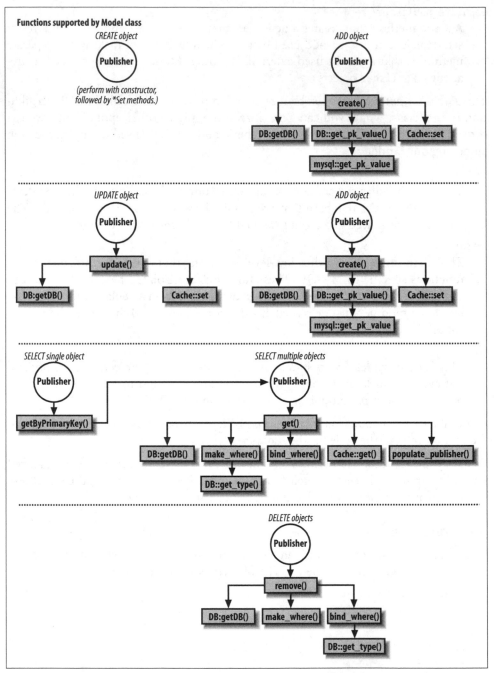

Figure 9-1. Function hierarchy

Methods that build and execute SQL

The create( ), get( ), remove( ), and update( ) methods are fairly short and simple. They check the types of their input arguments, build SQL queries or updates in the ways shown earlier in this chapter, and execute the SQL. They also interact with the cache. Example 9-6 demonstrates this.

Example 9-6. Methods that build and execute SQL

```
##################################################
# create() - Inserts the object into the database.
# Parameters: None.
# Returns: A Publisher object (redundantly, because
# this method is called on that same object).
sub create {
    my $self = shift;
    my $dbh = CBDB::DB::getDB( );
    my $query = "INSERT INTO publisher ( name, id ) VALUES ( ?, ? )";
    my $sth = $dbh->prepare($query);
    my $pk_id = undef;

    $sth->bind_param(1, $self->getName( ), {TYPE=>1});
    $sth->bind_param(2, undef, {TYPE=>4});
    $sth->execute;
    $sth->finish;

    $pk_id = CBDB::DB::get_pk_value($dbh, 'publisher_id');
    $self->setId( $pk_id);

    $dbh->disconnect;
    CBDB::Cache::set('publisher', $self->getId( ), $self);
    return $self;
}


##################################################
# get() - Retrieves objects from the database.
# Parameters: Optional WHERE clause.
# Returns: Array of Publisher objects.
sub get {
    my $wheres = undef;
    my $do_all = 1;
    if (ref($_[0]) eq 'ARRAY') { $wheres = shift; $do_all = shift if @_; }
    else { $do_all = shift; }

    my $dbh = CBDB::DB::getDB( );
    my $where .= ' WHERE  ' . make_where( $wheres );
    my $query = qq{
SELECT publisher.name as publisher_name,
publisher.id as publisher_id
    FROM publisher
$where
};
    my $sth = $dbh->prepare($query);
```

Example 9-6. Methods that build and execute SQL (continued)

```perl
    bind_where( $sth, $wheres );
    $sth->execute;
    my @publishers;
    while (my $Ref = $sth->fetchrow_hashref) {
    my $publisher = undef;
    if (CBDB::Cache::has('publisher', $Ref->{publisher_id})) {
        $publisher = CBDB::Cache::get('publisher', $Ref->{publisher_id});
    } else {
        $publisher = CBDB::Publisher::populate_publisher( $Ref );

    CBDB::Cache::set('publisher',
        $Ref->{publisher_id}, $publisher);
    }
    push(@publishers, $publisher);
    }
    $sth->finish;
    $dbh->disconnect;
    return @publishers;
}


#################################################
# remove() - Removes an object from the database.
# This method can be called on an object to delete
# that object, or statically, with a WHERE clause,
# to delete multiple objects.
# Parameters: An optional where clause.
# Returns: Nothing.
sub remove {
    my $self = undef;
    my $where = undef;
    my $is_static = undef;
    if ( ref($_[0]) and $_[0]->isa("CBDB::Publisher") ) {
    $self = shift;
    $where = "WHERE id = ?";
    } elsif (ref($_[0]) eq 'HASH') {
    $is_static = 1;
    $where = 'WHERE ' . make_where($_[0]);
    } else {
    die "CBDB::Publisher::remove: Unknown parameters: " . join(' ', @_);
    }

    my $dbh = CBDB::DB::getDB( );
    my $query = "DELETE FROM publisher $where";

    my $sth = $dbh->prepare($query);

    if ($is_static) {
    bind_where($sth, $_[0]);
    } else {
    $sth->bind_param(1, $self->getId( ), {TYPE=>4});
    }
```

Example 9-6. Methods that build and execute SQL (continued)

```
    $sth->execute;
    $sth->finish;
    $dbh->disconnect;
}


##################################################
# update() - Updates this object in the database.
# Parameters: None.
# Returns: Nothing.
sub update {
    my $self = shift;
    my $dbh = CBDB::DB::getDB();
    my $query = "UPDATE publisher SET name = ?, id = ? WHERE id = ?";
    my $sth = $dbh->prepare($query);

    $sth->bind_param(1, $self->getName(), {TYPE=>1});
    $sth->bind_param(2, $self->getId(), {TYPE=>4});
    $sth->bind_param(3, $self->getId(), {TYPE=>4});
    $sth->execute;
    $sth->finish;
    $dbh->disconnect;
    CBDB::Cache::set('publisher', $self->getId(), $self);

}
```

Methods that handle WHERE clauses

The make_where() and bind_where() methods are the most complex in our Model, because they must unpack and process complex data structures: Perl hashes, sometimes containing nested hashes. The make_where() method takes the Perl hash as input and converts its contents to a string containing a valid WHERE clause. The bind_where() method is even more complicated. It takes a statement handle and an array (sometimes containing nested arrays) of bind variables. It issues bind_param() calls to bind values to the proper places in the statement handle.

The WHERE clause used by the get and remove methods is in the form of a array reference. Each element of the array is either a single WHERE element or a reference to another array. If it is a reference to another array, the elements in that array are recursively embedded into the WHERE clause to allow clauses such as:

    element AND (*element* OR (*element* AND *element*))

A single WHERE element is a hash reference that has at least the keys column and value. These contain the column name and value of the WHERE element. Other optional keys include type, which is the SQL operator used to join this element with the next element (it defaults to AND) and operator, which is the SQL operator used between the column name and the value (it defaults to an equals sign). Example 9-7 shows methods that handle WHERE clauses.

Example 9-7. Methods that handle WHERE clauses

```perl
###################################################
# make_where() - Construct a WHERE clause from a well-defined hash ref.
# Parameters: WHERE clause reference.
# Returns: WHERE clause string.
sub make_where {
    my $where_ref = shift;
    if ( ref($where_ref) ne 'ARRAY' ) {
    die "CBDB::Publisher::make_where: Unknown parameters: " .
    join(' ', @_);
    }
    my @wheres = @$where_ref;
    my $element_counter = 0;
    my $where = "";
    for my $element_ref (@wheres) {
    if (ref($element_ref) eq 'ARRAY') {
        $where .= make_where($element_ref);
    } elsif (ref($element_ref) ne 'HASH') {
        die "CBDB::Publisher::make_where: malformed WHERE parameter: "
        . $element_ref;
    }
    my %element = %$element_ref;
    my $type = 'AND';
    if (not $element_counter and scalar keys %element == 1 and
        exists($element{'TYPE'})) {
        $type = $element{'TYPE'};
    } else {
        my $table = "publisher";
        my $operator = "=";
        if (exists($element{'table'})) { $table = $element{'table'}; }
        if (exists($element{'operator'}))
        { $operator = $element{'operator'}; }
        if ($element_counter) { $where .= " $type "; } else
        { $element_counter = 1; }
        for my $term ( grep !/^(table|operator)$/, keys %element ) {
            $where .= "$table.$term $operator ?";
        }
    }
  }
  return $where;
}


###################################################
# bind_where() - Executes the handle->bind method that binds the
# where element.
# Parameters: WHERE clause array ref and a scalar
# ref to a counter number that tells the method
# which parameter to bind to.
# Returns: Nothing.
sub bind_where {
    my $sth = shift;
    my $where_ref = shift;
    my $counter_ref = shift || undef;
    my $counter = (ref($counter_ref) eq 'Scalar')?  $$counter_ref : 1;
```

Example 9-7. Methods that handle WHERE clauses (continued)

```perl
    if ( not $sth->isa('DBI::st') or ref($where_ref) ne 'ARRAY' ) {
    die "CBDB::Publisher::make_where: Unknown parameters: "
        . join(' ', @_);
    }
    my @wheres = @$where_ref;
    for my $element_ref (@wheres) {
    if (ref($element_ref) eq 'ARRAY') {
        bind_where($sth, $element_ref, \$counter);
    } elsif (ref($element_ref) ne 'HASH') {
        die "CBDB::Publisher::make_where: malformed WHERE parameter: "
            . $_;
    }
    my %element = %$element_ref;
    unless (not $counter and scalar keys %element == 1 and
            exists($element{'TYPE'})) {
        my $table = "publisher";
        if (exists($element{'table'})) {
            $table = $element{'table'};
        }
        for my $term ( grep !/^(table|operator)$/, keys %element ) {
            $sth->bind_param($counter, $element{$term},
                {TYPE=>CBDB::DB::getType($table,$term)});
            $counter++;
        }
    }
  }
 }
}
```

Getter/setter methods

The getId( ), setId( ), getName( ), and setName( ) methods are typical object-oriented methods for accessing properties of the object. Example 9-8 demonstrates this.

Example 9-8. Getter/setter methods

```perl
################################################
# getId( ) - Return Id for this publisher.
# Parameters: None.
# Returns: ID.
sub getId {
    my $self = shift;
    return $self->{Id};
}


################################################
# setId( ) - Set Id for this publisher.
# Parameters: An Id number.
# Returns: Nothing.
sub setId {
    my $self = shift;
    my $pId = shift or die "publisher.setId( Id ) requires a value.";
    $self->{Id} = $pId;
}
```

Example 9-8. Getter/setter methods (continued)

```
##################################################
# getName() - Return Name for this publisher.
# Parameters: None.
# Returns: Name.
sub getName {
    my $self = shift;
    return $self->{Name};
}


##################################################
# setName() - Set Name for this publisher.
# Parameters: A name.
# Returns: Nothing.
sub setName {
    my $self = shift;
    my $pName = shift || undef;
    $self->{Name} = $pName;
}
```

Primary key select method

The getByPrimaryKey( ) method retrieves data by its primary key, invoking the get( ) method previously shown. This is shown in Example 9-9.

Example 9-9. Primary Key Select Method

```
##################################################
# getByPrimaryKey() - Retrieves a single object from
# the database based on a primary key.
# Parameters: An Id.
# Returns: A Publisher object.
sub getByPrimaryKey {
    my $pId = shift or die "publisher.get()";
    my $where = [ {'id' => $pId } ];
    return ( get( $where, 1 ) )[0];
}
```

Constructors

The new( ) method is a typical, generic constructor, while the populate_publisher( ) method is used by the get( ) method to create a Publisher object. Example 9-10 shows constructors.

Example 9-10. Constructors

```
##################################################
# new() - Constructor.
# Example: CBDB::Publisher->new();
# Returns: blessed hash.
sub new {
    my $proto = shift;
```

Example 9-10. Constructors (continued)

```
    my $class = ref($proto) || $proto;
    my $self = {};
    bless($self, $class);

    return $self;
}

##################################################
# populate_publisher() - Return a publisher object
# populated from a result set.
# Parameters: Data from a DBI fetch.
# Returns: A Publisher object.
sub populate_publisher {
    my $Ref = shift;
    my $publisher = CBDB::Publisher->new();
    $publisher->setName($Ref->{publisher_name});
    $publisher->setId($Ref->{publisher_id});

    return $publisher;
}

1; # This always terminates a class definition.
```

The DB class

This class provides utility functions related to databases. It also invokes a database-specific class, mysql. It contains, as a static variable, a hash that lists all the columns in all the application's tables along with their data types.

getDB( )

> This method creates a connection to the database and returns the database handle. This method is used by the Publisher methods that build and execute SQL.

get_pk_value( )

> This method returns the most recent value assigned to a primary key through the auto-increment feature of the database. It invokes a method by the same name from mysql.

get_type( )

> This method returns the SQL type of a column within a table, using the class's hash of columns.

Example 9-11 demonstrates the DB class.

Example 9-11. The DB class

```
package CBDB::DB;

use strict;
use BM::mysql;

my $VERSION = '0.1';
use constant DSN => "dbi:mysql:database=Books;host=localhost";
```

Example 9-11. The DB class (continued)

```perl
use constant USER => "andy";
use constant PASSWORD => "ALpswd";

my $types = {
    'creator' => { 'name' => 1, 'id' => 4 },
    'book' => { 'title' => 1, 'publisher_id' => 4, 'date' => 11, 'id' => 4 },
    'book_creator' => { 'book_id' => 4, 'creator_id' => 4, 'role_id' => 4 },
    'publisher' => { 'name' => 1, 'id' => 4 },
    'role' => { 'name' => 1, 'id' => 4 },
};

######################################################################
# getDB() - Returns a database handle connection for the database.
# Parameters: None.
# Returns: DBH Connection Handle.
sub getDB {
    my $dbh = DBI->connect(DSN,USER,PASSWORD,{PrintError => 1,RaiseError => 1});
    return $dbh;
}

######################################################################
# get_pk_value() - Returns the most recent auto_increment value for a PK.
# Parameters: Database Handle.
# Returns: Primary key value.
sub get_pk_value {
    my $dbh = shift or die "DB::get_pk_value needs a Database Handle...";

    my $dbd = BM::mysql->new();
    return $dbd->get_pk_value( $dbh );
}

######################################################################
# getType() - Returns the type of a column within a table.
# Parameters: Table name and column name.
# Returns: DBI Type code.
sub getType {
    my $table = shift;
    my $col = shift;
    return $types->{$table}{$col};
}

1;
```

The mysql class

In this class, we have tried to extract and isolate calls to methods that are specific to a particular database server.

new( )

> This is the generic object constructor.

is_pk( )

> This method determines whether a field is part of the primary key of the table.

---

is_auto_increment( )

This method determines whether the primary key of the table is an AUTO_ INCREMENT field.

get_pk_value( )

This method returns the value of the most recently inserted AUTO_INCREMENT field.

Example 9-12 demonstrates the mysql class.

Example 9-12. The mysql class

```perl
package BM::mysql;

use strict;

###############
# CONSTRUCTOR #
###############
sub new {
    my $proto = shift;
    my $class = ref($proto) || $proto;
    my $self = { };
    bless($self, $class);
    return $self;
}


#################################################
# is_pk() - Determines if a column is a primary key.
# Parameters: DBI statement handle and a column
# number from that handle.
# Returns: true or false.

sub is_pk ($$$) {
    my $self = shift;
    my $sth = shift;
    my $i = shift;

    return 1 if $$sth->{mysql_is_pri_key}->[$i];
    return 0;
}


#################################################
# is_auto_increment() - Determines if a column is an
# AUTO_INCREMENT column.
# Parameters: DBI statement.
# handle and a column number from that handle.
# Returns: true or false.
sub is_auto_increment($$$) {
    my $self = shift;
    my $sth = shift;
    my $i = shift;

    return 1 if $$sth->{mysql_is_auto_increment}->[$i];
    return 0;
}
```

Example 9-12. The mysql class (continued)

```
#################################################
# get_pk_value() - Returns the last AUTO_INCREMENT
# value for this connection.
# Paramaters: DBI database handle.
# Returns: PK value.
sub get_pk_value {
    my $self = shift;
    my $dbh = shift or die "mysql::get_pk needs a Database Handle...";
    my $mysqlPk = "Select last_insert_id() as pk";
    my $mysqlSth = $dbh->prepare($mysqlPk);
    $mysqlSth->execute();
    my $mysqlHR = $mysqlSth->fetchrow_hashref;
    my $pk = $mysqlHR->{"pk"};
    $mysqlSth->finish;
    return $pk;
}

1;
```

The Cache class

This class contains a static hash of all the Model objects used by the application. The cache is organized by class name (the first-order hash) and primary key (the second-order, or nested, hash).

Besides increasing performance, the cache also allows multiple objects to exist that represent the same row of data in the underlying table. Because each object's code uses references to the cached objects, the object automatically reflects changes made to other objects.

set( )
   Adds an object to the cache.

get( )
   Retrieves an object from the cache.

has( )
   Checks to see whether the object already exists in the cache.

Example 9-13 demonstrates the Cache class.

Example 9-13. The Cache class

```
package CBDB::Cache;

# This file keeps a copy of all active objects,
#s with records of their primary keys.
use strict;

my %cache = ();

sub set {
    $cache{$_[0]}{$_[1]} = $_[2];
```

Example 9-13. The Cache class (continued)

```perl
}
sub get {
    return $cache{$_[0]}{$_[1]};
}
sub has {
    return exists $cache{$_[0]}{$_[1]};
}

1;
```

Example of the Model's Use

Now that we've seen the Model class and all its supporting classes, let's look at how it is used in practice. The following snippets of code would be part of the Controller layer of the application: the layer that performs all the logic. Note how all the actual database calls are hidden from this layer. It uses just calls to the Model class.

Each file in the Controller layer indicates that it will use the Publisher class:

```perl
use CBDB::Publisher;
my $VERSION = 1.0;
```

A new object is created as follows:

```perl
my $pub = new CBDB::Publisher();
```

Now let's set some data. The following creates a new publisher in our program (but not the database). We're in a hurry, so we can't be bothered with good spelling.

```perl
$pub->setName("Joe's Boks");
```

Note that we didn't set the id field of the publisher. The ID is an auto-increment field taken care of automatically by the database. A more abstract way of understanding our approach is that the ID is not a real-world property of this object. It exists only because the object-relational model we're using internally requires it. Therefore, at the controller level, we don't have to worry about assigning it or making sure it's unique.

We'll see what we just created:

```perl
print 'Our new publisher is ' . $pub->getName() . "\n";
```

If the program were to terminate at this point, this object's data would be lost. To make it persistent, we need to save it to the database:

```perl
$pub->create();
```

Now the object has been created in the database and can be retrieved by another application, or by our application during a subsequent run. The database has assigned a primary key, which we can store for later use to find the object again:

```perl
my $new_id = $pub->getId();
```

Suppose we want to retrieve the object in another part of our program. We'll use the getByPrimaryKey( ) call with the ID we stored earlier. The getByPrimaryKey( ) is static; we call it on the Publisher class itself instead of on an object from that class.

```
my $pub2 = CBDB::Publisher::getByPrimaryKey($new_id);
```

Because of the caching mechanism, $pub2 is the same object in memory as $pub. We can check this identity, if we're curious.

```
if ($pub2 != $pub) {
    print "Whoops! Something isn't working right!\n"
}
```

Let's change some data. For instance, we can fix the typo we introduced at the beginning of this section.

```
$pub2->setName("Joe's Books");
```

At this point, the data has been changed in the object only, not in the underlying database. However, because all active instances of this object in our program are references to the same object, this change takes place everywhere in the application immediately. Thus, the following statement will print Joe's Books, not Joe's Boks, even though we didn't explicitly touch the data to which $pub points.

```
print "The publisher's name is now " . $pub->getName() . "\n";
```

Now let's save these changes to the database. We can use either $pub or $pub2 to indicate the data.

```
$pub2->update();
```

Later, we decide we're finished with this data and need to delete the row from the database.

```
$pub->remove();
```

The underlying row in the database has now been deleted. However, this object (as well as $pub2) still contains the data until the program terminates or destroys the objects. This may be useful in case we want to refer to some property that the publisher used to have, as we do in the informational message below.

```
print "The publisher " . $pub->getName() . " was just erased.\n";
```

We hope that this little tour has shown the value of planning your program's structure so it is flexible and maintainable. Underneath DBI and CGI and the MVC methodology, it's just a bunch of INSERT, SELECT, and other SQL statements.

## CHAPTER 10

Python

If you do a lot of Perl programming but are not familiar with Python, you should definitely take a look at it. Python is an object-oriented scripting language that combines the strengths of languages such as Perl and Tcl with a clear syntax that lends itself to applications that are easy to maintain and extend. *Learning Python*, by Mark Lutz and David Asher (O'Reilly), provides an excellent introduction to Python programming. This chapter assumes you have a working understanding of the Python language.

To follow the content of this chapter, you will need to download and install MySQLdb, the MySQL version of DB-API. You can find the module at *http:// dustman.net/andy/python/MySQLdb*. Chapter 20 includes directions on how to install MySQLdb.

DB-API

Like Java and Perl, Python has developed a unified API for database access: DB-API. This database API was developed by a Python Special Interest Group (SIG) called the Database SIG. The Database SIG is a group of influential Python developers interested in implementing Python access to various databases. On the positive side, DB-API is a very small, simple API. On the negative side, it has design flaws. Part of its problem is that, being small, it does not support many of the more complex features database programmers expect in a database API. It also fails to achieve true database independence. As a comprehensive database access API, it still leaves a lot to be desired and does not compete with more mature APIs such as Perl DBI and Java JDBC. You should therefore expect significant changes in this API over time.

The Database Connection

The entry point into DB-API is really the only part of the API tied to a particular database engine. By convention, all modules supporting DB-API are named after the database they support with a *db* extension. The MySQL implementation is thus called MySQLdb. Similarly, the Oracle implementation is called oracledb and the

Sybase implementation sybasedb. Each module contains a connect( ) method that returns a DB-API connection object. This method returns an object that has the same name as the module:

```
import MySQLdb;
conn = MySQLdb.connect(host='carthage', user='test',
                       passwd='test', db='test');
```

This example connects using the username/password pair test/test to the MySQL database test hosted on the machine carthage. In addition to these four arguments, you can specify a custom port, the location of a Unix socket to use for the connection, and an integer representing client connection flags. All arguments must be passed to connect( ) as keyword/value pairs, as in the example above.

The API for a connection object is very simple. You basically use it to gain access to cursor objects and manage transactions. When you are done, you should close the connection:

```
conn.close( );
```

Cursors

Cursors represent SQL statements and their results. The connection object provides your application with a cursor via the cursor( ) method:

```
cursor = conn.cursor( );
```

This cursor is the center of your Python database access. Through the execute( ) method, you send SQL to the database and process any results. The simplest form of database access is, of course, a simple insert:

```
conn = MySQLdb.connect(host='carthage', user='test', passwd='test', db='test');
cursor = conn.cursor( );
cursor.execute("INSERT INTO test (test_id, test_char) VALUES (1, 'test')");
print "Affected rows: ", cursor.rowcount;
```

In this example, the application inserts a new row into the database using the cursor generated by the MySQL connection. It then verifies the insert by printing out the number of rows affected. For inserts, this value should always be 1.

Query processing is a little more complex. Again, you use the execute( ) method to send SQL to the database. Instead of checking the affected rows, however, you grab the results from the cursor using one of many fetch methods. Example 10-1 shows a Python program processing a simple query.

Example 10-1. A simple query

```
import MySQLdb;

connection = None;
try:
    connection = MySQLdb.connect(host="carthage", user="user",
                                 passwd="pass", db="test");
```

Example 10-1. A simple query (continued)

```
    cursor = connection.cursor();
    cursor.execute("SELECT test_id, test_val FROM test ORDER BY test_id");
    for row in cursor.fetchall():
        print "Key: ", row[0];
        print "Value: ", row[1];
      connection.close();
  except:
    if connection:
        connection.close();
```

The cursor object actually provides several fetch methods: fetchone( ), fetchmany( ), and fetchall( ). For each of these methods, a row is represented by a Python tuple. In Example 10-1, the fetchall( ) method fetches all the results from the query into a list of Python tuples. This method, like all the fetch methods, will throw an exception if the SQL was not a query.

Of course, fetching all the rows at once can be inefficient for large result sets. You can instead fetch each row one by one by using the fetchone( ) method. The fetchone( ) method returns a single row as a tuple where each element represents a column in the returned row. If you have already fetched all the rows of the result set, fetchone( ) will return None.

The final fetch method, fetchmany( ), is middle ground between fetchone( ) and fetchall( ). It enables an application to fetch a predefined number of rows at once. You can either pass in the number of rows you wish to see or rely on the value of cursor.arraysize to provide a default value.

Parameterized SQL

DB-API includes a mechanism for executing parameterized SQL statements using the execute( ) method as well as a more complex method called executemany( ). Parameterized SQL is an SQL statement with placeholders to which you can pass arguments. As with a simple SQL execution, the first argument to execute( ) is an SQL string. Unlike the simple form, this SQL has placeholders for parameters specified by the second argument. A simple example is:

```
    cursor.execute('INSERT INTO COLORS (COLOR, ABBR) VALUES (%s, %s)',
                   ('BLUE', 'BL'));
```

In this example, %s is placed in the SQL as a placeholder for values passed as the second argument. The first %s matches the first value in the paramter tuple, and the second %s matches the second value in the tuple.

 MySQLdb treats all values as string values, even when their underlying database type is BIGINT, DOUBLE, DATE, etc. Thus, all conversion parameters should be %s even though you might think they should be %d or %f.

DB-API actually has several ways of marking SQL parameters. You can specify the format you wish to use by setting MySQLdb.paramstyle. The above example is MySQLdb.paramstyle = "format". The "format" value is the default for MySQLdb when a tuple of parameters is passed to execute( ) and is basically the set of placeholders from the ANSI C printf( ) function. Another possible value for MySQLdb.paramstyle is "pyformat". This value is the default when you pass a Python mapping as the second argument.

DB-API actually allows several other formats, but MySQLdb does not support them. This lack of support is particularly unfortunate since it is common practice in database applications in other languages to mark placeholders with a ?.

The utility of parameterized SQL becomes apparent when you use the executemany( ) method. This method enables you to execute the same SQL statement with multiple sets of parameters. For example, consider this code snippet that adds three rows to the database using execute( ):

```
cursor.execute("INSERT INTO COLOR (COLOR, ABBREV) VALUES ('BLUE', 'BL')");
cursor.execute("INSERT INTO COLOR (COLOR, ABBREV) VALUES ('PURPLE', 'PPL')");
cursor.execute("INSERT INTO COLOR (COLOR, ABBREV) VALUES ('ORANGE', 'ORN')");
```

That same functionality using executemany( ) looks like this:

```
cursor.executemany("INSERT INTO COLOR ( COLOR, ABBREV ) VALUES (%s, %s )",
                    (("BLUE", "BL"), ("PURPLE", "PPL"), ("ORANGE", "ORN")));
```

This one line executes the same SQL three times using different values in place of the placeholders. This can be extremely useful if you are using Python in batch processing.

Other Objects

DB-API provides a host of other objects to help encapsulate common SQL data types so they may be passed as parameters to execute( ) and executemany( ) and relieve developers of the burden of formatting them for different databases. These objects include Date, Time, Timestamp, and Binary. MySQLdb supports these objects up to a point. Specifically, when MySQLdb binds parameters, it converts each paramter to a string (via __str__) and places it in the SQL. The Timestamp object, in particular, includes fractional seconds, which MySQL considers illegal input.

It is important to note that MySQLdb does not properly implement the Date( ), Time( ), and Timestamp( ) constructors for their respective objects. You instead have to use the DateFromTicks( ), TimeFromTicks( ), and TimestampFromTicks( ) methods to get a reference to the desired object. The argument for each of these methods is the number of seconds since the epoch.

The following code creates a Date for the current time and updates the database:

```
import time;
d = MySQLdb.DateFromTicks(time.time( ));
cursor.execute("UPDATE test SET test_date = %s WHERE test_id = 1", (d,));
```

Proprietary Operations

In general, you should stick to the published DB-API specification when writing database code in Python. There will be some instances, however, when you may need access to MySQL-specific functionality. MySQLdb is actually built on top of the MySQL C API and exposes that API to programs that wish to use it. This ability is particularly useful for applications that want metadata about the MySQL database.

Basically, MySQLdb exposes most C methods except those governing result set processing, because cursors are a better interface for that functionality. Example 10-2 shows a trivial application that uses the list_dbs() and list_tables() methods from the C API to loop through all the tables in all the databases on the MySQL server and print out the first row from each table. Needless to say, do not run this application against a production machine.

Example 10-2. A Python application using proprietary functionality

```
import MySQLdb;

conn = None;
try:
    conn = MySQLdb.connect(host="carthage", user="test",
                           passwd="test", db="test");
    for db in conn.list_dbs():
        for tbl in conn.list_tables(db[0]):
            cursor = conn.cursor();
            cursor.execute("SELECT * FROM " + tbl[0]);
            print cursor.fetchone();
            cursor.close();
except:
    if conn:
        conn.close();
```

Chapter 20 lists the proprietary APIs exposed by MySQLdb.

Applied DB-API

So far, we have walked you through the DB-API and showed you its basic functionality. Now we will go through a practical example of a Python database application using the DB-API.

Our example is a batch routine that pulls stale orders from an order database and builds an XML file. Business partners can then download this XML file and import the order information into their databases. Example 10-3 shows a sample generated XML file.

Example 10-3. An XML file containing order information for a fictitious manufacturer

```
<?xml version="1.0"?>

<order orderID="101" date="2000" salesRepID="102">
  <customer customerID="100">
    <name>Wibble Retail</name>
    <address>
      <lines>
        <line>
          1818 Harmonika Rd.
        </line>
      </lines>
      <city>Osseo</city>
      <state>MN</state>
      <country>US</country>
      <postalCode>55369</postalCode>
    </address>
  </customer>
  <lineItem quantity="2">
    <unitCost currency="USD">12.99</unitCost>
    <product productID="104">
      <name>Wibble Scarf</name>
    </product>
  </lineItem>
  <lineItem quantity="1">
    <unitCost currency="USD">24.95</unitCost>
    <product productID="105">
      <name>Wibble Hat</name>
    </product>
  </lineItem>
</order>
```

The XML enables the business partners to trade information about orders without having to know anything about our data model. Every night, a Python script runs to look for orders that have not been converted to XML in the previous day. Any such orders are then read from the database and converted to XML.

The Python script, *xmlgen.py*, starts with a few simple imports:

```
import sys, os;
import traceback;
import MySQLdb;
```

Much of the script defines Python objects that encapsulate the business objects in the database. Example 10-4 contains the code for these business objects.

Example 10-4. Business objects for the XML generator

```
class Address:
    def __init__(self, l1, l2, cty, st, ctry, zip):
        self.line1 = l1;
        self.line2 = l2;
        self.city = cty;
        self.state = st;
```

Example 10-4. Business objects for the XML generator (continued)

```
            self.country = ctry;
            self.postalCode = zip;

    def toXML(self, ind):
        xml = ('%s<address>\r\n' % ind);
        xml = ('%s%s  <lines>\r\n' % (xml, ind));
        if self.line1:
            xml = ('%s%s    <line>\r\n%s        %s\r\n%s    </line>\r\n' %
                    (xml, ind, ind, self.line1, ind));
        if self.line2:
            xml = ('%s%s    <line>\r\n%s        %s\r\n%s    </line>\r\n' %
                    (xml, ind, ind, self.line2, ind));
        xml = ('%s%s  </lines>\r\n' % (xml, ind));
        if self.city:
            xml = ('%s%s  <city>%s</city>\r\n' % (xml, ind, self.city));
        if self.state:
            xml = ('%s%s  <state>%s</state>\r\n' % (xml, ind, self.state));
        if self.country:
            xml = ('%s%s  <country>%s</country>\r\n' % (xml,ind,self.country));
        if self.postalCode:
            xml = ('%s%s  <postalCode>%s</postalCode>\r\n' %
                    (xml, ind, self.postalCode));
        xml = ('%s%s</address>\r\n' % (xml, ind));
        return xml;

class Customer:
    def __init__(self, cid, nom, addr):
        self.customerID = cid;
        self.name = nom;
        self.address = addr;

    def toXML(self, ind):
        xml = ('%s<customer customerID="%s">\r\n' % (ind, self.customerID));
        if self.name:
            xml = ('%s%s  <name>%s</name>\r\n' % (xml, ind, self.name));
        if self.address:
            xml = ('%s%s' % (xml, self.address.toXML(ind + '  ')));
        xml = ('%s%s</customer>\r\n' % (xml, ind));
        return xml;

class LineItem:
    def __init__(self, prd, qty, cost):
        self.product = prd;
        self.quantity = qty;
        self.unitCost = cost;

    def toXML(self, ind):
        xml = ('%s<lineItem quantity="%s">\r\n' % (ind, self.quantity));
        xml = ('%s%s  <unitCost currency="USD">%s</unitCost>\r\n' %
                (xml, ind, self.unitCost));
        xml = ('%s%s' % (xml, self.product.toXML(ind + '  ')));
        xml = ('%s%s</lineItem>\r\n' % (xml, ind));
        return xml;
```

Example 10-4. Business objects for the XML generator (continued)

```
class Order:
    def __init__(self, oid, date, rep, cust):
        self.orderID = oid;
        self.orderDate = date;
        self.salesRep = rep;
        self.customer = cust;
        self.items = [];

    def toXML(self, ind):
        xml = ('%s<order orderID="%s" date="%s" salesRepID="%s">\r\n' %
                (ind, self.orderID, self.orderDate, self.salesRep));
        xml = ('%s%s' % (xml, self.customer.toXML(ind + '  ')));
        for item in self.items:
            xml = ('%s%s' % (xml, item.toXML(ind + '  ')));
        xml = ('%s%s</order>\r\n' % (xml, ind));
        return xml;

class Product:
    def __init__(self, pid, nom):
        self.productID = pid;
        self.name = nom;

    def toXML(self, ind):
        xml = ('%s<product productID="%s">\r\n' % (ind, self.productID));
        xml = ('%s%s  <name>%s</name>\r\n' % (xml, ind, self.name));
        xml = ('%s%s</product>\r\n' % (xml, ind));
        return xml;
```

Each business object defines two basic methods. The first, the constructor, does nothing more than assign values to the object's attributes. The second method, toXML( ), converts the business object to XML. So far, we have kept all database access separate from our business objects. This is a very critical design element of good database programming.

All database access comes in a module method called executeBatch( ). The purpose of this method is to find out which orders need XML generated and load them from the database into business objects. It then takes these loaded orders and sends the return value of toXML( ) to an XML file. Example 10-5 shows the executeBatch( ) method.

Example 10-5. Database access for the XML generator

```
def executeBatch(conn):
    try:
        cursor = conn.cursor();
        cursor.execute("SELECT ORDER_ID FROM ORDER_EXPORT " +
                        "WHERE LAST_EXPORT <> CURRENT_DATE( )");
        orders = cursor.fetchall( );
        cursor.close( );
    except:
        print "Error retrieving orders.";
        traceback.print_exc( );
```

Example 10-5. Database access for the XML generator (continued)

```
        conn.close( );
        exit(0);

for row in orders:
    oid = row[0];
    try:
        cursor = conn.cursor( );
        cursor.execute("SELECT CUST_ORDER.ORDER_DATE, " +
                    "CUST_ORDER.SALES_REP_ID, " +
                    "CUSTOMER.CUSTOMER_ID, " +
                    "CUSTOMER.NAME, " +
                    "CUSTOMER.ADDRESS1, " +
                    "CUSTOMER.ADDRESS2, " +
                    "CUSTOMER.CITY, " +
                    "CUSTOMER.STATE, " +
                    "CUSTOMER.COUNTRY, " +
                    "CUSTOMER.POSTAL_CODE " +
                    "FROM CUST_ORDER, CUSTOMER " +
                    "WHERE CUST_ORDER.ORDER_ID = %s " +
                    "AND CUST_ORDER.CUSTOMER_ID = CUSTOMER.CUSTOMER_ID",
                    ( oid ) );
        row = cursor.fetchone( );
        cursor.close( );
        addr = Address(row[4], row[5], row[6], row[7], row[8], row[9]);
        cust = Customer(row[2], row[3], addr);
        order = Order(oid, row[0], row[1], cust);
        cursor = conn.cursor( );
        cursor.execute("SELECT LINE_ITEM.PRODUCT_ID, " +
                    "LINE_ITEM.QUANTITY, " +
                    "LINE_ITEM.UNIT_COST, " +
                    "PRODUCT.NAME " +
                    "FROM LINE_ITEM, PRODUCT " +
                    "WHERE LINE_ITEM.ORDER_ID = %s " +
                    "AND LINE_ITEM.PRODUCT_ID = PRODUCT.PRODUCT_ID",
                    oid);
        for row in cursor.fetchall( ):
            prd = Product(row[0], row[3]);
            order.items.append(LineItem(prd, row[1], row[2]));
    except:
        print "Failed to load order: ", oid;
        traceback.print_exc( );
        exit(0);

    try:
        cursor.close( );
    except:
        print "Error closing cursor, continuing...";
        traceback.print_exc( );

    try:
        fname = ('%d.xml' % oid);
        xmlfile = open(fname, "w");
        xmlfile.write('<?xml version="1.0"?>\r\n\r\n');
```

Example 10-5. Database access for the XML generator (continued)

```
            xmlfile.write(order.toXML(''));
            xmlfile.close( );
        except:
            print ("Failed to write XML file: %s" % fname);
            traceback.print_exc( );

        try:
            cursor = conn.cursor( );
            cursor.execute("UPDATE ORDER_EXPORT " +
                    "SET LAST_EXPORT = CURRENT_DATE( ) " +
                    "WHERE ORDER_ID = %s", ( oid ));
        except:
            print "Failed to update ORDER_EXPORT table, continuing";
            traceback.print_exc( );
```

The first try/except block looks in the ORDER_EXPORT table for all orders that have not had XML generated in the previous day. If that fails for any reason, the script bails completely.

Each row returned from fetchall( ) represents an order in need of exporting. The script therefore loops through each of the rows and loads all the data for the order represented by the row. Inside the for loop, the script executes SQL to pull order and customer data from the ORDER and CUSTOMER tables. With those columns in hand, it can construct Order, Customer, and Address objects for the order, its associated customer, and the customer's address. Because ORDER to LINE_ITEM is a one-to-many relationship, we need a separate query to load the LineItem objects. The next query looks for all the line items associated with the current order ID and loads business objects for them.

With all the data loaded into business objects, the script opens a file and writes out its XML conversion to that file. Once the write is successful, the script goes back to the database to note that the XML is now up to date with the database. The script then goes to the next order and continues processing until there are no more orders.

The last part missing from the script is the functionality to call executeBatch( ):

```
    if __name__ == '__main__':
        try:
            conn = MySQLdb.connect(host='carthage', user='test', passwd='test',
                            db='Test');
        except:
            print "Error connecting to MySQL:";
            traceback.print_exc( );
            exit(0);

        executeBatch(conn);
```

This script, along with the SQL to generate the tables and data behind, it are available with the rest of the examples from this book at the O'Reilly web site.

## CHAPTER 11

PHP

The triad of PHP, MySQL, and the Apache web server is one of the most popular web development platforms. There are several good reasons for PHP's popularity as a web scripting language: it is easy to include PHP scripts in HTML documents, PHP is free in a monetary and open source sense, it has over a hundred function libraries, and it shares syntax with C or Perl-like languages.

This chapter introduces you to building web database applications with PHP. To show PHP in action, we present a simple application: a wedding gift registry. The application shows how common database functions are used in practice, along with how to secure a system, pass data between scripts, and add login and logout features.

We introduce the following concepts in this chapter:

- An introduction to the PHP language and a short guide to installing PHP on your platform
- How common MySQL library functions are used to access the MySQL DBMS
- How to handle MySQL DBMS errors, use include files to modularize code, and secure user data
- How to write data to databases, manage sessions in applications, and control the web browser
- Other resources for learning more about developing PHP and MySQL web database applications

Chapter 18 presents a complete reference to the PHP MySQL library functions.

Introducing PHP

PHP is a scripting language designed to be embedded into the HTML markup used for web pages. Web pages that contain PHP scripts are preprocessed by the PHP scripting engine and the source code replaced with the output of the script. Indeed, the acronym PHP suggests just that; PHP: Hypertext Preprocessor.

Consider a simple PHP script embedded in an HTML document:

```
<!DOCTYPE HTML PUBLIC
   "-//W3C//DTD HTML 4.0 Transitional//EN"
   "http://www.w3.org/TR/html4/loose.dtd" >
<html>
  <head>
    <title>Hello, world</title>
  </head>
<body>
  <?php echo "Hello, world"; ?>
</body>
</html>
```

When preprocessed by the PHP scripting engine, the short (and not very useful) script:

```
<?php echo "Hello, world"; ?>
```

is replaced with its output:

```
Hello, world
```

The text before and after the script is HTML; the first three lines define that HTML Version 4 is being used.

You can embed any number of PHP scripts in a single HTML document, as long as each PHP script is surrounded by the begin tag `<?php` and the end tag `?>`. Other tags can also be used to delimit PHP scripts, but these are the most common and reliable.

One of the best language features of PHP is how it decodes user data and automatically initializes variables. Consider an example script stored in the file *printuser.php*:

```
<!DOCTYPE HTML PUBLIC
   "-//W3C//DTD HTML 4.0 Transitional//EN"
   "http://www.w3.org/TR/html4/loose.dtd" >
<html>
  <head>
    <title>Saying hello</title>
  </head>
<body>
  <?php
    echo "Hello, $username";
  ?>
</body>
</html>
```

Let's assume that the file is stored in the *document root* of the web server. If the web server is Apache and the machine runs a variant of the Unix operating system, the document root is the directory */usr/local/apache/htdocs*. The script can then be retrieved using a web browser—if it is running on the same machine as the web server—by requesting the URL *http://localhost/printuser.php?username=Selina*. In response to the request, the PHP engine replaces the script:

```
<?php
  echo "Hello, $username";
?>
```

with the output:

```
Hello, Selina
```

The URL is automatically decoded. Also, a variable $username, that matches the name of the attribute in the URL is initialized, and its value is set to Selina. This automatic registration of variables is an excellent feature, but one that has security problems in some cases. How to guard against them is discussed in the Section "Securing User Data."

Files that contain PHP scripts usually have the extension *.php* instead of the HTML file extensions *.html* or *.htm*. The *.php* extension is the trigger for the web server to invoke the PHP scripting engine to preprocess the file. This is controlled by a directive in the web server's configuration file and is discussed in more detail in the Section "Installing PHP."

Passing variables and values using the URL is one way of transferring data from a web browser to a web server. However, the most common technique is to use an HTML <form> such as the following:

```
<!DOCTYPE HTML PUBLIC
   "-//W3C//DTD HTML 4.0 Transitional//EN"
   "http://www.w3.org/TR/html4/loose.dtd" >

<html>
  <head>
     <title>Saying hello</title>
  </head>

<body>
<form method="GET" action="printuser.php">
Enter your name: <input type="text" name="username">
<br><input type="submit" value="Print it!">
</body>

</html>
```

When this HTML document is rendered by a web browser, the user is able to enter a name into an input widget. Below the widget is a button labeled Print It!. When the user presses the button, the script listed as the action attribute of the <form> tag is requested, and the data in the input widget is sent to the server as part of the URL. For example, if the user enters the name Selina into the input widget and clicks on the Print It! button, the URL *http://localhost/printuser.php?username=Selina* is requested, and the output of the script is the same as before:

```
Hello, Selina
```

A Short Language Primer

This section introduces the basic syntax of PHP. If you're familiar with high-level languages such as C, Java, JavaScript, or Perl, you'll be at home with PHP. The current version of PHP is PHP 4, and some details we present here are specific to this version.

As discussed previously, PHP scripts are surrounded by the PHP start tag <?php and the end tag ?>. You'll often see the start tag abbreviated as <?, but this conflicts with the emerging XHTML standard and should be avoided.

Statements in a script are terminated with a semicolon. Statements can be formatted for readability by including any amount of whitespace—such as space characters, tab characters, or blank lines—in a script.

Comments can be included in a PHP script using the following styles:

```
// One line comment

# Another one line comment

/* A
   multiple line
   comment */
```

Data can be output with the statements print, echo, and printf. The first two are often interchangeable, but echo has an advantage in that it can take more than one argument. The printf statement is used for more complex output and is identical to that used in other programming languages such as C and scripting languages such as *awk*. Consider a few examples:

```
// These are the same
echo "This is output";
print "This is output";

// echo can output more than one argument
echo 123, "is a number";

// printf can be used to control formatting
// This outputs 3.14
printf("pi is %.2f\n", 3.14159);
```

Variables are identified by the prefix dollar sign ($) and variable names are case sensitive. Variables are declared and given a type when they're first used. For example, the following creates a variable $x of type integer:

```
$x = 4;
```

The type of a variable can change in a script. For example, the following is valid:

```
// $x is an integer
$x = 4;

// Now it is a string
$x = "Selina";
```

PHP has four scalar variable types: integer, Boolean, string, and float. There are two compound types: object and array. Compound types contain elements that are scalar variables, and their types can be mixed. The object type isn't discussed in this chapter, but here are examples of the other five types:

```
// $x is an integer
$x = 4;

// $x is a float
$x = 3.142;

// $x is a string
$x = "Richmond";

// $x and $y are Boolean
$x = true;
$y = false;

// $x is an array of strings
$x = array("one", "two", "three", "four", "five");
```

Arrays can be accessed by their numeric index or associatively. Index elements are numbered from zero. Consider two example arrays:

```
// This is an associative array
$x = array("one" => 1,
           "two" => 2,
           "three" => 3);

// This prints 1
echo $x["one"];

// This is a numerically indexed array
$x = array(1, 2, 3);

// This prints 2
echo $x[1];
```

Two functions are useful for checking the state of a variable:

```
// Has the variable been declared?
if (isset($x))
  echo "x is set";

// Is the variable empty?
if (empty($x))
  echo "x is empty";
```

A variable that doesn't exist is always empty. However, a variable that's empty may or may not exist. If it does, it has a NULL value.

Variables are assigned with a single = character, and equality is tested with the double equals (==) syntax:

```
$x = 4;

if ($x == 4)
  echo "x is four!";
```

A triple equals (===) can be used to test if the parameters are equal and of the same type:

```
$x = 0;

// This is true
if ($x == false)
  echo "$x is false";

// This is false
if ($x === false)
  echo "$x is false";
```

The arithmetic shortcuts that work in many other languages also work in PHP:

```
$x = 4;

// add one to $x in three different ways
$x++;
$x = $x + 1;
$x += 1;

// subtract one in three different ways
$x--;
$x = $x - 1;
$x -= 1;
```

The standard loop constructs are for, while, and do...while:

```
for ($x=0; $x<10; $x++)
  echo $x;

$x = 0;
while ($x < 10)
{
  echo $x;
  $x++;
}

$x = 0;
do
{
  echo $x;
  $x++;
} while ($x < 10);
```

The foreach statement is used to iterate through an array:

```
// $x is an array of strings
$x = array("one", "two", "three", "four", "five");

// This prints out each element of the array
foreach ($x as $element)
  echo $element;
```

The if and switch statements are the most frequently used conditionals:

```
if ($x < 5)
  echo "x is less than 5";

switch ($x)
{
  case 1:
     echo "x is 1";
     break;
  case 2:
     echo "x is 2";
     break;
  case 3:
     echo "x is 3";
     break;
  default:
     echo "x is not 1, 2, or 3";
}
```

There is other basic syntax that isn't discussed here. There are also over a hundred libraries that can be used for tasks as diverse as string manipulation, network communications, data compression, and disk access. If you'd like more detail, a list of references is included at the end of this chapter in the section "Where to Find Out More."

Installing PHP

PHP works on almost all Unix platforms and with Microsoft Windows 32-bit environments. In Unix environments, PHP can be used to develop three different types of software:

Command-line scripts
> PHP can be used as an alternative to Perl, Tcl, shell scripts, and other scripting languages.

GUI Windowing applications
> With the PHP-GTK extension, PHP can be used to develop window-based applications.

Server-side scripts
> PHP can be used to process scripts that are requested with a web browser

PHP was designed for the third alternative. To use it in this environment, a web server is required. We focus on integrating MySQL with the web environment in this chapter.

PHP can be used for web scripting by integrating it as a module of a supported web server such as Apache, Microsoft Internet Information Server (IIS), or iPlanet. For web servers that do not support module integration—those that do not support SAPI or ISAPI direct module interfacing—the PHP executable can be used as a CGI processor. The Common Gateway Interface (CGI) allows a web server to run any executable, but this is a much slower method of running the PHP engine than integrating it as a server module. In either case, to use PHP to access the MySQL DBMS, it must be compiled with MySQL support.

Getting Started Under Unix

Before installing PHP, you should check whether you already have a web server that supports PHP and whether your PHP engine supports MySQL. For example, many Linux distributions now include the Apache web server with preconfigured PHP support for accessing the MySQL DBMS.

The simplest way to check if your web server supports PHP, and if the PHP module supports MySQL, is to create a file *phpinfo.php* in the web server document root. Create this file so that it has only one line with the following contents:

```
<?php phpinfo(); ?>
```

For most systems that are running the Apache web server, the document root is the directory: */usr/local/apache/htdocs/*.

After creating the file, run the script by requesting the following URL with a web browser that is running on the same machine as the web server: *http://localhost/phpinfo.php*.

If you see output—not the script contents—then your web server has PHP support. The Configure Command section near the top of the output will include the option *--with-mysql* if MySQL support is built-in; scrolling down through the output should also show a section headed *mysql*.

If this checks out, you're ready to start with PHP and MySQL. If not, then additional configuration is required. Suggested steps are included in this section.

Here are three possible ways to get started with a web server, PHP, and MySQL support:

- The easiest approach is to obtain an installation package. NuSphere has a free, downloadable installation package for Linux, Sun Solaris, and Microsoft Windows environments. They also sell integrated Apache, PHP, and MySQL bundles with software support. The NuSphere web site is *http://www.nusphere.com/*.

- Another easy approach is to add packages to your system using, for example, the RPM package manager for RedHat Linux, the Debian package manager for Debian Linux, or Fink for Mac OS X. For Linux installs, the Apache package usually includes the PHP module, which usually has preconfigured MySQL support.

- Obtain the source code to Apache, PHP, and MySQL and compile the source. This is the most complex option, but it allows you to choose the libraries you include in PHP and how PHP is loaded as a module into the web server. Apache and PHP must be installed after MySQL, and PHP must be built with the *--with-mysql=/usr/local/mysql* option (assuming MySQL is installed in the directory */usr/local/mysql*). Concise instructions for installing PHP and Apache can be found at *http://www.php.net/manual*. Instructions for installing MySQL can be found in Chapter 2. An excellent, in-depth guide to installing from source can be found at *http://www.delouw.ch/linux/apache.phtml*.

Installation problems

If you have a MySQL installation that you're happy with, but don't have a web server and PHP, then the easiest approach is to install a web server and PHP package. The best choice is the Apache web server, because it's popular, free, and flexible in its integration with PHP. We focus on Apache in this section.

If you have an Apache web server that appears not to support PHP, it's worth double-checking. There are three common problems that can give the wrong impression:

- Your PHP test files don't have the extension *.php*. If this is the case, your web server will deliver the source code and not run the scripts.
- Your web server isn't configured to run the PHP engine when a file with the *.php* extension is requested. In Apache, this is controlled by a line in the *httpd.conf* file usually found in the directory */usr/local/apache/conf*:

      AddType application/x-httpd-php .php

  If this line is commented, uncomment it, and restart the web server. Apache can usually be restarted by running apachectl restart. The *apachectl* script is usually found in */usr/local/apache/bin/*.
- Your PHP module is a DSO (DSOs are explained below), but the module isn't being loaded by Apache. Check that the following line is present and not commented out in the *httpd.conf* file:

      LoadModule php4_module   libexec/libphp4.so

  If you change the httpd.conf file, restart the web server.

If you have Apache and PHP, but not MySQL support, you need to find out whether your PHP module is a web server *dynamic shared object* (DSO). To check if your PHP is a DSO, take a look at the output of the *phpinfo.php* script you created in the previous section. If the Configure Command section contains the string *--with-apache=*, your PHP is not a DSO. If it contains the string *--with-apxs=*, your PHP is a DSO.

If your PHP module isn't a DSO, you need to rebuild your PHP and Apache to include MySQL support. This is the disadvantage of having a *statically linked* PHP module. The advantage of static linking is that the module is preloaded when the web server starts up, and a static-linked module is faster. Instructions for rebuilding a static-linked module version can be found at: *http://www.php.net/manual/en/install.unix.php*. As discussed earlier, ensure that you include the *--with-mysql=* directive in the PHP build process and that the directive includes the path to your MySQL installation.

If your PHP is a DSO, the upgrade process is simpler. This is the primary advantage of a DSO. You only need to rebuild the PHP module by rerunning the configure script with the addition of the *--with-mysql=* directive; again, make sure you include the path to MySQL with the *--with-mysql=* directive. Run *make* and *make install* to complete the process. You then need to restart your web server so that the new PHP module is loaded.

Getting Started Under Microsoft Windows

The easiest approach to getting started in a Microsoft Windows environment is to use an installation package that includes Apache, PHP, and MySQL. NuSphere sells an install package with support and offers a free package without support. Their web site is *http://www.nusphere.com/*. Another excellent, free installation package is PHP Triad for Windows, available from *http://sourceforge.net/projects/phptriad/*.

To install without an installation package, instructions can be found in the installation section of the PHP manual at *http://www.php.net/manual/*.

Accessing the MySQL DBMS with PHP

This section shows you how to connect to and query the MySQL DBMS using PHP. The examples are illustrated with the first of three scripts from a simple but useful PHP application: a wedding gift registry that allows guests to log in, view a list of gifts wanted by the bride and groom, and reserve gifts that they plan to purchase by putting them on a shopping list. The complete application—including the database, scripts, and instructions on how to install it on your web site—is available at *http://www.webdatabasebook.com/wedding/*.

The gift registry application illustrates the basics of interacting with MySQL using PHP. It shows how to:

- Call PHP library functions to connect to the MySQL DBMS, execute queries through the DBMS connection, and retrieve query result sets
- Present query results using HTML
- Interact with the user, and preprocess user data to minimize security risks
- Add session support to an application so that a user can log in and out
- Pass data between scripts by creating embedded hypertext links in HTML, develop HTML <form> environments, and use HTTP headers
- Handle MySQL errors with PHP
- Manage DBMS credentials with include files

This section introduces the basics of interacting with MySQL using PHP. The script described here displays the gifts that are unreserved and the gifts that have been reserved by the current user. The output of the script rendered by a Netscape browser is shown in Figure 11-1. The script assumes the guest has already logged in. The script for logging in is discussed later in the section "Using the HTML <form> Environment." The script that adds and removes gifts from the guest's shopping list is discussed in the section "Writing Data with PHP."

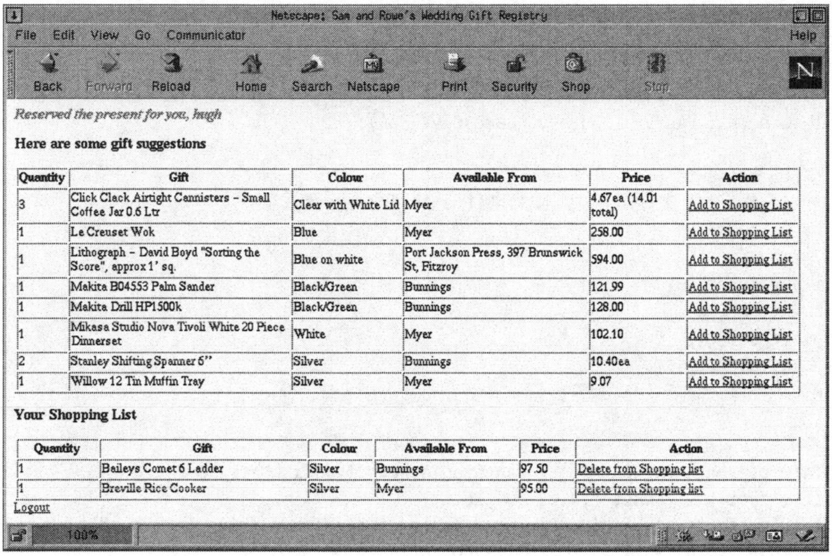

Figure 11-1. The wedding gift registry

The scripts in the gift registry use only the common PHP MySQL library functions. Chapter 18 is a reference to PHP's complete MySQL function library.

The Wedding Gift Registry Database

Example 11-1 is a file that contains the SQL statements (and the MySQL use command) to create and populate the wedding database. The database contains only two tables: presents, which stores data about gifts, including a unique identifier, description, desired quantity, color, place of purchase, price, and the user who reserved the gift, and people, which stores a unique username and password for each guest.

A one-to-many relationship is maintained between the two tables; each guest stored in the people table can reserve zero or more gifts in the presents table. When the gifts are initially inserted in the wedding database using the statements in Example 11-1, the people_id in the presents table is set to NULL so that all gifts are unreserved. If a guest reserves a gift, the NULL value is replaced with the guest's people_id. For example, if the guest hugh reserves the gift with a present_id of 2 (such as the Richmond Tigers autographed print (unframed)), the people_id of that gift is set to hugh.

Example 11-1. The statements to create and populate the wedding database

```sql
create database wedding;
use wedding;

CREATE TABLE people (
  people_id varchar(30) DEFAULT '' NOT NULL,
  passwd varchar(30),
  PRIMARY KEY (people_id)
);

INSERT INTO people VALUES ('hugh','huw8o3cEvVS8o');

CREATE TABLE presents (
  present_id int(11) DEFAULT '0' NOT NULL auto_increment,
  present varchar(255),
  shop varchar(100),
  quantity varchar(30),
  colour varchar(30),
  price varchar(30),
  people_id varchar(30),
  PRIMARY KEY (present_id)
);

INSERT INTO presents VALUES (1,'Mikasa Studio Nova Tivoli White 20 Piece
Dinnerset','Myer','1','White','102.10',NULL);
INSERT INTO presents VALUES (2,'Richmond Tigers autographed print (unframed)',
'www.greatmoments.com.au','1','NA','375.00',NULL);
INSERT INTO presents VALUES (3,'Breville Rice Cooker','Myer','1',
'Silver','95.00','NULL');
INSERT INTO presents VALUES (4,'Krups - Nespresso 986 coffee machine','Myer','1',
'Black','608.00',NULL);
INSERT INTO presents VALUES (5,'Click Clack Airtight Cannisters - Small Coffee Jar
0.6 Ltr','Myer','3','Clear with White Lid','4.67ea (14.01 total)',NULL);
INSERT INTO presents VALUES (6,'Avanti Twin Wall Mixing Bowls 2.8 Ltr','Myer','2',
'Silver','41.65ea (83.30 total)',NULL);
INSERT INTO presents VALUES (7,'Lithograph - David Boyd 'Sorting the Score',
approx 1" sq.','Port Jackson Press, 397 Brunswick St, Fitzroy','1',
'Blue on white','594.00',NULL);
INSERT INTO presents VALUES (8,'Le Creuset Wok','Myer','1','Blue','258.00',NULL);
INSERT INTO presents VALUES (9,'Willow 12 Tin Muffin Tray','Myer','1',
'Silver','9.07',NULL);
INSERT INTO presents VALUES (10,'Baileys Comet 6 Ladder','Bunnings','1',
'Silver','97.50',NULL);
INSERT INTO presents VALUES (11,'Makita Drill HP1500k','Bunnings','1',
'Black/Green','128.00',NULL);
INSERT INTO presents VALUES (12,'Makita BO4553 Palm Sander','Bunnings','1',
'Black/Green','121.99',NULL);
INSERT INTO presents VALUES (13,'Stanley Shifting Spanner 6""','Bunnings','2',
'Silver','10.40ea',NULL);
```

The MySQL DBMS that maintains the gift registry has a user fred who has a password shhh. This user is set up using the following SQL GRANT statement:

```
GRANT SELECT, INSERT, DELETE, UPDATE
ON wedding.*
TO fred@localhost
IDENTIFIED by 'shhh';
```

In our environment, the web server and the MySQL DBMS are running on the same machine, so the user fred needs access only from the local host. Having the DBMS and web server on the same machine is a good decision for small- to medium-size web database applications because there is no network communications overhead between the DBMS and the web server. For high-traffic or complex web database applications, it may be desirable to have dedicated hardware for each application.

Opening and Using a Database Connection

Several PHP library functions are used to connect to a MySQL DBMS, run queries, retrieve results, and handle any errors that occur along the way. The *presents.php* script shown in Example 11-2 illustrates five of these functions in action.

Example 11-2. Querying a MySQL DBMS using PHP to display the gift registry

```php
<?php
  // Show the user the available presents and the presents in their shopping
  // list

  // Include the DBMS credentials
  include 'db.inc';

  // Check if the user is logged in
  // (this also starts the session)
  logincheck();

  // Show the user the gifts
  //
  // Parameters:
  // (1) An open $connection to the DBMS
  // (2) Whether to show the available gifts with the option to add
  //     them to the shopping list ($delete = false) or to show the current
  //     user's shopping list with the option to remove the gifts ($delete = true)
  // (3) The $user name
  function showgifts($connection, $delete, $user)
  {

    // If we're showing the available gifts, then set up
    // a query to show all unreserved gifts (where people IS NULL)
    if ($delete == false)
      $query = "SELECT *
                FROM presents
                WHERE people_id IS NULL
                ORDER BY present";
    else
```

Example 11-2. Querying a MySQL DBMS using PHP to display the gift registry (continued)

```
// Otherwise, set up a query to show all gifts reserved by
// this user
   $query = "SELECT *
             FROM presents
             WHERE people_id = \"{$user}\"
             ORDER BY present";

// Run the query
if (!($result = @ mysql_query ($query, $connection)))
   showerror();

// Did we get back any rows?
if (@ mysql_num_rows($result) != 0)
{
   // Yes, so show the gifts as a table
   echo "\n<table border=1 width=100%>";

   // Create some headings for the table
   echo "\n<tr>" .
        "\n\t<th>Quantity</th>" .
        "\n\t<th>Gift</th>" .
        "\n\t<th>Colour</th>" .
        "\n\t<th>Available From</th>" .
        "\n\t<th>Price</th>" .
        "\n\t<th>Action</th>" .
        "\n</tr>";

   // Fetch each database table row of the results
   while($row = @ mysql_fetch_array($result))
   {
      // Display the gift data as a table row
      echo "\n<tr>" .
           "\n\t<td>{$row["quantity"]}</td>" .
           "\n\t<td>{$row["present"]}</td>" .
           "\n\t<td>{$row["colour"]}</td>" .
           "\n\t<td>{$row["shop"]}</td>" .
           "\n\t<td>{$row["price"]}</td>";

      // Should we offer the chance to remove the gift?
      if ($delete == true)
         // Yes. So set up an embedded link that the user can click
         // to remove the gift to their shopping list by running
         // action.php with action=delete
         echo "\n\t<td><a href=\"action.php?action=delete&amp;" .
              "present_id={$row["present_id"]}\">Delete from Shopping list</a>";
      else
         // No. So set up an embedded link that the user can click
         // to add the gift from their shopping list by running
         // action.php with action=insert
         echo "\n\t<td><a href=\"action.php?action=insert&amp;" .
              "present_id={$row["present_id"]}\">Add to Shopping List</a>";
   }
   echo "\n</table>";
```

Example 11-2. Querying a MySQL DBMS using PHP to display the gift registry (continued)

```
    }
    else
    {
        // No data was returned from the query.
        // Show an appropriate message
        if ($delete == false)
            echo "\n<h3><font color=\"red\">No gifts left!</font></h3>";
        else
            echo "\n<h3><font color=\"red\">Your Basket is Empty!</font></h3>";
    }
  }
?>
<!DOCTYPE HTML PUBLIC
  "-//W3C//DTD HTML 4.0 Transitional//EN"
  "http://www.w3.org/TR/html4/loose.dtd">
<html>
<head>
  <title>Sam and Rowe's Wedding Gift Registry</title>
</head>
<body bgcolor=#ffffff>
<?php

  // Secure the user data
  $message = clean($message, 128);

  // If there's a message to show, output it
  if (!empty($message))
      echo "\n<h3><font color=\"red\"><em>{$message}</em></font></h3>";

  // Connect to the MySQL DBMS
  if (!($connection = @ mysql_pconnect($hostName, $username, $password)))
      showerror();

  // Use the wedding database
  if (!mysql_select_db($databaseName, $connection))
      showerror();

  echo "\n<h3>Here are some gift suggestions</h3>";

  // Show the gifts that are still unreserved
  showgifts($connection, false, $user);

  echo "\n<h3>Your Shopping List</h3>";

  // Show the gifts that have been reserved by this user
  showgifts($connection, true, $user);

  // Show a logout link
  echo "<a href=\"logout.php\">Logout</a>";
?>
</body>
</html>
```

The script in Example 11-2 shows the current user a list of gifts that are not reserved by any of the guests and a list of gifts reserved by the current user. Using this script (and the script *action.php* that we discuss later in the section "Writing Data with PHP") the user can add and remove gifts from her shopping list by clicking on the links next to each gift. Figure 11-1 shows the output of the script rendered in a Netscape browser.

The user must be logged in (the `logincheck()` function is discussed later) and a `message` parameter is expected by the script. As discussed earlier, parameters can be passed with a URL, or a user can enter the data into an HTML form. At this point, it's not important how the data is passed (we discuss this later in the section "Using the HTML <form> Environment") but that a $message variable is set.

The example has two parts: the main body and a function `showgifts()`. To begin, let's focus on the MySQL library functions that are prefixed with the string `mysql_`. The main body has two MySQL function calls:

```
// Connect to the MySQL DBMS
if (!($connection = @ mysql_pconnect($hostName, $username, $password)))
    showerror();

// Use the wedding database
if (!mysql_select_db($databaseName, $connection))
    showerror();
```

The function `mysql_pconnect()` is used to establish a connection to the DBMS. In the example, three parameters are passed to the function: the values of variables $hostName, $username, and $password. These variables are initialized in an auxiliary include file and are set to localhost, fred, and shhh respectively. The function returns a *connection resource handle*. A handle is a value that can be used to access information associated with the connection.

Connections opened with `mysql_pconnect()` can be reused in other scripts. The p stands for persistent, which means that after the script ends, the connection is kept in a pool of open connections. The connection can then be reused by any other script that requires a connection with the same host, username, and password. Connections in the pool that are unused for five seconds are closed to save resources. The time restriction is a MySQL parameter that can be changed with the *--set-variable connect_timeout* parameter when the MySQL server is started.

The `mysql_select_db()` function is then used to access the required database. Two parameters are passed to the function in this example: the $databaseName (set to wedding in the auxiliary include file) and the $connection handle that was returned from `mysql_pconnect()`.

The main script also calls the `showgifts()` function that runs the queries and processes the results. It calls three MySQL library functions. The first runs a query:

```
// Run the query
if (!($result = @ mysql_query ($query, $connection)))
    showerror();
```

The function takes two parameters: the SQL query and the DBMS connection to use. The query is a string created at the beginning of showgifts( ). The connection parameter is the value returned from the earlier call to mysql_pconnect( ). The function mysql_query( ) returns a result set handle resource that is used to retrieve the output of the query.

Handling Results

The second MySQL library function called in showgifts( ) returns the number of rows that have been output by the query:

```
// Did we get back any rows?
if (@ mysql_num_rows($result) != 0)
{
```

The function takes one parameter, the result set handle returned from mysql_query( ).

The last MySQL function called in showgifts( ) fetches the data:

```
// Fetch each database table row of the results
while($row = @ mysql_fetch_array($result))
{
```

This function retrieves row data, taking only the result set handle returned from mysql_query( ) as a parameter. Each call to mysql_fetch_array( ) fetches the next row of results and returns an array. In this example, the attributes are stored in the array $row. The function returns false when there are no more rows to fetch.

The attribute data stored in the array $row can be accessed associatively, that is, the attribute name can be used as a key to retrieve its value. For example, the following code prints the values of each presents table attribute as an HTML table row:

```
// Display the gift data as a table row
echo "\n<tr>" .
    "\n\t<td>{$row["quantity"]}</td>" .
    "\n\t<td>{$row["present"]}</td>" .
    "\n\t<td>{$row["colour"]}</td>" .
    "\n\t<td>{$row["shop"]}</td>" .
    "\n\t<td>{$row["price"]}</td>";
```

The name of the attribute from the presents table—for example, quantity—is used as an index in the statement {$row["quantity"]}. The braces are a new feature in PHP that allow all variables to be included directly into strings that are delimited by double quotation marks; if a variable can be unambiguously parsed from within a double-quoted string, the braces can be omitted.

Here's an example of the output of the above code fragment:

```
<tr>
  <td>1</td>
  <td>Baileys Comet 6 Ladder</td>
  <td>Silver</td>
  <td>Bunnings</td>
  <td>97.50</td>
```

The code in `showgifts()` also uses associative array access to produce embedded links for each gift, such as:

```
<td><a href="action.php?action=insert&amp;present_id=10">Add to Shopping List</a>
```

In this example, when the user clicks the link, the script *action.php* is requested, and two parameters are passed: `action=insert` and `present_id=10`. In response to these parameters, the script *action.php* inserts the gift with the `present_id` of 10 into the shopping list of the guest who's logged in. The script is discussed later in the section "Writing Data with PHP."

There are three tricks to accessing data returned from `mysql_fetch_array()`:

- When both a table and attribute name are used in a SELECT statement, only the attribute name is used to access the data associatively. For example, after executing the statement:

  ```
  SELECT presents.quantity FROM presents
  ```

  the data is accessed associatively as `$row["quantity"]`. If two attributes have the same name, you must use aliases so that both can be accessed in the associative array. For example, the attributes in the following query:

  ```
  SELECT cust.name AS cname, stock.name AS sname FROM cust, stock
  ```

  can be accessed in an array as `$row["cname"]` and `$row["sname"]`.

- Aggregate functions such as SELECT count(*) FROM presents are associatively accessed as `$row["count(*)"]`.

- Prior to PHP 4.0.5, NULL values were not returned into the array. This doesn't affect associative access but causes renumbering for numeric access. If a present has a `color` attribute that is NULL, the array that is returned has six elements instead of seven. The missing element can still be referenced as `$row["color"]` since referencing a nonexistent element returns NULL. However, if you want to avoid arrays of different lengths being returned, ensure that all attributes have a value or upgrade to a new release of PHP.

Other MySQL library functions can be used to process result sets differently. These are discussed in Chapter 18. However, all of the basic techniques needed to develop a simple application are shown by the functions in this chapter.

Frequently Used MySQL Library Functions

This chapter develops applications using the following PHP calls:

resource mysql_pconnect([string *host[:port]*], [string *username*], [string *password*])

> Used to establish a connection to the MySQL DBMS. Upon success, the function returns a connection resource handle that can be used to access databases through subsequent function calls. It returns `false` on failure.

The function has three optional parameters. The first is the *host* name of the DBMS and an optional *port* number; a default port of 3306 for MySQL is assumed if the port is omitted. The *host* parameter is usually set to localhost when the MySQL DBMS and the web server are running on the same machine.

The *username* and *password* are MySQL DBMS username and password credentials. These are the same username and password used to access the DBMS though the command-line monitor mysql.

int mysql_select_db (string *database,* [resource *connection*])

Use the specified *database* through the *connection*. The connection is a resource handle returned from mysql_pconnect(). The second parameter is optional but always recommended in practice. The function returns true on success and false on failure.

resource mysql_query(string SQL, [resource *connection*])

Run an SQL statement through a MySQL DBMS *connection*. The second parameter is optional but always recommended in practice. On success, the function returns a query result resource that can be used to fetch data. The function returns false on failure.

The SQL statement does not need to be terminated with a semicolon, and any SQL statement is allowed, including SELECT, INSERT, DELETE, UPDATE, DROP, and CREATE.

int mysql_num_rows(resource *query_handle*)

Returns the number of rows associated with the *query_handle* returned from mysql_query(). The function works only for SELECT queries; the number of rows affected by an SQL INSERT, UPDATE, or DELETE statement can be determined using the function mysql_affected_rows().

array mysql_fetch_array(resource *query_handle,* [int *result_type*])

Retrieves as an array the next available row from the result set associated with the parameter *query_handle*. The *query_handle* is returned from a prior call to mysql_query(). The function returns false when no more rows are available.

Each row is returned as an array. The second parameter *result_type* controls whether associative access, numeric access, or both are possible on the array. Since the default is MYSQL_BOTH, there is no reason to supply or change the parameter.

int mysql_errno(resource *connection*)

Returns the error number of the last error on the *connection* resource. Error handling is discussed in the next section.

string mysql_error(resource *connection*)

Returns a string that describes the last error on the *connection*. Error handling is discussed in the next section.

```
int mysql_affected_rows([resource connection])
```
Returns the number of rows affected by the last UPDATE, DELETE, or INSERT SQL statement on the *connection* resource passed as a parameter. The parameter is optional but always recommended in practice. The function does not work for SELECT statements; in this case, mysql_num_rows() should be used instead. The function is discussed later in the section "Writing Data with PHP."

Handling MySQL Errors

The script in Example 11-2 includes MySQL error handling. Errors can occur in many different cases. For example, the MySQL DBMS might be unavailable, it might not be possible to establish a connection because the DBMS user's credentials are incorrect, or an SQL query might be incorrectly formed.

Consider a fragment from Example 11-2:

```
// Run the query
if (!($result = @ mysql_query ($query, $connection)))
    showerror();
```

If the mysql_query() function returns false, the function showerror() is called to output details of the error:

```
// Show an error and stop the script
function showerror()
{
    if (mysql_error())
        die("Error " . mysql_errno() . " : " . mysql_error());
    else
        die("Could not connect to the DBMS");
}
```

If a MySQL error has occurred, the script outputs the error number and a descriptive string, and the PHP engine stops. If the error isn't a MySQL error, there is a problem connecting to the DBMS with mysql_pconnect(). The showerror() function is part of the *db.inc* include file.

When a function such as showerror() is used, MySQL function calls are usually prefixed with the @ operator. The @ stops the PHP engine from outputting its own internal error messages. If the @ is omitted, the output of showerror() is shown interleaved with the PHP engine's internal error messages, which can be confusing to debug.

Include Files

Example 11-3 shows the *db.inc* file that is included in each of the gift registry scripts. The include directive allows the variables and functions in *db.inc* to be used by each script without duplicating the code. Note that the code in include files must always be surrounded by PHP start and end tags.

Example 11-3. The db.inc include file

```php
<?php

// These are the DBMS credentials and the database name
$hostName = "localhost";
$databaseName = "wedding";
$username = "fred";
$password = "shhh";

// Show an error and stop the script
function showerror()
{
   if (mysql_error())
      die("Error " . mysql_errno() . " : " . mysql_error());
   else
      die("Could not connect to the DBMS");
}

// Secure the user data by escaping characters and shortening the input string
function clean($input, $maxlength)
{
  $input = substr($input, 0, $maxlength);
  $input = EscapeShellCmd($input);
  return ($input);
}

// Check if the user is logged in. If not, send him to the login page
function logincheck()
{
   session_start();

   if (!session_is_registered("user"))
      // redirect to the login page
      header("Location: index.php");
}
?>
```

The *db.inc* include file stores the four variables that are used in connecting to the DBMS and selecting the database. The showerror() function is discussed in the previous section. The clean() function is discussed below. The logincheck() function is discussed in the section "Managing Sessions."

The include file has an *.inc* extension, which presents a minor security problem. If the user creates a URL to request the include file, the source of the include file will be shown in the browser. The user can then see the DBMS credentials and some of the source code. These details should be secure.

You can secure your *.inc* files by configuring the web server so that retrieval of files with that extension is forbidden. With Apache, you can do this by adding the following to the *httpd.conf* file and restarting the web server:

```
<Files ~ "\.inc$">
    Order allow,deny
```

```
      Deny from all
      Satisfy All
   </Files>
```

Other approaches that achieve the same result are renaming the include file with a *.php* extension—so that the source is no longer output—or moving the include files outside of the web server's document tree.

Securing User Data

The clean( ) function in the include file *db.inc* makes user input secure. The function is shown in Example 11-3, and it takes two parameters: the user $input and the maximum length $maxlength that is expected. It returns the clean user data.

The clean( ) function uses the PHP library string function substr( ) to reduce the length of the $input to its desired maximum. It then uses the PHP library function EscapeShellCmd( ) to insert backslash characters before selected characters—such as semicolons, backslashes, greater-thans, and less-thans—so that their special meanings in Unix shells are nullified or *escaped*. These two steps are usually sufficient to ensure that users cannot maliciously add extra clauses to SQL queries and cannot manipulate other MySQL library functions.

Never trust user input or network data.

You should preprocess all user data by escaping special shell characters and ensuring that the data does not exceed a maximum length. A function such as clean( ) in our *db.inc* include file is useful for this task.

The automatic initialization of variables by the PHP engine also presents a minor security risk. The engine initializes variables in a certain order (defined in PHP's configuration file *php.ini*), which presents the possibility that a variable can be initialized twice, with the second value overwriting the first. For example, by default, the PATH environment variable, which tells the PHP engine where to look for programs, is one of the first that is initialized. If the user passes through a parameter with the name PATH, the user's value will overwrite the system default. This can be undesirably exploited.

A simple solution is to turn off the automatic initialization of variables by setting register_globals = off in the *php.ini* configuration file. However, if you do disable automatic initialization, you can still access the user data by associative array access. Any user variables passed through with the GET method are elements of the array $HTTP_GET_VARS. For example, to access the value of a user-supplied parameter message, you can access the element of the array as $HTTP_GET_VARS["message"].

We don't discuss the <form> POST method, environment variables, server variables, or cookies in detail in this chapter. However, these variables can be found in the following arrays:

- Parameters passed with the <form> POST method are found in $HTTP_POST_VARS.
- Environment variables can be found in the array $HTTP_ENV_VARS.
- Session variables can be found in the array $HTTP_SESSION_VARS.
- Cookie variables can be found in the array $HTTP_COOKIE_VARS.
- Server variables can be found in the array $HTTP_SERVER_VARS.

You should also be careful how you use data that is received from the browser. For example, it is unwise to use the price of an item from a <form> widget to calculate an invoice; even if the price is hidden or read-only, the user can still change it by modifying the <form> or authoring a URL. The correct approach is to verify the price against the database before calculating the invoice. Similarly, don't embed SQL in HTML—even if it is hidden—because the user can browse the HTML source, figure out the database structure, and modify the statements.

Managing Sessions

The Web was designed for browsing documents, where each request from a web browser to a web server is independent of every other interaction. To develop applications for the Web, additional logic is required so that different requests can be related. For example, this logic is required to allow users to log in, use the gift registry application, and log out when they're finished. In PHP, the logic is provided by the sessions library.

Sessions allow variables to be stored on the server so the variables can be restored each time a user requests a script. Consider a short example:

```php
<?php
  session_start();

  if (session_is_registered("count"))
  {
    echo "Hello! You've visited {$count} times";
    $count++;
  }
  else
  {
    echo "Welcome new user!";
    session_register("count");
    $count = 1;
  }
?>
```

When the user requests the script for the first time, a new session is created. Then, a variable $count is registered and stored on the web server with its associated value of 1. When the script is requested again, the variable is automatically restored by the PHP engine and the count incremented. For example, on the fifth request of the script the output is:

```
Hello! You've visited 5 times
```

With its default configuration, the sessions library relies on cookies. *Cookies* are strings that are passed back and forth between the web server and browser and are used in sessions to maintain a unique key. This key is used on the server to locate the variables associated with the session. If cookies are disabled or unsupported by the browser, then sessions won't work; this problem can be solved by storing the session key in the URL, but we don't discuss that here.

All sessions have a timeout. This means that if a user doesn't access the server for a predetermined period, the session is destroyed. Session timeouts are necessary because there is no guarantee in a web environment that a user will log out. By default, the timeout is set to 1,440 seconds, or 24 minutes. This can be adjusted—along with other session parameters—through the *php.ini* configuration file that is normally stored in the directory */usr/local/lib* on Unix servers.

You can also allow a user to destroy a session by adding a logout feature to an application. In our gift registry, the user can click on a Logout embedded link, which runs the following script stored in the file *logout.php*:

```php
<?php
  // Log out of the system

  session_start();
  session_destroy();

  // Redirect to the confirmation page.
  header("Location: logout.html");
?>
```

A session must be started before it can be destroyed. The script doesn't produce HTML output but instead makes use of a popular web trick. The following code fragment sends an HTTP header back to the web browser using the PHP library header( ) function:

```
// Redirect to the confirmation page.
header("Location: logout.html");
```

The Location: header instructs the web browser to immediately request another resource; in this case, the *logout.html* page. Therefore, when the user clicks on the link to log out, the *logout.php* script destroys the session, and the *logout.html* page is displayed. We use this redirection so that if the user reloads or refreshes the *logout.html* page, no unnecessary session activity occurs. The page thanks the user for using the application.

The header( ) function causes a very common error in which the PHP engine complains that it cannot add header information because the headers have already been sent.

The error occurs because the web server sends headers as soon as any HTML is output. If you leave a blank line or even a single space before the PHP start tag, the headers are sent, because these are treated as HTML (albeit not very interesting HTML).

In the gift registry application, the session variable $user is registered when a guest logs in, and its value is set to his people_id. This variable is then used throughout the application both as the source of the guest's identity and to indicate that the guest is logged in. The function logincheck( ) is called at the beginning of the *presents.php* and *action.php* scripts to check if the user is logged in:

```
function logincheck( )
{
    session_start( );

    if (!session_is_registered("user"))
        // redirect to the login page
        header("Location: index.php");
}
```

If the user hasn't logged on or the session has timed-out, then the header( ) function redirects the browser to the login page, which we discuss later in the section "Using the HTML <form> Environment."

Writing Data with PHP

In this chapter, we've covered the basic techniques for connecting to and reading data from a MySQL DBMS using PHP. In this section, we extend this to writing data.

Example 11-4 shows the *action.php* script that adds and removes gifts from a guest's shopping list. The script uses the MySQL library functions we discussed earlier. If the user-supplied $action variable has the value insert, an attempt is made to reserve the gift with the value in $present_id for the current guest. If $action is set to delete, an attempt is made to remove the gift from the guest's shopping list. As discussed in the previous section, the guest's people_id is maintained in the $user session variable.

The script first checks the status of the gift with the identifier $present_id. If the gift is already reserved, the current guest can't reserve it; this can happen if another guest is using the application and beats the current guest to it. Likewise, the script checks that the gift is reserved by the current guest before actually unreserving it; this check should never fail, unless the same user is logged in twice. Defensive programming, or thinking through all the possibilities that can occur, is wise when developing for the Web, since each script is independent, and there are no time limits or controls in our application on when a user can request a script.

Example 11-4. The action.php script reserves gifts or removes them from a shopping list

```php
<?php
  // Add or remove a gift from the user's shopping list
  //
  // This script expects two parameters:
  // (1) The $present_id of the present they'd like to reserve
  //     or remove from their shopping list
  // (2) The $action to carry out: insert or delete
  // It carries out its requested action, and then redirects back
  // to presents.php. This script produces no output.

  // Include the DBMS credentials
  include "db.inc";

  // Check if the user is logged in
  // (this also starts the session)
  logincheck();

  // Secure the user data
  $present_id = clean($present_id, 5);
  $action = clean($action,6);

  // Connect to the MySQL DBMS
  if (!($connection = @ mysql_pconnect($hostName, $username, $password)))
    showerror();

  // Use the wedding database
  if (!mysql_select_db($databaseName, $connection))
    showerror();

  // LOCK the presents table for writing
  $query = "LOCK TABLES presents WRITE";

  // Run the query
  if (!($result = @ mysql_query($query, $connection)))
    showerror();

  // Create a query to retrieve the gift.
  $query = "SELECT *
            FROM presents WHERE
            present_id = {$present_id}";

  // Run the query
  if (!($result = @ mysql_query($query, $connection)))
    showerror();

  // Get the matching gift row (there's only one)
  $row = @ mysql_fetch_array($result);

  // Does the user want to add a new item to their shopping list?
  if ($action == "insert")
  {
    // Yes, an insert.
```

Example 11-4. The action.php script reserves gifts or removes them from a shopping list (continued)

```php
    // Has someone already reserved this? (a race condition)
    if (!empty($row["people_id"]) && $row["people_id"] != $user)
        // Yes. So, record a message to show the user
        $message = "Oh dear... Someone just beat you to that present!";
    else
    {
        // No. So, create a query that reserves the gift for this user
        $query = "UPDATE presents
                  SET people_id = \"{$user}\"
                  WHERE present_id = {$present_id}";

        // Run the query
        if (!($result = @ mysql_query($query, $connection)))
            showerror();

        // Create a message to show the user
        if (mysql_affected_rows() == 1)
            $message = "Reserved the present for you, {$user}";
        else
            $message = "There was a problem updating. Please contact the administrator.";
    }
}
else
{
    // No, it's a delete action.

    // Double-check they actually have this gift reserved
    if (!empty($row["people_id"]) && $row["people_id"] != $user)
        // They don't, so record a message to show the user
        $message = "That's not your present, {$user}!";
    else
    {
        // They do have it reserved. Create a query to unreserve it.
        $query = "UPDATE presents
                  SET people_id = NULL
                  WHERE present_id = {$present_id}";

        // Run the query.
        if (!($result = @ mysql_query($query, $connection)))
            showerror();

        // Create a message to show the user
        if (mysql_affected_rows() == 1)
            $message = "Removed the present from your shopping list, {$user}";
        else
            $message = "There was a problem updating. Please contact the administrator.";
    }
}

// UNLOCK the presents table
$query = "UNLOCK TABLES";

// Run the query
```

Example 11-4. The action.php script reserves gifts or removes them from a shopping list (continued)

```
  if (!($result = @ mysql_query($query, $connection)))
    showerror();

  // Redirect the browser back to presents.php
  header("Location: presents.php?message=" . urlencode($message));
?>
```

The script uses the MySQL library function mysql_affected_rows( ). The function reports the number of rows affected by the most recently executed SQL UPDATE, DELETE, or INSERT statement. In the script in Example 11-4, the function should return 1 in both cases, since one row is updated when the people_id is changed; if the returned value isn't 1, an unexpected error has occurred.

In other applications, mysql_affected_rows( ) can report that zero rows were affected, even if an SQL statement executes successfully. This occurs if, for example, an UPDATE statement doesn't actually change the database, or there are no matching rows to DELETE. The function can't be used with SELECT statements; mysql_num_rows( ) should be used instead.

The header( ) function is used to redirect the web browser back to the *presents.php* script. So when the user clicks on a link on the presents page, the *action.php* script is requested, and the browser is redirected to the presents page. The overall impression the user has is that she never left the presents page.

A message is sent back to the presents page as part of the URL. The urlencode( ) library function is used to convert characters that are not permitted in URLs—such as spaces, tabs, and reserved characters—into hexadecimal values that can be sent safely. This is necessary because the message contains spaces.

Using the HTML <form> Environment

The final script in our gift registry application is the first the user sees. It shows the guest a login <form> in which he can enter his username and password. The source of the script is shown in Example 11-5, and its output is shown in Figure 11-2.

When the guest has entered his credentials and clicks on the Log In button, the script is re-requested to validate the credentials. If the username already exists in the people table, the password is validated. If the password matches, the session variable $user is registered with the guest's people_id as its value. Then the header( ) function with the Location: parameter is used to redirect the browser to the *presents.php* script, along with a welcome message. If the password doesn't match, then the script is re-requested, and an error message is shown.

If the username doesn't exist, it is added to the people table along with the user-supplied password. This allows a new guest to use the system, decide on his own username and password, and log in. For applications in which security is important, the usernames and passwords would be added to the people table by an administrator.

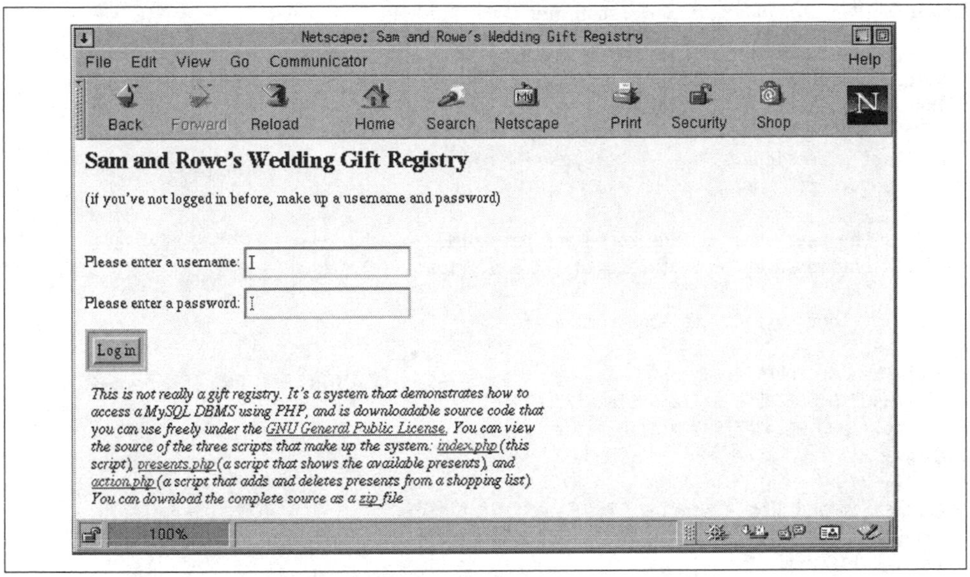

Figure 11-2. The initial login screen of the gift registry

Passwords are encrypted. The PHP library function crypt( ) is a one-way encryption function that takes two parameters: the string to be encrypted and a *salt*. The salt in our example is two characters from the username. It adds security by ensuring that a password is encrypted to a different string when it is provided by different users. Because crypt( ) is one-way, the encrypted string cannot be decoded. Therefore, when a returning user attempts to log in, the password they've supplied is encrypted and compared to the stored string: if they're the same, the password is correct.

The gift registry application isn't secure. Passwords are transferred between the web browser and web server as unencrypted text. While this isn't important for a simple application, additional security and authentication features are often required in web database applications. For such applications, communications should be encrypted by a secure sockets layer (SSL) software package that can be added to a web server.

Example 11-5. The index.php script

```php
<?php
    // Show the user the login screen for the application, or
    // try and log the user in.
    //
    // Three optional parameters:
    // (1) $login name that has been entered into the <form>
    // (2) $password that has been entered into the <form>
    // (3) $message to display

    // Include database parameters
    include "db.inc";
```

Example 11-5. The index.php script (continued)

```php
  // Pre-process the user data for security
  $user = clean($user, 30);
  $passwd = clean($passwd, 30);

  // Start a session
  session_start();

  // Has the user entered a username and password?
  if (isset($message) || empty($login) || empty($passwd))
  {
    // No, they haven't, so show them a <form>
?>
<!DOCTYPE HTML PUBLIC
  "-//W3C//DTD HTML 4.0 Transitional//EN"
  "http://www.w3.org/TR/html4/loose.dtd">
<html>
<head>
  <title>Sam and Rowe's Wedding Gift Registry</title>
</head>
<body bgcolor=#ffffff>
<h2>Sam and Rowe's Wedding Gift Registry</h2>
<?php
  // If an error message is stored, show it...
  if (isset($message))
    echo "<h3><font color=\"red\">{$message}</font></h3>";
?>
(if you've not logged in before, make up a username and password)
<form action="index.php" method="POST">
<br>Please enter a username: <input type="text" name="login">
<br>Please enter a password: <input type="password" name="passwd">
<br><input type="submit" value="Log in">
</form><br>
<?php require "disclaimer"; ?>
</body>
</html>
<?php
  } else
  {
    // Connect to the MySQL DBMS - credentials are in the file db.inc
    if (!($connection = @ mysql_pconnect($hostName, $username, $password)))
      showerror();

    // Use the wedding database
    if (!mysql_select_db($databaseName, $connection))
      showerror();

    // Create a query to find any rows that match the username the user entered
    $query = "SELECT people_id, passwd
              FROM people
              WHERE people_id = \"{$login}\"";

    // Run the query through the connection
    if (!($result = @ mysql_query($query, $connection)))
```

Example 11-5. The index.php script (continued)

```
        showerror();

    // Were there any matching rows?
    if (mysql_num_rows($result) == 0)
    {
        // No. So insert the new username and password into the table
        $query = "INSERT INTO people
                    SET people_id = \"{$login}\",
                        passwd    = \"" . crypt($passwd, substr($user, 0, 2)) .  "\"";

        // Run the query
        if (!($result = @ mysql_query($query, $connection)))
            showerror();
    }
    else
    {
        // Yes. So fetch the matching row
        $row = @ mysql_fetch_array($result);

        // Does the user-supplied password match the password in the table?
        if (crypt($passwd, substr($login, 0, 2)) != $row["passwd"])
        {
            // No, so create an error message
            $message = "This user exists, but the password is incorrect. Choose another
username, or fix the password.";

            // Now, redirect the browser to the current page
            header("Location: index.php?message=" . urlencode($message));
            exit;
        }
    }

    // Save the user's login name in the session
    if (!session_is_registered("user"))
        session_register("user");
    $user = $login;

    $message = "Welcome! Please select gift suggestions from the list to add" .
                " to your shopping list!";

    // Everything went ok. Redirect to the presents.php page.
    header("Location: presents.php?message=" . urlencode($message));
}
?>
```

Where to Find Out More

Chapter 18 contains a complete reference to the MySQL library functions. However, there are many other excellent resources available for you to learn more about PHP, its libraries, web servers, and building web database applications. We list a few of these resources in this section.

To find out more about the Apache web server, we recommend the following:

- The Apache web site: *http://httpd.apache.org/*
- B. Laurie and P. Laurie, *Apache: The Definitive Guide*, O'Reilly and Associates, Second Edition, 1999.

For PHP and web database applications, try the following books:

- H. E. Williams and D. Lane, *Web Database Applications with PHP and MySQL*, O'Reilly and Associates, 2002.
- W. Gilmore, *A Programmer's Introduction to PHP 4.0*, Apress publishing, 2000.
- P. Moulding, *PHP Black Book*, The Coriolis Group, 2001.
- Z. Greant, G. Merrall, T. Wilson, and B. Michlitsch, *PHP Functions Essential Reference*, New Riders Publishing, 2001.
- L. Welling and L. Thomson, *PHP and MySQL Web Development*, SAMS, 2001.
- J. Parise, H. Rawat, J. Moore, L. Argerich, D. Thomas, D. O'Dell et al., *Professional PHP4 Programming*,Wrox Press Inc, 2001.
- S. Hughes and A. Zmievski, *PHP Developer's Cookbook*, SAMS, 2000.

There are also many useful web sites that include tutorials, example code, online discussion forums, and links to example PHP applications. The official PHP site links page at *http://www.php.net/links.php* points to many of these sites. A few of the ones we use are:

- *http://www.phpbuilder.com/*
- *http://www.devshed.com/Server_Side/PHP/*
- *http://www.hotscripts.com/PHP/*
- *http://php.resourceindex.com/*

## CHAPTER 12

C API

In this book, we examine several different programming languages: Python, Java, Perl, PHP, and C. Among these languages, C is by far the most challenging. With the other languages, your primary concern is the formulation of SQL, the passing of that SQL to a function call, and the manipulation of the resulting data. C adds the complex issue of memory management into the mix.

MySQL provides C libraries that enable the creation of MySQL database applications. MySQL's API is derived heavily from mSQL to take advantage of the many tools that existed only for mSQL in MySQL's early days. In this chapter, we dive into basic programming with MySQL C's API.

 You can use MySQL's C API for C++ programming as well. If you are looking for a more object-oriented approach, however, you should leverage the recently developed MYSQL++ API.

API Overview

The following list shows the function calls of the MySQL C API. Chapter 19 lists each of these methods with detailed prototype information, return values, and descriptions.

```
mysql_affected_rows( )
mysql_close( )
mysql_connect( )
mysql_create_db( )
mysql_data_seek( )
mysql_drop_db( )
mysql_eof( )
mysql_error( )
mysql_fetch_field( )
mysql_fetch_lengths( )
mysql_fetch_row( )
```

```
mysql_field_count( )
mysql_field_seek( )
mysql_free_result( )
mysql_get_client_info( )
mysql_get_host_info( )
mysql_get_proto_into( )
mysql_get_server_info( )
mysql_init( )
mysql_insert_id( )
mysql_list_dbs( )
mysql_list_fields( )
mysql_list_processes( )
mysql_list_tables( )
mysql_num_fields( )
mysql_num_rows( )
mysql_query( )
mysql_real_query( )
mysql_reload( )
mysql_select_db( )
mysql_shutdown( )
mysql_stat( )
mysql_store_result( )
mysql_use_result( )
```

You may notice that many of the function names do not seem directly related to accessing database data. In many cases, MySQL actually only provides an API interface into database administration functions. By reading the function names, you might have gathered that any database application you write might look something like this:

Connect
Select DB
Query
Fetch row
Fetch field
Close

Example 12-1 shows a simple select statement that retrieves data from a MySQL database using the MySQL C API.

Example 12-1. A program that selects all data in a test database and displays the data

```
#include <stdio.h>
#include <mysql.h>

int main(char **args) {
```

Example 12-1. A program that selects all data in a test database and displays the data (continued)

```
MYSQL_RES *result;
MYSQL_ROW row;
MYSQL *connection, mysql;
int state;

/* connect to the MySQL database at localhost */
mysql_init(&mysql);
connection = mysql_real_connect(&mysql,"localhost", "orausr", "orapw",
                                "oradb", 0, 0, 0);
/* check for a connection error */
if (connection == NULL) {
/* print the error message */
printf(mysql_error(&mysql));
return 1;
}
state = mysql_query(connection,
"SELECT test_id, test_val FROM test");
if (state != 0) {
printf(mysql_error(connection));
return 1;
}
/* must call mysql_store_result() before you can issue
     any other query calls */
   result = mysql_store_result(connection);
   printf("Rows: %d\n", mysql_num_rows(result));
   /* process each row in the result set */
   while ( ( row = mysql_fetch_row(result)) != NULL ) {
       printf("id: %s, val: %s\n",
           (row[0] ? row[0] : "NULL"),
           (row[1] ? row[1] : "NULL"));
}
/* free the result set */
mysql_free_result(result);
/* close the connection */
mysql_close(connection);
printf("Done.\n");
}
```

Of the included header files, both *mysql.h* and *stdio.h* should be obvious to you. The *mysql.h* header contains the prototypes and variables required for MySQL, and *stdio.h* the prototype for printf( ). On FreeBSD, you can compile this program for MySQL 3. 23 with the GNU C compiler using the command line:

```
gcc -L/usr/local/lib/mysql -I/usr/local/include/mysql -o select select.c\
     -lmysqlclient
```

On Mac OS X, compiling MySQL 4.0 requires linking to zlib:

```
cc -L/usr/local/lib/mysql -I/usr/local/include/mysql -o select select.c\
     -lmysqlclient -lz
```

You should of course substitute the directory where you have MySQL installed for */usr/local/lib/mysql* and */usr/local/include/mysql* in the preceding code.

The `main( )` function follows the steps we outlined earlier: it connects to the server, selects a database, issues a query, processes the result sets, and cleans up the resources it used. We will cover each of these steps in detail as the chapter progresses. For now, read the code and get a feel for what it does.

The Connection

An application should call `mysql_init( )` before performing any other operation. This method initializes a database handler used by many of the functions—including the connection and error handling functions. In the above example, we created a handler in the declaration:

```
MYSQL *connection, mysql;
```

The pointer to the handler, `connection`, will represent our actual connection once it is made; the allocated handler, `mysql`, represents a null connection until we actually make the database connection. Our first step is to initialize this handler through the `mysql_init( )` function:

```
mysql_init(&mysql);
```

This function takes a reference to an allocated null handler. The MySQL API requires this hocus-pocus with a null handler to support operations such as error handling that occur outside the context of a physical database connection. The first function needing this handler is the actual connection API: `mysql_real_connect( )`.

 At first glance over the API list, you may be tempted to use the `mysql_connect( )` function. The odd name of the `mysql_real_connect( )` function exists because it is a replacement for the long-deprecated `mysql_connect( )` function. The old `mysql_connect( )` provided compatibility for mSQL applications; you should never use it in modern applications.

The `mysql_real_connect( )` function takes several arguments:

null handler
The connection handler allocated and subsequently initialized through `mysql_init( )`.

host
The name of the machine on which the MySQL server is running.

user
The user ID of the MySQL user to connect under.

password
The password that identifies the user you are connecting under.

database
The name of the database on the MySQL server to connect to.

port

The port number MySQL is listening to. If you specify 0, it will connect to MySQL on MySQL's default port number.

unix socket

A pointer to the Unix socket or null. Under Windows, you should be certain to pass in NULL and not a null string—i.e., use (char *)NULL and not (char *)"".

client flag

A number including a set of flags for the connection. You will generally pass in 0 here.

Upon success, the `mysql_real_connect( )` function returns a pointer to an actual MySQL connection. To verify success, your application should check for a null value:

```
if( connection == NULL ) {
    /* An error! */
}
```

If you run into an error during a connection, it becomes clear why you needed that null handler we created in `mysql_init( )`. It provides you with access to the error:

```
printf("%s\n", mysql_error(&mysql));
```

We will go into more detail on error handling later in the chapter.

Queries and Results

Now that you have a physical connection to the database, you can interact with MySQL. The above example used the `mysql_query( )` function to get all of the rows from the test table in our sample database:

```
state = mysql_query(connection, "SELECT test_id, test_val FROM test");
```

This function returns nonzero on error. Once you send a query, you should therefore check the return code to make sure the query executed properly.

```
if(state != 0 ) {
    /* Error! */
}
```

If the return code is 0, you can access any results through the `mysql_store_result( )` function:

```
result = mysql_store_result(connection);
```

This function returns a pointer to the result set generated by the previous query executed against the specified connection. If that query did not generate results, or if you encounter an error getting to the results, this function returns null. The earlier example does not look for these states—we will go into them in more detail when we cover error handling later in the chapter.

The results given to you by the mysql_store_result( ) function are now under your control. They will exist in memory until you explicitly free them through the mysql_free_result( ) function. In this case, you should step through each row of the results and print the row's values:

```
while( (row = mysql_fetch_row(result)) != NULL ) {
    printf("id: %s, val: %s\n", (row[0] ? row[0] : "NULL"),
           (row[1] ? row[1] : "NULL"));
}
```

Even though the test_id column in our database is a numeric column, we still treat it as a null-terminated string in the results. We have to do this since the MYSQL_RES typedef is, in fact, nothing more than an array of null-terminated strings—regardless of their underlying MySQL type. We will perform some more complex result set handling that includes binary data later in this chapter.

Once you are done with the results, you must tell MySQL to free the memory they use:

```
mysql_free_result(result);
```

Closing the Connection

The final step of any database application is to free the database resources it uses. In MySQL, you free your database resources through the mysql_close( ) function:

```
mysql_close(connection);
```

If you attempt to use that connection at any point after closing it, you will encounter an error.

The C API in Practice

What you have seen so far will take you a long way. If you want to understand what is going on in more detail, understand proper error handling, or work with binary data, however, we need to drop down a level and look at the API in a practical example. To these ends, we will look to an API that provides callers with access to delayed stock quotes stored in a MySQL database. The application leverages a single MySQL table, Stock, with the following schema:

```
CREATE TABLE Stock (
    symbol    CHAR(5) NOT NULL PRIMARY KEY,
    openPrice REAL    NOT NULL,
    currPrice REAL    NOT NULL,
    high52    REAL    NOT NULL,
    low52     REAL    NOT NULL
);
```

Our library needs two basic functions:

```
void assign_stock(Stock *stock);
```
    Assigns the values in the Stock structure to the database

```
Stock *get_stock(char *symbol);
```
    Retrieves the Stock structure for the specified stock

These functions naturally depend on a struct that mirrors the database schema for the stock quotes.

Support Functions

Our example includes three simple helper functions to support its work. The first initializes everything:

```
MySQL * connection, mysql;

int init_api() {
    mysql_init(&mysql);
    connection = mysql_real_connect(&mysql, "localhost", "orausr",
                                    "orapw", "oradb", 0, 0, 0);
    if( connection == NULL ) {
        return -1;
    }
    else {
        return 0;
    }
}
```

This function does the MySQL initialization we covered earlier in the chapter. It specifically establishes a connection to the database. If any error occurs while making the connection, it returns −1.

The second support function is the opposite of the initialization function; it closes everything:

```
void close_api() {
    if( connection != NULL ) {
        mysql_close(connection);
        connection = NULL;
    }
}
```

The last support function will be used many times in the example. It returns a message for the last error.

```
char *error;

char *get_error() {
    return error;
}
```

Any time the API encounters an error condition, it sets the error variable to the appropriate error message. Applications calling this API therefore call this function to retrieve the last error message. You should always copy any error messages into storage managed by your application if you wish to save them for later use.

Quote Retrieval

The get_stock( ) function provides all stock information from MySQL for the stock with the specified symbol. It formulates a query based on the ticker symbol and sticks the results into a Stock structure.

```c
Stock *get_stock(char *symbol) {
    char *query = "SELECT symbol, openPrice, currPrice, high52, low52, \
                   FROM Stock WHERE symbol = '%s'";
    char *sql;
    int state;

    error = (char *)NULL;
    sql = (char *)malloc((strlen(query) + strlen(symbol) + 1) * sizeof(char));
    sprintf(sql, query, symbol);
    state = mysql_query(connection, sql);
    free(sql);
    if( state != 0 ) {
        error = mysql_error(connection);
        return (Stock *)NULL;
    }
    else {
        MYSQL_RES *result;
        Stock *stock;
        MYSQL_ROW row;

        result = mysql_store_result(connection);
        if( result == (MYSQL_RES *)NULL ) {
            error = mysql_error(connection);
            return (Stock *)NULL;
        }
        stock = (Stock *)malloc(sizeof(Stock));
        row = mysql_fetch_row(result);
        if( !row ) {
            error = "Invalid symbol.";
            return (Stock *)NULL;
        }
        stock->symbol = row[0];
        stock->open_price = atof(row[1]);
        stock->current_price = atof(row[2]);
        stock->high52 = atof(row[3]);
        stock->low52 = atof(row[4]);
        return stock;
    }
}
```

The first line of the function is where we prepare the query. It includes the entire query except for a %s placeholder for the ticker symbol. We will insert this into the string later using sprintf().

The function next clears out the error message used by the get_error() helper function. Clearing out the error message is critical since MySQL actually manages the memory allocated to MySQL error messages. If this function failed to clear out the error message, and the client calling this API tried to call get_error() when no error occurred, it would be possible for the error message to point to garbage memory.

To make sure the final SQL has enough memory allocated to it, the function allocates enough space for the query with the placeholder, the ticker symbol, and a final null terminator. Using sprintf(), the query is assembled into its final SQL.

In applications in which the stock symbol may come from data entered by a user, either your application or—perhaps more appropriately—the API should check the ticker symbol for validity. In other words, you should scan it for SQL, especially single quotes. If you fail to check for these things, users may inadvertently cause errors in the database calls or—even worse—exploit the error to corrupt the database.

Immediately after running the query, the API frees the memory allocated for the query and proceeds to error handling. As we illustrated earlier, you check the error on a query by checking its return value. If the return value is nonzero, an error occurred. This API sets the value of the current error message to whatever mysql_error() has set and returns NULL to the calling application.

On success, the function retrieves the results of the query. For this query, it is looking for one and only one result. The call to mysql_store_result() gets the result set from MySQL. The mysql_store_result() function returns NULL under two conditions:

- The original SQL was not a query (i.e., it was an INSERT, UPDATE, or DELETE).
- The function encountered an error.

Because we know we sent a query to the database, this situation can mean only that an error has occurred. We therefore set the error message and return null.

We are now ready to allocate a Stock struct and assign it values. This example actually does row processing in a different manner from what we did earlier. It specifically calls mysql_fetch_row() instead of directly accessing the data through the MYSQL_RES struct. Though both methods are proper, mysql_fetch_row() is technically more proper. It enables you to step through a result set row by row and get metadata for the row. Though we care about neither issue in this case, we still use that function.

The mysql_fetch_row() function will return a MYSQL_ROW struct if there are more rows in the result set. For this query, there should be only one row. If the call to mysql_fetch_row() returns NULL, the symbol simply is not in the database. We therefore check that it is in the database and begin assigning values to the Stock struct based on the data in the result set.

Adding Symbols

Adding a new symbol to the database is simpler than a query in that you have no results to process, yet more complex in that you have more mucking around with memory allocation for strings in building the query. We take the same approach in building the insert that we took in building SELECT for get_stock( ) except that we do not bother calculating how much memory we need; 255 characters should be more than enough for this example. Nothing about adding the stock is new.

```
int assign_stock(Stock *stock) {
    char *query = "INSERT INTO Stock ( symbol, openPrice, \
                    currPrice, high52, low52 ) \
                    VALUES ('%s', %f, %f, %f, %f)";
    char *sql;
    int state;

    sql = (char *)malloc(255 * sizeof(char));
    error = (char *)NULL;
    sprintf(sql, query,
            stock->symbol, stock->open_price, stock->current_price,
            stock->high52, stock->low52);
    state = mysql_query(connection, sql);
    free(sql);
    if( state != 0 ) {
        error = mysql_error(connection);
        return -1;
    }
    return 0;
}
```

Advanced Issues

The MySQL C API provides the tools for manipulating queries and results using their lengths rather than null termination. This feature is useful if you have strings encoded with nulls in them.

```
char *sql = (char *)malloc(3246);

...
state = mysql_real_query(connection, sql, 3246);
```

This function behaves just like mysql_query( ) but requires you to specify the string length.

Of course, if you are intent on using MySQL to store binary data, you need to worry about a lot more than nulls in your query data. You need to worry about all of the special characters interpreted by MySQL. The mysql_escape_string( ) function is critical to getting around this concern.

The following example shows how to load an MP3 from a file in MySQL:

```
void add_mp3(char *song, FILE *f) {
    unsigned int read;
    char sql[1024000];
    char mp3[1024000];
    char *p;

    sprintf(sql, "INSERT INTO MP3 ( title, song ) VALUES ( '%s', '", song);
    p = sql + strlen(sql);
    while( (read = fread(mp3, 1, sizeof(mp3), f)) > 0 ) {
        if( (p + (2*read) + 3) > (sql + sizeof(sql)) ) {
            // reallocate memory
        }
        p += mysql_escape_string(p, mp3, read);
    }
    strcpy(p, "')");
    if( mysql_query(connection, sql) != 0 ) {
        printf("%s\n", mysql_error(connection));
    }
}
```

In this example, the application reads an MP3 from a file. Instead of placing it directly into the query string, however, it runs the binary data read from the file through the mysql_escape_string( ) function. This function takes a pointer to a position in a string and places escaped data from the second argument into that string. In other words, where the program read a null from the file, it will place the special sequence '\0' into the query string. Because each special character is replaced with two characters, we need to assume that each character will be escaped when checking whether the memory we have allocated for the query string can accept the data. The function finally adds a null to the end of your string to create a null-terminated string.

A more mundane use of this feature is to deal with the problem of arbitrary user input we discussed earlier in the chapter. You can pass user input through this function and get a string that is safe to stick in your query.

## CHAPTER 13

Java

Java is one of the simplest languages in which you can write MySQL applications. Its database access API, Java Database Connectivity (JDBC), is one of the more mature database-independent APIs for database access in common use. Most of what we cover in this chapter can be applied to Oracle, Sybase, MS SQL Server, mSQL, and any other database engine, as well as MySQL. In fact, almost none of the MySQL-specific information in this chapter has anything to do with coding. Instead, the "proprietary" information relates only to downloading MySQL support for JDBC and configuring the runtime environment. Everything else is largely independent of MySQL.

In this chapter, we assume you have a basic understanding of the Java programming language and Java concepts. If you do not already have this background, we strongly recommend taking a look at *Learning Java*, by Pat Niemeyer and Jonathan Knudsen (O'Reilly). For more details on how to build the sort of three-tier database applications we discussed in Chapter 8, take a look at *Database Programming with JDBC and Java*, by George Reese (O'Reilly).

The JDBC API

Like all Java APIs, JDBC is a set of classes and interfaces that work together to support a specific set of functionality. In the case of JDBC, this functionality is database access. The classes and interfaces that make up the JDBC API are thus abstractions from concepts common to database access for any kind of database. A Connection, for example, is a Java interface representing a database connection. Similarly, a ResultSet represents a result set of data returned from an SQL SELECT. Java combines the classes that form the JDBC API in the *java.sql* package, which Sun introduced in JDK 1.1.

The underlying details of database access naturally differ from vendor to vendor. JDBC does not actually deal with those details. Most of the classes in the *java.sql* package are in fact interfaces with no implementation details. Individual database vendors provide implementations of these interfaces in the form of something called a JDBC driver. As a database programmer, however, you need to know only a few details about the driver you are using—the rest you manage via the JDBC interfaces.

The first database-dependent thing you need to know is what drivers exist for your database. Different people provide different JDBC implementations for a variety of databases. As a database programmer, you should select a JDBC implementation that will provide the greatest stability and performance for your application. Though it may seem counterintuitive, JDBC implementations provided by the database vendors are generally at the bottom of the pack when it comes to stability and flexibility. As an open source project, however, MySQL relies on drivers provided by other developers in the community.

Sun has created four classifications of JDBC drivers based on their architectures. Each JDBC driver classification represents a trade-off between performance and flexibility.

Type 1

Type 1 drivers use a bridging technology to access a database. The JDBC-ODBC bridge that comes with JDK 1.2 is the most common example of this kind of driver. It provides a gateway to the ODBC API. Implementations of the ODBC API, in turn, perform the actual database access. Though useful for learning JDBC and quick testing, bridging solutions are rarely appropriate for production environments.

Type 2

Type 2 drivers are native API drivers. "Native API" means that the driver contains Java code that calls native C or C++ methods provided by the database vendor. In the context of MySQL, a Type 2 driver is one that uses MySQL's C API under the hood to talk to MySQL on behalf of your application. Type 2 drivers generally provide the best performance, but they require the installation of native libraries on clients that need to access the database. Applications using Type 2 drivers have a limited degree of portability.

Type 3

Type 3 drivers provide a client with a pure Java implementation of the JDBC API in which the driver uses a network protocol to talk to middleware on the server. This middleware, in turn, performs the actual database access. The middleware may or may not use JDBC for its database access. The Type 3 architecture is actually more of a benefit to driver vendors than application architects since it enables the vendor to write a single implementation and claim support for any database that has a JDBC driver. Unfortunately, it has weak performance and unpredictable stability.

Type 4

Using network protocols built into the database engine, Type 4 drivers talk directly to the database using Java sockets. This is a pure Java solution. Because these network protocols are almost never documented, most Type 4 drivers come from the database vendors. The open source nature of MySQL, however, has enabled several independent developers to write different Type 4 MySQL drivers.

Practically speaking, Type 2 and Type 4 drivers are the only viable choices for a production application. At an abstract level, the choice between Type 2 and Type 4 comes down to a single issue: is platform independence critical? By platform independence, we mean that the application can be bundled up into a single jar and run on any platform. Type 2 drivers have a hard time with platform independence since you need to package platform-specific libraries with the application. If the database access API has not been ported to a client platform, your application will not run on the platform. On the other hand, Type 2 drivers tend to perform better than Type 4 drivers.

Knowing the driver type provides only a starting point for making a decision about which JDBC driver to use in your application. The decision really comes down to knowing the drivers that exist for your database of choice and how they compare to each other. Table 13-1 lists the JDBC drivers available for MySQL. Of course, you can use any ODBC bridge to talk to MySQL as well—but we do not recommend it under any circumstance for MySQL developers.

Table 13-1. JDBC drivers for MySQL

Driver name[a]	OSI[b] license	JDBC version	Home page
mm (GNU)	LGPL	1.x and 2.x	*http://mmmysql.sourceforge.net/*
twz	None	1.x	*http://www.voicenet.com/~zellert/tjFM/*
Caucho	QPL	2.x	*http://www.caucho.com/projects/jdbc-mysql/index.xtp*

[a] These are all Type 4 drivers.
[b] This stands for Open Source Initiative (*http://www.opensource.org*). For drivers released under an OSI-approved license, the specific license is referenced.

Of the three MySQL JDBC drivers, twz sees the least amount of development and thus does not likely serve the interests of most programmers these days. The GNU driver (also known as mm MySQL), on the other hand, has been under constant development and is the most mature of the three JDBC drivers. Not to be outdone, Caucho claims significant performance benefits over the GNU driver.

The JDBC Architecture

We have already mentioned that JDBC is a set of interfaces implemented by different vendors. Figure 13-1 shows how database access works from an application's perspective. Essentially, the application simply makes method calls to the JDBC interfaces. Under the hood, the implementation being used by that application performs the actual database calls.

JDBC is divided into two Java packages: *java.sql* and *javax.sql*. The *java.sql* package was the original package that contained all the JDBC classes and interfaces. JDBC 2. 0, however, introduced something called the JDBC Optional Package—the *javax.sql*

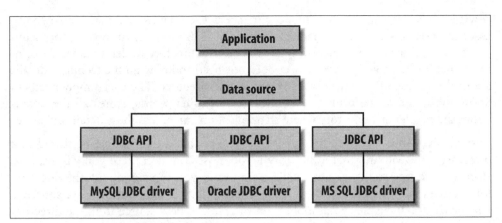

Figure 13-1. The JDBC architecture

package—with interfaces that a driver does not have to implement. In fact, the interfaces themselves are not even part of the J2SE as of JDK 1.3 (though it has always been part of the J2EE).

As it turns out, some of the functionality in the JDBC Optional Package is so important that it is no longer "optional" and should instead be part of the J2SE with the release of JDK 1.4. For backwards compatibility, the Optional Package classes remain in *javax.sql*.

Connecting to MySQL

JDBC represents a connection to a database through the Connection interface. Thus, connecting to MySQL requires you to get an instance of the Connection interface from your JDBC driver. JDBC supports two ways of getting access to a database connection:

- Through a JDBC data source
- Using the JDBC driver manager

The data source method is preferred for connecting to a database. Data sources come from the Optional Package, so support for them is still spotty. No matter what environment you are in, you can rely on driver manager connectivity.

Data source connectivity

Data source connectivity is very simple. In fact, the following code makes a connection to any database; it is not specific to MySQL:

```
Context ctx = new InitialContext();
DataSource ds = (DataSource)ctx.lookup("jdbc/myds");
Connection conn = ds.getConnection("userid", "password");
```

The first line in this example actually comes from the Java Naming and Directory Interface (JNDI) API. JNDI is an API that provides access to naming and directory services.* Naming and directory services are specialized data stores that enable you to associate related data under a familiar name. In a Windows environment, for example, a network printer is stored in Microsoft ActiveDirectory under a name. To print to the networked color printer, a user does not need to know all the technical details about the printer. Those details are stored in the directory. The user simply needs to know the name of the printer. The directory, in other words, stores all the details about the printer in a directory where an application can access these details by name.

Though data source connectivity does not require that a data source be stored in a directory, you will find that a directory is the most common place you will want to store data source configuration details. As a result, you can simply ask the directory for the data source by name. In the above example, the name of the data source is *jdbc/myds*. JNDI enables your application to grab the data source from the directory by its name without worrying about all the configuration details.

Though this sounds simple enough, you are probably wondering how the data source got in the directory in the first place. Someone had to put it there. Programmatically, putting the data source in the directory can be as simple as the following code:

```
SomeDataSourceClass ds = new SomeDataSourceClass();
Context ctx = new InitialContext();

// configure the DS by setting configuration attributes
ctx.bind("jdbc/myds", ds);
```

We have two bits of "magic" in this code. The first bit of magic is the SomeDataSourceClass class. In short, it is an implementation of the javax.sql. DataSource interface. In some cases, this implementation may come from the JDBC vendor—but not always. In fact, none of the MySQL drivers currently ship with a DataSource implementation. If you are using an application server such as Orion or WebLogic, it will provide a DataSource implementation for you that will work with MySQL.

Configuring your data source depends on the properties demanded by the data source implementation class. In most cases, a data source implementation will want to know the JDBC URL and name of the java.sql.Driver interface implementation for the driver. We will cover these two things in the section on driver manager connectivity.

Though we have been vague about configuring a JDBC data source programmatically, do not despair. You should never have to configure a JDBC data source programmatically. The vendor that provides your data source implementation should provide you with a configuration tool capable of publishing the configuration for a data source to a directory. All application servers come with such a tool. A tool of

---

* A full discussion of JNDI is way beyond the scope of this chapter. At the very least, you need a JNDI service provider (analogous to a JDBC driver), and you must set some environment variables to support that service provider. You also need a directory service to talk to. If you do not have access to a directory service, you can always practice using the filesystem service provider available on the JNDI home page at *http://java.sun.com/ products/jndi* or use the driver manager approach.

this sort will prompt you for the values to enter a new data source in a directory, then allow you to save that configuration to the directory. Your application can then access the data source by name, as shown earlier in the chapter.

Driver manager connectivity

One of the few implementation classes in the *java.sql* package is the `DriverManager` class. It maintains a list of implementations of the JDBC `java.sql.Driver` class and provides you with database connections based on the JDBC URLs you provide. A JDBC URL is in the form of *jdbc:protocol:subprotocol*. It tells a `DriverManager` which database engine you wish to connect to and provides the `DriverManager` with enough information to make a connection.

 JDBC uses the word "driver" in multiple contexts. When lowercase, a JDBC driver is the collection of classes that together implement all the JDBC interfaces and provide an application with access to at least one database. When uppercase, the `Driver` is the class that implements `java.sql.Driver`. Finally, JDBC provides a `DriverManager` that can be used to keep track of all the different `Driver` implementations.

The protocol part of the URL refers to a given JDBC driver. The protocol for the Caucho MySQL driver, for example, is *mysql-caucho*, while the GNU driver uses *mysql*. The subprotocol provides the implementation-specific connection data. Every MySQL driver requires a hostname and database name to make a connection. It also requires a port if your database engine is not running on the default port. Table 13-2 shows the configuration information for the MySQL JDBC drivers.

Table 13-2. Configuration information for MySQL JDBC drivers

Driver	Implementation	URL
Caucho	com.caucho.jdbc.mysql.Driver	*jdbc:mysql-caucho://HOST[:PORT]/DB*
GNU	org.gjt.mm.mysql.Driver	*jdbc:mysql://[HOST][:PORT]/ DB[?PROP1=VAL1][&PROP2=VAL2]...*
twz	twz1.jdbc.mysql.jdbcMysqlDriver	*jdbc:z1MySQL://HOST[:PORT]/ DB[?PROP1=VAL1][&PROP2=VAL2]...*

As you can see, the URLs for the GNU driver and twz driver are very different from that of the Caucho driver. As a general rule, the format of the Caucho driver is preferred, because it allows you to specify properties separately.

Your first task is to register the driver implementation with the JDBC `DriverManager`. There are two key ways to register a driver:

- Specify the names of the drivers you want to register on the command line of your application using the `jdbc.drivers` property:

  ```
  java -Djdbc.drivers=com.caucho.jdbc.mysql.Driver MyAppClass
  ```

- Explicitly load the class in your program by executing a new statement or a Class.forName( ):

```
Class.forName("twz1.jdbc.mysql.jdbcMysqlDriver").newInstance( ).
```

For portability's sake, we recommend that you put all configuration information in some sort of configuration file, such as a properties file, then load the configuration data from that configuration file. By taking this approach, your application will not rely on MySQL or the JDBC driver you are using. You can simply change the values in the configuration file to move from the GNU driver to Caucho or from MySQL to Oracle.

Once you have registered your driver, you can ask the DriverManager for a Connection by calling the getConnection( ) method in the driver with the information identifying the desired connection. This information minimally includes a JDBC URL, user ID, and password. You may optionally include a set of parameters:

```
Connection conn = DriverManager.getConnection("jdbc:mysql-caucho://carthage/Web",
    "someuser", "somepass");
```

This code returns a connection associated with the database Web on the MySQL server on the machine carthage using the Caucho driver under the user ID someuser and authenticated with somepass. Though the Caucho driver has the simplest URL, connecting with the other drivers is not much more difficult. They just ask that you specify connection properties such as the user ID and password as part of the JDBC URL. Table 13-3 lists the URL properties for the GNU driver, and Table 13-4 lists them for the twz driver.

Table 13-3. URL properties for the GNU (mm) JDBC driver

Name	Default	Description
autoReconnect	false	Causes the driver to attempt a reconnect when the connection dies.
characterEncoding	None	The Unicode encoding to use when Unicode is the character set.
initialTimeout	2	The initial time between reconnects in seconds when autoReconnect is set.
maxReconnects	3	The maximum number of times the driver should attempt a reconnect.
maxRows	0	The maximum number of rows to return for queries. Zero means return all rows.
password	None	The password to use in connecting to MySQL.
useUnicode	false	Specifies Unicode as the character set to be used for the connection.
user	None	The user to use for the MySQL connection.

Table 13-4. URL properties for the twz JDBC driver

Name	Default	Description
autoReX	true	Manages automatic reconnect for data update statements.
cacheMode	memory	Dictates where query results are cached.

Table 13-4. URL properties for the twz JDBC driver (continued)

Name	Default	Description
cachePath	.	The directory to which result sets are cached if cacheMode is set to disk.
connectionTimeout	120	The amount of time, in seconds, that a thread will wait for action by a connection before throwing an exception.
db	mysql	The MySQL database to which the driver is connected.
dbmdDB	<connection>	The MySQL database to use for database metadata operations.
dbmdMaxRows	66536	The maximum number of rows returned by a database metadata operation.
dbmdPassword	<connection>	The password to use for database metadata operations.
dbmdUser	<connection>	The user ID to use for database metadata operations.
dbmdXcept	false	Causes exceptions to be thrown on unsupported database metadata operations instead of the JDBC-compliant behavior of returning an empty result.
debugFile	None	Enables debugging to the specified file.
debugRead	false	When debugging is enabled, data read from MySQL is dumped to the debug file. This will severely degrade the performance of the driver.
debugWrite	false	When debugging is enabled, data written to MySQL is dumped to the debug file. This will severely degrade the performance of the driver.
host	localhost	The host machine on which MySQL is running.
maxField	65535	The maximum field size for data returned by MySQL. Any extra data is silently truncated.
maxRows	Integer.MAX_VALUE	The maximum number of rows that can be returned by a MySQL query.
moreProperties	None	Tells the driver to look for more properties in the named file.
multipleQuery	true	Will force the caching of the result set, allowing multiple queries to be open at once.
password	None	The password used to connect to MySQL.
port	3306	The port on which MySQL is listening.
socketTimeout	None	The time in seconds that a socket connection will block before throwing an exception.
user	None	The user connected to MySQL.
RSLock	false	Enables locking of result sets for a statement for use in multiple threads.

As a result, connections for the GNU driver commonly look like:

```
Connection conn = DriverManager.getConnection("jdbc:mysql://carthage/
Web?user=someuser&password=somepass");
```

or for twz:

```
Connection conn =
    DriverManager.getConnection("jdbc:z1MySQL://carthage/
Web?user=someuser&password="somepass");
```

Instead of passing the basic connection properties of user and password as a second and third argument to getConnection( ), GNU and twz pass them as part of the URL. In fact, you can pass any of the properties as part of the URL. JDBC, however, has a standard mechanism for passing driver-specific connection properties to getConnect():

```
Properties p = new Properties( );
Connection conn;

p.put("user", "someuser");
p.put("password", "somepass");
p.put("useUnicode", "true");
p.put("characterEncoding", "UTF-8");
conn = DriverManager.getConnection(url, p);
```

Unfortunately, the way in which MySQL supports these optional properties is a bit inconsistent. So it is best to go with the preferred manner for your driver, however unwieldy it makes the URLs.

Example 13-1 shows how to make a connection to MySQL using the GNU driver.

Example 13-1. A complete sample of making a JDBC connection

```java
import java.sql.*;

public class Connect {
    public static void main(String argv[]) {
        Connection con = null;

        try {
            // here is the JDBC URL for this database
            String url = "jdbc:mysql://athens.imaginary.com/
                         Web?user=someuser&password=somepass";
            // more on what the Statement and ResultSet classes do later
            Statement stmt;
            ResultSet rs;

            // either pass this as a property, i.e.
            // -Djdbc.drivers=org.gjt.mm.mysql.Driver
            // or load it here as we are doing in this example
            Class.forName("org.gjt.mm.mysql.Driver");
            // here is where the connection is made
            con = DriverManager.getConnection(url);
        }
        catch( SQLException e ) {
            e.printStackTrace( );
        }
        finally {
            if( con != null ) {
                try { con.close( ); }
                catch( Exception e ) { }
            }
        }
    }
}
```

The line `con = DriverManager.getConnection(url)` makes the database connection in this example. In this case, the JDBC URL and `Driver` implementation class names are actually hardcoded into this application. The only reason this is acceptable is because this application is an example driver. As we mentioned earlier, you want to get this information from a properties file or the command line in real applications.

Maintaining Portability Using Properties Files

Though our focus is on MySQL, it is good Java programming practice to make your applications completely portable. To most people, portability means that you do not write code that will run on only one platform. In the Java world, however, the word "portable" is a much stronger term. It means no hardware resource dependencies, and that means no database dependencies.

We discussed how the JDBC URL and `Driver` name are implementation dependent, but we did not discuss the details of how to avoid hardcoding them. Because both are simple strings, you can pass them on the command line as runtime arguments or as parameters to applets. While that solution works, it is hardly elegant since it requires command-line users to remember long command lines. A similar solution might be to prompt the user for this information; but again, you are requiring that the user remember a JDBC URL and a Java class name each time he runs an application.

Properties files

A more elegant solution than either of those mentioned would be to use a properties file. Properties files are supported by the `java.util.ResourceBundle` and its subclasses to enable an application to extract runtime-specific information from a text file. For a JDBC application, you can stick the URL and `Driver` name in the properties file, leaving the details of the connectivity up to an application administrator. Example 13-2 shows a properties file that provides connection information.

Example 13-2. The SelectResource.properties file with connection details for a connection

```
Driver=org.gjt.mm.mysql.Driver
URL=jdbc:mysql://athens.imaginary.com/Web?user=someuser&password=somepass
```

Example 13-3 shows the portable `Connect` class.

Example 13-3. Using a properties file to maintain portability

```
import java.sql.*;
import java.util.*;

public class Connect {
    public static void main(String argv[]) {
        Connection con = null;
        ResourceBundle bundle = ResourceBundle.getBundle("SelectResource");
```

Example 13-3. Using a properties file to maintain portability (continued)

```
    try {
        String url = bundle.getString("URL");
        Statement stmt;
        ResultSet rs;

         Class.forName(bundle.getString("Driver"));
         // here is where the connection is made
         con = DriverManager.getConnection(url);
    }
    catch( SQLException e ) {
        e.printStackTrace( );
    }
    finally {
        if( con != null ) {
            try { con.close( ); }
            catch( Exception e ) { }
        }
    }
  }
}
```

We have gotten rid of anything specific to MySQL or the GNU driver in the sample connection code. One important issue still faces portable JDBC developers. JDBC requires that all drivers support the SQL2 entry level standard. This is an ANSI standard for minimum SQL support. As long as you use SQL2 entry level SQL in your JDBC calls, your application will be 100% portable to other database engines. Fortunately, MySQL is SQL2 entry level, even though it does not support many of the advanced SQL2 features.

Data sources revisited

Earlier in the chapter, we fudged a bit on how data sources were configured. Specifically, we stated that you can configure a data source using either a tool or through Java code. In most cases you will use a tool. The way you configure a data source is dependent on the vendor providing the data source. Now that you have a greater appreciation of connection properties, you should have a good idea of what you will need to configure a data source to support MySQL.

To better illustrate how a data source can be set up for an application, it helps to look at a real-world application environment. Orion is a J2EE compliant application server that is free for noncommercial use. In this application, it is serving up Java Server Pages (JSPs) that issue statements against a MySQL database. The JSP makes the following JDBC call to do its database work:

```
InitialContext ctx = new InitialContext( );
DataSource ds = (DataSource)ctx.lookup("jdbc/AddressBook");
Connection = ds.getConnection( );
```

This looks familiar so far? Of course, it begs the question: how exactly does jdbc/ AddressBook get configured? In Orion, you configure the data source by editing a file called *data-sources.xml*. Here is the entry for jdbc/AddressBook:

```
<data-source connection-driver="org.gjt.mm.mysql.Driver"
             class="com.evermind.sql.DriverManagerDataSource"
             name="AddressBook"
             url="jdbc:mysql://carthage/Address?user=test&amp;password=test"
             location="jdbc/AddressBook"/>
```

Simple Database Access

The Connect example did not do much. It simply showed you how to connect to MySQL. A database connection is useless unless you actually talk to the database. The simplest forms of database access are SELECT, INSERT, UPDATE, and DELETE statements. Under the JDBC API, you use your database Connection instance to create Statement instances. A Statement represents any kind of SQL statement. Example 13-4 shows how to insert a row into a database using a Statement.

Example 13-4. Inserting a row into MySQL using a JDBC Statement object

```
import java.sql.*;
import java.util.*;

public class Insert {
    // We are inserting into a table that has two columns: TEST_ID (int)
    // and TEST_VAL (char(55))
    // args[0] is the TEST_ID and args[1] the TEST_VAL
    public static void main(String argv[]) {
        Connection con = null;
        ResourceBundle bundle = ResourceBundle.getBundle("SelectResource");

        try {
            String url = bundle.getString("URL");
            Statement stmt;

            Class.forName(bundle.getString("Driver"));
            // here is where the connection is made
            con = DriverManager.getConnection(url, "user", "pass");
            stmt = con.createStatement();
            stmt.executeUpdate("INSERT INTO TEST (TEST_ID, TEST_VAL) " +
                        "VALUES(" + args[0] + ", '" + args[1] + "')");
        }
        catch( SQLException e ) {
            e.printStackTrace();
        }
        finally {
            if( con != null ) {
                try { con.close(); }
                catch( Exception e ) { }
```

Example 13-4. Inserting a row into MySQL using a JDBC Statement object (continued)

```
            }
        }
    }
}
```

If this were a real application, we would of course verify that the user entered an INT for the TEST_ID, that it was not a duplicate key, and that the TEST_VAL entry did not exceed 55 characters. This example nevertheless shows how simple it is to perform an insert. The createStatement( ) method does just what it says: it creates an empty SQL statement associated with the Connection in question. The executeUpdate( ) method then passes the specified SQL on to the database for execution. As its name implies, executeUpdate( ) expects SQL that will modify the database in some way. You can use it to insert new rows, as shown earlier, or to delete rows, update rows, create new tables, or do any other database modification.

Queries and Result Sets

Queries are a bit more complicated than updates because queries return information from the database in the form of a ResultSet. A ResultSet is an interface that represents zero or more rows matching a database query. A JDBC Statement has an executeQuery( ) method that works like the executeUpdate( ) method, except it returns a ResultSet from the database. Exactly one ResultSet is returned by executeQuery( ). JDBC supports the retrieval of multiple result sets, but MySQL does not. You may notice code for multiple result sets if you look at code written for another database.

Example 13-5 shows a simple query. Figure 13-2 shows the data model behind the test table.

Example 13-5. A simple query

```
import java.sql.*;
import java.util.*;

public class Select {
    public static void main(String argv[]) {
        Connection con = null;
        ResourceBundle bundle =
                ResourceBundle.getBundle("SelectResource");

        try {
            String url = bundle.getString("URL");
            Statement stmt;
            ResultSet rs;

             Class.forName(bundle.getString("Driver"));
            // here is where the connection is made
            con = DriverManager.getConnection(url, "user", "pass");
```

Example 13-5. A simple query (continued)

```
            stmt = con.createStatement();
            rs = stmt.executeQuery("SELECT * from TEST ORDER BY TEST_ID");
            System.out.println("Got results:");
            while(rs.next()) {
                int a= rs.getInt("TEST_ID");
                String str = rs.getString("TEST_VAL");

                System.out.print(" key= " + a);
                System.out.print(" str= " + str);
                System.out.print("\n");
            }
            stmt.close();
        }
        catch( SQLException e ) {
            e.printStackTrace();
        }
        finally {
            if( con != null ) {
                try { con.close(); }
                catch( Exception e ) { }
            }
        }
    }
}
```

Figure 13-2. The test table from the sample database

The Select application executes the query and loops through each row in the ResultSet using the next( ) method. Until the first call to next( ), the ResultSet does not point to any row. Each call to next( ) points the ResultSet to the subsequent row. You are done processing rows when next( ) returns false.

You can specify that your result set is scrollable, meaning you can move around in the result set—not just forward on a row-by-row basis. The ResultSet instances generated by a Statement are scrollable if the statement was created to support scrollable result sets. Connection enables this through an alternate form of the createStatement( ) method:

```
Statement stmt = conn.createStatement(ResultSet.TYPE_SCROLL_SENSITIVE,
                                      ResultSet.CONCUR_READ_ONLY);
```

The first argument says that any result sets of the newly created statement should be scrollable. By default, a statement's result sets are not scrollable. The second argument relates to an advanced feature of JDBC, updatable result sets, which lie beyond the scope of this book. They are described in *Database Programming with JDBC and Java*, by George Reese (O'Reilly).

With a scrollable result set, you can make calls to previous() to navigate backwards through the results and to absolute() and relative() to move to arbitrary rows. Like next(), previous() moves one row through the result set, except in the opposite direction. The previous() method returns false when you attempt to move before the first row. Finally, absolute() moves the result set to a specific row, whereas relative() moves the result set a specific number of rows before or after the current row.

Dealing with a row means getting the values for each of its columns. Whatever the value in the database, you can use the getter methods in the ResultSet to retrieve the column value as the Java data type you want. In the Select application, the call to getInt() returned the TEST_ID column as an int, and the call to getString() returned the TEST_VAL column as a String. These getter methods accept either the column number—starting with column 1—or the column name. You should, however, avoid retrieving values using a column name because it is much slower than retrieving them by column number.

One area of mismatch between Java and MySQL lies in the concept of an SQL NULL. Specifically, SQL is able to represent some data types as null that Java cannot represent as null. In particular, Java has no way of representing primitive data types as nulls. As a result, you cannot immediately determine whether a 0 returned from MySQL through getInt() means a 0 is in that column or no value is in that column.

JDBC addresses this mismatch through the wasNull() method. As its name implies, wasNull() returns true if the last value fetched was SQL NULL. For calls returning a Java object, the value will generally be NULL when an SQL NULL is read from the database. In these instances, wasNull() may appear somewhat redundant. For primitive datatypes, however, a valid value—such as 0—may be returned on a fetch. The wasNull() method gives you a way to see if that value was NULL in the database.

Error Handling and Clean Up

All JDBC method calls can throw SQLException or one of its subclasses if something happens during a database call. Your code should be set up to catch this exception, deal with it, and clean up any database resources that have been allocated. Each of the JDBC classes mentioned so far has a close() method associated with it. Practically speaking, however, you only really need to make sure you close things whose calling processes might remain open for a while. In the examples we have seen so far, you only really need to close your database connections. Closing the database connection closes any statements and result sets associated with it automatically. If you intend to leave a connection open for any period of time, however, it is a good idea to close the statements you create using that connection when you finish with them. In the JDBC examples you have seen, this clean up happens in a `finally` clause. You do this since you want to make sure to close the database connection no matter what happens.

Dynamic Database Access

So far, we have dealt with applications in which you know exactly what needs to be done at compile time. If this were the only kind of database support that JDBC provided, no one could ever write tools like the *mysql* interactive command-line tool that determines SQL calls at runtime and executes them. The JDBC `Statement` class provides the execute( ) method for executing SQL that can be either a query or an update. Additionally, `ResultSet` instances provide runtime information about themselves in the form of an interface called `ResultSetMetaData`, which you can access via the getMetaData( ) call in the `ResultSet`.

Metadata

The term metadata sounds officious, but it is really nothing more than extra data about some object that would otherwise waste resources if it were actually kept in the object. For example, simple applications do not need the name of the columns associated with a `ResultSet`—the programmer probably knew that when the code was written. Embedding this extra information in the `ResultSet` class is thus not considered by JDBC's designers to be part of the core of `ResultSet` functionality. Data such as the column names, however, is very important to some database programmers—especially those writing dynamic database access. The JDBC designers provide access to this extra information—the metadata—via the `ResultSetMetaData` interface. This class specifically provides:

- The number of columns in a result set
- Whether `NULL` is a valid value for a column
- The label to use for a column header
- The name for a given column
- The source table for a given column
- The data type of a given column

Example 13-6 shows some of the source code from a command-line tool that accepts arbitrary user input and sends it to MySQL for execution. The rest of the code for this example can be found at the O'Reilly web site with the other examples from this book.

Example 13-6. An application for executing dynamic SQL

```java
import java.sql.*;

public class Exec {
    public static void main(String args[]) {
        Connection con = null;
        String sql = "";

        for(int i=0; i<args.length; i++) {
            sql = sql + args[i];
            if( i < args.length - 1 ) {
                sql = sql + " ";
            }
        }
        System.out.println("Executing: " + sql);
        try {
            Class.forName("com.caucho.jdbc.mysql.Driver").newInstance( );
            String url = "jdbc:mysql-caucho://athens.imaginary.com/TEST";
            con = DriverManager.getConnection(url, "test", "test");
            Statement s = con.createStatement( );

            if( s.execute(sql) ) {
                ResultSet r = s.getResultSet( );
                ResultSetMetaData meta = r.getMetaData( );
                int cols = meta.getColumnCount( );
                int rownum = 0;

                while( r.next() ) {
                    rownum++;
                    System.out.println("Row: " + rownum);
                    for(int i=0; i<cols; i++) {
                        System.out.print(meta.getColumnLabel(i+1) + ": "
                                        + r.getObject(i+1) +  ", ");
                    }
                    System.out.println("");
                }
            }
            else {
                System.out.println(s.getUpdateCount( ) + " rows affected.");
            }
            s.close( );
            con.close( );
        }
        catch( Exception e ) {
            e.printStackTrace( );
        }
        finally {
            if( con != null ) {
                try { con.close(); }
                catch( SQLException e ) { }
            }
        }
    }
}
```

Each result set provides a ResultSetMetaData instance via the getMetaData( ) method. In the case of dynamic database access, we need to find out how many columns are in a result set so we are certain to retrieve each column as well as the names of each column for display to the user. The metadata for our result set provides all of this information via the getColumnCount( ) and getColumnLabel( ) methods.

Processing Dynamic SQL

The overriding concept introduced in Example 13-6 is the dynamic SQL call. Because we do not know whether we will be processing a query or an update, we need to pass the SQL call through the execute( ) method. This method returns true if the statement returned a result set or false if none was produced. In the example, if it returns true, the application gets the returned ResultSet through a call to getResultSet( ). The application can then go on to do normal result set processing. If, on the other hand, the statement performed some sort of database modification, you can call getUpdateCount( ) to find out how many rows were modified by the statement.

A Guest Book Servlet

You have probably heard quite a bit about Java applets. We discussed in Chapter 8, however, how doing database access in the client is a really bad idea. We have packaged with the examples in this book a servlet that uses the JDBC knowledge we have discussed in this chapter to store the comments from visitors to a web site in a database and display the comments in the database. While servlets are not in themselves part of the three-tier solution we discussed in Chapter 8, this example should provide a useful example of how JDBC can be used. For this example, all you need to know about servlets is that the doPost( ) method handles HTTP POST events, and doGet( ) handles HTTP GET events. The rest of the code is either simple Java code or an illustration of the database concepts from this chapter. You can see the servlet in action at *http://www.imaginary.com/~george/guestbook.shtml*.

## CHAPTER 14

Extending MySQL

Within the spectrum of relational database management systems, MySQL has always occupied a unique position. Its open source nature and fast performance have made it the most popular database server for small-to-medium web-based applications. However, its lack of support for features such as transactions, foreign keys, row-level locking, and stored procedures have made many pass over it for other applications, though its performance would otherwise be beneficial.

As MySQL has matured over time, various solutions have emerged for all these problems. Through alternative table types such as Berkeley DB and InnoDB, MySQL now supports transactions and row-level locking. Thanks to the InnoDB table type, the MySQL team has added support for foreign keys.

One of MySQL's virtues is that it is intended to be extended. For example, stored procedures remain the most requested Oracle/SQL Server/Sybase feature lacking in MySQL. Though MySQL currently has no support for stored procedures (it probably will by the time you read this book), you can extend MySQL by writing your own user-defined functions (UDFs). In this chapter, we examine how to write your own functions and add character sets to MySQL.

User-Defined Functions

UDFs are simply native programming functions. MySQL links to the libraries containing them and executes them as SQL functions in the same way you have used the PASSWORD( ) and NOW( ) functions. MySQL gives these functions access to the internals of MySQL and empowers them to manipulate data.

You will generally write UDFs in C. The examples in this chapter are all in C. However, because MySQL accesses your functions through shared libraries, you can write them in any language that you can compile into a native-code shared library. In other words, you can write a UDF in C, C++, Objective C, C#, Java, VisualBasic, or even Pascal.

MySQL supports two types of UDFs: standard and aggregate. MySQL applies standard functions to each row in the result set. PASSWORD( ) and DAYNAME( ) are examples of two common standard functions built into MySQL. If you execute the SQL in the mysql database:

```
SELECT UPPER(User) FROM user;
```

you will see the name of each user in your database in all capital letters.

An aggregate function operates on groups of rows. You generally execute aggregate functions in conjunction with the SQL GROUP BY clause. This clause causes MySQL to group result sets into sections, in which each section is a single row. An aggregate function operates on all of the values of each group. AVG( ) and MAX( ) are examples of two common aggregate functions built into MySQL:

```
SELECT AVG(age) FROM People GROUP BY city;
```

The result of this query is a single column containing the average of all age values for people who live in the same city.

You create aggregate and standard functions in much the same manner—aggregate functions simply have two extra routines.

Standard Functions

Create a standard UDF in three steps, two of which are optional:

init
> When an SQL query calls a UDF, the init routine for that function is called first, if it exists. This routine is responsible for allocating data and setting certain parameters for the main routine.

main
> After the init routine is called, the main routine for the desired UDF is called. This is the only routine required to exist to define a UDF. This routine is responsible for processing the data and returning the result of the function.

deinit
> Once the main routine is finished and the result is returned to the user, MySQL will call a deinit routine for the function, if it exists. The purpose of this routine is to deallocate any memory allocated by the init routine and clean up as necessary.

When an SQL query calls a standard function, these routines are called in the following manner:

```
init
   main
   main
   main
   ...
deinit
```

MySQL calls the main routine once for each row returned by the SQL query. The return values of the main routine comprise the results of the UDF as a whole.

When creating a UDF, all three routines must reside in the same library. You can, however, bundle multiple functions in the same library.

 We use the terms "routine" and "function" in a specific manner in this section to reduce the possibility of confusion. The problem is that multiple native functions make up a single UDF. When we refer to a routine, we mean one of the native functions that make up the UDF. When we refer to a function, we mean the UDF itself.

The init routine

The init routine is the first routine called when a user attempts to execute a UDF within a SQL query. For a function with the name remove_html( ), the init routine must have the name remove_html_init( ). The init function must have the following signature:

```
my_bool func_name_init(UDF_INIT *initid, UDF_ARGS *args, char *message);
```

The three parameters passed to the init routine are all pointers to modifiable data that will be made available to the main function.

initid

    This parameter is the main data structure used by the UDF engine. This structure will be made available to all three routines for a particular UDF. Any changes that need to be made to the default values of this structure should be made here in the init routine so they will be available for the main routine. The structure has the following members:

maybe_null

    This Boolean value indicates whether the function can return an SQL NULL value. By default, this value is false unless any of the function arguments are nullable, in which case the default is true. To be safe, if you want the function to return an SQL NULL value, set the value of this attribute to true within the init routine.

decimals

    This integer value indicates the maximum number of decimals in the result returned by this function. This attribute is used only if the function returns a numeric result. The default value of this attribute is determined by the arguments passed into the function. The number of decimals in the numeric argument with the most decimal places is used as the default. Since there is no way of knowing which values will be passed into the function, if you want to limit the number of decimals returned, set this attribute within the init routine.

max_length

This integer value indicates the maximum number of characters (or digits) in the result returned by this function. The default value depends on the type of function and the arguments passed to it. For a string function, the default value is the length of the longest string argument. For an integer function, the default is 21 digits (one of which will be a sign character, if necessary). For a decimal function, the default is 13 digits or other characters (including any sign character or decimal point) plus the value of the decimals attribute (see above). There is no performance penalty for setting this value to a large number (in case the function returns a BLOB or other large value).

ptr

This generic pointer can be used arbitrarily by the routines for a UDF. It is most useful to pass some data between the three routines of the function or to include a reference to some data from another part of the application. If this pointer will be used for new data (that is, not a reference to some existing data), the memory should be allocated here in the init routine. The main routine will then receive the allocated pointer to use as it will.

args

This array contains the arguments passed in from the SQL query. Because the actual processing of the arguments is performed in the main routine, this structure is rarely touched during the init routine. There are two attributes of this structure that are sometimes accessed within the init routine:

arg_type

This attribute is an array of values that correspond to the constants STRING_RESULT, INT_RESULT, and REAL_RESULT. Within the main routine, this array indicates the types of arguments the routine is receiving. These types may not always be what the routine is expecting. Instead of returning an error, it is possible to force the arguments passed by the user into the types that the main routine will need. This is done by setting the value within the arg_type array in the init routine. For example, if the first argument needs to be a STRING-type argument, set the first element of this array to STRING_RESULT. This will cause any value passed in by the user (even an integer or real value) to be coerced into a string value before the main routine is called.

lengths

This attribute is an array of values that correspond to the length of each argument passed in by the user. Within the main routine, the attribute describes the actual length values of the arguments being passed in, row by row. Within the init routine, this attribute describes maximum possible length values for string arguments.

message

> This value is a character pointer used to store a user-level message about any error that occurs during the execution of the function. This preallocated character buffer is 200 characters wide by default. However, convention dictates keeping the message short enough to fit on one line. The message string must be terminated by a null byte.

The return value of the init routine is a my_bool (Boolean) type. If the initialization completes successfully, the routine should return 0 (false). If an error occurs, the routine should return 1 (true). In addition, in the case of an error, a user-level error message should be placed into the message argument.

The main routine

The main routine is the heart of the UDF. In fact, if no special initialization or cleanup is required, this routine is the only one needed to create a UDF. For a function with the name remove_html( ), the main routine should have the same name: remove_html( ).

The signature of the main routine depends on the return value of the UDF. There are three different SQL return values possible for UDFs: STRING, INTEGER, and REAL. The main routine for each of these types has the following signatures.

For a STRING:

```
char *func_name(UDF_INIT *initid, UDF_ARGS *args,
 char *result, unsigned long *length,
 char *is_null, char *error)
```

For an INTEGER:

```
long long func_name(UDF_INIT *initid, UDF_ARGS *args,
 char *is_null, char *error)
```

For a REAL:

```
double func_name(UDF_INIT *initid, UDF_ARGS *args,
 char *is_null, char *error)
```

All the different routine signatures handle incoming arguments the same way. The differences lie in how each routine returns the result. We will consider the four parameters that are identical among the signatures first:

initid

> This is the main data structure used by the UDF engine. It is a UDF_INIT structure, which is described in the previous section. Any of the attributes set during the init routine (including the generic data ptr attribute) are available during the main routine. Although there are no hard rules on the matter, the attributes of these structures should be accessed read-only from within the main routine. This is because all the initialization is done during the init routine, and all the deinitialization is done during the deinit routine. Therefore, in the middle, there is no need to modify these values.

args

> These are the arguments passed in from the SQL query as a UDF_ARGS structure with the following attributes:

arg_count

> This is the number of arguments passed into the UDF from the SQL query. If you want the UDF to have a fixed number of arguments, you can check the value here and return an error if the number is not correct. Otherwise, UDFs can support variable numbers of arguments.

arg_type

> This is an array of type identifiers that indicate the SQL type of each argument. The number of elements in this array is equal to the arg_count attribute. Checking the values of the arg_type array in the main routine allows strict type checking of the incoming arguments. However, as mentioned in the previous section, it is generally more flexible to set the desired types in the init routine. This will transform them from whatever the user passed in to whatever types the main routine is expecting. The values of the arg_type attribute correspond to the constants STRING_RESULT, INT_RESULT, and REAL_RESULT, defined in the MySQL development headers.

args

> This is an array of the actual arguments passed to the function. As mentioned above, the number of elements in this array is given by the arg_count property. The values of the arguments depend on two factors: the type of the argument and whether the argument was a constant value. Table 14-1 contains a mapping of types to C types. To accommodate these different possibilities, the elements of the args array are passed around as generic void pointers. You must therefore cast them to the appropriate C type.

Table 14-1. The mapping of MySQL result types to C types

Result type	C type
STRING_RESULT	char *
INT_RESULT	long long
REAL_RESULT	double

lengths

> This value is an array of the lengths of the arguments passed to the UDF. As with the other array attributes (arg_type and args), the length of the array is given by the arg_count attribute. Each value of the array is the length of that argument (and hence the length of the corresponding element in the args array). For string arguments, the value is the accurate length of the string for that particular call to the function. Because the function will be called once for each row in the SQL query, this value will change to reflect the length of

a string argument each time. Integer and decimal arguments have fixed lengths that are either defaults or set within the init routine.

is_null

This argument is a pointer to an integer value. If the UDF is returning a NULL value for a particular call to the function, set the value of this integer to 1. Otherwise, leave it at the default of 0.

error

This argument is a pointer to an integer value. If an error occurs during the main routine of the UDF, set the value of this integer to 1. This will return a NULL value for this particular call to the function. In addition, the main routine will not be called for any subsequent rows of data in the query that called the UDF, and NULL will be returned for each row.

There are two additional arguments specific to UDF that return STRING results:

result

This argument is a pointer to a character array. The return value of the UDF should be placed in the string referenced by this pointer. In addition, the pointer should be returned as the return value of the main routine (explained later). The MySQL UDF engine allocates 255 bytes as the buffer for a string return value. If the result fits within this limit, simply place the result into this buffer and return the pointer. If the result is bigger, you must use a string buffer that you have allocated. This allocation should be done by using the generic ptr attribute within the init routine. The result string should then be placed into this pointer, which should be returned as the return value of the function. If you take this route, the memory allocated for the pointer within the init routine should be deallocated in the deinit routine.

length

This argument is a pointer to an integer value. The value referenced by this pointer should be set to the length of the return value of the UDF. This does not include any trailing null characters. That is, if the return value of the function is the string make, the integer referenced by length should be set to 6.

The return value of the main routine depends upon the return value of the UDF as a whole. For INTEGER_RETURN functions, the main routine should return the return value of the function as a long long integer value. For REAL_RETURN functions, the main routine should return the return value of the function as a double value. For STRING_RETURN functions, the main routine should return the return value of the function as a pointer to a character array. As mentioned above, if the resulting value is less than 255 characters, this pointer should be the result pointer passed into the main routine. Otherwise, it should be a pointer allocated within the init routine.

The deinit routine

The deinit routine is responsible for freeing any memory allocated by the init routine and performing any other necessary cleanup. For a UDF with the name remove_html( ), the deinit routine must have the name remove_html_deinit( ). It has the following signature:

```
void func_name_deinit(UDF_INIT *initid)
```

The deinit routine takes one argument, the main UDF_INIT structure used by all three routines. This structure contains the generic ptr pointer that is available for generic use throughout the routines. If this pointer was allocated during the init routine, this deinit routine is responsible for freeing that memory. The deinit routine returns no value.

Example 14-1 shows a UDF that returns the contents of an image file, given the filename of that image. This function could be used to efficiently access image data without storing that data as a BLOB in the database.

Example 14-1. A UDF that returns the contents of an image file based on its filename

```
#include <mysql/my_global.h>
#include <mysql/my_sys.h>
#include <mysql/mysql.h>
#include <mysql/m_ctype.h>
#include <mysql/m_string.h>

#define MAX_IMAGE_SIZE 1048576
#define MAX_FILE_NAME 1024

/* Our 'init' routine is responsible for some simple set-up:
        - Check the argument count. This function must have exactly
                one argument, the filename, so we return an error
                if there are any other number.
        - Coerce the types of the arguments. Theoretically, the
                image names could be stored as integer IDs
                (and thus stored in files with simple numbers
                for names in the filesystem). Therefore, we want
                to allow any type of argument, and coerce it to a string.
        - Allocate the data buffer to hold the image data. This is a fairly large
                buffer to accommodate images of differing sizes.
*/
my_bool getImage_init(UDF_INIT *initid, UDF_ARGS *args, char *message) {
    if (args->arg_count != 1) {
        strmov(message,"Usage: getImage( fileName )");
        return 1;
    }
    args->arg_type[0] = STRING_RESULT;
    if ( !(initid->ptr =
        (char *) malloc( sizeof(char) * MAX_IMAGE_SIZE ) ) ) {
        strmov(message, "Couldn't allocate memory!");
        return 1;
    }
}
```

Example 14-1. A UDF that returns the contents of an image file based on its filename (continued)

```
        bzero( initid->ptr, sizeof(char) * MAX_IMAGE_SIZE );
        return 0;
}


/* This routine frees the memory allocated by the image buffer */
void getImage_deinit(UDF_INIT *initid) {
    if (initid->ptr)
        free(initid->ptr);
}

/* The main routine does most of the work for this function. The argument
   passed to the function is the filename of an image file. This function first
   uses 'chdir' to set the directory to the directory of the image file. This
   prevents misuse of this function by using it to read an arbitrary file on
   the filesystem. (We also remember the old working directory so that we can
   reset it at the end.)

   Once we've set the current directory, we open the image file using the
   Filename passed in as the argument. If the image opens successfully, we read
   the contents of the file into the empty data buffer.

   Before returning the data, we set the length pointer to tell MySQL how
   Large our image buffer is. Finally, we return the pointer to the data
   as the string result of this function.
*/
char *getImage(UDF_INIT *initid, UDF_ARGS *args, char *result,
               unsigned long *length, char *is_null, char *error) {
    FILE *img_file;
    size_t img_size;
    char filename[MAX_FILE_NAME];
    char old_dir[MAX_FILE_NAME];

    bzero(filename, MAX_FILE_NAME);
    bzero(old_dir, MAX_FILE_NAME);

    getcwd(old_dir, MAX_FILE_NAME);
    chdir("/path/to/my/pictures");
    strncpy( filename, args->args[0], args->lengths[0] );
    img_file = fopen( filename, "r" );
    if (! img_file ) {
        *is_null = 1;
        return 0;
    }

    img_size =
        fread( (void *)initid->ptr, sizeof(char),
            MAX_IMAGE_SIZE, img_file );

    *length = (unsigned long)img_size;
    chdir(old_dir);
    fclose(img_file);
    return initid->ptr;
}
```

Aggregate Functions

As mentioned earlier, aggregate functions work just like standard functions except that they have a couple of extra routines. Those routines drive the aggregation for each group of data:

reset

> This routine is called at the beginning of each group of data. It resets any local data used to aggregate the data so that each group starts with an empty aggregation.

add

> This routine is called for each row of data within a group. The purpose of the function is to perform any data aggregation required for the group.

The order in which routines are called illustrates the differences between standard and aggregate functions:

```
init
  reset
      add
      add
      add
      ...
      main
  reset
      add
      add
      add
      ...
      main
  reset
      add
      add
      add
      ...
      main
  ...
  deinit
```

While a standard function is comprised of a single loop, an aggregate function is a loop of loops. For a standard function, the main routine is called for each row of data, which corresponds directly with each row of the result set. For an aggregate function, the rows of the result set are made up of groups, in which each row represents a group of rows of data. The add routine is called for each row of data (except the first), while the main routine is called only once for each group (resulting in one row of the result set).

While the signatures of the routines called within a standard function do not differ for an aggregate function, their roles are somewhat different.

init

Unlike a standard function, the init function is almost always used for aggregate functions. The `initid->ptr` generic pointer plays an important role, which it does not always do for other UDFs. This pointer is initialized to store data about a single group of data. As the rows are processed by the add routine, the data structure is populated. When the main routine is finally called for each group, it accesses the populated structure to perform the desired calculation.

All the other abilities of the init routine are also available for aggregate functions, such as forcing the arguments' types and sizes and indicating the return type.

reset

The reset routine works as a sort of init routine that is called once per group. For a function named calc_interest( ), the reset routine must be named `calc_interest_reset( )`. It has the following signature:

```
void func_name_reset(UDF_INIT* initid, UDF_ARGS* args,
                     char* is_null, char *error )
```

The arguments are those already covered under the main routine. The reset routine returns no value. At the beginning of each group, this routine is called to clear out any data that is used on per-group data. This is generally stored in the `initid->ptr` pointer as a data structure that contains the aggregated group data. This routine should zero out or otherwise clear this structure to prepare for a new group of data.

Because of an oddity in the MySQL UDF engine, the add routine does not get called for the first row of data in every group. Therefore, if your aggregate function needs to act upon every row of data (and most will), it is necessary to explicitly call the add routine from the reset routine. This is because this first row of data is passed to the reset routine, which can then pass it to the add routine. For each subsequent row of the group, the add routine will be called directly.

add

The add routine is called on every row of data except the first within every group of the SQL query. For a function named calc_interest( ), the add routine must be named calc_interest_add( ). It has the following signature:

```
void func_name_add(UDF_INIT* initid, UDF_ARGS* args,
                   char* is_null, char *error )
```

The arguments are those already covered under the main routine. The add routine returns no value. The purpose of the add routine is to aggregate the data from the rows that comprise each group specified in the SQL query. This is generally done by taking the data from the rows and accumulating it in a data structure (in some matter that makes sense to the operation). The data structure is usually stored in the `initid->ptr` pointer, allocated by the init routine.

main

As mentioned earlier, the purpose of the main routine is significantly different from that of a standard UDF. Instead of operating on single rows of data, the main routine operates on aggregated data collected by the add routine. This data is generally stored in a data structure referenced by the initid->ptr pointer, allocated by the init routine. The main routine takes the data from this structure and performs any calculation needed on the aggregated data.

The main routine returns the result in the same manner as a standard UDF.

deinit

The deinit routine works identically to that of a standard function. It will almost always exist for an aggregate function, because there is almost always an allocated initid->ptr structure to free.

Aggregate example

Example 14-2 is a UDF that calculates the average distance from the center of a range of points. This function takes two arguments, which correspond to the x and y coordinates of points on a graph. The function then aggregates all the points given to it by the SQL query and returns the distance from the center of the graph (x=0, y=0) to the average of all the points.

Example 14-2. An aggregate UDF that calculates the distance from the center of a graph

```
#include <mysql/my_global.h>
#include <mysql/my_sys.h>
#include <mysql/mysql.h>
#include <mysql/m_ctype.h>
#include <mysql/m_string.h>

/* This is the structure that defines the aggregate of all of the points
 * It contains the sum of all 'x' values, the sum of all 'y' values,
 * and the total number of points counted (for a single group).
 */
struct point {
    double x;
    double y;
    long count;
};

/* Our 'init' routine has several duties, this time:
        - Check the argument count. This function must have exactly
            two arguments, x and y, so we return an error if there are
            any other number.
        - Coerce the types of the arguments. Since we are dealing with decimal
            values, we don't want to penalize the user for passing in
            integers, or even numeric values stored within a string, so
            we coerce the incoming arguments into a 'real' type.
```

Example 14-2. An aggregate UDF that calculates the distance from the center of a graph (continued)

```
          - Set the 'maybe_null' flag to zero. This function will never return
                  a null value. Maybe a 'zero' value, but not null.
          - Set the 'decimals' flag to 5 and the 'max_length' flag to 10.
                  This will cause the results to be in the format +/-###.#####
                  with a guarantee of 5 decimal places and up to three integer
                  places.
          - Allocate the point structure. This structure will be used to house
                  the aggregate point data as we accumulate it.
*/
my_bool distanceFromCenter_init( UDF_INIT* initid, UDF_ARGS* args,
    char* message ) {

    /* Check number of arguments */
    if (args->arg_count != 2) {
        strmov(message,"Usage: distanceFromCenter( x, y )");
        return 1;
    }

    /* Coerce arguments to 'real' */
    args->arg_type[0] = REAL_RESULT;
    args->arg_type[1] = REAL_RESULT;

  /* Set flags */
    initid->maybe_null = 0;
    initid->decimals = 5;
    initid->max_length = 10;

    /* Allocate pointer */
    initid->ptr = malloc( sizeof( struct point ) );
    if (! initid->ptr ) {
        strmov(message, "Cannot allocate memory for 'point' structure");
        return 1;
    }
    return 0;
}

/* The 'deinit' routine only has to de-allocate the 'point' structure */
void distanceFromCenter_deinit( UDF_INIT* initid ) {
    free(initid->ptr);
}

/* The 'add' routine is called once for each row of data. It is responsible
   for aggregating the point information. It simply adds the 'x' and 'y'
   values to the totals stored in the point structure and then increments
   the count in the same structure.
*/
void distanceFromCenter_add( UDF_INIT* initid, UDF_ARGS* args,
    char* is_null, char *error ) {
    ((struct point *)initid->ptr)->x += *((double *)args->args[0]);
    ((struct point *)initid->ptr)->y += *((double *)args->args[0]);
    ((struct point *)initid->ptr)->count++;
}
```

Example 14-2. An aggregate UDF that calculates the distance from the center of a graph (continued)

```
/* The 'reset' routine is called at the beginning of each group. It simply
   zeros out the information  in the point structure in preperation for a new
   group of data. As mentioned earlier, this is the only routine called on the
   first row of data in a group. Therefore, we must also call the 'add' routine
   from this routine, to include the first row of data in the aggregate set.
*/
void distanceFromCenter_reset( UDF_INIT* initid, UDF_ARGS* args,
    char* is_null, char *error ) {
    ((struct point *)initid->ptr)->x = 0.0;
    ((struct point *)initid->ptr)->y = 0.0;
    ((struct point *)initid->ptr)->count = 0;
    distanceFromCenter_add( initid, args, is_null, error );
}

/* The 'main' routine has a very simple role here. It just has to take the
   aggregate data from the point structure and calculate a point (x,y) value
   for that data. It then runs the classic a^2 + b^2 = c^2 formula to determine
   the distance to the center of the grid for that point.
double distanceFromCenter( UDF_INIT* initid, UDF_ARGS* args,
    char* is_null, char *error ) {
    double avg_x, avg_y;

    /* Calculate the average 'x' and the average 'y' */
    avg_x = ((struct point *)initid->ptr)->x /
        (double)((struct point *)initid->ptr)->count;
    avg_y = ((struct point *)initid->ptr)->y /
        (double)((struct point *)initid->ptr)->count;

    /* Return the square root of a^2 + b^2 */
    return sqrt( avg_x * avg_x + avg_y * avg_y );
}
```

Calling a UDF

Now that we have successfully created the routines necessary for a UDF, the next step is to call those functions from an SQL query. This is accomplished in three steps:

1. Compiling the function routines
2. Loading the UDF
3. Running the UDF

As discussed earlier, the routines that make up a UDF can be implemented in any programming language that can be compiled into an operating system–level shared library. On most Unix-based systems, a shared library is indicated by a *.so* extension. In Microsoft Windows, shared libraries have *.dll* extensions.

Once the routines are written, use whatever procedure is generally followed for compiling source code into a shared library. For example, compiling a shared library from a C or C++ file using the GNU C Compiler on a Unix-based system can be accomplished with the following command:

```
gcc -shared -o myfunc.so myfunc.c
```

The -shared flag indicates that a shared library should be created from the functions within the source file. Different compilers, operating systems, and programming languages will have different methods for creating a shared library.

As mentioned earlier, multiple UDFs can be defined and implemented within a single shared library file. However, all the routines necessary for each function must be present within that file. That is, you can place multiple functions within a single shared library, but you cannot split the routines necessary for a single function between multiple libraries.

Once a shared library has been created, it should be placed somewhere on the operating system's filesystem that is designated for shared libraries. On Unix-based systems, this generally means the /lib and /usr/lib directories as well as any directories specified in the LD_LIBRARY_PATH environment variable (although the name of the environment variable differs on some Unix-based systems). For Microsoft Windows systems, this generally means the WINDOWS\System32 directory (where WINDOWS is the main Windows directory, often C:\Winnt for Windows NT and 2000 systems).

Finally, it may be necessary to restart the MySQL server for it to find the shared library file. This may not be necessary, though, so if restarting the MySQL server is an issue, first try to load the function library without restarting.

Once the shared library file is in a place that is accessible to the MySQL server, it is possible to access the UDF directly from MySQL. To do this, the UDF must be loaded, which generally means loading the shared library into MySQL's memory so it can access the function routines.

Loading a new UDF is accomplished through the SQL CREATE FUNCTION statement:

```
CREATE [AGGREGATE] FUNCTION function_name
RETURNS {STRING|REAL|INTEGER}
SONAME shared_library_name
```

Basically, this statement indicates the name of the UDF, its return type, and the shared library where it is located. The optional AGGREGATE keyword indicates that the function is an aggregate function.

The name of the function must be the name of the main routine used to implement the function. The name is case sensitive, so it must be capitalized the same way it is in the shared library.

The return type of the function is specified by one of the keywords STRING, REAL, or INTEGER. This value must match the return type of the main routine.

The shared library is given as an SQL literal string. It should be only the filename (not a directory path), and it is case sensitive. The shared library given here must be accessible to MySQL.

Behind the scenes, loading a UDF involves adding and removing data from the func table of the system mysql database. Therefore, to execute the CREATE FUNCTION statement, a user must have INSERT and DELETE privileges for that table (or for the whole database). In general, this should be restricted to administrative users, because loading arbitrary UDFs can give a user almost complete control over the MySQL system. (Imagine loading a function that kills the main MySQL process. Because the function is run from MySQL itself, nothing will stop it from shutting down the system abruptly.)

The following SQL calls add two UDFs, one standard and the other aggregate:

```
CREATE FUNCTION getImage RETURNS STRING SONAME 'myfuncs.so';
CREATE AGGREGATE FUNCTION distanceFromCenter
                RETURNS REAL SONAME 'myfuncs.so';
```

Once a UDF has been loaded into MySQL, it can be accessed just as if it were a built-in MySQL function, because MySQL functions are case insensitive. Even though it was necessary to specify the correct case when loading the function, once loaded, the function can be executed with any case:

```
SELECT GETIMAGE( image_name ) AS image FROM Product;
SELECT distanceFromCenter( x, y ) FROM Point GROUP BY shape_id
```

Alternative Character Sets

A character set defines the basic alphabet supported by a database. An encoding then maps the character set to the 1s and 0s understood by a computer. MySQL comes with support for a variety of character sets and encodings. Unfortunately, this support is very peculiar. MySQL ties the concepts of character set, encoding, and sorting rules together so that these three normally distinct concepts cannot be separated. While this scheme works well if you use one of the supported character sets with the built-in sorting rules, you may need to go to some extra lengths if the character sets that come with MySQL do not meet your needs.

First, you need to determine whether the character set needs special string collating routines for sorting and whether it needs multi-byte character support. If it needs either of these, it will need to be compiled in. Otherwise, support for the character set can be added by simply modifying the configuration.

Simple Character Sets

Additional character sets may be configured into MySQL if they don't require multi-byte character support or string collating routines. Adding a character set through configuration requires the following steps:

1. Add the new character set to the file *sql/share/charsets/Index.*[*]
2. Create the configuration file for the new character set in *sql/share/charsets*.
3. Edit your *configure.in* file to include the character set in the next compile.
4. Recompile MySQL.

In this example, we will add a special character set called *elvish*. We first need to add it to the character set index file. The file looks like this:

```
$ cat sql/share/charsets/Index
# sql/share/charsets/Index
#
# This file lists all of the available character sets. Please keep this
# file sorted by character set number.


big5            1
czech           2
dec8            3
 .
 .
 .
latin5          30
latin1_de       31
```

To add a new character set, simply add the character set to the end of the file with a unique index:

```
latin5          30
latin1_de       31
elvish          32
```

The next step is to create a configuration file in *sql/share/charsets* for your character set. You can base it on *sql/share/charsets/latin1.conf*.

```
$ cd sql/share/charsets
$ cp latin1.conf elvish.conf
$ vi elvish.conf
```

There are four array definitions in the configuration file. You need to edit each of these arrays to configure your character set. A # in the configuration file indicates a comment.

---

[*] The *charsets* directory may have different locations depending on your installation. This file might also be *share/mysql/charsets*, for example.

---

ctype*

The ctype array defines the features of each character in the character set. It consists of 257 hexadecimal words. Each word corresponds to a character in the character set, plus an additional character for EOF (for legacy reasons), and is a bitmask that defines the features of its corresponding characters. Table 14-2 shows the possible features. These are also defined in *include/m_ctype.h*. The ctype value for each character is the union of all the features that describe it. For example, "A" is an uppercase character (0001) and a hexadecimal digit (0200), so its ctype is 0001 + 0200 = 0201 octal. In hexadecimal, this is 81. So ctype['A' + 1] should contain 0x81.

Table 14-2. Character feature bitmask values

Feature	Bitmask (in octal)
Uppercase	0001
Lowercase	0002
Numeral (digit)	0004
Whitespace	0010
Punctuation	0020
Control character	0040
Blank	0100
Hexadecimal digit	0200

to_lower *and* to_upper

The to_lower and to_upper arrays contain, for each character, the corresponding upper- and lowercase character. So, for example to_lower['A'] should contain 'a', and to_upper['a'] should contain 'A'.

sort_order

MySQL uses the sort_order array to determine the sort order of characters in your character set. For character sets in which you want the sorting to be case insensitive, this will be the same as the to_upper array. If the sorting rules for your character set are too complicated to be handled by a simple table, you will need to compile in support for your character set.

Once you have configured your character set, you are ready to compile MySQL to include it. Before recompiling MySQL, you need to edit *configure.in* and add your new character set to CHARSETS_AVAILABLE:

```
CHARSETS_AVAILABLE="big5 cp1251 cp1257
                croat czech danish dec8 dos estonia euc_kr gb2312 gbk
                german1 greek hebrew hp8 hungarian koi8_ru koi8_ukr
```

---

* Note that the ctype array contains 257 words while the to_lower, to_upper, and sort_order arrays all contain 256 words. The ctype array is indexed by character value +1, while the others are indexed by character value.

```
            latin1 latin1_de latin2 latin5 sjis swe7 tis620 ujis
            usa7 win1250 win1251ukr elvish"
```

The last step is to compile MySQL:

```
$ make
$ make install
```

Complex Character Sets

Character sets requiring special string collating routines for sorting or multi-byte
character support will need custom work a configuration file simply cannot handle.
To accomplish this task, you will need to be familiar with C programming, as you
will need to create several C source files. If you plan to attempt this, it is highly recommended that you study the existing *ctype-*.c* files and base yours on these.

As with simple character sets, you need to edit the *sql/share/charsets/Index* and *con-
figure.in* files. Instead of a configuration file, however, you need to create a C source
file called *ctype-charset.c*. In our case, this file will be *ctype-elvish.c*. You can get a
head start with your character set file by copying the source file for a similar character set.

The first task in this source file is to define ctype, to_lower, to_upper, and sort_
order. These are the same arrays you configured in the previous section, except they
are defined as C arrays. You'll need to create:

- ctype_*charset*
- to_upper_*charset*
- to_lower_*charset*
- sort_order_*charset*

For our example, we need to create ctype_elvish, to_upper_elvish, to_lower_elvish,
and sort_order_elvish.

If you need string collating functions, you must write your own custom string collating functions. These functions should be named:

- my_strnncoll_*charset*
- my_strnxfrm_*charset*
- my_strcoll_*charset*
- my_strxfrm_*charset*
- my_like_range_*charset*

We therefore need to create my_strnncoll_elvish, my_strnxfrm_elvish, my_strcoll_
elvish, my_strxfrm_elvish, and my_like_range_elvish.

Multi-byte support requires the coding of special multi-byte functions:

- ismbchar_*charset*
- ismbhead_*charset*
- mbcharlen_*charset*

We need to create ismbchar_elvish, ismbhead_elvish, and mbcharlen_elvish.

With your coding complete, you need to create a comment header for your ctype file. This header should look like this:

```
/*
 * This comment is parsed by configure to create ctype.c,
 * so don't change it unless you know what you are doing.
 *
 * .configure. number_charset=[character set index number from Index file]
 * .configure. strxfrm_multiply_charset=[max ratio that strings may grow
 *                                      during my_strxfrm_charset - a
 *                                      positive integer]
 * .configure. mbmaxlen_charset=[size in bytes of largest char in set]
 */
```

For our example, this might look like:

```
 * .configure. number_elvish=32
 * .configure. strxfrm_multiply_elvish=1
 * .configure. mbmaxlen_elvish=2
```

Finally, compile MySQL and install your new binaries supporting the custom character set.

MySQL Reference

Part IV provides reference materials for the APIs we have covered in this book.

## CHAPTER 15

SQL Syntax for MySQL

In this chapter, we cover the full range of SQL supported by MySQL. MySQL supports the ANSI SQL2 standard. If you are interested in compatibility with other SQL databases, you should avoid using any proprietary MySQL extensions to the SQL standard.

Basic Syntax

SQL is a kind of controlled English language consisting of verb phrases. Each of these verb phrases begins with an SQL command followed by other SQL keywords, literals, identfiers, or punctuation. Keywords are never case sensitive. Identifiers for database names and table names are case sensitive when the underlying filesystem is case sensitive (this includes all Unix except Mac OS X) and case insensitive when the underlying filesystem is case insensitive (this includes Mac OS X and Windows). You should, however, avoid referring to the same database or table name in a single SQL statement using different cases—even if the underlying operating system is case insensitive. For example, the following SQL is troublesome:

```
SELECT TBL.COL FROM tbl;
```

Table aliases are case sensitive, but column aliases are case insensitive.

If all this case sensitivity nonsense is annoying, you can force MySQL to convert all table names to lowercase by starting *mysqld* with the argument *-O lower_case_table_names=1*.

Literals

Literals come in the following varieties:

String literals
   String literals may be enclosed either by single or double quotes. If you wish to be ANSI compatible, you should always use single quotes. Within a string literal, you may represent special characters through escape sequences. An escape

sequence is a backslash followed by another character to indicate to MySQL that the second character has a meaning other than its normal meaning. Table 15-1 shows the MySQL escape sequences. Quotes can also be escaped by doubling them up: `'This is a ''quote'''`. However, you do not need to double up on single quotes when the string is enclosed by double quotes: `"This is a 'quote'"`.

Binary literals

Like string literals, binary literals are enclosed in single or double quotes. You must use escape sequences in binary data to escape NUL (ASCII 0), " (ASCII 34), ' (ASCII 39), and \ (ASCII 92).

Number literals

Numbers appear as a sequence of digits. Negative numbers are preceded by a - sign and a . indicates a decimal point. You may also use scientific notation, as in: −45198.2164e+10.

Hexadecimal literals

MySQL also supports the use of hexadecimal literals in SQL. The way in which that hexadecimal is interpreted is dependent on the context. In a numeric context, the hexadecimal literal is treated is a numeric value. In a non-numeric context, it is treated as a binary value. For example, 0x1 + 1 is 2, but 0x4d7953514c by itself is MySQL.

Null

The special keyword NULL signifies a null literal in SQL. In the context of import files, the special escape sequence \N signifies a null value.

Table 15-1. MySQL escape sequences

Escape Sequence	Value
\0	NUL
\'	Single quote
\"	Double quote
\b	Backspace
\n	Newline
\r	Carriage return
\t	Tab
\z	Ctrl-z (workaround for Windows use of Ctrl-z as EOF)
\\	Backslash
\%	Percent sign (only in contexts where a percent sign would be interpreted as a wildcard)
_	Underscore (only in contexts where an underscore would be interpreted as a wildcard)

Identifiers

Identifiers are names you make up to reference database objects. In MySQL, database objects consist of databases, tables, and columns. These objects fit into a hierarchical namespace whose root element is the database in question. You can reference any given object on a MySQL server—assuming you have the proper rights—using one of the following conventions:

Absolute naming

Absolute naming is specifying the full tree of the object you are referencing. For example, the column `BALANCE` in the table `ACCOUNT` in the database `BANK` would be referenced absolutely as:

```
BANK.ACCOUNT.BALANCE
```

Relative naming

Relative naming allows you to specify only part of the object's name, with the rest of the name being assumed based on your current context. For example, if you are currently connected to the `BANK` database, you can reference the `BANK.ACCOUNT.BALANCE` column simply as `ACCOUNT.BALANCE`. In an SQL query where you have specified that you are selecting from the `ACCOUNT` table, you can reference the column using only `BALANCE`. You must provide an extra layer of context whenever relative naming might result in ambiguity. An example of such ambiguity would be a `SELECT` statement pulling from two tables that both have `BALANCE` columns.

Aliasing

Aliasing enables you to reference an object using an alternate name that helps avoid both ambiguity and the need to fully qualify a long name.

In general, MySQL allows you to use any character in an identifier.[*] This rule is limited, however, for databases and tables, because these values must be treated as files on the local filesystem. You can therefore use only characters valid for the underlying filesystem's filenaming conventions in a database or table name. Specifically, you may not use / or . in a database or table name. You can never use NUL (ASCII 0) or ASCII 255 in an identifier.

Given these rules, it is very easy to shoot yourself in the foot when naming things. As a general rule, it is a good idea to stick to alphanumeric characters from whatever character set you are using.

When an identifier is also an SQL keyword, you must enclose the identifier in backticks:

```
CREATE TABLE `select` ( `table` INT NOT NULL PRIMARY KEY AUTO_INCREMENT);
```

Since Version 3.23.6, MySQL supports the quoting of identifiers using both backticks and double quotes. For ANSI compatibility, however, you should use double quotes for quoting identifiers. You must, however, be running MySQL in ANSI mode.

---

[*] Older versions of MySQL limited identifiers to valid alphanumeric characters from the default character set as well as $ and _.

Comments

You can introduce comments in your SQL to specify text that should not be interpreted by MySQL. This is particularly useful in batch scripts for creating tables and loading data. MySQL specifically supports three kinds of commenting: C, shell-script, and ANSI SQL commenting.

C commenting treats anything between /* and */ as comments. Using this form of commenting, your comments can span multiple lines. For example:

```
/*
 * Creates a table for storing customer account information.
 */
DROP TABLE IF EXISTS ACCOUNT;

CREATE TABLE ACCOUNT ( ACCOUNT_ID BIGINT NOT NULL PRIMARY KEY AUTO_INCREMENT,
                       BALANCE DECIMAL(9,2) NOT NULL );
```

Within C comments, MySQL still treats single quotes and double quotes as a start to a string literal. In addition, a semicolon in the comment will cause MySQL to think you are done with the current statement.

Shell-script commenting treats anything from a # character to the end of a line as a comment:

```
CREATE TABLE ACCOUNT ( ACCOUNT_ID BIGINT NOT NULL PRIMARY KEY AUTO_INCREMENT,
                       BALANCE DECIMAL(9,2) NOT NULL ); # Not null ok?
```

MySQL does not really support ANSI SQL commenting, but it comes close. ANSI SQL commenting is distinguished by adding -- to the end of a line. MySQL supports two dashes and a space ('-- ') followed by the comment. The space is the non-ANSI part:

```
DROP TABLE IF EXISTS ACCOUNT; -- Drop the table if it already exists
```

SQL Commands

In this section, we present the full syntax of all commands accepted by MySQL.

ALTER TABLE

Syntax

```
ALTER [IGNORE] TABLE table action_list
```

Description

The ALTER statement covers a wide range of actions that modify the structure of a table. This statement is used to add, change, or remove columns from an existing table as well as to remove indexes. To perform modifications on the table, MySQL creates a copy of the table and changes it, meanwhile queuing all table altering queries. When the change is done, the old table is removed and the new table put in its place. At this point the queued queries are performed.

As a safety precaution, if any of the queued queries create duplicate keys that should be unique, the ALTER statement is rolled back and cancelled. If the IGNORE keyword is present in the statement, duplicate unique keys are ignored and the ALTER statement proceeds as if normal. Be warned that using IGNORE on an active table with unique keys is inviting table corruption.

Possible actions in action_list include:

ADD [COLUMN] *create_clause* [FIRST | AFTER *column*]
ADD [COLUMN] (*create_clause, create_clause,...*)
> Adds a new column to the table. The *create_clause* is the SQL that would define the column in a normal table creation (see CREATE TABLE for the syntax and valid options). The column will be created as the first column if the FIRST keyword is specified. Alternately, you can use the AFTER keyword to specify which column it should be added after. If neither FIRST nor AFTER is specified, the column is added at the end of the table's column list. You may add multiple columns at once by enclosing multiple create clauses separated with commas, inside parentheses.

ADD [CONSTRAINT *symbol*] FOREIGN KEY *name* (*column, ...*) [*reference*]
> Currently applies only to the InnoDB table type, which supports foreign keys.

ADD FULLTEXT [*name*] (*column, ...*)
> Adds a new full text index to the table using the specified columns.

ADD INDEX [*name*] (*column, ...*)
> Adds an index to the altered table, indexing the specified columns. If the name is omitted, one will be chosen automatically by MySQL.

ADD PRIMARY KEY (*column, ...*)
> Adds a primary key consisting of the specified columns to the table. An error occurs if the table already has a primary key.

ADD UNIQUE[*name*] (*column, ...*)
> Adds a unique index to the altered table; similar to the ADD INDEX statement.

ALTER [COLUMN] *column* SET DEFAULT *value*
> Assigns a new default value for the specified column. The COLUMN keyword is optional and has no effect.

ALTER [COLUMN] *column* DROP DEFAULT
> Drops the current default value for the specified column. A new default value will be assigned to the column based on the CREATE statement used to create the table. The COLUMN keyword is optional and has no effect.

DISABLE KEYS
> Tells MySQL to stop updating indexes for MyISAM tables. This clause applies only to non-unique indexes. Because MySQL is more efficient at rebuilding its keys than it is at building them one at a time, you may want to disable keys while performing bulk inserts into a database. You should avoid this trick, however, if you have read operations going against the table while the inserts are running.

ENABLE KEYS
> Recreates the indexes no longer being updated because of a prior call to DISABLE KEYS.

CHANGE [COLUMN] *column create_clause*
MODIFY [COLUMN] *create_clause [FIRST | AFTER column]*
> Alters the definition of a column. This statement is used to change a column from one type to a different type while affecting the data as little as possible. The create clause is the same syntax as in the CREATE TABLE statement. This includes the name of the column. The MODIFY version is the same as CHANGE if the new column has the same name as the old. The COLUMN keyword is optional and has no effect. MySQL will try its best to perform a reasonable conversion. Under no circumstance will MySQL give up and return an error when using this statement; a conversion of some sort will always be done. With this in mind you should make a backup of the data before the conversion and immediately check the new values to see if they are reasonable.

DROP [COLUMN] *column*
> Deletes a column from a table. This statement will remove a column and all its data from a table permanently. There is no way to recover data destroyed in this manner other than from backups. All references to this column in indexes will be removed. Any indexes where this was the sole column will be destroyed as well. (The COLUMN keyword is optional and has no effect.)

DROP PRIMARY KEY
> Drops the primary key from the table. If no primary key is found in the table, the first unique key is deleted.

DROP INDEX *key*
> Removes an index from a table. This statement will completely erase an index from a table. This statement will not delete or alter any of the table data itself, only the index data. Therefore, an index removed in this manner can be recreated using the ALTER TABLE ... ADD INDEX statement.

RENAME [AS] *new_table*
RENAME [TO] *new_table*
> Changes the name of the table. This operation does not affect any of the data or indexes within the table, only the table's name. If this statement is performed alone, without any other ALTER TABLE clauses, MySQL will not create a temporary table as with the other clauses, but simply perform a fast Unix-level rename of the table files.

ORDER BY *column*
> Forces the table to be reordered by sorting on the specified column name. The table will no longer be in this order when new rows are inserted. This option is useful for optimizing tables for common sorting queries.

table_options
> Enables a redefinition of the tables options such as the table type.

Multiple ALTER statements may be combined into one using commas, as in the following example:

```
ALTER TABLE mytable DROP myoldcolumn, ADD mynewcolumn INT
```

To perform any of the ALTER TABLE actions, you must have SELECT, INSERT, DELETE, UPDATE, CREATE, and DROP privileges for the table in question.

Examples

```
# Add the field 'address2' to the table 'people' and make
# it of type 'VARCHAR' with a maximum length of 100.
ALTER TABLE people ADD COLUMN address2 VARCHAR(100)
# Add two new indexes to the 'hr' table, one regular index for the
# 'salary' field and one unique index for the 'id' field. Also, continue
# operation if duplicate values are found while creating
# the 'id_idx' index (very dangerous!).
ALTER TABLE hr ADD INDEX salary_idx ( salary )
ALTER IGNORE TABLE hr ADD UNIQUE id_idx ( id )
# Change the default value of the 'price' field in the
# 'sprockets' table to $19.95.
ALTER TABLE sprockets ALTER price SET DEFAULT '$19.95'
# Remove the default value of the 'middle_name' field in the 'names' table.
ALTER TABLE names ALTER middle_name DROP DEFAULT
# Change the type of the field 'profits' from its previous value (which was
# perhaps INTEGER) to BIGINT. The first instance of 'profits'
# is the column to change, and the second is part of the create clause.
ALTER TABLE finances CHANGE COLUMN profits profits BIGINT
# Remove the 'secret_stuff' field from the table 'not_private_anymore'
ALTER TABLE not_private_anymore DROP secret_stuff
# Delete the named index 'id_index' as well as the primary key from the
# table 'cars'.
ALTER TABLE cars DROP INDEX id_index, DROP PRIMARY KEY
# Rename the table 'rates_current' to 'rates_1997'
ALTER TABLE rates_current RENAME AS rates_1997
```

ANALYZE TABLE

Syntax

```
ANALYZE TABLE table1, table2, ..., tablen
```

Description

Acquires a read lock on the table and performs an analysis on it for MyISAM and BDB tables. The analysis examines the key distribution in the table. It returns a result set with the following columns:

Table
> The name of the table.

Op
> The value analyze.

Msg_type
> One of status, error, or warning.

Msg_text
> The message resulting from the analysis.

CREATE DATABASE

Syntax

CREATE DATABASE [IF NOT EXISTS] *dbname*

Description

Creates a new database with the specified name. You must have the proper privileges to create the database. Running this command is the same as running the *mysqladmin create* utility.

Example

    CREATE DATABASE Bank;

CREATE FUNCTION

Syntax

CREATE [AGGREGATE] FUNCTION *name*
RETURNS *return_type* SONAME *library*

Description

The CREATE FUNCTION statement allows MySQL statements to access precompiled executable functions known as user-defined functions (UDFs). These functions can perform practically any operation, since they are designed and implemented by the user. The return value of the function can be STRING, for character data; REAL, for floating point numbers; or INTEGER, for integer numbers. MySQL will translate the return value of the C function to the indicated type. The library file that contains the function must be a standard shared library that MySQL can dynamically link into the server. See Chapter 14 for more information.

Example

    CREATE FUNCTION multiply RETURNS REAL SONAME mymath

CREATE INDEX

Syntax

CREATE [UNIQUE|FULLTEXT] INDEX *name*
ON *table* (*column, ...*)

Description

The CREATE INDEX statement is provided for compatibility with other implementations of SQL. In older versions of SQL this statement does nothing. As of 3.22, this statement is equivalent to the ALTER TABLE ADD INDEX statement. To perform the CREATE INDEX statement, you must have INDEX privileges for the table in question.

The UNIQUE keyword constrains the table to having only one row in which the index columns have a given value. If the index is multicolumn, individual column values may be repeated; the whole index must be unique.

The FULLTEXT keyword enables keyword searching on the indexed column or columns.

Example

```
CREATE UNIQUE INDEX TransIDX ON Translation ( language, locale, code );
```

CREATE TABLE

Syntax

```
CREATE [TEMPORARY] TABLE [IF NOT EXISTS] table
(create_clause, ...) [table_options]
[[IGNORE|REPLACE] select]
```

Description

The CREATE TABLE statement defines the structure of a table within the database. This statement is how all MySQL tables are created. If the TEMPORARY keyword is used, the table exists only as long as the current client connection exists, or until you explicitly drop the table.

The IF NOT EXISTS clause tells MySQL to create the table only if the table does not already exist. If the table does exist, nothing happens. If the table exists and IF NOT EXISTS and TEMPORARY are not specified, an error will occur. If TEMPORARY is specified and the table exists but IF NOT EXISTS is not specified, the existing table will simply be invisible to this client for the duration of the new temporary table's life.

The CREATE clause can either define the structure of a specific column or define a meta-structure for the column. A CREATE clause that defines a column consists of the name of the new table followed by any number of field definitions. The syntax of a field definition is:

```
column type [NOT NULL | NULL] [DEFAULT value]
[AUTO_INCREMENT] [PRIMARY KEY] [reference]
```

MySQL supports the data types described in Chapter 16. The modifiers in this syntax are:

AUTO_INCREMENT

Indicates that the column should be automatically incremented using the current greatest value for that column. Only whole number columns may be auto-incremented.

DEFAULT value

This attribute assigns a default value to a field. If a row is inserted into the table without a value for this field, this value will be inserted. If a default is not defined, a null value is inserted, unless the field is defined as NOT NULL in which case MySQL picks a value based on the type of the field.

NOT NULL

This attribute guarantees that every entry in the column will have some non-null value. Attempting to insert a NULL value into a field defined with NOT NULL will generate an error.

NULL

This attribute specifies that the field is allowed to contain NULL values. This is the default if neither this nor the NOT NULL modifier are specified. Fields that are contained within an index cannot contain the NULL modifier. (The attribute will be ignored, without warning, if it does exist in such a field.)

PRIMARY KEY

This attribute automatically makes the field the primary key (see later) for the table. Only one primary key may exist for a table. Any field that is a primary key must also contain the NOT NULL modifier.

REFERENCES *table* [(*column*,...)] [MATCH FULL | MATCH PARTIAL] [ON DELETE *option*]
[ON UPDATE *option*]

Currently applies only to the InnoDB table type.

You may specify meta-structure such as indexes and constraints via the following clauses:

FULLTEXT (column, ...)

Since MySQL 3.23.23, MySQL has supported full text indexing. The use and results of this search are described in the online MySQL reference manual. To create a full text index, use the FULLTEXT keyword:

```
CREATE TABLE Item ( itemid INT NOT NULL PRIMARY KEY,
        name VARCHAR(25) NOT NULL,
        description TEXT NOT NULL,
        FULLTEXT ( name, description )
);
```

INDEX [*name*] (*column*, ...)

Creates a regular index of all of the named columns (KEY and INDEX, in this context, are synonyms). Optionally the index may be given a name. If no name is provided, a name is assigned based on the first column given and a trailing number, if necessary, for uniqueness. If a key contains more than one column, leftmost subsets of those columns are also included in the index. Consider the following index definition.

```
INDEX idx1 ( name, rank, serial );
```

When this index is created, the following groups of columns will be indexed:

- name, rank, serial
- name, rank
- name

KEY [*name*] (*column*, ...)

Synonym for INDEX.

PRIMARY KEY

Creates the primary key of the table. A primary key is a special key that can be defined only once in a table. The primary key is a UNIQUE key with the name PRIMARY. Despite its privileged status, it behaves the same as every other unique key.

UNIQUE [*name*] (*column*, ...)

Creates a special index where every value contained in the index (and therefore in the fields indexed) must be unique. Attempting to insert a value that already exists into a unique index will generate an error. The following would create a unique index of the nicknames field:

```
UNIQUE (nicknames);
```

When indexing character fields (CHAR, VARCHAR, and their synonyms only), it is possible to index only a prefix of the entire field. For example, the following will create an index of the numeric field id along with the first 20 characters of the character field address:

```
INDEX adds ( id, address(20) );
```

When performing any searches of the field address, only the first 20 characters will be used for comparison, unless more than one match is found that contains the same first 20 characters, in which case a regular search of the data is performed. Therefore, it can be a big performance bonus to index only the number of characters in a text field that you know will make the value unique.

Fields contained in an index must be defined with the NOT NULL modifier. When adding an index as a separate declaration, MySQL will generate an error if NOT NULL is missing. However, when defining the primary key by adding the PRIMARY KEY modifier to the field definition, the NOT NULL modifier is added automatically (without a warning) if it is not explicitly defined.

In addition to the above, MySQL supports the following special "types," and the team is working on adding functionality to support them:

- FOREIGN KEY *(name (column, [column2, . . .])*
- CHECK

As of MySQL 3.23, you can specify table options at the end of a CREATE TABLE statement. These options are:

AUTO_INCREMENT = *start*
> Specifies the first value to be used for an AUTO_INCREMENT column.

AVG_ROW_LENGTH = *length*
> An option for tables containing large amounts of variable-length data. The average row length is an optimization hint to help MySQL manage this data.

CHECKSUM = 0 or 1
> When set to 1, this option forces MySQL to maintain a checksum for the table to improve data consistency. This option creates a performance penalty.

COMMENT = *comment*
> Provides a comment for the table. The comment may not exceed 60 characters.

DELAY_KEY_WRITE = 0 or 1
> For MyISAM tables only. When set, this option delays key table updates until the table is closed.

MAX_ROWS = *rowcount*
> The maximum number of rows you intend to store in the table.

MIN_ROWS = *rowcount*
> The minimum number of rows you intend to store in the table.

PACK_KEYS = 0 or 1
> For MyISAM and ISAM tables only. This option provides a performance booster for read-heavy tables. Set to 1, this option causes smaller keys to be created and thus slows down writes while speeding up reads.

PASSWORD = '*password*'

> Available only to MySQL customers with special commercial licenses. This option uses the specified password to encrypt the table's *.frm* file. This option has no effect on the standard version of MySQL.

ROW_FORMAT = DYNAMIC or STATIC

> For MyISAM tables only. Defines how the rows should be stored in a table.

TYPE = *rowtype*

> Specifies the table type of the database. If the selected table type is not available, the closest table type available is used. For example, BDB is not available yet for Mac OS X. If you specified TYPE=BDB on a Mac OS X system, MySQL will instead create the table as a MyISAM table. Table 15-2 contains a list of supported table types and their advanatages. For a more complete discussion of MySQL tables types, see the MySQL table type reference.

Table 15-2. MySQL table types

Type	Transactional	Description
BDB	Yes	Transaction-safe tables with page locking
Berkeley_db	Yes	Alias for BDB
HEAP	No	Memory-based table; not persistent
ISAM	No	Obsolete format; replaced by MyISAM
InnoDB	Yes	Transaction-safe tables with row locking
MERGE	No	A collection of MyISAM tables merged as a single table
MyISAM	No	A newer table type to replace ISAM that is portable

You must have CREATE privileges on a database to use the CREATE TABLE statement.

Examples

```
# Create the new empty database 'employees'
CREATE DATABASE employees;
# Create a simple table
CREATE TABLE emp_data ( id INT, name CHAR(50) );
# Create a complex table
CREATE TABLE IF NOT EXISTS emp_review (
    id INT NOT NULL PRIMARY KEY AUTO_INCREMENT,
    emp_id INT NOT NULL REFERENCES emp_data ( id ),
    review TEXT NOT NULL,
    INDEX ( emp_id ),
    FULLTEXT ( review )
) AUTO_INCREMENT = 1, TYPE=InnoDB;
# Make the function make_coffee (which returns a string value and is stored
# in the myfuncs.so shared library) available to MySQL.
CREATE FUNCTION make_coffee RETURNS string SONAME "myfuncs.so";
```

DELETE

Syntax
```
DELETE [LOW_PRIORITY | QUICK]
FROM table [WHERE clause] [ORDER BY column, ...]
[LIMIT n]

DELETE [LOW_PRIORITY | QUICK]
table1[.*], table2[.*], ..., tablen[.*]
FROM tablex, tabley, ..., tablez [WHERE clause]

DELETE [LOW_PRIORITY | QUICK]
FROM table1[.*], table2[.*], ..., tablen[.*]
USING references
[WHERE clause]
```

Description
Deletes rows from a table. When used without a WHERE clause, this will erase the entire table and recreate it as an empty table. With a WHERE clause, it will delete the rows that match the condition of the clause. This statement returns the number of rows deleted.

As mentioned above, omitting the WHERE clause will erase this entire table. This is done by using an efficient method that is much faster than deleting each row individually. When using this method, MySQL returns 0 to the user because it has no way of knowing how many rows it deleted. In the current design, this method simply deletes all the files associated with the table except for the file that contains the actual table definition. Therefore, this is a handy method of zeroing out tables with unrecoverably corrupt data files. You will lose the data, but the table structure will still be in place. If you really wish to get a full count of all deleted tables, use a WHERE clause with an expression that always evaluates to true:

```
DELETE FROM TBL WHERE 1 = 1;
```

The LOW_PRIORITY modifier causes MySQL to wait until no clients are reading from the table before executing the delete. QUICK causes the table handler to suspend the merging of indexes during the DELETE, to enhance the speed of the DELETE.

The LIMIT clause establishes the maximum number of rows that will be deleted in a single shot.

When deleting from MyISAM tables, MySQL simply deletes references in a linked list to the space formerly occupied by the deleted rows. The space itself is not returned to the operating system. Future inserts will eventually occupy the deleted space. If, however, you need the space immediately, run the OPTIMIZE TABLE statement or use the *myisamchk* utility.

The second two syntaxes are new multi-table DELETE statements that enable the deletion of rows from multiple tables. The first is new as of MySQL 4.0.0, and the second was introduced in MySQL 4.0.2.

In the first multi-table DELETE syntax, the FROM clause does not name the tables from which the DELETEs occur. Instead, the objects of the DELETE command are the tables to delete from. The FROM clause in this syntax works like a FROM clause in a SELECT in that it names all of the tables that appear either as objects of the DELETE or in the WHERE clause.

We recommend the second multi-table DELETE syntax because it avoids confusion with the single table DELETE. In other words, it deletes rows from the tables specified in the FROM clause. The USING clause describes all the referenced tables in the FROM and WHERE clauses. The following two DELETEs do the exact same thing. Specifically, they delete all records from the emp_data and emp_review tables for employees in a specific department.

```
DELETE emp_data, emp_review
FROM emp_data, emp_review, dept
WHERE dept.id = emp_data.dept_id
AND emp_data.id = emp_review.emp_id
AND dept.id = 32;

DELETE FROM emp_data, emp_review
USING emp_data, emp_review, dept
WHERE dept.id = emp_data.dept_id
AND emp_data.id = emp_review.emp_id
AND dept.id = 32;
```

You must have DELETE privileges on a database to use the DELETE statement.

Examples

```
# Erase all of the data (but not the table itself) for the table 'olddata'.
DELETE FROM olddata
# Erase all records in the 'sales' table where the 'syear' field is '1995'.
DELETE FROM sales WHERE syear=1995
```

DESCRIBE

Syntax

```
DESCRIBE table [column]
DESC table [column]
```

Description

Gives information about a table or column. While this statement works as advertised, its functionality is available (along with much more) in the SHOW statement. This statement is included solely for compatibility with Oracle SQL. The optional column name can contain SQL wildcards, in which case information will be displayed for all matching columns.

Example

```
# Describe the layout of the table 'messy'
DESCRIBE messy
# Show the information about any columns starting
# with 'my_' in the 'big' table.
# Remember: '_' is a wildcard, too, so it must be
# escaped to be used literally.
DESC big my\_%
```

DESC

Synonym for DESCRIBE.

DROP DATABASE

Syntax

DROP DATABASE [IF EXISTS] *name*

Description

Permanently remove a database from MySQL. Once you execute this statement, none of the tables or data that made up the database are available. All the support files for the database are deleted from the filesystem. The number of files deleted will be returned to the user. This statement is equivalent to running the *mysqladmin drop* utility. As with running *mysqladmin*, you must be the administrative user for MySQL (usually root or *mysql*) to perform this statement.You may use the IF EXISTS clause to prevent any error message that would result from an attempt to drop a nonexistent table.

DROP FUNCTION

Syntax

DROP FUNCTION *name*

Description

Will remove a user-defined function from the running MySQL server process. This does not actually delete the library file containing the function. You may add the function again at any time using the CREATE FUNCTION statement. In the current implementation, DROP FUNCTION simply removes the function from the function table within the MySQL database. This table keeps track of all active functions.

DROP INDEX

Syntax

DROP INDEX *idx_name* ON *tbl_name*

Description

Provides compatibility with other SQL implementations. In older versions of MySQL, this statement does nothing. As of 3.22, this statement is equivalent to ALTER TABLE ... DROP INDEX. To perform the DROP INDEX statement, you must have SELECT, INSERT, DELETE, UPDATE, CREATE, and DROP privileges for the table in question.

DROP TABLE

Syntax

```
DROP TABLE [IF EXISTS] name [, name2, ...]
[RESTRICT | CASCADE]
```

Description

Will erase an entire table permanently. In the current implementation, MySQL simply deletes the files associated with the table. As of 3.22, you may specify IF EXISTS to make MySQL not return an error if you attempt to remove a table that does not exist. The RESTRICT and CASCADE keywords do nothing; they exist solely for ANSI compatibility. You must have DELETE privileges on the table to use this statement.

 DROP is by far the most dangerous SQL statement. If you have drop privileges, you may permanently erase a table or even an entire database. This is done without warning or confirmation. The only way to undo a DROP is to restore the table or database from backups. The lessons to be learned here are: (1) always keep backups; (2) don't use DROP unless you are really sure; and (3) always keep backups.

EXPLAIN

Syntax

```
EXPLAIN [table_name | sql_statement]
```

Description

Used with a table name, this command is an alias for SHOW COLUMNS FROM table_name.

Used with an SQL statement, this command displays verbose information about the order and structure of a SELECT statement. This can be used to see where keys are not being used efficiently. This information is returned as a result set with the following columns:

table
   The name of the table referenced by the result set row explaining the query.

type
   The type of join that will be performed. See Chapter 5 for an explanation of the output.

possible_keys
   Indicates which indexes MySQL could use to build the join. If this column is empty, there are no relevant indexes and you should probably build some to enhance performance.

key
   Indicates which index MySQL decided to use.

key_len
   Provides the length of the key MySQL decided to use for the join.

ref
   Describes which columns or constants were used with the key to build the join.

rows

> Indicates the number of rows MySQL estimates it will need to examine to perform the query.

Extra

> Additional information indicating how MySQL will perform the query. See Chapter 5 for an explanation of the output.

Example

```
EXPLAIN SELECT customer.name, product.name FROM customer, product, purchases
WHERE purchases.customer=customer.id AND purchases.product=product.id
```

FLUSH

Syntax

```
FLUSH option[, option...]
```

Description

Flushes or resets various internal processes depending on the options given. You must have RELOAD privileges to execute this statement. The option can be any of the following:

DES_KEY_FILE

> Reloads the DES keys from the file originally specified with the *--des-key-file* option.

HOSTS

> Empties the cache table that stores hostname information for clients. This should be used if a client changes IP addresses, or if there are errors related to connecting to the host.

LOGS

> Closes all the standard log files and reopens them. This can be used if a log file has changed its inode number. If no specific extension has been given to the update log, a new update log will be opened with the extension incremented by one.

PRIVILEGES

> Reloads all the internal MySQL permissions grant tables. This must be run for any changes to the tables to take effect.

QUERY CACHE

> For better memory use, this command defragments the query cache but it does not delete queries from the cache.

STATUS

> Resets the status variables that keep track of the current state of the server.

TABLE *table*
TABLES *table, table2, ..., tablen*

> Flushes only the specified tables.

TABLES [WITH READ LOCK]

> Closes all currently open tables and flushes any cached data to disk. With a read lock, it acquires a read lock that will not be released until UNLOCK TABLES is issued.

GRANT

Syntax

```
GRANT privilege
[ (column, ...) ] [, privilege [( column, ...) ] ...]
ON {table} TO user [IDENTIFIED BY 'password']
[, user [IDENTIFIED BY 'password'] ...]
[REQUIRE [{SSL | X509}] [CIPHER cipher [AND]]
[ISSUER issuer [AND]]
[SUBJECT subject]]
[WITH [GRANT OPTION | MAX_QUERIES_PER_HOUR=limit]]
```

Description

Previous to MySQL 3.22.11, the GRANT statement was recognized but did nothing. In current versions, GRANT is functional. This statement enables access rights to a user (or users). Access can be granted per database, table or individual column. The table can be given as a table within the current database; use * to affect all tables within the current database, *.* to affect all tables within all databases or database.* to affect all tables within the given database.

The following privileges are currently supported:

ALL PRIVILEGES/ALL
    Assigns all privileges except FILE, PROCESS, RELOAD, and SHUTDOWN

ALTER
    To alter the structure of tables

CREATE
    To create new tables

DELETE
    To delete rows from tables

DROP
    To delete entire tables

FILE
    To create and remove entire databases as well as manage log files

INDEX
    To create and delete indexes from tables

INSERT
    To insert data into tables

PROCESS
    To kill process threads

REFERENCES
    Not implemented (yet)

RELOAD
    To refresh various internal tables (see the FLUSH statement)

SELECT
    To read data from tables

SHUTDOWN
    To shut down the database server

UPDATE
To alter rows within tables

USAGE
No privileges at all

The user variable is of the form *user@hostname*. Either the user or the hostname can contain SQL wildcards. If wildcards are used, either the whole name must be quoted, or just the parts with the wildcards (e.g., joe@"%.com " and "joe@%.com" are both valid). A user without a hostname is considered to be the same as user@"%".

If you have a global GRANT privilege, you may specify an optional INDENTIFIED BY modifier. If the user in the statement does not exist, it will be created with the given password. Otherwise, the existing user will have her password changed.

The GRANT privilege is given to a user with the WITH GRANT OPTION modifier. If this is used, the user may grant any privilege she has to another user. You may alternately chose to limit the number of queries made by a particular user ID through the MAX_QUERIES_PER_HOUR option.

Support for secure SSL encryptions, as well as X.509 authentication, has recently been added to MySQL. The REQUIRE clause enables you to require a user to authenticate in one of these manners and identify the credentials to be used. Just specifying REQUIRE SSL tells MySQL that the user can connect to MySQL using only an SSL connection. Similarly, REQUIRE X509 requires the user to authenticate using an X.509 certificate. You can place the following restrictions on the connection

ISSUER *issuer*
Demands that the certificate have the issuer specified.

SUBJECT *subject*
Not only does the user have to have a valid certificate, but it must have a certificate for the specified subject.

CIPHER *cipher*
Enables MySQL to enforce a minimum encryption strength. The connection must use one of the ciphers specified here.

Examples

```
# Give full access to joe@carthage for the Account table
GRANT ALL ON bankdb.Account TO joe@carthage;
# Give full access to jane@carthage for the
# Account table and create a user ID for her
GRANT ALL ON bankdb.Account TO jane@carthage IDENTIFIED BY 'mypass';
# Give joe the ability
# to SELECT from any table on the webdb database
GRANT SELECT ON webdb.* TO joe;
# Give joe on the local machine access to everything in webdb but
# require some special security
GRANT ALL on webdb.* TO joe@localhost
IDENTIFIED BY 'mypass'
REQUIRE SUBJECT 'C=US, ST=MN, L=Minneapolis, O=My Cert,
CN=Joe Friday/Email=joe@localhost'
AND ISSUER='C=US, ST=MN, L=Minneapolis, O=Imaginet,
CN=Joe Friday/Email=joe@localhost'
AND CIPHER='RSA-DES-3DES-SHA';
```

INSERT

Syntax

```
INSERT [DELAYED | LOW_PRIORITY ] [IGNORE]
[INTO] table [ (column, ...) ]
VALUES ( values [, values... ])

INSERT [DELAYED | LOW_PRIORITY] [IGNORE]
[INTO] table [ (column, ...) ]
SELECT ...

INSERT [DELAYED | LOW_PRIORITY] [IGNORE]
[INTO] table
SET column=value, column=value,...
```

Description

Inserts data into a table. The first form of this statement simply inserts the given values into the given columns. Columns in the table that are not given values are set to their default values or NULL. The second form takes the results of a SELECT query and inserts them into the table. The third form is simply an alternate version of the first form that more explicitly shows which columns correspond with which values. If the DELAYED modifier is present in the first form, all incoming SELECT statements will be given priority over the insert, which will wait until the other activity has finished before inserting the data. In a similar way, using the LOW_PRIORITY modifier with any form of INSERT will cause the insertion to be postponed until all other operations from the client have been finished.

When using a SELECT query with the INSERT statement, you cannot use the ORDER BY modifier with the SELECT statement. Also, you cannot insert into the same table from which you are selecting.

Starting with MySQL 3.22.5, it is possible to insert more than one row into a table at a time. This is done by adding additional value lists to the statement separated by commas.

You must have INSERT privileges to use this statement.

Examples

```
# Insert a record into the 'people' table.
INSERT INTO people ( name, rank, serial_number )
VALUES ( 'Bob Smith', 'Captain', 12345 );
# Copy all records from 'data' that are older than a certain date into
# 'old_data'. This would usually be followed by deleting the old data from
# 'data'.
INSERT INTO old_data ( id, date, field )
SELECT ( id, date, field)
FROM data
WHERE date < 87459300;
# Insert 3 new records into the 'people' table.
INSERT INTO people (name, rank, serial_number )
VALUES ( 'Tim O\'Reilly', 'General', 1),
       ('Andy Oram', 'Major', 4342),
       ('Randy Yarger', 'Private', 9943);
```

KILL

Syntax

KILL *thread_id*

Description

Terminates the specified thread. The thread ID numbers can be found using SHOW PROCESSES. Killing threads owned by users other than yourself requires PROCESS privilege.

Example

```
# Terminate thread 3
KILL 3
```

LOAD

Syntax

```
LOAD DATA [LOW_PRIORITY | CONCURRENT] [LOCAL]
INFILE file [REPLACE|IGNORE]
INTO TABLE table [delimiters] [(columns)]
```

Description

Reads a text file and inserts its data into a database table. This method of inserting data is much quicker than using multiple INSERT statements. Although the statement may be sent from all clients like any other SQL statement, the file referred to in the statement is assumed to be located on the server unless the LOCAL keyword is used. If the filename does not have a fully qualified path, MySQL looks under the directory for the current database of the file.

With no delimiters specified, LOAD DATA INFILE will assume that the file is tab delimited with character fields, special characters escaped with backslashes (\), and lines terminated with newline characters.

In addition to the default behavior, you may specify your own delimiters using the following keywords. Delimiters apply to all tables in the statement.

FIELDS TERMINATED BY 'c'
> Specifies the character used to delimit the fields. Standard C language escape codes can be used to designate special characters. This value may contain more than one character. For example, FIELDS TERMINATED BY ',' denotes a comma-delimited file and FIELDS TERMINATED BY '\t' denotes tab delimited. The default value is tab delimited.

FIELDS ENCLOSED BY 'c'
> Specifies the character used to enclose character strings. For example, FIELD ENCLOSED BY '"' would mean that a line containing "one, two", "other", "last" would be taken to have three fields:
> - one, two
> - other
> - last
>
> The default behavior is to assume that no quoting is used in the file.

FIELDS ESCAPED BY 'c'

Specifies the character used to indicate that the next character is not special, even though it would usually be a special character. For example, with FIELDS ESCAPED BY '^' a line consisting of First,Second^,Third,Fourth would be parsed as three fields: "First", "Second,Third", and "Fourth". The exceptions to this rule are the null characters. Assuming the FIELDS ESCAPED BY value is a backslash, \0 indicates an ASCII NUL (character number 0) and \N indicates a MySQL NULL value. The default value is the backslash character. Note that MySQL itself considers the backslash character to be special. Therefore, to indicate backslash in that statement, you must backslash the backslash like this: FIELDS ESCAPED BY '\\'.

IGNORE number LINES

Ignores the specified number of lines before it loads.

LINES TERMINATED BY 'c'

Specifies the character that indicates the start of a new record. This value can contain more than one character. For example, with LINES TERMINATED BY '.', a file consisting of a,b,c.d,e,f.g,h,k. would be parsed as three separate records, each containing three fields. The default is the newline character. This means that by default, MySQL assumes that each line is a separate record.

By default, if a value read from the file is the same as an existing value in the table for a field that is part of a unique key, an error is given. If the REPLACE keyword is added to the statement, the value from the file will replace the one already in the table. Conversely, the IGNORE keyword will cause MySQL to ignore the new value and keep the old one.

The word NULL encountered in the data file is considered to indicate a null value unless the FIELDS ENCLOSED BY character encloses it.

Using the same character for more than one delimiter can confuse MySQL. For example, FIELDS TERMINATED BY ',' ENCLOSED BY ',' would produce unpredictable behavior.

If a list of columns is provided, the data is inserted into those particular fields in the table. If no columns are provided, the number of fields in the data must match the number of fields in the table, and they must be in the same order as the fields are defined in the table.

You must have SELECT and INSERT privileges on the table to use this statement.

Example

```
# Load in the data contained in 'mydata.txt' into the table 'mydata'. Assume
# that the file is tab delimited with no quotes surrounding the fields.
LOAD DATA INFILE 'mydata.txt' INTO TABLE mydata
# Load in the data contained in 'newdata.txt' Look for two comma delimited
# fields and insert their values into the fields 'field1' and 'field2' in
# the 'newtable' table.
LOAD DATA INFILE 'newdata.txt'
INTO TABLE newtable
FIELDS TERMINATED BY ','
( field1, field2 )
```

LOCK

Syntax

```
LOCK TABLES name
[AS alias] {READ | [READ LOCAL] | [LOW_PRIORITY] WRITE}
[, name2 [AS alias] {READ | [READ LOCAL] | LOW_PRIORITY] WRITE, ...]
```

Description

Locks a table for the use of a specific thread. This command is generally used to emulate transactions. If a thread creates a READ lock, all other threads may read from the table, but only the controlling thread can write to the table. If a thread creates a WRITE lock, no other thread may read from or write to the table.

 Using locked and unlocked tables at the same time can cause the process thread to freeze. You must lock all the tables you will be accessing during the time of the lock. Tables you access only before or after the lock do not need to be locked. The newest versions of MySQL generate an error if you attempt to access an unlocked table while you have other tables locked.

Example

```
# Lock tables 'table1' and 'table3' to prevent updates, and block all access
# to 'table2'. Also create the alias 't3' for 'table3' in the current thread.
LOCK TABLES table1 READ, table2 WRITE, table3 AS t3 READ
```

OPTIMIZE

Syntax

```
OPTIMIZE TABLE name
```

Description

Recreates a table, eliminating any wasted space and sorting any unsorted index pages. Also updates any statistics that are not currently up to date. This task is performed by creating the optimized table as a separate, temporary table and then replacing the current table with it. This command currently works only for MyISAM and BDB tables. If you want the syntax to work no matter what table type you use, you should run *mysqld* with *--skip-new* or *--safe-mode* on. Under these circumstance, OPTIMIZE TABLE is an alias for ALTER TABLE.

Example

```
OPTIMIZE TABLE mytable
```

REPLACE

Syntax

```
REPLACE [DELAYED | LOW_PRIORITY]
INTO table [(column, ...)]
VALUES (value, ...)

REPLACE [DELAYED | LOW_PRIORITY]
INTO table [(column, ...)]
SELECT select_clause

REPLACE [DELAYED | LOW_PRIORITY]
INTO table
SET column=value, column=value, ...
```

Description

Inserts data into a table, replacing any old data that conflicts. This statement is identical to INSERT except that if a value conflicts with an existing unique key, the new value replaces the old one. The first form of this statement simply inserts the given values into the given columns. Columns in the table that are not given values are set to their default values or to NULL. The second form takes the results of a SELECT query and inserts them into the table.

Examples

```
# Insert a record into the 'people' table.
REPLACE INTO people ( name, rank, serial_number )
VALUES ( 'Bob Smith', 'Captain', 12345 )
# Copy all records from 'data' that are older than a certain date into
# 'old_data'. This would usually be followed by deleting the old data from
# 'data'.
REPLACE INTO old_data ( id, date, field )
SELECT ( id, date, field)
FROM data
WHERE date < 87459300
```

REVOKE

Syntax

```
REVOKE privilege [(column, ...)] [, privilege [(column, ...) ...]
ON table FROM user
```

Description

Removes a privilege from a user. The values of privilege, table, and user are the same as for the GRANT statement. You must have the GRANT privilege to be able to execute this statement.

SELECT

Syntax

```
SELECT [STRAIGHT_JOIN]
[SQL_SMALL_RESULT] [SQL_BIG_RESULT] [SQL_BUFFER_RESULT]
[SQL_CACHE | SQL_NO_CACHE] [SQL_CALC_FOUND_ROWS]
[HIGH_PRIORITY]
[DISTINCT | | DISTINCTROW | ALL]
column [[AS] alias][, ...]
[INTO {OUTFILE | DUMPFILE} 'filename' delimiters]
[FROM table [[AS] alias]
[USE INDEX (keys)] [IGNORE INDEX (keys)][, ...]
[constraints]]
[UNION [ALL] select substatement]
```

Description

Retrieves data from a database. The SELECT statement is the primary method of reading data from database tables.

If the DISTINCT keyword is present, only one row of data will be output for every group of rows that is identical. The ALL keyword is the opposite of DISTINCT and displays all returned data. The default behavior is ALL. DISTINCT and DISTINCTROWS are synonyms.

MySQL provides several extensions to the basic ANSI SQL syntax that help modify how your query runs:

HIGH_PRIORITY
> Increases the priority with which the query is run, even to the extent of ignoring tables locked for update. You can cause the database to grind to a halt if you use this option with long-running queries.

STRAIGHT_JOIN
> If you specify more than one table, MySQL will automatically join the tables so that you can compare values between them. In cases where MySQL does not perform the join in an efficient manner, you can specify STRAIGHT_JOIN to force MySQL to join the tables in the order you enter them in the query.

SQL_BUFFER_RESULT
> Forces MySQL to store the result in a temporary table.

SQL_CALC_FOUND_ROWS
> Enables you to find out how many rows the query would return without a LIMIT clause. You can retrieve this value using SELECT FOUND_ROWS().

SQL_BIG_RESULT
SQL_SMALL_RESULT
> Tells MySQL what size you think the result set will be for use with GROUP BY or DISTINCT. With small results, MySQL will place the results in fast temporary tables instead of using sorting. Big results, however, will be placed in disk-based temporary tables and use sorting.

`SQL_CACHE`
`SQL_NO_CACHE`

> `SQL_NO_CACHE` dictates that MySQL should not store the query results in a query cache. `SQL_CACHE`, on the other hand, indicates that the results should be stored in a query cache if you are using cache on demand (`SQL_QUERY_CACHE_TYPE=2`).

The selected columns' values can be any one of the following:

Aliases

> Any complex column name or function can be simplified by creating an alias for it. The value can be referred to by its alias anywhere else in the `SELECT` statement (e.g., `SELECT DATE_FORMAT(date,"%W, %M %d %Y") as nice_date FROM calendar`). You should not use aliases in `WHERE` clauses, as their values may not be calculated at that point.

Column names

> These can be specified as `column`, `table.column` or `database.table.column`. The longer forms are necessary only to disambiguate columns with the same name, but can be used at any time (e.g., `SELECT name FROM people; SELECT mydata.people.name FROM people`).

Functions

> MySQL supports a wide range of built-in functions such as `SELECT COS(angle) FROM triangle` (see later). In addition, user defined functions can be added at any time using the `CREATE FUNCTION` statement.

By default, MySQL sends all output to the client that sent the query. It is possible however, to have the output redirected to a file. In this way you can dump the contents of a table (or selected parts of it) to a formatted file that can either be human readable, or formatted for easy parsing by another database system.

The `INTO OUTFILE 'filename'` modifier is the means in which output redirection is accomplished. With this, the results of the `SELECT` query are put into *filename*. The format of the file is determined by the `delimiters` arguments, which are the same as the `LOAD DATA INFILE` statement with the following additions:

- The `OPTIONALLY` keyword may be added to the `FIELDS ENCLOSED BY` modifier. This will cause MySQL to thread enclosed data as strings and non-enclosed data as numeric.

- Removing all field delimiters (i.e., `FIELDS TERMINATED BY '' ENCLOSED BY ''`) will cause a fixed-width format to be used. Data will be exported according to the display size of each field. Many spreadsheets and desktop databases can import fixed-width format files.

The default behavior with no delimiters is to export tab-delimited data using backslash (\) as the escape character and to write one record per line. You may optionally specify a `DUMPFILE` instead of an `OUTFILE`. This syntax will cause a single row to be placed into the file with no field or line separators. It is used for outputting binary fields.

The list of tables to join may be specified in the following ways:

Table1, Table2, Table3, . . .

> This is the simplest form. The tables are joined in the manner that MySQL deems most efficient. This method can also be written as `Table1 JOIN Table2 JOIN Table3, ....`

The CROSS keyword can also be used, but it has no effect (e.g., Table1 CROSS JOIN Table2) Only rows that match the conditions for both columns are included in the joined table. For example, SELECT * FROM people, homes WHERE people.id=homes.owner would create a joined table containing the rows in the people table that have id fields that match the owner field in the homes table.

 Like values, table names can also be aliased (e.g., SELECT t1.name, t2.address FROM long_table_name t1, longer_table_name t2)

Table1 INNER JOIN *Table2* {[ON *expr*] | [USING (*columns*)]}

Performs a standard inner join. This method is identical to the method just described, except you specify the USING clause to describe the join columns instead of a WHERE clause.

Table1 STRAIGHT_JOIN *Table2*

This is identical to the first method, except that the left table is always read before the right table. This should be used if MySQL performs inefficient sorts by joining the tables in the wrong order.

Table1 LEFT [OUTER] JOIN *Table2* ON *expression*

This checks the right table against the clause. For each row that does not match, a row of NULLs is used to join with the left table. Using the previous example, SELECT * FROM people, homes LEFT JOIN people, homes ON people.id=homes.owner, the joined table would contain all the rows that match in both tables, as well as any rows in the people table that do not have matching rows in the homes table; NULL values would be used for the homes fields in these rows. The OUTER keyword is optional and has no effect.

Table1 LEFT [OUTER] JOIN *Table2* USING (*column[, column2 . . .]*)

This joins the specified columns only if they exist in both tables (e.g., SELECT * FROM old LEFT OUTER JOIN new USING (id)).

Table1 NATURAL LEFT [OUTER] JOIN *Table2*

This joins only the columns that exist in both tables. This would be the same as using the previous method and specifying all the columns in both tables (e.g., SELECT rich_people.salary, poor_people.salary FROM rich_people NATURAL LEFT JOIN poor_people).

{ oj *Table1* LEFT OUTER JOIN *Table2* ON *clause* }

This is identical to *Table1* LEFT JOIN *Table2* ON *clause* and is included only for ODBC compatibility.

MySQL also supports right joins using the same syntax as left joins. For portability, however, it is recommended that you formulate your joins as left joins.

If no constraints are provided, SELECT returns all the data in the selected tables. You may also optionally tell MySQL whether to use or ignore specific indexes on a join using USE INDEX and IGNORE INDEX.

The search constraints can contain any of the following substatements:

WHERE *statement*

The WHERE statement construct is the most common way of searching for data in SQL. This statement is usually a comparison of some type but can also include any of the functions listed below, except for the aggregate functions. Named values, such as column names and aliases, and literal numbers and strings can be used in the statement. The syntax and common operators are described in Chapter 3.

FOR UPDATE

Creates a write lock on the rows returned by the query. This constraint is useful if you intent to immediately modify the query data and update the database.

LOCK IN SHARE MODE

Creates a shared mode lock on the read so that the query returns no data that is part of an uncommitted transaction.

GROUP BY *column*[*, column2,...*]

This gathers all the rows that contain data from a certain column. This allows aggregate functions to be performed on the columns (e.g., SELECT name,MAX(age) FROM people GROUP BY name). The column value may be an unsigned integer or a formula, instead of an actual column name.

HAVING *clause*

This is the same as a WHERE clause except it is performed upon the data that has already been retrieved from the database. The HAVING statement is a good place to perform aggregate functions on relatively small sets of data that have been retrieved from large tables. This way, the function does not have to act upon the whole table, only the data that has already been selected (e.g., SELECT name,MAX(age) FROM people GROUP BY name HAVING MAX(age)>80).

ORDER BY *column* [*ASC|DESC*][*, column2* [*ASC|DESC*],...]

Sorts the returned data using the given column(s). If DESC is present, the data is sorted in descending order, otherwise ascending order is used (e.g., SELECT name, age FROM people ORDER BY age DESC). Ascending order can also be explicitly stated with the ASC keyword. As with GROUP BY, the column value may be an unsigned integer or a formula, instead of the column name.

LIMIT [*start,*] *rows*

Returns only the specified number of rows. If the start value is supplied, that many rows are skipped before the data is returned. The first row is number 0 (e.g., SELECT url FROM links LIMIT 5,10 returns URLs numbered 5 through 14).

PROCEDURE *name*

In early versions of MySQL, this does not do anything. It was provided to make importing data from other SQL servers easier. Starting with MySQL 3.22, this substatement lets you specify a procedure that modifies the query result before returning it to the client.

SELECT supports functions. MySQL defines several built-in functions that can operate on the data in the table, returning the computed value(s) to the user. With some functions, the value returned depends on whether the user wants to receive a numerical or string value. This is regarded as the "context" of the function. When selecting values to be displayed to the user, only text context is used, but when selecting data to be inserted into a field, or to be used as the argument of another function, the context depends upon what the receiver is expecting. For instance, selecting data to be inserted into a numerical field will place the function into a numerical context. MySQL functions are detailed in full in Chapter 17.

MySQL 4.0 introduced support for unions. A UNION clause enables the results from two SELECT statements to be joined as a single result set. The two queries should have columns that match in type and number.

Examples

```
# Find all names in the 'people' table where the 'state' field is 'MI'.
SELECT name FROM people WHERE state='MI'
# Display all of the data in the 'mytable' table.
SELECT * FROM mytable
```

SET

Syntax

SET OPTION SQL_OPTION=*value*

Description

Defines an option for the current session. Values set by this statement are not in effect anywhere but the current connection, and they disappear at the end of the connection. The following options are currently supported:

AUTOCOMMIT=0 or 1

When set to the default value of 1, each statement sent to the database is automatically committed unless preceded by BEGIN. Otherwise, you need to send a COMMIT or ROLLBACK to end a transaction.

CHARACTER SET *charsetname* or DEFAULT

Changes the character set used by MySQL. Specifying DEFAULT will return to the original character set.

LAST_INSERT_ID=*number*

Determines the value returned from the LAST_INSERT_ID( ) function.

PASSWORD=PASSWORD('password')

Sets the password for the current user.

PASSWORD FOR user = PASSWORD('password')

Sets the password for the specified user.

SQL_AUTO_IS_NULL= 0 or 1

When set to the default value of 1, you can find the last inserted row in a table with WHERE auto_increment_column IS NULL.

SQL_BIG_SELECTS=0 or 1

Determines the behavior when a large SELECT query is encountered. If set to 1, MySQL will abort the query with an error, if the query would probably take too long to compute. MySQL decides that a query will take too long if it will have to examine more rows than the value of the max_join_size server variable. The default value of the variable is 0, which allows all queries.

`SQL_BIG_TABLES=0 or 1`

Determines the behavior of temporary tables (usually generated when dealing with large data sets). If this value is 1, temporary tables are stored on disk, which is slower than primary memory but can prevent errors on systems with low memory. The default value is 0, which stores temporary tables in RAM.

`SQL_BUFFER_RESULT=0 or 1`

A value of 1 is the same as specifying `SQL_BUFFER_RESULT` for every `SELECT` statement. It forces MySQL to place results into a temporary table.

`SQL_LOG_OFF=0 or 1`

When set to 1, turns off standard logging for the current session. This does not stop logging to the ISAM log or the update log. You must have `PROCESS LIST` privileges to use this option. The default is 0, which enables standard logging.

`SQL_LOG_UPDATE=0 or 1`

Enables a client to turn off its update log only if the client has `PROCESS` privileges.

`SQL_LOW_PRIORITY_UPDATES=0 or 1`

Tells MySQL to wait until no pending `SELECT` or `LOCK TABLE READ` is occuring on an affected table before executing a `write` statement.

`SQL_MAX_JOIN_SIZE=value or DEFAULT`

Prohibits MySQL from executing queries that will likely need more than the specified number of row combinations. If you set this value to anything other than the default, it will cause `SQL_BIG_SELECTS` to be reset. Resetting `SQL_BIG_SELECTS` will cause this value to be ignored.

`SQL_QUERY_CACHE_TYPE=value`

Tells MySQL not to cache or retrieve results (0 or `OFF`), to cache everything but `SQL_NO_CACHE` queries (1 or `ON`), or to cache only `SQL_CACHE` queries (2 or `DEMAND`).

`SQL_SAFE_UPDATES=0 or 1`

Prevents accidental executions of `UPDATE` or `DELETE` statements that do not have a `WHERE` clause or `LIMIT` set.

`SQL_SELECT_LIMIT=number`

The maximum number of records returned by a `SELECT` query. A `LIMIT` modifier in a `SELECT` statement overrides this value. The default behavior is to return all records.

`SQL_UPDATE_LOG=0 or 1`

When set to 0, turns off update logging for the current session. This does not affect standard logging or ISAM logging. You must have `PROCESS LIST` privileges to use this option. The default is 1, which enables update logging.

`TIMESTAMP=value or DEFAULT`

Determines the time used for the session. This time is logged to the update log and will be used if data is restored from the log. Specifying `DEFAULT` will return to the system time.

Example

```
# Turn off logging for the current connection.
SET OPTION SQL_LOG_OFF=1
```

SHOW

Syntax

```
SHOW [FULL] COLUMNS
    FROM table [FROM database] [LIKE clause]
SHOW DATABASES [LIKE clause]
SHOW FIELDS FROM table [FROM database] [LIKE clause]
SHOW GRANTS FOR user
SHOW INDEX FROM table [FROM database]
SHOW KEYS FROM table [FROM database]
SHOW LOGS
SHOW MASTER STATUS
SHOW MASTER LOGS
SHOW [FULL] PROCESSLIST
SHOW SLAVE STATUS
SHOW STATUS [LIKE clause]
SHOW TABLE STATUS [FROM database [LIKE clause]]
SHOW [OPEN] TABLES [FROM database] [LIKE clause]
SHOW VARIABLES [LIKE clause]
```

Description

Displays a lot of different information about the MySQL system. This statement can be used to examine the status or structure of almost any part of MySQL.

Examples

```
# Show the available databases
SHOW DATABASES
# Display information on the indexes on table 'bigdata'
SHOW KEYS FROM bigdata
# Display information on the indexes on table 'bigdata'
# in the database 'mydata'
SHOW INDEX FROM bigdata FROM mydata
# Show the tables available from the database 'mydata' that begin with the
# letter 'z'
SHOW TABLES FROM mydata LIKE 'z%'
# Display information about the columns on the table 'skates'
SHOW COLUMNS FROM stakes
# Display information about the columns on the table 'people'
# that end with '_name'
SHOW FIELDS FROM people LIKE '%\_name'
# Show server status information.
SHOW STATUS
# Display server variables
SHOW VARIABLES
```

TRUNCATE

Syntax
```
TRUNCATE TABLE table
```

Description
Drops and recreates the specified table.

Example
```
# Truncate the emp_data table
TRUNCATE TABLE emp_data;
```

UNLOCK

Syntax
```
UNLOCK TABLES
```

Description
Unlocks all tables that were locked using the LOCK statement during the current connection.

Example
```
# Unlock all tables
UNLOCK TABLES
```

UPDATE

Syntax
```
UPDATE [LOW_PRIORITY] [IGNORE] table
SET column=value, ...
[WHERE clause]
[LIMIT n]
```

Description
Alters data within a table. You may use the name of a column as a value when setting a new value. For example, UPDATE health SET miles_ran=miles_ran+5 would add five to the current value of the miles_ran column.

The syntax and common operators of the WHERE clause are shown in Chapter 3. The WHERE clause limits updates to matching rows. The LIMIT clause ensures that only *n* rows change. The statement returns the number of rows changed.

You must have UPDATE privileges to use this statement.

Example

```
# Change the name 'John Deo' to 'John Doe' everywhere in the people table.
UPDATE people SET name='John Doe' WHERE name='John Deo'
```

USE

Syntax

USE *database*

Description

Selects the default database. The database given in this statement is used as the default database for subsequent queries. Other databases may still be explicitly specified using the database.table.column notation.

Example

```
# Make db1 the default database.
USE db1
```

CHAPTER 16
MySQL Data Types

MySQL offers a wide variety of data types to support the storage of different kinds of data. This chapter lists the full range of these data types and describes their functionality, syntax, and data storage requirements. For each data type, the syntax shown uses square brackets ([]) to indicate optional parts of the syntax. The following example shows how BIGINT is explained in this chapter:

```
BIGINT[(display_size)]
```

This indicates that you can use BIGINT alone or with a display size value. The italics indicate that you do not enter display_size literally, but instead enter your own value. Thus, possible uses of BIGINT include:

```
BIGINT
BIGINT(20)
```

Like the BIGINT type above, many MySQL data types support the specification of a display size. Unless otherwise specified, this value must be an integer between 1 and 255.

Table 16-1 lists the data types and categorizes them as numeric, string, date, or complex. You can find the full description of each data type later in this chapter.

Table 16-1. MySQL data types

Data type	Classification
BIGINT	Numeric
BLOB	String
CHAR	String
CHARACTER	String
CHARACTER VARYING	String
DATE	Date
DATETIME	Date
DEC	Numeric
DECIMAL	Numeric

Table 16-1. MySQL data types (continued)

Data type	Classification
DOUBLE	Numeric
DOUBLE PRECISION	Numeric
ENUM	Complex
FLOAT	Numeric
INT	Numeric
INTEGER	Numeric
LONGBLOB	String
LONGTEXT	String
MEDIUMBLOB	String
MEDIUMINT	Numeric
MEDIUMTEXT	String
NCHAR	String
NATIONAL CHAR	String
NATIONAL CHARACTER	String
NATIONAL VARCHAR	String
NUMERIC	Numeric
REAL	Numeric
SET	Complex
SMALLINT	Numeric
TEXT	String
TIME	Date
TIMESTAMP	Date
TINYBLOB	String
TINYINT	Numeric
TINYTEXT	String
VARCHAR	String
YEAR	Date

In the following cases, MySQL silently changes the column type you specify in your table creation to something else:

VARCHAR -> CHAR

When the specified VARCHAR column size is less than four characters, it is converted to CHAR.

CHAR -> VARCHAR

When a table has at least one column of a variable length, all CHAR columns greater than three characters in length are converted to VARCHAR.

TIMESTAMP *display sizes*

Display sizes for TIMESTAMP fields must be an even value between 2 and 14. A display size of 0 or greater than 14 will convert the field to a display size of 14. An odd-valued display size will be converted to the next highest even value.

Numeric Data Types

MySQL supports all ANSI SQL2 numeric data types. MySQL numeric types break down into two groups: integer and floating point. Within each group, the types differ by the amount of storage required for them.

Numeric types allow you to specify a display size, which affects the way MySQL displays results. The display size bears no relation to the internal storage provided by each data type. In addition, the floating types allow you to optionally specify the number of digits that follow the decimal point. In such cases, the digits value should be an integer from 0 to 30 and at most two less than the display size. If you do make the digits value greater than two less than the display size, the display size will automatically change to two more than the digits value. For instance, MySQL automatically changes FLOAT(6,5) to FLOAT(7,5).

When you insert a value into a column that requires more storage than the data type allows, it will be clipped to the minimum (negative values) or maximum (positive values) value for that data type. MySQL will issue a warning when such clipping occurs during ALTER TABLE, LOAD DATA INFILE, UPDATE, and multirow INSERT statements.

The AUTO_INCREMENT attribute may be supplied for at most one column of an integer type in a table. The UNSIGNED attribute may be used with any numeric type. An unsigned column may contain only positive integers or floating-point values. The ZEROFILL attribute indicates that the column should be left padded with zeros when displayed by MySQL. The number of zeros padded is determined by the column's display width.

BIGINT

Syntax   BIGINT[(*display_size*)] [AUTO_INCREMENT] [UNSIGNED] [ZEROFILL]

Storage   8 bytes

Description

Largest integer type, supporting range of whole numbers from –9,223,372,036,854,775,808 to 9,223,372,036,854,775,807 (0 to 18,446,744,073,709,551,615 unsigned). BIGINT has some issues when you perform arithmetic on unsigned values. MySQL performs all arithmetic using signed BIGINT or DOUBLE values. You should therefore avoid performing any arithmetic operations on unsigned BIGINT values greater than 9,223,372,036,854,775,807. If you do, you may end up with imprecise results.

DEC

Synonym for DECIMAL.

DECIMAL

Syntax   DECIMAL[(*precision*, [*scale*])] [ZEROFILL]

Storage   *precision* + 2 bytes

Description

Stores floating-point numbers where precision is critical, such as for monetary values. DECIMAL types require you to specify the precision and scale. The precision is the number of significant digits in the value. The scale is the number of those digits that come after the decimal point. For example, a BALANCE column declared as DECIMAL(9, 2) would store numbers with nine significant digits, two of which are to the right of the decimal point. The range for this declaration would be –9,999,999.99 to 9,999,999.99. If you specify a number with more decimal points, it is rounded to fit the proper scale. Values beyond the range of the DECIMAL are clipped to fit within the range.

MySQL actually stores DECIMAL values as strings, not as floating-point numbers. It uses one character for each digit, one character for the decimal points when the scale is greater than 0, and one character for the sign of negative numbers. When the scale is 0, the value contains no fractional part. Prior to MySQL 3.23, the precision actually had to include space for the decimal and sign. This requirement is no longer in place, in accordance with the ANSI specification.

ANSI SQL supports the omission of precision and/or scale where the omission of scale creates a default scale of zero and the omission of precision defaults to an implementation-specific value. In the case of MySQL, the default precision is 10.

DOUBLE

Syntax   DOUBLE[(*display_size*, *digits*)] [ZEROFILL]

Storage   8 bytes

Description

A double-precision floating-point number. This type stores large floating-point values. DOUBLE columns can store negative values between –1.7976931348623157E+308 and –2.2250738585072014E-308, 0, and positive numbers between 2.2250738585072014E-308 and 1.7976931348623157E+308.

DOUBLE PRECISION

Synonym for DOUBLE.

FLOAT

Syntax	FLOAT[(*display_size, digits*)] [ZEROFILL]
Storage	4 bytes

Description

A single-precision floating-point number. This type is used to store small floating-point numbers. FLOAT columns can store negative values between −3.402823466E+38 and −1.175494351E-38, 0, and positive values between 1.175494351E-38 and 3.402823466E+38.

INT

Syntax	INT[(*display_size*)] [AUTO_INCREMENT] [UNSIGNED] [ZEROFILL]
Storage	4 bytes

Description

A basic whole number with a range of −2,147,483,648 to 2,147,483,647 (0 to 4,294,967,295 unsigned).

INTEGER

Synonym for INT.

MEDIUMINT

Syntax	MEDIUMINT[(*display_size*)] [AUTO_INCREMENT] [UNSIGNED] [ZEROFILL]
Storage	3 bytes

Description

A basic whole number with a range of −8,388,608 to 8,388,607 (0 to 16,777,215 unsigned).

NUMERIC

Synonym for DECIMAL.

REAL

Synonym for DOUBLE.

SMALLINT

Syntax   SMALLINT[(*display_size*)] [AUTO_INCREMENT] [UNSIGNED] [ZEROFILL]

Storage   2 bytes

Description

A basic whole number with a range of −32,768 to 32,767 (0 to 65,535 unsigned).

TINYINT

Syntax   TINYINT[(*display_size*)] [AUTO_INCREMENT] [UNSIGNED] [ZEROFILL]

Storage   1 byte

Description

A basic whole number with a range of −128 to 127 (0 to 255 unsigned).

String Data Types

String data types store various kinds of text data. There are several types to accommodate data of different sizes. For each size, there is a type that sorts and compares entries in a case-insensitive fashion in accordance with the sorting rules for the default character set and a corresponding binary type that does simple byte-by-byte sorts and comparisons. In other words, binary values are case sensitive. For CHAR and VARCHAR, the binary types are declared using the BINARY attribute. The TEXT types, however, have corresponding BLOB types as their binary counterparts.

BLOB

Binary form of TEXT.

CHAR

Syntax   CHAR(*size*) [BINARY]

Size   Specified by the *size* value in a range of 0 to 255 (1 to 255 prior to MySQL 3.23)

Storage   *size* bytes

Description

A fixed-length text field. String values with fewer characters than the column's size will be right padded with spaces. The right padding is removed on retrieval of the value from the database.

CHAR(0) fields are useful for backward compatibility with legacy systems that no longer store values in the column.

CHARACTER

Synonym for CHAR.

CHARACTER VARYING

Synonym for VARCHAR.

LONGBLOB

Binary form of LONGTEXT.

LONGTEXT

Syntax	LONGTEXT
Size	0 to 4,294,967,295
Storage	Length of value + 4 bytes

Description

Storage for large text values. While the theoretical limit on the size of the text that can be stored in a LONGTEXT column exceeds 4 GB, the practical limit is much less due to limitations of the MySQL communication protocol and the amount of memory available on both the client and server ends of the communication.

MEDIUMBLOB

Binary form of MEDIUMTEXT.

MEDIUMTEXT

Syntax   MEDIUMTEXT

Size   0 to 16,777,215

Storage   Length of value + 3 bytes

Description

Storage for medium-sized text values.

NCHAR

Synonym of CHAR.

NATIONAL CHAR

Synonym of CHAR.

NATIONAL CHARACTER

Synonym of CHAR.

NATIONAL VARCHAR

Synonym of VARCHAR.

TEXT

Syntax   TEXT

Size   0 to 65,535

Storage   Length of value + 2 bytes

Description

Storage for most text values.

TINYBLOB

Binary form of TINYTEXT.

TINYTEXT

Syntax   TINYTEXT

Size   0 to 255

Storage   Length of value + 1 byte

Description

Storage for short text values.

VARCHAR

Syntax   VARCHAR(*size*) [BINARY]

Size   Specified by the *size* value in a range of 0 to 255 (1 to 255 prior to MySQL 3.23)

Storage   Length of value + 1 byte

Description

Storage for variable-length text. Trailing spaces are removed from VARCHAR values when stored in a database that conflicts with the ANSI specification.

Date Data Types

MySQL date types are extremely flexible tools for storing date information. They are also extremely forgiving in the belief that it is up to the application, not the database, to validate date values. MySQL only checks that months range from 0 to 12 and dates range from 0 to 31. February 31, 2001, is therefore a legal MySQL date. More useful, however, is the fact that February 0, 2001, is a legal date. In other words, you can use 0 to signify dates in which you do not know a particular piece of the date.

Though MySQL is somewhat forgiving on the input format, you should actually attempt to format all date values in your applications in MySQL's native format to avoid any confusion. MySQL always expects the year to be the left-most element of a date format. If you assign an illegal value in an SQL operation, MySQL will insert a zero for that value.

MySQL will also perform automatic conversion of date and time values to integer values when used in an integer context.

DATE

Syntax   DATE

Format   YYYY-MM-DD (2001-01-01)

Storage   3 bytes

Description

Stores a date in the range of January 1, 1000 ('1000-01-01') to December 31, 9999 ('9999-12-31') in the Gregorian calendar.

DATETIME

Syntax   DATETIME

Format   YYYY-MM-DD hh:mm:ss (2001-01-01 01:00:00)

Storage   8 bytes

Description

Stores a specific time in the range of 12:00:00 AM, January 1, 1000 ('1000-01-01 00:00:00') to 11:59:59 P.M., December 31, 9999 ('9999-12-31 23:59:59') in the Gregorian calendar.

TIME

Syntax   TIME

Format   hh:mm:ss (06:00:00)

Storage   3 bytes

Description

Stores a time value in the range of midnight ('00:00:00') to one second before midnight ('23:59:59').

TIMESTAMP

Syntax   TIMESTAMP[(*display_size*)]

Format   YYYYMMDDhhmmss (20010101060000)

Storage   4 bytes

Description

A simple representation of a point in time down to the second in the range of midnight on January 1, 1970, to one minute before midnight on December 31, 2037. Its primary utility is keeping track of table modifications. When you insert a NULL value into a TIMESTAMP column, the current date and time are inserted instead. When you modify any value in a row with a TIMESTAMP column, the first TIMESTAMP column will be automatically updated with the current date and time.

YEAR

Syntax	YEAR
Format	YYYY (2001)
Storage	1 byte

Description

Stores a year of the Gregorian calendar in the range of 1900 to 2155.

Complex Data Types

MySQL's complex data types ENUM and SET are really nothing more than special string types. We break them out because they are conceptually more complex and represent a lead into the SQL3 data types that MySQL may support one day.

ENUM

Syntax	ENUM(*value1, value2, ...*)
Storage	1–255 members: 1 byte 256–65,535 members: 2 bytes

Description

Stores one value of a predefined list of possible strings. When you create an ENUM column, you provide a list of all possible values. Inserts and updates are allowed to set the column to values only from that list. Any attempt to insert a value that is not part of the enumeration will cause an empty string to be stored instead.

You may reference the list of possible values by index where the index of the first possible value is 0. For example:

```
SELECT COLID FROM TBL WHERE COLENUM = 0;
```

Assuming COLID is a primary key column and COLENUM is the column of type ENUM, this SQL will retrieve the primary keys of all rows in which the COLENUM value equals the first value of that list. Similarly, sorting on ENUM columns happens according to index, not string value.

The maximum number of elements allowed for an ENUM column is 65,535.

SET

Syntax   SET(*value1, value2, ...*)

Storage   1–8 members: 1 byte
9–16 members: 2 bytes
17–24 members: 3 bytes
25–32 members: 4 bytes
33–64 members: 8 bytes

Description

A list of values taken from a predefined set of values. A field can contain any number—including none—of the strings specified in the SET statement. A SET is basically an ENUM that allows each field to contain more than one of the specified values. A SET, however, is not stored according to index but as a complex bit map. Given a SET with the members Orange, Apple, Pear, and Banana, each element is represented by an "on" bit in a byte, as shown in Table 16-2.

Table 16-2. MySQL representations of set elements

Member	Decimal value	Bitwise representation
Orange	1	0001
Apple	2	0010
Pear	4	0100
Banana	8	1000

The values Orange and Pear are therefore stored in the database as 5 (0101).

You can store a maximum of 64 values in a SET column. Though you can assign the same value multiple times in an SQL statement updating a SET column, only a single value will actually be stored.

## CHAPTER 17

Operators and Functions

Like any other programming language, SQL carries among its core elements operators and named procedures. This reference lists all those operators and functions and explains how they evaluate into useful expressions.

Operators

MySQL offers three kinds of operators: arithmetic, comparison, and logical.

Rules of Precedence

When your SQL contains complex expressions, the subexpressions are evaluated based on MySQL's rules of precedence. Of course, you may always override MySQL's rules of precedence by enclosing an expression in parentheses.

1. BINARY
2. NOT
3. - (unary minus)
4. * / %
5. + -
6. << >>
7. &
8. |
9. < <= > >= = <=> <> IN IS LIKE REGEXP
10. BETWEEN
11. AND
12. OR

Arithmetic Operators

Arithmetic operators perform basic arithmetic on two values.

+   Adds two numerical values

-    Subtracts two numerical values

*   Multiplies two numerical values

/   Divides two numerical values

%   Gives the modulo of two numerical values

| Performs a bitwise OR on two integer values

&   Performs a bitwise AND on two integer values

<<   Performs a bitwise left shift on an integer value

>>   Performs a bitwise right shift on an integer value

Comparison Operators

Comparison operators compare values and return 1 if the comparison is true and 0 otherwise. Except for the <==> operator, NULL values cause a comparison operator to evaluate to NULL.

<> or !=
: Match rows if the two values are not equal.

<=
: Match rows if the left value is less than or equal to the right value.

<
: Match rows if the left value is less than the right value.

>=
: Match rows if the left value is greater than or equal to the right value.

>
: Match rows if the left value is greater than the right value.

value BETWEEN *value1* AND *value2*
: Match rows if *value* is between *value1* and *value2*, or equal to one of them.

value IN (*value1,value2,...*)
: Match rows if *value* is among the values listed.

value NOT IN (*value1, value2,...*)
: Match rows if *value* is not among the values listed.

value1 LIKE *value2*
: Compares *value1* to *value2* and matches the rows if they match. The righthand value can contain the wildcard '%', which matches any number of characters (including 0), and '_', which matches exactly one character. This is probably the

single most used comparison in SQL. Its most common use is comparing a field value with a literal containing a wildcard (e.g., SELECT name FROM people WHERE name LIKE 'B%').

value1 NOT LIKE *value2*

Compares *value1* to *value2* and matches the rows if they differ. This is identical to NOT (value1 LIKE value2).

value1 REGEXP/RLIKE *value2*

Compares *value1* to *value2* using the extended regular expression syntax and matches the rows if the two values match. The righthand value can contain full Unix regular expression wildcards and constructs (e.g., SELECT name FROM people WHERE name RLIKE '^B.*').

value1 NOT REGEXP *value2*

Compares *value1* to *value2* using the extended regular expression syntax and matches the rows if they differ. This is identical to NOT (value1 REXEXP value2).

Logical Operators

Logical operators check the truth value of one or more expressions. In SQL terms, a logical operator checks whether its operands are 0, nonzero, or NULL. A 0 value means false, nonzero means true, and NULL means no value.

NOT *or* !

Performs a logical not (returns 1 if the value is 0 or NULL; otherwise, returns 0)

OR *or* ||

Performs a logical or (returns 1 if any of the arguments are nonzero and non-NULL; otherwise, returns 0)

AND *or* &&

Performs a logical and (returns 0 if any of the arguments are 0 or NULL; otherwise, returns 1)

Functions

MySQL provides built-in functions that perform special operations.

Aggregate Functions

Aggregate functions operate on a set of data. These are usually used to perform some action on a complete set of returned rows. For example, SELECT AVG(height) FROM kids would return the average of all the values of the height field in the kids table.

AVG(*expression*)

Returns the average value of the values in *expression* (e.g., SELECT AVG(score) FROM tests).

BIT_AND(*expression*)

Returns the bitwise AND aggregate of all the values in *expression* (e.g., SELECT BIT_AND(flags) FROM options). A bit will be set in the result if and only if the bit is set in every input field.

BIT_OR(*expression*)

Returns the bitwise OR aggregate of all the values in *expression* (e.g., SELECT BIT_OR(flags) FROM options). A bit is set in the result if it is set in at least one of the input fields.

COUNT(*expression*)

Returns the number of times *expression* was not null. COUNT(*) will return the number of rows with some data in the entire table (e.g., SELECT COUNT(*) FROM folders).

MAX(*expression*)

Returns the largest value in *expression* (e.g., SELECT MAX (elevation) FROM mountains).

MIN(*expression*)

Returns the smallest value in *expression* (e.g., SELECT MIN(level) FROM toxic_waste).

STD(*expression*)/STDDEV(*expression*)

Returns the standard deviation of the values in *expression* (e.g., SELECT STDDEV(points) FROM data).

SUM(*expression*)

Returns the sum of the values in *expression* (e.g., SELECT SUM(calories) FROM daily_diet).

General Functions

General functions operate on one or more discrete values. We have omitted a few rarely used functions with very specialized applications.

ABS(*number*)

Returns the absolute value of *number* (e.g., ABS(-10) returns 10).

ACOS(*number*)

Returns the inverse cosine of *number* in radians (e.g., ACOS(0) returns 1.570796).

ADDDATE(*date*, INTERVAL *amount type*)

Synonym for DATE_ADD.

ASCII(*char*)

Returns the ASCII value of the given character (e.g., ASCII('h') returns 104).

ASIN(*number*)

Returns the inverse sine of *number* in radians (e.g., ASIN(0) returns 0.000000).

ATAN(*number*)

Returns the inverse tangent of number in radians (e.g., ATAN(1) returns 0.785398).

ATAN2(*X, Y*)

Returns the inverse tangent of the point (*X*,*Y*) (for example, ATAN(-3,3) returns −0.785398).

BENCHMARK(*num, function*)

Runs *function* over and over *num* times and reports the total elapsed clock time.

BIN(*decimal*)

Returns the binary value of the given decimal number (e.g., BIN(8) returns 1000). This is equivalent to the function CONV(decimal,10,2) .

BIT_COUNT(*number*)

Returns the number of bits that are set to 1 in the binary representation of the number (e.g., BIT_COUNT(17) returns 2).

BIT_LENGTH(*string*)

Returns the number of bits in *string* (the number of characters times 8, for single-byte characters).

CASE *value* WHEN *choice* THEN *returnvalue* ... ELSE *returnvalue* END

Compares *value* to a series of *choice* values or expressions. The first *choice* to match the *value* ends the function and returns the corresponding *returnvalue*. The ELSE *returnvalue* is returned if no *choice* matches.

CEILING(*number*)

Returns the smallest integer greater than or equal to *number* (e.g., CEILING (5.67) returns 6).

CHAR(*num1*[,*num2*,. . .])

Returns a string made from converting each number to the character corresponding to that ASCII value (e.g., CHAR(122) returns 'z').

CHAR_LENGTH(*string*)

Synonym for LENGTH().

CHARACTER_LENGTH(*string*)

Synonym for LENGTH().

COALESCE(*expr1, expr2, ...*)

Returns the first non-null expression in the list (e.g., COALESCE(NULL, NULL, 'cheese', 2) returns 3).

CONCAT(*string1,string2*[,*string3*,. . .])

Returns the string formed by joining together all of the arguments (e.g., CONCAT('Hi',' ','Mom','!') returns "Hi Mom!").

CONCAT_WS(*sep, string1, [string2, ...]*)

Returns all strings as a single string, separated by *sep*.

CONNECTION_ID()

Returns the ID of the current connection.

CONV(*number, base1, base2*)

Returns the value of *number* converted from *base1* to *base2*. *number* must be an integer value (either as a bare number or as a string). The bases can be any integer from 2 to 36. Thus, CONV(8,10,2) returns 1000, which is the number 8 in decimal converted to binary.

COS(*radians*)

Returns the cosine of the given number, which is in radians (e.g., COS(0) returns 1.000000).

COT(*radians*)

Returns the cotangent of the given number, which must be in radians (e.g., COT(1) returns 0.642093).

CURDATE( )

Returns the current date. A number of the form YYYYMMDD is returned if this is used in a numerical context; otherwise, a string of the form 'YYYY-MM-DD' is returned (e.g., CURDATE( ) could return "1998-08-24").

CURRENT_DATE( )

Synonym for CURDATE( ).

CURRENT_TIME( )

Synonym for CURTIME( ).

CURRENT_TIMESTAMP( )

Synonym for NOW( ).

CURTIME( )

Returns the current time. A number of the form HHMMSS is returned if this is used in a numerical context; otherwise, a string of the form HH:MM:SS is returned (e.g., CURTIME( ) could return 13:02:43).

DATABASE( )

Returns the name of the current database (e.g., DATABASE( ) could return "mydata").

DATE_ADD(*date,* INTERVAL *amount type*)

Returns a date formed by adding the given amount of time to the given date. The time element to add can be one of the following: SECOND, MINUTE, HOUR, DAY, MONTH, YEAR, MINUTE_SECOND (as "minutes:seconds"), HOUR_MINUTE (as "hours:minutes"), DAY_HOUR (as "days hours"), YEAR_MONTH (as "years-months"), HOUR_SECOND (as "hours:minutes:seconds"), DAY_MINUTE (as "days hours:minutes") and DAY_SECOND (as "days hours:minutes:seconds"). Except for those time elements with forms specified above, the amount must be an integer value (e.g., DATE_ADD("1998-08-24 13:00:00", INTERVAL 2 MONTH) returns "1998-10-24 13:00:00").

DATE_FORMAT(*date, format*)

Returns the date formatted as specified. The format string prints as given with the following values substituted:

%a   Short weekday name (Sun, Mon, etc.)

%b   Short month name (Jan, Feb, etc.)

%D   Day of the month with ordinal suffix (1st, 2nd, 3rd, etc.)

%d   Day of the month

%H   24-hour hour (always two digits, e.g., 01)

%h/%I

12-hour hour (always two digits, e.g., 09)

%i   Minutes

%j   Day of the year

%k   24-hour hour (one or two digits, e.g., 1)

%l   12-hour hour (one or two digits, e.g., 9)

%M   Name of the month

%m   Number of the month (January is 1)

%p   A.M. or P.M.

%r   12-hour total time (including A.M./P.M.)

%S   Seconds (always two digits, e.g., 04)

%s   Seconds (one or two digits, e.g., 4)

%T   24-hour total time

%U   Week of the year (new weeks begin on Sunday)

%W   Name of the weekday

%w   Number of weekday (0 is Sunday)

%Y   Four-digit year

%y   Two-digit year

%%   A literal % character

DATE_SUB(*date*, INTERVAL *amount type*)

Returns a date formed by subtracting the given amount of time from the given date. The same interval types are used as with DATE_ADD (e.g., SUBDATE("1999-05-20 11:04:23", INTERVAL 2 DAY) returns "1999-05-18 11:04:23").

DAYNAME(*date*)

Returns the name of the day of the week for the given date (e.g., DAYNAME('1998-08-22') returns "Saturday").

DAYOFMONTH(*date*)

Returns the day of the month for the given date (e.g., DAYOFMONTH('1998-08-22') returns 22).

DAYOFWEEK(*date*)

Returns the number of the day of the week (1 is Sunday) for the given date (e.g., DAY_OF_WEEK('1998-08-22') returns 7).

DAYOFYEAR(*date*)

Returns the day of the year for the given date (e.g., DAYOFYEAR('1983-02-15') returns 46).

DECODE(*blob, passphrase*)

Decodes encrypted binary data using the specified passphrase. The encrypted binary is expected to be encrypted with the ENCODE( ) function:

```
mysql> SELECT DECODE(ENCODE('open sesame', 'please'), 'please');
+---------------------------------------------------+
| DECODE(ENCODE('open sesame', 'please'), 'please') |
+---------------------------------------------------+
| open sesame                                       |
+---------------------------------------------------+
1 row in set (0.01 sec)
```

DEGREES(*radians*)

Returns the given argument converted from radians to degrees (e.g., DEGREES(2*PI( )) returns 360.000000).

ELT(*number,string1,string2, . . .*)

Returns *string1* if *number* is 1, *string2* if *number* is 2, etc. A null value is returned if *number* does not correspond with a string (e.g., ELT(3, "once","twice","thrice","fourth") returns "thrice").

ENCODE(*secret, passphrase*)

Creates a binary encoding of the *secret* using the *passphrase*. You may later decode the secret using DECODE( ) and the passphrase.

ENCRYPT(*string[, salt]*)

Password-encrypts the given string. If a salt is provided, it is used to add extra obfusticating characters to the encrypted string (e.g., ENCRYPT('mypass','3a') could return "3afi4004idgv").

EXP(*power*)

Returns the number *e* raised to the given power (e.g., EXP(1) returns 2.718282).

EXPORT_SET(*num, on, off, [separator, [num_bits]]*)

Examines a number and maps the on and off bits in that number to the strings specified by the on and off arguments. In other words, the first string in the output indicates the on/off value of the first (low-order) bit of *num*, the second string reflects the second bit, and so on. Examples:

```
mysql> SELECT EXPORT_SET(5, "y", "n", "", 8);
+--------------------------------+
| EXPORT_SET(5, "y", "n", "", 8) |
+--------------------------------+
| ynynnnnn                       |
+--------------------------------+
1 row in set (0.00 sec)

mysql> SELECT EXPORT_SET(5, "y", "n", ",", 8);
+---------------------------------+
| EXPORT_SET(5, "y", "n", ",", 8) |
+---------------------------------+
| y,n,y,n,n,n,n,n                 |
+---------------------------------+
1 row in set (0.00 sec)
```

EXTRACT(interval FROM datetime)

Returns the specified part of a DATETIME (e.g., EXTRACT(YEAR FROM '2001-08-10 19:45:32') returns 2001).

FIELD(string,string1,string2, . . .)

Returns the position in the argument list (starting with *string1*) of the first string that is identical to *string*. Returns 0 if no other string matches *string* (e.g., FIELD('abe','george','john','abe','bill') returns 3).

FIND_IN_SET(string,set)

Returns the position of *string* within *set*. The *set* argument is a series of strings separated by commas (e.g., FIND_IN_SET ('abe', 'george, john, abe, bill') returns 3).

FLOOR(number)

Returns the largest integer less than or equal to *number* (e.g., FLOOR(5.67) returns 5).

FORMAT(number, decimals)

Neatly formats the given number, using the given number of decimals (e.g., FORMAT(4432.99134,2) returns "4,432.99").

FROM_DAYS(days)

Returns the date that is the given number of days (in which day 1 is Jan 1 of year 1) (e.g., FROM_DAYS(728749) returns "1995-04-02").

FROM_UNIXTIME(seconds[, format])

Returns the date (in GMT) corresponding to the given number of seconds since the epoch (January 1, 1970 GMT). For example, FROM_UNIXTIME(903981584) returns "1998-08-24 18:00:02". If a format string (using the same format as DATE_FORMAT) is given, the returned time is formatted accordingly.

GET_LOCK(name,seconds)

Creates a named user-defined lock that waits for the given number of seconds until timeout. This lock can be used for client-side application locking between programs that cooperatively use the same lock names. If the lock is successful, 1 is returned. If the lock times out while waiting, 0 is returned. All others errors return NULL values. Only one named lock may be active at a time during a single session. Running GET_LOCK( ) more than once will silently remove any previous locks. For example: GET_LOCK("mylock",10) could return 1 within the following 10 seconds.

GREATEST(*num1, num2*[*, num3*, . . .])

Returns the numerically highest of all the arguments (for example, GREATEST(5,6,68,1,-300) returns 68).

HEX(*decimal*)

Returns the hexadecimal value of the given decimal number (e.g., HEX(90) returns "3a"). This is equivalent to the function CONV(decimal,10,16).

HOUR(*time*)

Returns the hour of the given time (e.g., HOUR('15:33:30') returns 15).

IF(*test, value1, value2*)

If *test* is true, returns *value1*, otherwise returns *value2* (e.g., IF(1> 0,"true","false") returns true).

IFNULL(*value, value2*)

Returns *value* if it is not null; otherwise, returns *value2* (e.g., IFNULL(NULL, "bar") returns "bar").

INSERT(*string,position,length,new*)

Returns the string created by replacing the substring of *string* starting at *position* and going *length* characters with the string *new* (e.g., INSERT('help',3,1,' can jum') returns "he can jump").

INSTR(*string,substring*)

Identical to LOCATE except that the arguments are reversed (e.g., INSTR('makebelieve','lie') returns 7).

INTERVAL(*A,B,C,D*, . . .)

Returns 0 if *A* is the smallest value, 1 if *A* is between *B* and *C*, 2 if *A* is between *C* and *D*, etc. All values except for *A* must be in order (e.g., INTERVAL(5,2,4,6,8) returns 2, because 5 is in the second interval, between 4 and 6).

ISNULL(*expression*)

Returns 1 if the expression evaluates to NULL; otherwise, returns 0 (e.g., ISNULL(3) returns 0).

LAST_INSERT_ID( )

Returns the last value that was automatically generated for an AUTO_INCREMENT field (e.g., LAST_INSERT_ID( ) could return 4).

LCASE(*string*)
> Synonym for LOWER().

LEAST(*num1, num2*[*, num3, . . .*])
> Returns the numerically smallest of all the arguments (for example, LEAST(5,6,68,1,-20) returns –20).

LEFT(*string,length*)
> Returns *length* characters from the left end of *string* (e.g., LEFT("12345",3) returns "123").

LENGTH(*string*)
> Returns the length of *string* (e.g., CHAR_LENGTH('Hi Mom!') returns 7). In character sets that use multi-byte characters (such as Unicode and several Asian character sets), one character may take up more than one byte. In these cases, MySQL's string functions should correctly count the number of characters, not bytes, in the string. However, in versions prior to 3.23, this did not work properly and the function returned the number of bytes.

LOAD_FILE(*filename*)
> Reads the contents of the specified file as a string. This file must exist on the server and be world readable. Naturally, you must also have FILE privileges.

LOCATE(*substring,string*[*,number*])
> Returns the character position of the first occurrence of *substring* within *string* (e.g., LOCATE('SQL','MySQL') returns 3). If *substring* does not exist in *string*, 0 is returned. If a numerical third argument is supplied to LOCATE, the search for *substring* within *string* does not start until the given position within *string*.

LOG(*number*)
> Returns the natural logarithm of *number* (e.g., LOG(2) returns 0.693147).

LOG10(*number*)
> Returns the common logarithm of *number* (e.g., LOG10(1000) returns 3.000000).

LOWER(*string*)
> Returns *string* with all characters turned into lowercase (e.g., LOWER('BoB') returns "bob").

LPAD(*string,length,padding*)
> Returns *string* with padding added to the left end until the new string is *length* characters long (e.g., LPAD(' Merry X-Mas',18,'Ho') returns "HoHoHo Merry X-Mas").

LTRIM(*string*)
> Returns *string* with all leading whitespace removed (e.g., LTRIM(' Oops') returns "Oops").

MAKE_SET(*bits, string1, string2, ...*)

Creates a MySQL SET based on the binary representation of a number by mapping the on bits in the number to string values. The first string will appear in the output if the first (low-order) bit of *bits* is set, the second string will appear if the second bit is set, and so on. Example:

```
mysql> SELECT MAKE_SET(5, "a", "b", "c", "d", "e", "f");
+---------------------------------------------+
| MAKE_SET(5, "a", "b", "c", "d", "e", "f")   |
+---------------------------------------------+
| a,c                                         |
+---------------------------------------------+
1 row in set (0.01 sec)
```

MD5(*string*)

Creates an MD5 checksum for the specified string. The MD5 checksum is always a string of 32 hexadecimal numbers.

MID(*string,position,length*)

Synonym for SUBSTRING() with three arguments.

MINUTE(*time*)

Returns the minute of the given time (e.g., MINUTE('15:33:30') returns 33).

MOD(*num1, num2*)

Returns the modulo of *num1* divided by *num2*. This is the same as the % operator (e.g., MOD(11,3) returns 2).

MONTH(*date*)

Returns the number of the month (1 is January) for the given date (e.g., MONTH('1998-08-22') returns 8).

MONTHNAME(*date*)

Returns the name of the month for the given date (e.g., MONTHNAME('1998-08-22') returns "August").

NOW()

Returns the current date and time. A number of the form YYYYMMDDHHMMSS is returned if this is used in a numerical context; otherwise, a string of the form 'YYYY-MM-DD HH:MM:SS' is returned (e.g., NOW() could return "1998-08-24 12:55:32").

NULLIF(*value, value2*)

Return NULL if *value* and *value2* are equal, or else returns *value* (e.g., NULLIF((5+3)18,1) returns NULL).

OCT(*decimal*)

Returns the octal value of the given decimal number (e.g., OCT(8) returns 10). This is equivalent to the function CONV(decimal,10,8).

OCTET_LENGTH(*string*)

Synonym for LENGTH().

ORD(*string*)

Returns a numeric value corresponding to the first character in *string*. Treats a multi-byte string as a number in base 256. Thus, an 'x' in the first byte is worth 256 times as much as an 'x' in the second byte.

PASSWORD(*string*)

Returns a password-encrypted version of the given string (e.g., PASSWORD('mypass') could return "3afi4004idgv").

PERIOD_ADD(*date,months*)

Returns the date formed by adding the given number of months to *date* (which must be of the form YYMM or YYYYMM) (e.g., PERIOD_ADD(9808,14) returns 199910).

PERIOD_DIFF(*date1, date2*)

Returns the number of months between the two dates (which must be of the form YYMM or YYYYMM) (e.g., PERIOD_DIFF(199901,8901) returns 120).

PI( )

Returns the value of pi: 3.141593.

POSITION(*substring,string*)

Synonym for LOCATE() with two arguments.

POW(*num1, num2*)

Returns the value of *num1* raised to the *num2* power (e.g., POWER(3,2) returns 9.000000).

POWER(*num1, num2*)

Synonym for POW().

QUARTER(*date*)

Returns the number of the quarter of the given date (1 is January–March) (e.g., QUARTER('1998-08-22') returns 3).

RADIANS(*degrees*)

Returns the given argument converted from degrees to radians (e.g., RADIANS(-90) returns −1.570796).

RAND([*seed*])

Returns a random decimal value between 0 and 1. If an argument is specified, it is used as the seed of the random number generator (e.g., RAND(3) could return 0.435434).

RELEASE_LOCK(*name*)

Removes the named lock created with the GET_LOCK function. Returns 1 if the release is successful, 0 if it failed because the current thread did not own the lock, and a null value if the lock did not exist. For example, RELEASE_LOCK("mylock").

REPEAT(*string,number*)

Returns a string consisting of the original *string* repeated *number* times. Returns an empty string if *number* is less than or equal to zero (e.g., REPEAT('ma',4) returns 'mamamama').

REPLACE(*string,old,new*)

Returns a string that has all occurrences of the substring *old* replaced with *new* (e.g., REPLACE('*black jack*','*ack*','*oke*') returns "bloke joke").

REVERSE(*string*)

Returns the character reverse of *string* (e.g., REVERSE('my bologna') returns "angolob ym").

RIGHT(*string,length*)

Synonym for SUBSTRING() with FROM argument (e.g., RIGHT("string",1) returns "g").

ROUND(*number[,decimal]*)

Returns *number* rounded to the given number of decimals. If no *decimal* argument is supplied, *number* is rounded to an integer (e.g., ROUND(5.67,1) returns 5.7).

RPAD(*string,length,padding*)

Returns *string* with *padding* added to the right end until the new string is *length* characters long (e.g., RPAD('Yo',5,'!') returns "Yo!!!").

RTRIM(*string*)

Returns *string* with all trailing whitespace removed (e.g., RTRIM('Oops   ') returns "Oops").

SECOND(*time*)

Returns the seconds of the given time (e.g., SECOND('15:33:30') returns 30).

SEC_TO_TIME(*seconds*)

Returns the number of hours, minutes, and seconds in the given number of seconds. A number of the form HHMMSS is returned if this is used in a numerical context; otherwise, a string of the form HH:MM:SS is returned (e.g., SEC_TO_TIME(3666) returns "01:01:06").

SESSION_USER( )

Synonym for USER().

SIGN(*number*)

Returns −1 if *number* is negative, 0 if it's zero, or 1 if it's positive (e.g., SIGN(4) returns 1).

SIN(*radians*)

Returns the sine of the given number, which is in radians (e.g., SIN(2*PI( )) returns 0.000000).

SOUNDEX(*string*)

Returns the Soundex code associated with string (e.g., SOUNDEX('Jello') returns "J400").

SPACE(*number*)

Returns a string that contains *number* spaces (e.g., SPACE(5) returns "   ").

SQRT(*number*)

Returns the square root of *number* (e.g., SQRT(16) returns 4.000000).

STRCMP(*string1, string2*)

Returns 0 if the strings are the same, −1 if *string1* would sort before *string2*, or 1 if *string1* would sort after *string2* (e.g., STRCMP('bob','bobbie') returns −1).

SUBDATE(*date,* INTERVAL *amount type*)

Synonym for DATE_SUB().

SUBSTRING(*string,position*)

Returns all of *string* starting at *position* characters (e.g., SUBSTRING("123456",3) returns "3456").

SUBSTRING(*string,position,length*)/SUBSTRING(*string* FROM *position* FOR *length*)

Returns the substring formed by taking *length* characters from *string*, starting at *position* (e.g., SUBSTRING('12345',2,3) returns "234").

SUBSTRING(string FROM length)

Returns *length* characters from the right end of *string* (e.g., SUBSTRING("12345" FROM 3) returns "345").

SUBSTRING_INDEX(*string,character,number*)

Returns the substring formed by counting *number* of *character* within *string* and then returns everything to the left if the count is positive, or everything to the right if the count is negative (e.g., SUBSTRING_INDEX('1,2,3,4,5',',',3) returns "1,2,3").

SYSDATE()

Synonym for NOW().

SYSTEM_USER()

Synonym for USER().

TAN(*radians*)

Returns the tangent of the given number, which must be in radians (e.g., TAN(0) returns 0.000000).

TIME_FORMAT(*time, format*)

Returns the given time using a format string. The format string is of the same type as DATE_FORMAT, as shown earlier.

TIME_TO_SEC(*time*)

Returns the number of seconds in the *time* argument (e.g., TIME_TO_SEC('01:01:06') returns 3666).

TO_DAYS(*date*)

Returns the number of days (in which day 1 is Jan 1 of year 1) to the given date. The date may be a value of type DATE, DATETIME, or TIMESTAMP, or a number of the form YYMMDD or YYYYMMDD (e.g., TO_DAYS(19950402) returns 728749).

TRIM([BOTH|LEADING|TRAILING] [*remove*] [FROM] *string*)

With no modifiers, returns *string* with all trailing and leading whitespace removed. You can specify to remove the leading or trailing whitespace, or both. You can also specify a character other than space to be removed (e.g., TRIM(both '-' from '---look here---') returns "look here").

TRUNCATE(*number, decimals*)

Returns *number* truncated to the given number of decimals (for example, TRUNCATE(3.33333333,2) returns 3.33).

UCASE(*string*)

Synonym for UPPER().

UNIX_TIMESTAMP([*date*])

Returns the number of seconds from the epoch (January 1, 1970 GMT) to the given date (in GMT). If no date is given, the number of seconds to the current date is used (e.g., UNIX_TIMESTAMP('1998-08-24 18:00:02') returns 903981584).

UPPER(*string*)

Returns *string* with all characters turned into uppercase (e.g., UPPER ('Scooby') returns "SCOOBY").

USER()

Returns the name of the current user (e.g., SYSTEM_USER() could return "ryarger@localhost").

VERSION()

Returns the version of the MySQL server itself (e.g., VERSION() could return "3.22.5c-alpha").

WEEK(*date*)

Returns the week of the year for the given date (e.g., WEEK('1998-12-29') returns 52).

WEEKDAY(*date*)

Returns the numeric value of the day of the week for the specified date. Day numbers start with Monday as 0 and end with Sunday as 6.

YEAR(*date*)

Returns the year of the given date (e.g., YEAR('1998-12-29') returns 1998).

## CHAPTER 18

MySQL PHP API Reference

In this chapter, we list the functions that allow you to access the MySQL DBMS from PHP. We begin by discussing two database-specific data types used in many of these functions. The functions are then presented alphabetically with descriptions, and each includes an example code fragment. An introduction to PHP and examples of using PHP to access a MySQL DBMS are presented in Chapter 11. This chapter is based on Version 4.1.2, which was the version of PHP available at the time this book was written, but some differences between versions are discussed.

Data Types

The following PHP data types are specialized types for database access:

cresource

> A *connection resource handle*. An integer returned from the functions mysql_connect( ), and mysql_pconnect( ). Both functions are used to establish a connection to a MySQL DBMS, and are described later in this chapter. The connection resource handle is used as a parameter to several functions (such as mysql_select_db( ), mysql_query( ), and mysql_affected_rows( )) to determine or change aspects of the connection.

qresource

> A *query resource handle*. An integer returned from functions such as mysql_query(), mysql_list_fields(), mysql_list_dbs(), and mysql_unbuffered_query(). These functions are used to execute a query through a connection resource handle, and are described later in this chapter. A query resource handle is used as a parameter to several functions (such as mysql_fetch_array(), mysql_tablename(), and mysql_num_rows()) to retrieve a query's output or information about the query.

Functions

mysql_affected_rows

int mysql_affected_rows([cresource *connection*])

Returns the number of rows affected by the most recent DELETE, INSERT, or UPDATE statement. If the most recent query failed, −1 is returned. There is an exception to this rule: if all rows are deleted from a table, the function returns zero. The function takes an optional *connection* resource handle as a parameter. If no parameter is passed, the most recently opened connection that is still open is assumed. The function cannot be used with SELECT statements, where mysql_num_rows( ) should be used instead.

The function may report that zero rows were affected. For example, the query:

```
DELETE FROM customer WHERE cust_id = 3
```

always executes, but mysql_affected_rows( ) returns zero if there is no matching row. Similarly, if an UPDATE doesn't change the database, the function returns zero.

Example

```php
<?php
  $query = "INSERT INTO people
             VALUES(\"selina\", \"" . crypt("sarah", "se") . "\")";

  $connection = mysql_connect("localhost", "fred", "shhh");
  mysql_select_db("wedding", $connection);

  $result = mysql_query($query, $connection);

  echo "Inserted " . mysql_affected_rows($connection) . " row(s)";

?>
```

mysql_change_user

int mysql_change_user(string *username*, string *password* [, string *database*
[, cresource *connection*]])

Changes the logged-in MySQL user to another *username* using that user's *password*. Optional *database* and *connection* resource handles may be specified. If the *database* and *connection* resource handles are omitted, the current database and most recently opened connection that is still open are assumed.

The function returns true on success and false on failure. If false is returned, the user that was authenticated prior to the function call remains current.

The function `mysql_change_user()` is available only through MySQL DBMS Version 3.23.3 and later. In addition, the function is missing from PHP Version 4 (up to and including the current PHP 4.1.2), with calls to the function reporting it as an undefined function. This is likely to be fixed in future PHP versions.

Example

```php
<?php
  $connection = mysql_connect("localhost", "fred", "shhh");
  mysql_select_db("wedding", $connection);

  // The database will still be "wedding" on the current connection
  if (mysql_change_user("richo", "twelve") == true)
    echo "Changed user to richo";
  else
    echo "Change to user richo failed!";
?>
```

mysql_close

boolean mysql_close([cresource *connection*])

Closes the most recently opened MySQL DBMS connection. The function takes an optional *connection* resource handle as a parameter. If no parameter is passed, the most-recently opened connection that is still open is assumed.

The function returns true on success and false on failure.

This function is rarely used, as nonpersistent connections opened with `mysql_connect()` are closed when a script ends. Connections opened with `mysql_pconnect()` cannot be closed. Therefore, the only practical use of this function is to close a nonpersistent connection in a script where resource use must be minimized.

Example

```php
<?php
  $query = "SELECT * FROM presents";

  $connection = mysql_connect("localhost", "fred", "shhh");
  mysql_select_db("wedding", $connection);

  $result = mysql_query($query, $connection);

  while ($row = mysql_fetch_array($result))
    echo $row["present"] . "\n";

  mysql_close($connection);
?>
```

mysql_connect

cresource mysql_connect([string *hostname* [, string *username* [, string *password*
[, boolean *new_connection*]]]])

Used to establish a connection to the MySQL DBMS. The function returns a connection resource handle on success that can be used to access databases through subsequent function calls. The function returns false on failure.

The function has four optional parameters. The first is the *hostname* of the DBMS that can include an optional *port* number. The *hostname* parameter is usually set to localhost when the MySQL DBMS and the web server are running on the same machine. A default port for MySQL of 3306 is assumed if the port is omitted.

The second and third parameters—a *username* and *password*—are MySQL DBMS username and password credentials. These are the same username and password used to access the DBMS though the command-line monitor mysql.

If a second call is made to the function in the same script with the same first three parameters, a new connection is not opened. Instead, the function just returns the connection resource handle of the existing open connection. In the upcoming PHP 4.2 release, you should be able to override this behavior by supplying a fourth *new_connection* parameter. When it is set to true, a new connection will always be opened.

If all parameters are omitted, the *hostname* and port default to localhost:3306, the *username* defaults to the name of the user that owns the MySQL DBMS server process, and the *password* defaults to an empty string. Because these parameters are unlikely to be valid credentials for accessing the MySQL DBMS, the first three parameters to mysql_connect( ) should be supplied in practice.

Example

```php
<?php

    // This is a typical function call
    // Local machine, user "fred" and password "shhh"
    // On a Unix machine, this defaults to Unix socket
    $connection1 = mysql_connect("localhost", "fred", "shhh");

    // Local machine, user "fred" and password "shhh"
    // Adding the port forces a TCP/IP connection
    // on a Unix machine
    $connection2 = mysql_connect("localhost:3306", "fred", "shhh");

    // Remote machine "blah.webdatabasebook.com" on port 4000
    $connection3 = mysql_connect("blah.webdatabasebook.com:4000", "fred", "shhh");

?>
```

mysql_create_db

boolean mysql_create_db (string *database* [, cresource *connection*])

Creates a new database with the name supplied as the *database* parameter. The function takes an optional *connection* resource handle as the second parameter. If no second parameter is passed, the most recently opened connection that is still open is assumed. To use the database after creating it, you must call mysql_select_db( ).

Returns true on success and false on failure.

Example

```php
<?php
  $connection = mysql_connect("localhost", "fred", "shhh");

  if (mysql_create_db("temp", $connection))
    echo "Created database 'temp'";
  else
    echo "Create database 'temp' failed!";
?>
```

mysql_data_seek

boolean mysql_data_seek (qresource *query*, int *row*)

Moves the internal pointer related to a *query* to a specific *row*, where zero refers to the first row in a result set. After calling this function, the next row that is retrieved through mysql_fetch_array( ), mysql_fetch_assoc( ), mysql_fetch_object( ), or mysql_fetch_row( ) will be the *row* specified.

The function returns true on success and false on failure. A common source of failure is that there are no rows in the result set associated with the *query* resource handle. A prior call to mysql_num_rows( ) can be used to determine if results were returned from the query.

Example

```php
<?php
  $query = "SELECT * FROM presents";

  $connection = mysql_connect("localhost", "fred", "shhh");
  mysql_select_db("wedding", $connection);

  $result = mysql_query($query, $connection);

  if (!mysql_data_seek($result, 7))
    echo "Could not seek to the eighth row!";

  $row = mysql_fetch_array($result);

  echo "Eighth row: " . $row["present"];
?>
```

mysql_db_name

string mysql_db_name (qresource *query*, int *row*[, mixed unused])

Returns the name of a database associated with a *query* resource handle returned from a prior call to mysql_list_dbs( ). The second argument is a *row* index into the *query* result set. The first database in the result set is numbered zero. The number of database names in the result set can be determined using mysql_num_rows( ).

This function returns false on error. A common source of error is supplying a *row* number that is greater than the number of databases available at the DBMS.

 This function is an alias to mysql_result( ). It is therefore possible to supply a third argument to this function, but it should not be used in practice with mysql_db_name( ).

Example

```php
<?php
  $connection = mysql_connect("localhost", "fred", "shhh");
  mysql_select_db("wedding", $connection);

  $result = mysql_list_dbs($connection);

  echo "The databases available are:\n";

  for ($x=0; $x < mysql_num_rows($result); $x++)
     echo mysql_db_name($result, $x) . "\n";
?>
```

mysql_drop_db

boolean mysql_drop_db(string *database* [, cresource *connection*])

Drops a *database*. An optional *connection* can be supplied; otherwise, the most recently opened connection resource handle that is still open is used. This function permanently deletes the database, its tables, and its data.

The function returns true on success and false on failure.

Example

```php
<?php
  $connection = mysql_connect("localhost", "fred", "shhh");

  if (mysql_drop_db("temp", $connection))
     echo "Dropped database 'temp'";
  else
     echo "Drop database 'temp' failed!";
?>
```

mysql_errno

```
int mysql_errno([resource connection])
```

Returns the error number of the most recently executed MySQL function or zero if no error occurred. An optional *connection* can be supplied; otherwise, the most-recently opened connection resource handle that is still open is used. Any successful MySQL-related function call resets the value of this function to zero, with the exceptions of mysql_error() and mysql_errno(), which do not change the value.

Example

```php
<?php
  $connection = mysql_connect("localhost", "fred", "shhh");

  mysql_select_db("not-a-database", $connection);

  // Prints MySQL reported error 1049
  if (mysql_errno())
     echo "MySQL reported error " . mysql_errno();
?>
```

mysql_error

```
string mysql_error([cresource connection])
```

Returns the text of the error message associated with the most recently executed MySQL function or '' (the empty string) if no error occurred. An optional *connection* can be supplied; otherwise, the most recently opened connection resource handle that is still open is used. Any successful MySQL-related function call resets the text to '' (the empty string), with the exceptions of mysql_error() and mysql_errno(), which do not change this value.

Example

```php
<?php
  $connection = mysql_connect("localhost", "fred", "shhh");

  mysql_select_db("not-a-database", $connection);

  // Prints MySQL reported error: Unknown database 'not-a-database'
  if (mysql_errno())
     echo "MySQL reported error: " . mysql_error();
?>
```

mysql_escape_string

```
string mysql_escape_string (string input)
```

Escapes an *input* string so it can be used as a parameter to mysql_query() or mysql_unbuffered_query(). The function returns a copy of the input string that has any special characters escaped so it is safe to use in an SQL query. Specifically, it escapes single quote, double quote, NULL, carriage return, line feed, and SUB (substitute) characters.

Example

```
<?php
  $person = "Steven O'Grady";
  $person = mysql_escape_string($person);

  // Prints: Steven O\'Grady
  echo $person;
?>
```

mysql_fetch_array

array mysql_fetch_array (qresource *query* [, int *array_type*])

Returns an array that contains the next available row from the result set associated with the parameter *query*. The internal pointer associated with the result set is then incremented, so that the next call to this function will retrieve the next row. The *query* resource handle is returned from a prior call to mysql_query( ) or mysql_unbuffered_query( ). The function returns false when no more rows are available.

Each row is returned as an array, and all elements of the array are of type string. The second parameter, *array_type*, controls whether associative access, numeric access, or both are possible on the array. When set to MYSQL_ASSOC, the function behaves identically to mysql_fetch_assoc( ). When set to MYSQL_NUM, the function behaves identically to mysql_fetch_row( ). The default is MYSQL_BOTH, which permits both associative and numeric array access.

If two or more attributes in the query have the same name, only the last-named attribute in the SELECT clause is available via the associative array. The other attributes with identical names must be accessed via their numeric indexes.

When both a table and attribute name are used in a SELECT statement, only the attribute name should be used to access the data associatively. For example, after executing the statement SELECT p.quantity FROM presents p, the attribute data is accessed associatively in the array $row that is returned from mysql_fetch_array( ) as $row["quantity"].

Attributes can be aliased and then retrieved using the alias name. For example, consider the following statement:

```
SELECT customer.cust_id AS c,
       orders.cust_id AS o
FROM orders, customer
WHERE customer.cust_id = orders.cust_id
```

The attribute data can be accessed in an associate array $row that is returned from mysql_fetch_array( ) as $row["c"] and $row["o"].

Aggregate functions are associatively referenced using the aggregate function name. For example, after executing the statement SELECT sum(quantity) FROM presents, the aggregate data is accessed associatively in the array $row that is returned from mysql_fetch_array( ) as $row["sum(quantity)"].

Prior to PHP 4.0.5, NULL values were not returned into the array, but this has been fixed in recent versions.

This bug doesn't affect associative access, but it causes renumbering for numeric access. If a table has a NULL attribute, the array returned has one fewer element. The missing element can still be referenced associatively, because referencing a nonexistent element correctly returns NULL. However, if you want to avoid having arrays of different lengths returned, ensure that all attributes have a value or upgrade to a new release of PHP.

Example

```php
<?php
  $query = "SELECT * FROM presents";

  $connection = mysql_connect("localhost", "fred", "shhh");
  mysql_select_db("wedding", $connection);

  $result = mysql_query($query, $connection);

  while ($row = mysql_fetch_array($result))
  {
      echo "ID:\t{$row["present_id"]}\n";
      echo "Quantity:\t{$row["quantity"]}\n";
      echo "Present:\t{$row["present"]}\n";
      echo "Shop:\t{$row["shop"]}\n\n";
  }
?>
```

mysql_fetch_assoc

array mysql_fetch_assoc (qresource *query*)

Returns an associative array that contains the next available row from the result set associated with the parameter *query*. The internal pointer associated with the result set is then incremented, so that the next call to this function will retrieve the next row. The *query* resource handle is returned from a prior call to mysql_query( ) or mysql_unbuffered_query( ). The function returns false when no more rows are available.

The function behaves identically to mysql_fetch_array( ) when its second parameter is set to MYSQL_ASSOC. See the description of mysql_fetch_array( ) for the limitations of associative access to query results.

Example

```php
<?php
  $query = "SELECT people_id FROM people";

  $connection = mysql_connect("localhost", "fred", "shhh");
  mysql_select_db("wedding", $connection);

  $result = mysql_query($query, $connection);
```

```
    echo "Users:\n";

    while ($row = mysql_fetch_assoc($result))
        echo $row["people_id"] . "\n";
?>
```

mysql_fetch_field

`object mysql_fetch_field(qresource` *query* `[, int` *attribute* `])`

Returns an object containing metadata about an attribute associated with a *query* resource handle. The first argument is a *query* resource handle returned from a prior call to mysql_list_fields( ), mysql_query( ), or mysql_unbuffered_query( ). The second optional parameter indicates which *attribute* in the result set is required. If no second argument is provided, metadata about the first attribute that has not yet been retrieved is returned. Thus, successive calls to mysql_fetch_fields( ) can be used to retrieve information about all the attributes in a query result set.

The properties of the object returned by the function are:

name
:   The attribute name

table
:   The name of the table to which the attribute belongs

max_length
:   The maximum length of the attribute

not_null
:   Set to one if the attribute cannot be NULL

primary_key
:   Set to one if the attribute forms part of a primary key

unique_key
:   Set to one if the attribute is a unique key

multiple_key
:   Set to one if the attribute is a non-unique key

numeric
:   Set to one if the attribute is a numeric type

blob
:   Set to one if the attribute is a BLOB type

type
:   The type of the attribute

unsigned
:   Set to one if the attribute is an unsigned numeric type

zerofill
:   Set to one if the numeric column is zero filled

Example

```php
<?php
  $connection = mysql_connect("localhost", "fred", "shhh");

  $result = mysql_list_fields("wedding", "presents");

  echo "Presents table attributes:\n";

  while ($row = mysql_fetch_field($result))
  {
     echo $row->name;
     echo " is an attribute of type " . $row->type . ".";
     if ($row->not_null == true)
        echo " It cannot be null.\n";
     else
        echo " It can be null.\n";
  }
?>
```

mysql_fetch_lengths

array mysql_fetch_lengths(qresource *query*)

Returns an array of attribute lengths associated with the most recently retrieved row of data. The argument to the function is a *query* result handle that has been used to retrieve at least one row. The elements of the returned array correspond to the length of the values in the array returned from the most recent call to mysql_fetch_row( ), mysql_fetch_array( ), mysql_fetch_object( ), or mysql_fetch_assoc( ).

This function returns the length of a value within the specific result set, not the maximum length of an attribute as defined in the database table. Use the function mysql_field_len( ) to retrieve the maximum length of an attribute as defined in the database table.

The function returns false on error.

Example

```php
<?php
  $query = "SELECT * FROM presents";

  $connection = mysql_connect("localhost", "fred", "shhh");
  mysql_select_db("wedding", $connection);

  $result = mysql_query($query, $connection);

  while ($row = mysql_fetch_row($result))
  {
     echo "The total length of this row is: ";
     $row2 = mysql_fetch_lengths($result);
```

```
        $length = 0;
        foreach ($row2 as $element)
            $length += $element;

        echo $length . "\n";
    }
?>
```

mysql_fetch_object

```
object mysql_fetch_object(qresource query [, int array_type])
```

Returns an object that contains the next available row from the result set associated with the parameter *query*. The internal pointer associated with the result set is then incremented, so that the next call to this function will retrieve the next row. The *query* resource handle is returned from a prior call to mysql_query( ) or mysql_unbuffered_query( ). The function returns false when no more rows are available.

Each row is returned as an object, and all member variables of the object are of type string. The second parameter *array_type* should be included and set to MYSQL_ASSOC. Numeric indexes cannot be used to access objects.

The same associative access limitations that apply to mysql_fetch_array( ) apply to mysql_fetch_object( ). There is one additional limitation: aggregate functions must be aliased for associative access, because parentheses and other special characters are invalid in member variable names. Thus, the sum( ) function in the statement SELECT sum(quantity) as total FROM presents can be accessed associatively in the object $row as $row->total.

Example

```
<?php
  $query = "SELECT * FROM presents";

  $connection = mysql_connect("localhost", "fred", "shhh");
  mysql_select_db("wedding", $connection);

  $result = mysql_query($query, $connection);

  while ($row = mysql_fetch_object($result, MYSQL_ASSOC))
  {
      echo "\n\nQuantity:\t" . $row->quantity;
      echo "\nPresent:\t" . $row->present;
      echo "\nShop:\t" . $row->shop;
  }
?>
```

mysql_fetch_row

```
array mysql_fetch_row(qresource query)
```

Returns a numerically indexed array that contains the next available row from the result set associated with the parameter *query*. The internal pointer associated with the result set is then incremented, so that the next call to this function will retrieve the next row. The *query* resource handle is returned from a prior call to mysql_query( ) or mysql_unbuffered_query( ). Returns false when no more rows are available.

The function behaves identically to mysql_fetch_array( ) when its second parameter is set to MYSQL_NUM. Unlike mysql_fetch_assoc( ) (and mysql_fetch_array( ) with the MYSQL_BOTH or MYSQL_ASSOC second parameter), the array returned by mysql_fetch_row( ) contains all the attributes of the result set, even if some attributes have the same name.

Example

```php
<?php
  $query = "SELECT * FROM presents";

  $connection = mysql_connect("localhost", "fred", "shhh");
  mysql_select_db("wedding", $connection);

  $result = mysql_query($query, $connection);

  while ($row = mysql_fetch_row($result))
  {
    for($x=0;$x<mysql_num_fields($result);$x++)
      echo $row[$x] . " ";
    echo "\n";
  }
?>
```

mysql_field_flags

string mysql_field_flags(qresource *query*, int *attribute*)

Returns a string containing any special flags associated with an attribute in a query result set. The first argument is a *query* resource handle returned from a prior call to mysql_list_fields( ), mysql_query( ), or mysql_unbuffered_query( ). The second argument is the ordinal number of the *attribute* in the SQL query. The first attribute is numbered zero.

The flags are returned as a string and are delimited with a space character. The following flags are reported:

not_null
> The attribute cannot contain a NULL value.

primary_key
> The attribute is a primary key.

unique_key
> The attribute is a unique key.

multiple_key
> The attribute is a non-unique key.

blob
> The attribute is a BLOB type.

unsigned

> The attribute is an unsigned integer.

zerofill

> The attribute is a zero-filled numeric.

binary

> The attribute may contain binary data and will use binary-safe comparisons.

enum

> The attribute is an enumeration, which can contain one of several predefined values.

auto_increment

> The attribute has the auto_increment modifier.

timestamp

> The attribute is an automatic timestamp field.

Example

```php
<?php
  $connection = mysql_connect("localhost", "fred", "shhh");

  $result = mysql_list_fields("wedding", "presents");

  for($x=0; $x < mysql_num_fields($result); $x++)
    echo mysql_field_name($result, $x) .
        " has the properties: " .
        mysql_field_flags($result, $x) . "\n";
?>
```

mysql_field_name

string mysql_field_name(qresource *query*, int *attribute*)

Returns the name of an attribute in a result set. The first parameter is a *query* resource handle returned from a prior call to mysql_list_fields( ), mysql_query( ), or mysql_unbuffered_query( ). The second argument is the ordinal number of the *attribute* in the SQL query. The first attribute is numbered zero.

Example

```php
<?php
  $connection = mysql_connect("localhost", "fred", "shhh");

  $result = mysql_list_fields("wedding", "presents");

  echo "The attributes of presents are: ";
  for($x=0; $x < mysql_num_fields($result); $x++)
    echo mysql_field_name($result, $x) . " ";
?>
```

mysql_field_len

`int mysql_field(qresource query, int attribute)`

Returns the defined maximum length of an attribute in a result set. The first parameter is a *query* resource handle returned from a prior call to mysql_list_fields( ), mysql_query( ), or mysql_unbuffered_query( ). The second argument is the ordinal number of the attribute in the SQL query. The first attribute is numbered zero.

This function returns the maximum length of the attribute as defined in the database table, not the length of a value within a specific result set. Use the function mysql_fetch_lengths( ) to retrieve the length of specific values.

Example

```php
<?php
  $connection = mysql_connect("localhost", "fred", "shhh");

  $result = mysql_list_fields("wedding", "presents");

  for($x=0; $x < mysql_num_fields($result); $x++)
     echo mysql_field_name($result, $x) .
        " has a maximum length of " .
        mysql_field_len($result, $x) . "\n";
?>
```

mysql_field_seek

`boolean mysql_field_seek(qresource query, int attribute)`

Sets the internal attribute pointer within a result set. The first parameter is a *query* resource handle returned from a prior call to mysql_query( ) or mysql_unbuffered_query( ). The second argument is the ordinal number of the attribute in the SQL query, where zero refers to the first attribute.

After the attribute pointer has been set using this function, the next call to mysql_fetch_field( ) will return the attribute at this pointer.

The function returns true on success and false on error.

Example

```php
<?php
  $connection = mysql_connect("localhost", "fred", "shhh");

  $result = mysql_list_fields("wedding", "presents");

  mysql_field_seek($result, 2);

  $field = mysql_fetch_field($result);

  echo "The third attribute is " . $field->name;
?>
```

mysql_field_table

```
string mysql_field_table(qresource query, int attribute)
```

Returns the name of the table that contains the specified attribute. The first parameter is a *query* resource handle returned from a prior call to mysql_query( ), mysql_list_fields( ), or mysql_unbuffered_query( ). The second argument is the ordinal number of the *attribute* in the SQL query, where zero refers to the first attribute.

Example

```php
<?php
  $query = "SELECT * FROM presents, people WHERE presents.people_id = people.people_
  id";

  $connection = mysql_connect("localhost", "fred", "shhh");
  mysql_select_db("wedding", $connection);

  $result = mysql_query($query, $connection);

  echo "The table associated with the first attribute is " . mysql_field_
  table($result, 1);
?>
```

mysql_field_type

```
string mysql_field_type(qresource query, int attribute)
```

Returns the PHP type of an attribute. The first parameter is a *query* resource handle returned from a prior call to mysql_list_fields( ), mysql_query( ), or mysql_unbuffered_query( ). The second argument is the ordinal number of the *attribute* in the SQL query, where zero refers to the first attribute.

Example

```php
<?php
  $query = "SELECT * FROM presents, people WHERE presents.people_id = people.people_
  id";

  $connection = mysql_connect("localhost", "fred", "shhh");
  mysql_select_db("wedding", $connection);

  $result = mysql_query($query, $connection);

  for($x=0;$x<mysql_num_fields($result);$x++)
      echo "The type of attribute $x is " . mysql_field_type($result, $x) . "\n";
?>
```

mysql_free_result

`boolean mysql_free_result(qresource query)`

Frees all memory used by a *query* resource handle. This occurs automatically at the end of a script, but this function may be useful in scripts where repeated querying is performed or memory is constrained.

The function returns true on success and false on error.

Example

```php
<?php
  $query = "SELECT * FROM presents";

  $connection = mysql_connect("localhost", "fred", "shhh");
  mysql_select_db("wedding", $connection);

  $result = mysql_query($query, $connection);

  while ($row = mysql_fetch_object($result, MYSQL_ASSOC))
  {
     echo "\n\nQuantity:\t" . $row->quantity;
     echo "\nPresent:\t" . $row->present;
     echo "\nShop:\t" . $row->shop;
  }

  mysql_free_result($result);
?>
```

mysql_get_client_info

`string mysql_get_client_info( )`

Returns a string that describes the MySQL client library used by PHP. This is currently the library version number. This function is available only in PHP 4.0.5 or later versions.

Example

```php
<?php
  // Prints (on our machine): This is the 3.23.44 MySQL client library.
  echo "This is the " . mysql_get_client_info( ) . " MySQL client library.";
?>
```

mysql_get_host_info

`string mysql_get_host_info([cresource connection])`

Returns a string that describes a MySQL server connection. The string contains the type of connection (TCP or Unix socket) and the hostname. An optional *connection* resource handle may be provided as the parameter; otherwise, the most recently opened connection that is still open is assumed. This function is available only in PHP 4.0.5 or later versions.

Example

```
<?php
  mysql_connect("localhost", "root", "drum");

  // Prints: This is a Localhost via UNIX socket connection to MySQL.
  echo "This is a " . mysql_get_host_info() . " connection to MySQL.";
?>
```

mysql_get_proto_info

int mysql_get_proto_info([cresource *connection*])

Returns an integer that is the protocol version used in a MySQL server connection. An optional *connection* resource handle may be provided as the parameter; otherwise, the most recently opened connection that is still open is assumed. This function is available only in PHP 4.0.5 or later versions.

Example

```
<?php
echo "You are connected to MySQL using protocol " . mysql_get_proto_info();
?>
```

mysql_get_server_info

string mysql_get_server_info([cresource *connection*])

Returns as a string the version of the MySQL DBMS. An optional *connection* resource handle may be provided as the parameter, otherwise, the most recently opened connection that is still open is assumed. This function is available only in PHP 4.0.5 or later versions.

Example

```
<?php
  mysql_connect("localhost", "fred", "shhh");

  // Prints (on our machine): This is MySQL version 3.23.44-log
  echo "This is MySQL version " . mysql_get_server_info();
?>
```

mysql_insert_id

int mysql_insert_id([cresource *connection*])

Returns the most recently generated AUTO_INCREMENT identifier value associated with a connection. An optional *connection* resource handle may be provided as the parameter; otherwise, the most recently opened connection that is still open is assumed.

This function works for a *connection* and not on a per-query basis. Subsequent INSERT statements through the same *connection* make it impossible to retrieve previous identifier values using this function. The return value is not affected by non-INSERT SQL statements.

The function returns false if there have been no AUTO_INCREMENT identifiers for the connection.

Example

```php
<?php
  $query = "INSERT INTO presents
            VALUES(NULL, \"Bike\", \"Fitzroy Cycles\", 1, \"Red\", \"350.00\",
NULL)";

  $connection = mysql_connect("localhost", "root", "drum");
  mysql_select_db("wedding", $connection);

  $result = mysql_query($query, $connection);

  echo "Inserted record " . mysql_insert_id($connection);
?>
```

mysql_list_dbs

qresource mysql_list_dbs([cresource *connection*])

Returns a query resource handle that can be used to retrieve the names of the databases available on a connection; the database names are retrieved with a subsequent call to mysql_db_name( ). An optional *connection* resource handle may be provided as the parameter; otherwise, the most recently opened connection that is still open is assumed.

Returns false on error.

Example

```php
<?php
  $connection = mysql_connect("localhost", "fred", "shhh");
  mysql_select_db("wedding", $connection);

  $result = mysql_list_dbs($connection);

  echo "The databases available are:\n";

  for ($x=0; $x < mysql_num_rows($result); $x++)
     echo mysql_db_name($result, $x) . "\n";
?>
```

mysql_list_fields

qresource mysql_list_fields(string *database*, string *table*[, cresource *connection*])

Returns a query resource handle that can be used to retrieve information about the attributes of the specified *table* within the given *database*. The attribute information can be

retrieved through the functions mysql_field_name( ), mysql_field_type( ), mysql_field_
len( ), and mysql_field_flags( ). An optional *connection* resource handle may be provided
as the third parameter; otherwise, the most recently opened connection that is still open is
assumed.

Returns false on failure.

Example

```php
<?php
  $connection = mysql_connect("localhost", "fred", "shhh");

  $result = mysql_list_fields("wedding", "presents");

  echo "The attributes of presents are: ";
  for($x=0; $x < mysql_num_fields($result); $x++)
    echo mysql_field_name($result, $x) . " ";
?>
```

mysql_list_tables

qresource mysql_list_tables(string *database*[, cresource *connection*])

Returns a query resource handle that can be used to retrieve information about the tables
within the given *database*. The table name information can be retrieved with the function
mysql_tablename( ). An optional *connection* resource handle may be provided as the second
parameter; otherwise, the most recently opened connection that is still open is assumed.

Returns false on failure.

Example

```php
<?php
  $connection = mysql_connect("localhost", "fred", "shhh");

  $result = mysql_list_tables("wedding", $connection);

  echo "The tables of wedding are: ";
  for($x=0; $x < mysql_num_rows($result); $x++)
    echo mysql_tablename($result, $x) . " ";
?>
```

mysql_num_fields

int mysql_num_fields(qresource *query*)

Returns the number of attributes in a row associated with the *query* resource handle parameter. The *query* resource handle is returned from a prior call to mysql_list_fields( ),
mysql_query( ), or mysql_unbuffered_query( ).

Example

```php
<?php
  $connection = mysql_connect("localhost", "fred", "shhh");

  $result = mysql_list_fields("wedding", "presents", $connection);

  echo "There are " . mysql_num_fields($result) . " attributes in presents";
?>
```

mysql_num_rows

int mysql_num_rows(qresource *query*)

Returns the number of rows associated with a *query* resource handle. The *query* resource handle is returned from a prior call to mysql_query(). The function does not work with mysql_unbuffered_query(). In addition, this function works only for SELECT queries; the number of rows affected by an SQL INSERT, UPDATE, or DELETE statement should be determined using the function mysql_affected_rows().

Example

```php
<?php
  $query = "SELECT * FROM presents WHERE present LIKE 'M%'";

  $connection = mysql_connect("localhost", "fred", "shhh");
  mysql_select_db("wedding", $connection);

  $result = mysql_query($query, $connection);

  echo "There are " . mysql_num_rows($result) . " presents that begin with M";
?>
```

mysql_pconnect

cresource mysql_pconnect([string *hostname* [, string *username* [, string *password*]]])

Used to establish or re-establish a connection to the MySQL DBMS. The function returns a connection resource handle on success that can be used to access databases through subsequent function calls. The function returns false on failure. The three parameters are identical to the first three parameters of mysql_connect().

This function should be called only once with the same parameters in a script: any subsequent calls to mysql_pconnect() in the same script with the same parameters return the same connection handle. Indeed, connections created with mysql_pconnect() are often reused across several scripts: the p stands for persistent, which means that after the script ends, the connection is kept in a pool. The connection can then be reused by any other script that requires a connection with the same *hostname*, *username*, and *password*.

Connections in the pool that remain unused are closed to save resources. How long a connection can remain unused is a MySQL parameter and is set to a default of five seconds. This can be changed with the *--set-variable connect_timeout* parameter to *safe_mysqld*.

Persistent connections are available only through a PHP module that is integrated into a web server. See Chapter 11 for details.

Example

```php
<?php
$query = "SELECT * FROM presents";

$connection = mysql_pconnect("localhost", "fred", "shhh");
mysql_select_db("wedding", $connection);

$result = mysql_query($query, $connection);

while ($row = mysql_fetch_array($result))
    echo $row["present"] . "\n";

?>
```

mysql_query

qresource mysql_query(string *query*[, cresource *connection*])

Executes an SQL *query* and (usually) returns a query resource handle that can be used to retrieve the result set. The *query* statement does not need to be terminated with a semicolon, and any valid SQL statement is permitted. If the *connection* resource handle parameter is omitted, the last opened connection that is still open is assumed. If no connection is open, an attempt is made to open one, just as when mysql_connect( ) is issued with no parameters.

On success, the function never returns a false value. For SELECT, SHOW, EXPLAIN, or DESCRIBE queries, the function returns a query result resource that can be used to fetch data. For other SQL queries, the function returns true on success. The function returns false on failure.

Example

```php
<?php
$query = "SELECT * FROM people WHERE people_id LIKE 'h%'";

$connection = mysql_connect("localhost", "fred", "shhh");
mysql_select_db("wedding", $connection);

$result = mysql_query($query, $connection);

while ($row = mysql_fetch_array($result))
    echo $row["people_id"] . "\n";

?>
```

mysql_result

string mysql_result(qresource *query*, int *row*[, mixed *attribute*])

Retrieves as a string attribute value from a *query* resource handle. The *row* that contains the attribute is the second parameter; rows are numbered starting at zero. By default, the first attribute of the row is returned. A specific *attribute* can be provided as the third parameter. This *attribute* can be specified by using the attribute's ordinal position in the SQL query (where the first attribute is numbered zero), its name as given in the SQL query, or the fully qualified SQL name of the attribute (using the *table.attribute* notation). The ordinal position alternative executes much faster than the other alternatives and should be used wherever possible.

mysql_result() is different from functions that return entire rows, such as mysql_fetch_row().

You should not mix calls to mysql_result() with calls to other functions that read data from a result set. Also, mysql_result() is much slower for reading row data than row-specific functions, and should not be used for this task.

Example

```php
<?php
  $query = "SELECT count(*) FROM people";

  $connection = mysql_connect("localhost", "fred", "shhh");
  mysql_select_db("wedding", $connection);

  $result = mysql_query($query, $connection);

  $count = mysql_result($result, 0);
  echo "There are " . $count . " rows in people";
?>
```

mysql_select_db

boolean mysql_select_db(string *database*[, cresource *connection*])

Use the specified *database* on a connection. Subsequent calls to query functions (such as mysql_query() or mysql_unbuffered_query()) will execute on this *database*. An optional *connection* resource handle may be provided; otherwise, the most recently opened connection that is still open is assumed. If no connection is open, an attempt is made to open one with a mysql_connect() call that has no parameters.

This function returns true on success and false on failure.

Example

```php
<?php
    $connection = mysql_connect("localhost", "fred", "shhh");
    mysql_select_db("wedding", $connection);
?>
```

mysql_tablename

string mysql_tablename(qresource *query*, int *table*[, mixed *unused*])

Returns the name of a table from a prior *query* with mysql_list_tables( ). The second argument is an ordinal *table* index into the *query* result set, where the first table in the result set is numbered zero. The number of table names in the result set can be determined using mysql_num_rows( ).

This function returns false on error. A common source of error is supplying a *table* number that is greater than the number of tables available in the database.

 This function is an alias to mysql_result( ). It is therefore possible to supply a third argument to this function, but it should not be used in practice with mysql_tablename( ).

Example

```php
<?php
    $connection = mysql_connect("localhost", "fred", "shhh");

    $result = mysql_list_tables("wedding", $connection);

    echo "The tables of wedding are: ";
    for($x=0; $x < mysql_num_rows($result); $x++)
        echo mysql_tablename($result, $x) . " ";
?>
```

mysql_unbuffered_query

qresource mysql_unbuffered_query(string *query*[, cresource *connection*])

Execute a query without retrieving and buffering the entire result set. This is useful for queries that return large results sets or that are slow to execute. The advantage is that you don't need the memory resources to store the complete result set, and the function will return before the SQL query has finished. In contrast, the function mysql_query( ) does not return until the query is finished and all of the results have been buffered for subsequent retrieval. The parameters and return values are identical to mysql_query( ).

The disadvantage of mysql_unbuffered_query( ) is that mysql_num_rows( ) cannot be called for the returned query resource handle, because the number of rows returned from the query is not known. The function is otherwise identical in behavior to mysql_query( ).

This function is available in PHP 4.0.6 or later versions.

Because of the internal MySQL workings of this function, it is important that you finish processing a result set created with `mysql_unbuffered_query( )` before creating a new query. Failure to do so may create unpredictable results.

Example

```php
<?php
  $query = "SELECT * FROM presents";

  $connection = mysql_pconnect("localhost", "fred", "shhh");
  mysql_select_db("wedding", $connection);

  $result = mysql_unbuffered_query($query, $connection);

  while ($row = mysql_fetch_array($result))
     echo $row["present"] . "\n";
?>
```

## CHAPTER 19

C Reference

The MySQL C API underlies all the APIs used by other languages to communicate with MySQL.

Data Types

The MySQL C API uses several defined data types beyond the standard C types. These types are defined in the *mysql.h* header file that must be included when compiling any program that uses the MySQL library.

MYSQL

> A structure representing a connection to the database server. The program allocates a variable of this type, initializes the variable through the mysql_init call, and passes the variable to subsequent calls. The elements of the structure contain the name of the current database and information about the client connection, among other things.

MYSQL_FIELD

> A structure containing all the information concerning a specific field in the table. Of all the types created for MySQL, this is the only one with member variables accessed directly from client programs. Therefore, you need to know the layout of the structure:

char *name
> The name of the field.

char *table
> The name of the table containing this field. For result sets that do not correspond to real tables, this value is null.

char *def
> The default value of this field, if one exists. This value is always null unless mysql_list_fields is called, after which it is the correct value for fields that have defaults.

enum enum_field_types type

The type of the field. The type is one of the internal MySQL SQL data types. The following field types (along with their corresponding common MySQL SQL data types) are currently defined:

- FIELD_TYPE_TINY (TINYINT)
- FIELD_TYPE_SHORT (SMALLINT)
- FIELD_TYPE_LONG (INTEGER)
- FIELD_TYPE_INT24 (MEDIUMINT)
- FIELD_TYPE_LONGLONG (BIGINT)
- FIELD_TYPE_DECIMAL (DECIMAL or NUMERIC)
- FIELD_TYPE_FLOAT (FLOAT)
- FIELD_TYPE_DOUBLE (DOUBLE or REAL)
- FIELD_TYPE_TIMESTAMP (TIMESTAMP)
- FIELD_TYPE_DATE (DATE)
- FIELD_TYPE_TIME (TIME)
- FIELD_TYPE_DATETIME (DATETIME)
- FIELD_TYPE_YEAR (YEAR)
- FIELD_TYPE_STRING (CHAR or VARCHAR)
- FIELD_TYPE_BLOB (BLOB or TEXT)
- FIELD_TYPE_SET (SET)
- FIELD_TYPE_ENUM (ENUM)
- FIELD_TYPE_NULL (NULL)
- FIELD_TYPE_CHAR (TINYINT) (Deprecated, replaced by FIELD_TYPE_TINY)

unsigned int length

The size of the field based on the field's type.

unsigned int max_length

If accessed after calling mysql_list_fields, this contains the length of the maximum value contained in the current result set. If the field is a BLOB-style field (e.g., BLOB, TEXT, LONGBLOB, MEDIUMTEXT, etc.), this value is always 8000 (~8 kB) if called before the actual data is retrieved from the result set (by using mysql_store_result( ), for example). Once the data has been retrieved, this field contains the actual maximum length.

unsigned int flags

Zero or more option flags. The following flags are currently defined:

NOT_NULL_FLAG

If defined, the field cannot contain a NULL value.

PRI_KEY_FLAG

    If defined, the field is a primary key.

UNIQUE_KEY_FLAG

    If defined, the field is part of a unique key.

MULTIPLE_KEY_FLAG

    If defined, the field is part of a key.

BLOB_FLAG

    If defined, the field is of type BLOB or TEXT.

UNSIGNED_FLAG

    If defined, the field is a numeric type with an unsigned value.

ZEROFILL_FLAG

    If defined, the application should fill any unused characters in a value of this field with zeros.

BINARY_FLAG

    If defined, the field is of type CHAR or VARCHAR with the BINARY flag.

ENUM_FLAG

    If defined, the field is of type ENUM.

AUTO_INCREMENT_FLAG

    If defined, the field has the AUTO_INCREMENT attribute.

TIMESTAMP_FLAG

    If defined, the field is of type TIMESTAMP.

SET_FLAG

    If defined, the field is of type SET.

NUM_FLAG

    If defined, the field is a numeric type (e.g., INT, DOUBLE, etc.).

PART_KEY_FLAG

    If defined, the field is part of a key. This flag is not meant for use by clients, and its behavior may change in the future.

GROUP_FLAG

    This flag is not meant for use by clients, and its behavior may change in the future.

UNIQUE_FLAG

    This flag is not meant for use by clients, and its behavior may change in the future.

unsigned int decimals

    When used with a numeric field, this lists the number of decimals used in the field.

The following macros are provided to help examine the MYSQL_FIELD data:

IS_PRI_KEY(*flags*)

> Returns true if the field is a primary key. This macro takes the flags attribute of a MYSQL_FIELD structure as its argument.

IS_NOT_NULL(*flags*)

> Returns true if the field is defined as NOT NULL. This macro takes the flags attribute of a MYSQL_FIELD structure as its argument.

IS_BLOB(*flags*)

> Returns true if the field is of type BLOB or TEXT. This macro takes the flags attribute of a MYSQL_FIELD structure as its argument.

IS_NUM(*type*)

> Returns true if the field type is numeric. This macro takes the type attribute of a MYSQL_FIELD structure as its argument.

IS_NUM_FIELD(*field*)

> Returns true if the field is numeric. This macro takes a MYSQL_FIELD structure as its argument.

MYSQL_FIELD_OFFSET

> A numerical type indicating the position of the "cursor" within a row.

MYSQL_RES

> A structure containing the results of a SELECT (or SHOW) statement. The actual output of the query must be accessed through the MYSQL_ROW elements of this structure. A series of mysql_fetch calls are provided to retrieve results.

MYSQL_ROW

> A single row of data returned from a SELECT query. Output of all MySQL data types are stored in this type (as an array of character strings).

my_ulonglong

> A numerical type used for MySQL return values. The value ranges from 0 to 1.8E19, with −1 used to indicate errors.

Functions

mysql_affected_rows

`my_ulonglong mysql_affected_rows(MYSQL *mysql)`

Returns the number of rows affected by the most recent query. When used with a non-SELECT query, it can be used after the mysql_query call that sent the query. With SELECT, this function is identical to mysql_num_rows. This function returns 0, as expected, for queries that affect or return no rows. In the case of an error, the function returns −1.

When an UPDATE query causes no change in the value of a row, that row is not usually considered to be affected. However, if the CLIENT_FOUND_ROWS flag is set when connecting to the MySQL server (see the mysql_real_connect function), any rows that match the WHERE clause of the UPDATE query are considered affected.

Example

```
/* Insert a row into the people table */
mysql_query(&mysql, "INSERT INTO people VALUES ('', 'Illyana Rasputin', 16)");
num = mysql_affected_rows(&mysql);
/* num should be 1 if the INSERT (of a single row) was successful, and -1 if
   there was an error */

/* Make any of 'HR', 'hr', 'Hr', or 'hR' into 'HR'. This is an easy way to
   force a consistent capitalization in a field.
mysql_query(&mysql, "UPDATE people SET dept = 'HR' WHERE dept LIKE 'HR'");
affected = mysql_affected_rows(&mysql);
/* By default, 'affected' will contain the number of rows that were changed.
   That is, the number of rows that had a dept value of 'hr', 'Hr' or 'hR'.
   If the CLIENT_FOUND_ROWS flag was used, 'affected' will contain the number
   of rows that matched the where. */
```

mysql_change_user

```
my_bool mysql_change_user(MYSQL *mysql, char *username, char *password,
                          char *database)
```

Changes the currently authenticated user and database. This function reauthenticates the current connection using the given username and password. It also changes the default database to the given database (which can be NULL if no default is desired). If the password is incorrect for the given username, or if the new user does not have rights to access the given database, a false value is returned, and no action is taken. Otherwise, the rights of the new user take effect, the default database is selected, and a true value is returned.

Example

```
if (! mysql_change_user( &mysql, new_user, new_pass, new_db ) ) {
    printf("Change of User unsuccessful!");
    exit(1);
}
/* At this point, the connection is operating under the access rights of the
   new username, and the new database is the default. */
```

mysql_character_set_name

```
char *mysql_character_set_name(MYSQL *mysql)
```

Returns the name of the default character set used by the MySQL server. A generic installation of the MySQL source uses the ISO-8859-1 character set by default.

Example

```
printf("This server uses the %s character set by default\n",
        mysql_character_set_name(&mysql));
```

mysql_close

```
void mysql_close(MYSQL *mysql)
```

Ends a connection to the database server. If there is a problem when the connection is broken, the error can be retrieved from the mysql_err function.

Example

```
mysql_close(&mysql);
/* The connection should now be terminated */
```

mysql_connect

```
MYSQL *mysql_connect(MYSQL *mysql, const char *host, const char *user,
                     const char *passwd)
```

Creates a connection to a MySQL database server. The first parameter must be a predeclared MYSQL structure. The second parameter is the hostname or IP address of the MySQL server. If the host is an empty string or localhost, a connection is made to the MySQL server on the same machine. The final two parameters are the username and password used to make the connection. The password should be entered as plain text, not encrypted in any way. The return value is the MYSQL structure that was passed as the first argument, or NULL if the connection failed. (Because the structure is contained as an argument, the only use for the return value is to check if the connection succeeded.)

 This function has been deprecated in the newer releases of MySQL, and the mysql_real_connect function should be used instead.

Example

```
/* Create a connection to the local MySQL server using the name "bob" and
   password "mypass" */
MYSQL mysql;
if(!mysql_connect(&mysql, "", "bob", "mypass")) {
                printf("Connection error!\n");
                exit(0);
}
/* If we've reached this point we have successfully connected to the database
   server. */
```

mysql_create_db

```
int mysql_create_db(MYSQL *mysql, const char *db)
```

Creates an entirely new database with the given name. The return value is 0 if the operation was successful and nonzero if there was an error.

 This function has been deprecated in the newer releases of MySQL. MySQL now supports the CREATE DATABASE SQL statement. This should be used, via the mysql_query function, instead.

Example

```
/* Create the database 'new_database' */
result = mysql_create_db(&mysql, "new_database");
```

mysql_data_seek

```
void mysql_data_seek(MYSQL_RES *res, unsigned int offset)
```

Moves to a specific row in a group of results. The first argument is the MYSQL_RES structure that contains the results. The second argument is the row number you wish to seek to, starting from 0. This function works only if the data was retrieved using mysql_store_result, because datasets retrieved with mysql_use_result are not guaranteed to be complete.

Example

```
/* Jump to the last row of the results */
mysql_data_seek(results, mysql_num_rows(results)-1);
```

mysql_debug

```
mysql_debug(char *debug)
```

Manipulates the debugging functions if the client was compiled with debugging enabled. MySQL uses the Fred Fish debugging library, which has far too many features and options to detail here.

Example

```
/* This is a common use of the debugging library. It keeps a trace of the
   client program's activity in the file "debug.out" */
mysql_debug("d:t:0,debug.out");
```

mysql_drop_db

```
int mysql_drop_db(MYSQL *mysql, const char *db)
```

Destroys the database with the given name. The return value is 0 if the operation was successful and nonzero if there was an error.

This function has been deprecated in the newer releases of MySQL. MySQL now supports the DROP DATABASE SQL statement. This should be used, via the mysql_query function, instead.

Example

```
/* Destroy the database 'old_database' */
result = mysql_drop_db(&mysql, "old_database");
```

mysql_dump_debug_info

```
int mysql_dump_debug_info(MYSQL *mysql)
```

This function causes the database server to enter debugging information about the current connection into its logs. You must have Process privilege in the current connection to use this function. The return value is 0 if the operation succeeded and nonzero if there was an error.

Example

```
result = mysql_dump_debug_info(&mysql);
/* The server's logs should now contain information about this connection.
   If something went wrong so that this is not the case, 'result' will have
   a false value.*/
```

mysql_eof

```
my_bool mysql_eof(MYSQL_RES *result)
```

Returns a nonzero value if there is no more data in the group of results being examined. If there is an error in the result set, 0 is returned. This function works only if the result set was retrieved with the mysql_use_result function (mysql_store_result retrieves the entire result set, making a call to mysql_eof unnecessary).

This function has been deprecated in the newer releases of MySQL. The mysql_errno and mysql_error functions return more information about any errors that occur, and they are more reliable.

Example

```
/* Read through the results until no more data comes out */
while((row = mysql_fetch_row(results))) {
        /* Do work */
}

if(!mysql_eof(results))
   printf("Error. End of results not reached.\n");
```

mysql_errno

```
unsigned int mysql_errno(MYSQL *mysql)
```

Returns the error number of the last error associated with the current connection. If there have been no errors in the connection, the function returns 0. The actual text of the error can be retrieved using the mysql_error function. The defined names for the client errors can be found in the *errmsg.h* header file. The defined names for the server error can be found in the *mysqld_error.h* header file.

Example

```
error = mysql_errno(&mysql);
printf("The last error was number %d\n", error);
```

mysql_error

```
char *mysql_error(MYSQL *mysql)
```

Returns the error message of the last error associated with the current connection. If there have been no errors in the connection, the function returns an empty string. Error messages originating on the server will always be in the language used by the server (chosen at startup time with the --*language* option). The language of the client error messages can be chosen when compiling the client library. At the time of this writing, MySQL supports the following languages: Czech, Danish, Dutch, English, Estonian, French, German, Greek, Hungarian, Italian, Japanese, Korean, Norwegian (standard and ny), Polish, Portuguese, Romanian, Russian, Slovak, Spanish, and Swedish.

Example

```
printf("The last error was '%s'\n", mysql_error(&mysql));
```

mysql_escape_string

```
unsigned int mysql_escape_string(char *to, const char *from, unsigned int length)
```

Encodes a string so that it is safe to insert into a MySQL table. The first argument is the receiving string, which must be at least one character greater than twice the length of the second argument: the original string. (That is, to must be greater then or equal to from*2+1.) The third argument indicates the number of bytes to be copied from the original string and encoded. The function returns the number of bytes in the encoded string, not including the terminating null character.

> While not officially deprecated, this function is generally inferior to the mysql_real_escape_string function, which does everything this function does, but also takes into account the character set of the current connection, which may affect certain escape sequences.

Example

```
char name[15] = "Bob Marley's";
char enc_name[31];
mysql_escape_string(enc_name, name);
/* enc_name will now contain "Bob Marley\'s" (the single quote is escaped).
```

mysql_fetch_field

`MYSQL_FIELD *mysql_fetch_field(MYSQL_RES *result)`

Returns a MYSQL_FIELD structure describing the current field of the given result set. Repeated calls to this function return information about each field in the result set in turn until there are no more fields left. It then returns a null value.

Example

```
MYSQL_FIELD *field;

while((field = mysql_fetch_field(results)))
{
    /* You can examine the field information here */
}
```

mysql_fetch_field_direct

`MYSQL_FIELD * mysql_fetch_field_direct(MYSQL_RES * result, unsigned int fieldno)`

This function is the same as mysql_fetch_field, except that you specify which field you wish to examine, instead of cycling through the fields. The first field in a result set is 0.

Example

```
MYSQL_FIELD *field;

/* Retrieve the third field in the result set for examination */
field = mysql_fetch_field_direct(results, 2);
```

mysql_fetch_fields

`MYSQL_FIELD *mysql_fetch_fields(MYSQL_RES * result)`

This function is the same as mysql_fetch_field, except that it returns an array of MYSQL_FIELD structures containing the information for every field in the result set.

Example

```
MYSQL_FIELD *field; /* A pointer to a single field */
MYSQL_FIELD *fields; /* A pointer to an array of fields */
```

```
/* Retrieve all the field information for the results */
fields = mysql_fetch_fields(results);
/* Assign the third field to 'field' */
field = fields[2];
```

mysql_fetch_lengths

`unsigned long *mysql_fetch_lengths(MYSQL_RES *result)`

Returns an array of the lengths of each field in the current row. A null value is returned in the case of an error. You must have fetched at least one row (with mysql_fetch_row) before you can call this function. This function provides the only way to determine the lengths of variable-length fields, such as BLOB and VARCHAR, before you use the data.

 This function is especially useful when reading binary data from a BLOB. Since all MySQL data is retrieved as strings (char *), it is common to use the strlen( ) function to determine the length of a data value. However, for binary data, strlen( ) returns inaccurate results, because it stops at the first null character. In these cases, you can use mysql_fetch_lengths to retrieve the accurate length for a data value.

Example

```
unsigned long *lengths;

row = mysql_fetch_row(results);
lengths = mysql_fetch_lengths(results);
printf("The third field is %d bytes long\n", lengths[2]);
```

mysql_fetch_row

`MYSQL_ROW mysql_fetch_row(MYSQL_RES *result)`

Retrieves the next row of the result and returns it as a MYSQL_ROW structure. A null value is returned if there are no more rows or if there is an error. In the current implementation, the MYSQL_ROW structure is an array of character strings that can be used to represent any data. If a data element is NULL within the database, the MYSQL_ROW array element for that data element is a null pointer. This is necessary to distinguish between a value that is NULL and a value that is simply an empty string (which is returned as a non-null pointer to a null value).

Example

```
MYSQL_ROW row;

row = mysql_fetch_row(results);
printf("The data in the third field of this row is: %s\n", row[2]);
```

mysql_field_count

```
unsigned int mysql_field_count(MYSQL *mysql)
```

Returns the number of columns contained in a result set. This function is most useful when checking the type of query last executed. If a call to `mysql_store_result` returns a null pointer for a result set, either the query was a non-SELECT query (such as UPDATE, INSERT, etc.) or there was an error. By calling `mysql_field_count`, you can determine which was the case, because a non-SELECT query always returns zero fields, and a SELECT query always returns at least one field. Even if the returned query has no rows, the fields of the SELECT query will be reflected here.

Example

```
MYSQL_FIELD field;
MYSQL_RES *result;

// A query has been executed and returned success
result = mysql_store_result();
if (! result ) {
    // Ooops, the result pointer is null, either the query was a non-SELECT
    // query or something bad happened!
    if ( mysql_field_count(&mysql) ) {
        // The number of columns queried is greater than zero, it must have
        // been a SELECT query and an error must have occurred.
    } else {
        // Since the number of columns queried is zero, it must have been
        // a non-SELECT query, so all is well...
    }
}
```

mysql_field_seek

```
MYSQL_FIELD_OFFSET mysql_field_seek(MYSQL_RES *result, MYSQL_ FIELD_OFFSET offset)
```

Moves the internal pointer of a result set to the given field of the current row. The position set by this function is used when `mysql_fetch_field` is called. The MYSQL_FIELD_OFFSET value passed should be the return value of a `mysql_field_tell` call (or another `mysql_field_seek`). If the value passed is 0, the function seeks to the beginning of the row. The return value is the position of the cursor before the function was called.

Example

```
MYSQL_FIELD field;

/* result is a MYSQL_RES structure containing a result set */
/* ... do some stuff */
/* Seek back to the beginning of the row */
old_pos = mysql_field_seek(results, 0);
/* Fetch the first field of the row */
field = mysql_fetch_field(results);
/* Go back to where you were */
mysql_field_seek(results, old_pos);
```

mysql_field_tell

```
MYSQL_FIELD_OFFSET mysql_field_tell(MYSQL_RES *result)
```

Returns the value of the current field position within the current row of the result set. This value is used with mysql_field_seek.

Example

```
MYSQL_FIELD field1, field2, field3;
/* results is a MYSQL_RES structure containing a result set */

/* Record my current position */
old_pos = mysql_field_tell(results);
/* Fetch three more fields */
field1 = mysql_fetch_field(results);
field2 = mysql_fetch_field(results);
field3 = mysql_fetch_field(results);
/* Go back to where you where */
mysql_field_seek(results, old_pos);
```

mysql_free_result

```
void mysql_free_result(MYSQL_RES *result)
```

Frees the memory associated with a MYSQL_RES structure. This must be called whenever you are finished using this type of structure, or else memory problems will occur. This should be used only on a pointer to an actual MYSQL_RES structure. For example, if a call to mysql_store_result returns a null pointer, this function should not be used.

Example

```
MYSQL_RES *results;
/* Do work with results */
/* free results... we know it's not null since we just did work with
   it, but we'll check just to be safe. */
if (results)
    mysql_free_result(results);
```

mysql_get_client_info

```
char *mysql_get_client_info(void)
```

Returns a string containing the MySQL library version used by the client program.

Example

```
printf("This program uses MySQL client library version %s\n",
       mysql_get_client_info( ));
```

mysql_get_host_info

```
char *mysql_get_host_info(MYSQL *mysql)
```

Returns a string containing the hostname of the MySQL database server and the type of connection used (e.g., Unix socket or TCP).

Example

```
printf("Connection info: %s", mysql_get_host_info(&mysql));
```

mysql_get_proto_info

```
unsigned int mysql_get_proto_info(MYSQL *mysql)
```

Returns the MySQL protocol version used in the current connection as an integer. As a general rule, the MySQL network protocol changes only between minor releases of MySQL. That is, all releases of MySQL 3.23.x should have the same protocol version number.

Example

```
printf("This connection is using MySQL connection protocol ver. %d\n",
       mysql_get_proto_info( ));
```

mysql_get_server_info

```
char *mysql_get_server_info(MYSQL *mysql)
```

Returns a string containing the version number of the MySQL database server used by the current connection.

Example

```
printf("You are currently connected to MySQL server version %s\n",
       mysql_get_server_info(&mysql);
```

mysql_info

```
char *mysql_info(MYSQL *mysql)
```

Returns a string containing information about the most recent query, if the query was of a certain type. Currently, the following SQL queries supply extra information via this function: INSERT INTO (when used with a SELECT clause or a VALUES clause with more than one record), LOAD DATA INFILE, ALTER TABLE, and UPDATE. If the most recent query provided no additional information (e.g., it was not one of the above queries), this function returns a null value.

The format of the returned string depends on the query. If the query is INSERT INTO or ALTER TABLE, the string is:

Records: *n* Duplicates: *n* Warnings: *n*

If the query is LOAD DATA INFILE, the string is:

Records: *n* Deleted: *n* Skipped: *n* Warnings: *n*

If the query is UPDATE, the string is:

Rows matched: *n* Changed: *n* Warnings: *n*

Example

```
/* We just sent LOAD DATA INFILE query reading a set of record from a file into
   an existing table */
printf("Results of data load: %s\n", mysql_info(&mysql));
/* The printed string looks like this:
Records: 30 Deleted: 0 Skipped: 0 Warnings: 0
*/
```

mysql_init

```
MYSQL *mysql_init(MYSQL *mysql)
```

Initializes a MYSQL structure for creating a connection to a MySQL database server. A call to this function, followed by one to mysql_real_connect, is currently the approved method of initializing a server connection. You can pass mysql_init either a pointer to a MYSQL structure that you declared or a null pointer. If you pass your own pointer, you are responsible for freeing its data when the time comes (which must be after the connection is closed).

If you pass a null pointer, mysql_init creates a MYSQL structure, initializes it, and returns a pointer to the structure. Structures created by this function are freed automatically when mysql_close is called. A null value is returned if there is not enough memory available to initialize the structure.

 As of the current release of MySQL, MySQL clients will crash on certain platforms (such as SCO Unix) when you pass in a pointer to a MYSQL structure that you allocated yourself. If this is happening to you, just pass in NULL and use the pointer created by the MySQL library. As a bonus, you don't have to worry about freeing the structure if you do this.

Example

```
MYSQL mysql;

if (!mysql_init(&mysql)) {
          printf("Error initializing MySQL client\n");
          exit(1);
}
/* Now you can call mysql_real_connect() to connect to a server... */
/* Alternative method: */
MYSQL *mysql;
```

```
mysql = mysql_init(NULL);
if (!mysql) {
    printf("Error initializing MySQL client\n");
    exit(1);
}
```

mysql_insert_id

`my_ulonglong mysql_insert_id(MYSQL *mysql)`

Returns the generated value for an AUTO_INCREMENT field if the last query created a new row. This function is usually called immediately after a value has been inserted into an AUTO_INCREMENT field to determine the value that was inserted. This value is reset to 0 after any query that does not insert a new auto-increment row.

 The MySQL-specific SQL function LAST_INSERT_ID( ) also returns the value of the most recent auto-increment. In addition, it is not reset after each query, so it can be called at any time to retrieve that value of the last auto-increment INSERT executed during the current session.

Example

```
/* We just inserted an employee record with automatically generated ID into
    a table */
id = mysql_insert_id(&mysql);
printf("The new employee has ID %d\n", id);
/* As soon as we run another query, mysql_insert_id will return 0 */
```

mysql_kill

`int mysql_kill(MYSQL *mysql, unsigned long pid)`

Attempts to kill the MySQL server thread with the specified process ID. This function returns 0 if the operation was successful and nonzero on failure. You must have Process privilege in the current connection to use this function.

The process IDs are part of the process information returned by the mysql_list_processes function.

Example

```
/* Kill thread 4 */
result = mysql_kill(&mysql, 4);
```

mysql_list_dbs

`MYSQL_RES *mysql_list_dbs(MYSQL *mysql, const char *wild)`

Returns a MYSQL_RES structure containing the names of all existing databases that match the pattern given by the second argument. This argument may be any standard SQL regular expression. If a null pointer is passed instead, all databases are listed. Like all `MYSQL_RES` structures, the return value of this function must be freed with `mysql_free_result`. This function returns a null value in the case of an error.

The information obtained from this function can also be obtained through an SQL query using the statement SHOW databases.

Example

```
MYSQL_RES databases;
databases = mysql_list_dbs(&mysql, (char *)NULL);
/* 'databases' now contains the names of all of the databases in the
   MySQL server */
/* ... */
mysql_free_result( databases );
/* Find all databases that start with 'projectName' */
databases = mysql_list_dbs(&mysql, "projectName%");
```

mysql_list_fields

`MYSQL_RES *mysql_list_fields(MYSQL *mysql, const char *table, const char *wild)`

Returns a `MYSQL_RES` structure containing the names of all existing fields in the given table that match the pattern given by the third argument. This argument may be any standard SQL regular expression. If a null pointer is passed instead, all fields are listed. Like all `MYSQL_RES` structures, the return value of this function must be freed with `mysql_free_result`. This function returns a null value in the case of an error.

The information obtained from this function can also be obtained through an SQL query using the statement SHOW COLUMNS FROM table.

Example

```
MYSQL_RES fields;
fields = mysql_list_fields(&mysql, "people", "address%");
/* 'fields' now contains the names of all fields in the 'people' table
   that start with 'address' */
/* ... */
mysql_free_result( fields );
```

mysql_list_processes

`MYSQL_RES *mysql_list_processes(MYSQL *mysql)`

Returns a `MYSQL_RES` structure containing information on all the threads currently running on the MySQL database server. (The term processes in the function name refers to the internal MySQL processes, or threads, not to any operating system–level process.) The information contained in the structure can be used with mysql_kill to remove faulty threads. Like all MYSQL_RES structures, the return value of this function must be freed with mysql_free_result. This function returns a null value in the case of an error.

The returned result set contains the information in the following order:

The MySQL process ID
> This is the ID used with mysql_kill to kill a thread.

Username
> The MySQL username of the user executing a thread.

Hostname
> The location of the client running a thread.

Database
> The current database for the client running a thread.

Action
> The type of action last run in a thread. All SQL queries of any type show up as Query, so this will be the most common value.

Time
> The amount of time taken (in seconds) to execute the last action in a thread.

State
> The state of the current thread. This indicates whether the thread is active (currently executing a command) or idle.

Info

> Any extra information about the thread. For SQL queries, this will contain the text of the query.

 The information obtained from this function can also be obtained through an SQL query using the statement SHOW PROCESSLIST.

Example

```
MYSQL_RES *threads;
MYSQL_ROW row
threads = mysql_list_processes(&mysql);

row = mysql_fetch_row( threads );
printf("The ID of the first active thread is %d\n", row[0]);
```

mysql_list_tables

MYSQL_RES *mysql_list_tables(MYSQL *mysql, const char *wild)

Returns a MYSQL_RES structure containing the names of all existing tables in the current database that match the pattern given by the second argument. This argument may be any standard SQL regular expression. If a null pointer is passed, all tables are listed. Like all MYSQL_RES structures, the return value of this function must be freed with mysql_free_result. This function returns a null value in the case of an error.

The information obtained from this function can also be obtained through an SQL query using the statement SHOW TABLES.

Example

```
MYSQL_RES tables;
tables = mysql_list_tables(&mysql, "p%");
/* 'tables' now contains the names of all tables in the current database
   that start with 'p' */
```

mysql_num_fields

unsigned int mysql_num_fields(MYSQL_RES *result)

Returns the number of fields contained in each row of the given result set. This is different from the mysql_field_count function, in that it operates on an actual result set, which is known to contain data, whereas mysql_field_count checks the last executed query (usually to determine if an error occurred).

Example

```
/* 'results' is a MYSQL_RES result set structure */
num_fields = mysql_num_fields(results);
printf("There are %d fields in each row\n", num_fields);
```

mysql_num_rows

int mysql_num_rows(MYSQL_RES *result)

Returns the number of rows of data in the result set. This function is accurate only if the result set was retrieved with mysql_store_result. If mysql_use_result was used, the value returned by this function is the number of rows accessed so far.

Example

```
/* 'results' is a MYSQL_RES result set structure */
num_rows = mysql_num_rows(results);
printf("There were %d rows returned, that I know about\n", num_rows);
```

mysql_odbc_escape_string

char *mysql_odbc_escape_string(MYSQL *mysql, char *result_string, unsigned long result_string_length, char *original_string, unsigned long original_string_length, void *parameters, char *(*extend_buffer))

Creates a properly escaped SQL query string from a given string. This function is intended for use with ODBC clients, and mysql_real_escape_string provides the same functionality with a simpler interface. This function takes the string given in the fourth argument (with the length given in the fifth argument, not including the terminating null character) and escapes it so that the resulting string (which is put into the address given in the second argument, with a maximum length given in the third argument) is safe to use as a MySQL SQL statement. This function returns a copy of the result string (the second argument). The seventh argument must be a pointer to a function that can be used to allocate memory for the result string. The function must take three arguments: a pointer to a set of parameters that control how the memory is allocated (these parameters are passed in as the sixth argument to the original function), a pointer to the result string, and a pointer to the maximum length of the result string.

Example

```
char *data = "\000\002\001";
int data_length = 3;
char *result;
int result_length = 5; /* We don't want the final string to be longer than 5.
  extend_buffer() is a function that meets the criteria given above. */
mysql_odbc_escape_string( &mysql, result, result_length, data, data_length,
    NULL, extend_buffer );
/* 'result' now contains the string '\\\000\002\001'
  (that is, a backslash, followed by ASCII 0, then ASCII 2 then ASCII 1. */
```

mysql_odbc_remove_escape

```
void mysql_odbc_remove_escape(MYSQL *mysql, char *string )
```

Removes escape characters from a string. This function is intended for ODBC drivers themselves, and not for general use. Given a string, this function removes the escape character (\) preceding any other escape characters. This modifies (and thus shortens) the original string that was passed in.

Example

```
char *escaped = "\\'an escaped quoted string.\\'";
/* escaped contains the string: \' and escaped quoted string.\' */
mysql_odbc_remove_escape(&mysql, escaped);
/* escaped now contains the string: 'an escaped quoted string.' */
```

mysql_options

```
int mysql_options(MYSQL *mysql, enum mysql_option option, void *value)
```

Sets a connect option for an upcoming MySQL connection. This function must be called after a MYSQL structure has been initialized using mysql_init and before a connection has actually been established using mysql_real_connect. This function can be called multiple times to set more than one option. The options affect the upcoming connection. The value of the third argument depends on the type of option. Some options require a character string as an argument, while others take a pointer to an integer, or nothing at all. The options are as follows (the type of the third argument is given in parentheses after the option name):

MYSQL_INIT_COMMAND (char *)

Specifies an SQL query to execute as soon as the connection is established. This query is reexecuted if the connection is lost and automatically reconnected.

MYSQL_OPT_COMPRESS ()

Causes the connection to use a compressed protocol with the server to increase speed.

MYSQL_OPT_CONNECT_TIMEOUT (unsigned int *)

Specifies the number of seconds to wait before giving up on connecting to the server.

MYSQL_OPT_NAMED_PIPE ()

Causes the connection to use named pipes, as opposed to TCP, to connect to a local MySQL server running on Windows NT.

MYSQL_READ_DEFAULT_FILE (char *)

Specifies the name of the file to read for default options, in place of the default file *my.cnf*.

MYSQL_READ_DEFAULT_GROUP (char *)

Specifies the name of a section within the configuration file to read for the connection options, in place of the default client. See Chapter 4 for information about the configuration file options.

Example

```
MYSQL mysql;
mysql_init( &mysql );
/* Prepare this connection to use the compressed protocol, execute the
   query "SHOW tables" upon connection, and read addition options from the
   'startup' stanze in the file .mysqlrc */
mysql_options(&mysql, MYSQL_OPT_COMPRESS, 0 );
mysql_options(&mysql, MYSQL_INIT_COMMAND, "SHOW tables" );
mysql_options(&mysql, MYSQL_READ_DEFAULT_FILE, ".mysqlrc" );
mysql_options(&mysql, MYSQL_READ_DEFAULT_GROUP, "startup" );
/* Now it is time to call mysql_real_connect( ) to make the connection using
   these options */
```

mysql_ping

```
int mysql_ping(MYSQL *mysql)
```

Checks to see if the connection to the MySQL server is still alive. If it is not, the client attempts to reconnect automatically. This function returns 0 if the connection is alive and nonzero if it cannot successfully contact the server.

Example

```
while(mysql_ping(&mysql)) printf("Error, attempting reconnection...\n");
```

mysql_query

```
int mysql_query(MYSQL *mysql, const char *query)
```

Executes the SQL query given in the second argument. If the query contains any binary data (particularly the null character), this function cannot be used, and mysql_real_query should be used instead. The function returns 0 if the query was successful and nonzero in the case of an error.

Once a query has been executed using this function, the result set can be retrieved using the `mysql_store_result` or `mysql_use_result` function.

Example

```
error = mysql_query(&mysql, "SELECT * FROM people WHERE name like 'Bill%'");
if (error) {
    printf("Error with query!\n");
    exit(1);
}
```

mysql_read_query_result

`int mysql_read_query_result(MYSQL *mysql)`

Processes the result of a query executed with the `mysql_send_query` command. Any data processed this way is not returned. Therefore, this function is useful only when running non-SELECT queries or for debugging (because the return value still accurately reports if there was an error). The function returns 0 on success and a nonzero number if an error occurred.

Example

```
mysql_send_query(&mysql, "SELECT * INTO OUTFILE results.out FROM mytable");
/* This executes the query, but does not process the results, which is necessary
    in order to write the values into the outfile */
mysql_read_query_result(&mysql);
/* Now the results have been processed and the data written to the outfile */
```

mysql_real_connect

```
MYSQL *mysql_real_connect(MYSQL *mysql, const char *host, const char *user,
                          const char *passwd, const char *db, uint port,
                          const char *unix_socket, uint client_flag)
```

Creates a connection with a MySQL database server. There are eight arguments to this function:

- An initialized MYSQL structure, created with `mysql_init`.
- The hostname or IP address of the MySQL database server (use an empty string or localhost to connect to the local MySQL server over a Unix socket).
- The username used to connect to the database server (an empty string indicates that the Unix login name of the person running the client should be used).
- The password used to authenticate the given user. If an empty string is used, only users with no passwords are checked for authentication. That is, if a user happened to have a password set to an empty string, he would never be authenticated.
- The initial database selected when you connect (an empty string indicates that no database should be selected).

- The port used to remotely connect to a MySQL database server over TCP. (0 may be used to accept the default port).
- The filename of the Unix socket used to connect to a MySQL server on the local machine (an empty string may be used to accept the default socket).
- Zero or more of a set of flags used under special circumstances:

CLIENT_FOUND_ROWS
> When using queries that change tables, returns the number of rows found in the table, not the number of rows affected.

CLIENT_IGNORE_SPACE
> Allows spaces after built-in MySQL functions in SQL queries. Traditionally, functions must be followed immediately by their arguments in parentheses. If this option is used, the function names become reserved words and cannot be used for names of tables, columns, or databases.

CLIENT_INTERACTIVE
> Causes the server to wait for a longer amount of time (specified by the interactive_ timeout server variable) before automatically breaking a connection. This is useful for interactive clients that do not allow the user to enter any data for significant periods of time.

CLIENT_NO_SCHEMA
> Prevents the client from using the full database.table.column form to specify a column from any database.

CLIENT_COMPRESS
> Causes the client to use compression when communicating with the server.

CLIENT_ODBC
> Tells the server the client is an ODBC connection.

CLIENT_SSL
> Tells the client to use SSL encryption to secure the connection. The server must have been compiled to support SSL.

Example

```
MYSQL *mysql;
mysql = mysql_init( NULL );
/* Connect to the server on the local host with standard options. */
if (! mysql_real_connect(&mysql, "localhost", "bob", "mypass", "", 0, "", 0))
{ print "Error connecting!\n";
  exit(1);
}

/* or... */
/* Connect to the server at my.server.com using a compressed, secure protocol */
if (! mysql_real_connect(&mysql, "my.server.com", "bob", "mypass",
                         "", 0, "", CLIENT_COMPRESS|CLIENT_SSL)) {
        print "Error connecting!\n";
        exit(1);
}
```

mysql_real_escape_string

```
unsigned long mysql_real_escape_string(MYSQL *mysql, char *result_string,
                                       char *original_string,
                                       unsigned long orginal_string_length)
```

Creates a properly escaped SQL query string from a given string. This function takes the string given in the third argument (with the length given in the fourth argument, not including the terminating null character) and escapes it so that the resulting string (which is put into the address given in the second argument) is safe to use as a MySQL SQL statement. This function returns the new length of the resulting string (not including the terminating null character). To be completely safe, the space allocated for the result string should be at least twice as big as the original string (in case each character has to be escaped) plus one (for the terminating null character).

 This function is safe to use with binary data. The string can contain null characters or any other binary data. This is why it is necessary to include the length of the string. Otherwise, the MySQL library could not determine how long the string was if any null characters were present.

Example

```
# Properly escape a query that contains binary data.
char *data = "\002\001\000";
int original_length = 4 # 3 characters plus one for the null.
char real_data[7]; # Twice as big as the original string (3)
                   # plus one for the null.
int new_length;

new_length = mysql_real_escape_string(&mysql, data, real_data, original_length);
/* real_query can now be safely used in as a SQL query. */
/* The returned length is '4' since the only character that needed escaping
   was \000 (the null character) */
```

mysql_real_query

```
int mysql_real_query(MYSQL *mysql, const char *query, unsigned int length)
```

Executes the SQL query given in the second argument. The length of the query (not including any terminating null character) must be given in the third argument. By supplying the length, you can use binary data, including null characters, in the query. This function is also faster than mysql_query. The function returns 0 if the query was successful and nonzero in the case of an error.

Once a query has been executed using this function, the result set can be retrieved using the mysql_store_result or mysql_use_result function.

Example

```
error = mysql_real_query(&mysql, "SELECT * FROM people WHERE name like 'Bill%'",
        44);
if (error) {
    printf("Error with query!\n");
    exit(1);
}
```

mysql_refresh

```
int mysql_refresh(MYSQL *mysql, unsigned int options)
```

Instructs the server to refresh various system operations. Which operations are refreshed depends on the second argument, which is a bitwise combination of any of the following options:

REFRESH_GRANT
> Reloads the permissions tables. This is the same as mysql_reload( ) or the FLUSH PRIVILEGES SQL command.

REFRESH_LOG
> Flushes the log files to disk and then closes and reopens them.

REFRESH_TABLES
> Flushes any open tables to disk.

REFRESH_READ_LOCK
> Reinstates the read lock on the database files stored on disk.

REFRESH_HOSTS
> Reloads the internal cache MySQL keeps of known hostnames to limit DNS lookup calls.

REFRESH_STATUS
> Refreshes the status of the server by checking the status of various internal operations.

REFRESH_THREADS
> Clears out any dead or inactive threads from the internal cache of threads.

REFRESH_MASTER
> Flushes, closes, and reopens the binary log that tracks all changes to MySQL tables. This log is sent to all slave servers for replication.

REFRESH_SLAVE
> Resets the connection with any slave servers that are replicating the master MySQL server.

Example

```
/* Flush the log files and the table data to disk */
if (!mysql_refresh( &mysql, REFRESH_LOG|REFRESH_TABLES )) {
    printf("Error sending refresh command...\n");
}
```

mysql_reload

```
int mysql_reload(MYSQL *mysql)
```

Reloads the permission tables on the MySQL database server. You must have Reload permission on the current connection to use this function. If the operation is successful, 0 is returned; otherwise, a nonzero value is returned.

 This function is deprecated and will be removed in a future version of the API. The same functionality can be obtained by using the SQL query FLUSH PRIVILEGES.

Example

```
/* Make some changes to the grant tables... */
result = mysql_reload(&mysql);
/* The changes now take effect... */
```

mysql_row_seek

```
MYSQL_ROW_OFFSET mysql_row_seek(MYSQL_RES *result, MYSQL_ROW_OFFSET offset)
```

Moves the pointer for a result set (MYSQL_RES structure) to a specific row and returns the original row number. This function requires that the offset be an actual MYSQL_ROW_OFFSET structure, not a simple row number. If you have only a row number, use the mysql_data_seek function. You can obtain a MYSQL_ROW_OFFSET structure from a call to either mysql_row_tell or mysql_row_seek.

This function is useful only if the result set contains all the data from the query. Therefore, it should be used in conjunction with mysql_store_result and not used with mysql_use_result.

Example

```
/* result is a result set pointer created with mysql_store_result( ) */
MYSQL_ROW_OFFSET where, other_place;
where = mysql_row_tell( result );
/* Do some more work with the result set... */
/* Go back to where you were before, but remember where you are now: */
other_place = mysql_row_seek( result, where );
/* Do some more work... */
/* Go back to the second marker: */
mysql_row_seek( result, other_place );
```

mysql_row_tell

```
MYSQL_ROW_OFFSET mysql_row_tell(MYSQL_RES *result)
```

Returns the value of the cursor as mysql_fetch_row reads the rows of a result set. The return value of this function can be used with mysql_row_seek to jump to a specific row in the result set. Values from the function are useful only if the result set was created with mysql_store_result (which contains all the data) and not mysql_use_result (which does not).

Example

```
/* results is a result set pointer created with mysql_store_result() */
MYSQL_ROW_OFFSET saved_pos = mysql_row_tell(results);
/* I can now jump back to this row at any time using mysql_row_seek() */
```

mysql_select_db

```
int mysql_select_db(MYSQL *mysql, const char *db)
```

Changes the current database. The user must have permission to access the new database. The function returns 0 if the operation was successful and nonzero in the case of an error.

Example

```
if ( mysql_select_db(&mysql, "newdb") ) {
    printf("Error changing database, you probably don't have permission.\n");
}
```

mysql_send_query

```
int mysql_send_query(MYSQL *mysql, char *query, unsigned int query_length)
```

Executes a single MySQL query, without providing any results to the user. This function is useful for quickly executing a non-SELECT statement that does not return any data to the user. This function is also useful for debugging, since the return value still accurately reports whether an error occurred. The function returns 0 on success and nonzero if an error occurred.

Example

```
/* Quickly insert a row into a table */
mysql_send_query(&mysql, "INSERT INTO mytable VALUES ('blah', 'fnor')");
```

mysql_shutdown

```
int mysql_shutdown(MYSQL *mysql)
```

Shuts down the MySQL database server. The user must have Shutdown privileges on the current connection to use this function. The function returns 0 if the operation was successful and nonzero in the case of an error.

Example

```
if ( mysql_shutdown(&mysql) ) {
        printf("Server not shut down... Check your permissions...\n");
} else {
        printf("Server successfully shut down!\n");
}
```

mysql_ssl_cipher

```
char *mysql_ssl_cipher(MYSQL *mysql)
```

Returns the name of the SSL cipher that is used (or will be used) with the current connection. This could be RSA, blowfish, or any other cipher supported by the server's SSL library (MySQL uses OpenSSL by default, if SSL is enabled). The MySQL server and client must both have been compiled with SSL support for this function to work properly.

Example

```
printf("This connection is using the %s cipher for security.\n",
        Mysql_ssl_cipher(&mysql));
```

mysql_ssl_clear

```
int mysql_ssl_clear(MYSQL *mysql)
```

Clears any SSL information associated with the current connection. If mysql_ssl_clear is called before the connection has been made, the connection will be made without SSL. The function returns 0 on success and nonzero if an error occurs. It must be called before mysql_real_connect to have any effect. The MySQL server and client must both have been compiled with SSL support for this function to work properly.

Example

```
/* init a MYSQL structure and set SSL options...*/
/* Changed my mind, I don't want this connection to use SSL: */
mysql_ssl_clear(&mysql);
```

mysql_ssl_set

```
int mysql_ssl_set(MYSQL *mysql, char *key, char *certificate, char *authority,
                char *authority_path)
```

Sets SSL information for the current connection and causes the connection to be made using SSL for encryption. This function must be called before mysql_real_connect to have any effect. The arguments are (beyond the pointer to the MYSQL structure) the text of the SSL public key used for the connection, the filename of the certificate used, the name of the authority that issued the certificate, and the directory that contains the authority's certificates.

The function returns 0 on success and nonzero if an error occurs. The MySQL server and client both must have been compiled with SSL support for this function to work properly.

Example

```
/* 'key' contains an SSL public key.
   'cert' contains the filename of a certificate
   'ca' contains the name of the certificate authority
   'capath' contains the directory containing the certificate
*/
```

```
/* Create an initialized MYSQL structure using mysql_init */
mysql_ssl_set(&mysql, key, cert, ca, capath);
/* Now, when mysql_real_connect is called, the connection will use SSL for
   encryption. */
```

mysql_stat

`char *mysql_stat(MYSQL *mysql)`

Returns information about the current operating status of the database server. This includes the uptime, the number of running threads, and the number of queries being processed, among other information.

Example

```
printf("Server info\n-----------\n%s\n", mysql_stat(&mysql));
/* Output may look like this:
Server info
-----------
Uptime: 259044  Threads: 1  Questions: 24  Slow queries: 0  Opens: 6
Flush tables: 1 Open tables: 0 Queries per second avg: 0.000
Everything below the row of hyphens is all on one line
*/
```

mysql_store_result

`MYSQL_RES *mysql_store_result(MYSQL *mysql)`

Reads the entire result of a query and stores it in a MYSQL_RES structure. Either this function or mysql_use_result must be called to access return information from a query. You must call mysql_free_result to free the MYSQL_RES structure when you are done with it.

The function returns a null value in the case of an error. The function also returns a null value if the query was not of a type that returns data (such as an INSERT or UPDATE query). If you receive a null pointer and are not sure if the query was supposed to return data or not, you can call mysql_field_count to find the number of fields the query was supposed to return. If zero, then it was a non-SELECT statement, and the pointer should be null. Otherwise, an error has occurred.

If the query was a SELECT-type statement, but happens to contain no data, this function will still return a valid (but empty) MYSQL_RES structure (it will not be a null pointer).

Example

```
MYSQL_RES results;
mysql_query(&mysql, "SELECT * FROM people");
results = mysql_store_result(&mysql);
/* 'results' should now contain all of the information from the 'people' table */
if (!results) { printf("An error has occurred!\n"); }

/* 'query' is some query string we obtained elsewhere,
   we're not sure what it is... */
```

```
    mysql_query(&mysql, query);
    results = mysql_store_result(&mysql);
    if (!results) { /* An error might have occurred,
                        or maybe this is just a non-SELECT statement */
        if (! mysql_field_count(&mysql) ) { /* Aha! This is zero so it was
                                                a non-SELECT statement */
                printf("No error here, just a non-SELECT statement...\n");
        } else {
                printf("An error has occurred!\n");
        }
    }
```

mysql_thread_id

`unsigned long mysql_thread_id(MYSQL * mysql)`

Returns the thread ID of the current connection. This value can be used with `mysql_kill` to terminate the thread in case of an error. The thread ID will change if you disconnect from the server and reconnect (which may happen automatically, without warning, if you use `mysql_ping`). Therefore, you should call this function immediately before you use the value.

Example

```
    thread_id = mysql_thread_id(&mysql);
    /* This number can be used with mysql_kill( ) to terminate the current thread. */
```

mysql_thread_safe

`unsigned int mysql_thread_safe(void)`

Indicates whether the MySQL client library is safe to use in a threaded environment. The function returns a true value if the library is thread safe and 0 (`false`) if it is not.

Example

```
    if (mysql_thread_safe( )) {
        printf("This library is thread safe... thread away!\n");
    } else {
        printf("This library is *not* thread safe, be careful!\n");
    }
```

mysql_use_result

`MYSQL_RES *mysql_use_result(MYSQL *mysql)`

Reads the result of a query row by row and allows access to the data through a MYSQL_RES structure. Either this function or `mysql_store_result` must be called to access return information from a query. Because this function does not read the entire data set all at once, it is faster and more memory efficient than `mysql_store_result`. However, when using this function, you must read all the rows of the data set from the server or else the next query will receive the leftover data. Also, you cannot run any other queries until you are done with the data in this query. Even worse, no other threads running on the server can access the tables used by the query until you are finished. For this reason, you should use this function only when you are certain you can read the data in a timely manner and release it. You must call mysql_free_result to free the MYSQL_RES structure when you are done with it.

The function returns a null value in the case of an error. The function also returns a null value if the query was not of a type that returns data (such as an INSERT or UPDATE query). If you receive a null pointer and are not sure if the query was supposed to return data or not, you can call mysql_field_count to find the number of fields the query was supposed to return. If zero, then it was a non-SELECT statement, and the pointer should be null. Otherwise, an error has occurred.

If the query was a SELECT-type statement, but happens to contain no data, this function still returns a valid (but empty) MYSQL_RES structure; i.e., it does not return a null pointer.

Example

```
MYSQL_RES results;
mysql_query(&mysql, "SELECT * FROM people");
results = mysql_store_result(&mysql);
/* 'results' will now allow access (using mysql_fetch_row) to the table
    data, one row at a time */
```

## CHAPTER 20

The Python DB-API

DB-API supports database-independent database access. The MySQL implementation of this API, MySQLdb, can be downloaded from *http://dustman.net/andy/python/MySQLdb*. It comes with a RedHat RPM Linux installer, a Win32 installer, and a Python script for other platforms. For those other platforms:

1. Uncompress the *.tar.gz* file that contains MySQLdb using the commands *gunzip FILENAME.tar.gz* and *tar xf FILENAME.tar*.

2. Change directories into the newly generated MySQLdb directory.

3. Issue the command: *python setup.py install*.

The MySQLdb module contains the standard DB-API methods and attributes as well as several proprietary methods and attributes. Proprietary APIs are marked with asterisks.

Module: MySQLdb

The entry point into the MySQL module is via the `MySQLdb.connect( )` method. The return value from this method represents a connection to a MySQL database that you can use for all of your MySQL operations.

Module Attributes

apilevel

Synopsis

A string constant storing the version of the DB-API that MySQLdb supports.

paramstyle

Synopsis

Defines the type of parameter placeholder in parameterized queries. DB-API supports many valid values for this attribute, but MySQLdb actually supports only `format` and `pyformat`. This attribute is largely meaningless to MySQL developers.

quote_conv

Synopsis

Maps Python types to MySQL literals via a dictionary mapping.

threadsafety

Synopsis

Specifies the level of thread safety supported by MySQLdb. Possible values are:

0   Threads may not share the module.
1   Threads may share the module but not the connections.
2   Threads may share the module and connections.
3   Threads may share the module, connections, and cursors.

type_conv

Synopsis

Maps MySQL types from strings to the desired mapping type. This value is initialized with:

```
{ FIELD_TYPE.TINY : int,
FIELD_TYPE.SHORT: int,
FIELD_TYPE.LONG: long,
FIELD_TYPE.FLOAT: float,
FIELD_TYPE.DOUBLE: float,
FIELD_TYPE.LONGLONG: long,
FIELD_TYPE.INT24: int,
FIELD_TYPE.YEAR: int }
```

Module Methods

MySQL.connect()

Signature

```
connection = MySQL.connect(params)
```

Synopsis

Connects to the MySQL database engine represented by the various connection keyword/value parameters. These parameters include:

host
>   The name of the server on which the MySQL database is running

user
>   The user ID for connecting to MySQL. MySQL should allow this user to make the connection.

passwd
>   The password to authenticate the user ID for the connection.

db
>   The MySQL database to which the application attempts to connect.

port
>   Directs MySQLdb to connect to a MySQL installation on a custom part. When left unspecified, the method will use the default MySQL port of 3306.

unix_socket
>   Identifies the location of a socket or named pipe to use if the host allows it.

client_flags
>   An integer specifying the client connection flags to use. These client connection flags are the same ones enumerated in Chapter 19 for the mysql_real_connect( ) method.

This method returns a Python object representing a connection to a MySQL database.

Example

```
connection = MySQLdb.connect(host='carthage', user='test',
                             passwd='test', db='test');
```

Connection Attributes

---

db

Synopsis

A window into the MySQL C API. MySQLdb uses this attribute to make calls to the underlying C API.

Connection Methods

---

close()

Signature

```
close( )
```

Synopsis

Closes the current connection to the database and releases any associated resources.

Example

```
connection = MySQLdb.connect(host='carthage', user='test',
                             passwd='test', db='test');
connection.close();
```

commit()

Signature

```
commit()
```

Synopsis

Commits the current transaction by sending a COMMIT to MySQL.

Example

```
connection = MySQLdb.connect(host='carthage', user='test',
                             passwd='test', db='test');
connection._transactional = 1;
cursor = connection.cursor();
cursor.execute("UPDATE TNAME SET COL = 1 WHERE PK = 2045");
cursor.execute("UPDATE TNAME SET COL = 1 WHERE PK = 3200");
connection.commit();
connection.close();
```

cursor()

Signature

```
cursor = cursor()
```

Synopsis

Creates a cursor associated with this connection. Transactions involving any statements executed by the newly created cursor are governed by this connection.

Example

```
connection = MySQLdb.connect(host='carthage', user='test',
                             passwd='test', db='test');
cursor = connection.cursor();
cursor.execute("UPDATE TNAME SET COL = 1 WHERE PK = 2045");
connection.close();
```

rollback( )

Signature

```
rollback( )
```

Synopsis

Rolls back any uncommitted statements. This works only if MySQL is set up for transactional processing in this context.

Example

```
connection = MySQLdb.connect(host='carthage', user='test',
                             passwd='test', db='test');
connection._transactional = 1;
cursor = connection.cursor();
cursor.execute("UPDATE TNAME SET COL = 1 WHERE PK = 2045");
try:
    cursor.execute("UPDATE TNAME SET COL = 1 WHERE PK = 3200");
    connection.commit();
except:
    connection.rollback();
connection.close();
```

Cursor Attributes

arraysize

Synopsis

Specifies the number of rows to fetch at a time with the fetchmany( ) method call. By default, this value is set to 1. In other words, fetchmany( ) fetches one row at a time by default.

description

Synopsis

Describes a result column as a read-only sequence of seven-item sequences. Each sequence contains the following values: name, type_code, display_size, internal_size, precision, scale, and null_ok.

rowcount

Synopsis

Provides the number of rows returned through the last executeXXX( ) call. This attribute is read-only and has a value of −1 when no executeXXX( ) call has been made, or the last operation does not provide a row count.

Cursor Methods

callproc( )

Signature

```
callproc(procname [,parameters])
```

Synopsis

This method is not supported by MySQL.

Method: close( )

Signature

```
close( )
```

Synopsis

Closes the cursor explicitly. Once closed, a cursor will throw a `ProgrammingError` if any operation is attempted on the cursor.

Example

```
cursor = connection.cursor( );
cursor.close( );
```

execute( )

Signature

```
cursor = execute(sql [,parameters])
```

Synopsis

Sends arbitrary SQL to MySQL for execution. If the SQL specified is parameterized, the optional second argument is a sequence or mapping containing parameter values for the SQL. Any results or other information generated by the SQL can then be accessed through the cursor.

The parameters of this method may also be lists of tuples to enable you to perform multiple operations at once. This usage is considered deprecated as of the DB-API 2.0 specification. You should use the executemany( ) method instead.

Example

```
connection = MySQLdb.connect(host='carthage', user='test',
                             passwd='test', db='test');
cursor = connection.cursor( );
cursor.execute('SELECT * FROM TNAME');
```

executemany( )

Signature

```
cursor.executemany(sql,parameters)
```

Synopsis

Prepares an SQL statement and sends it to MySQL for execution against all parameter sequences or mappings in the parameters sequence.

Example

```
connection = MySQLdb.connect(host='carthage', user='test',
                             passwd='test', db='test');
cursor = connection.cursor( );
cursor.executemany("INSERT INTO COLOR ( COLOR, ABBREV ) VALUES (%s, %s )",
                   (("BLUE", "BL"), ("PURPLE", "PPL"), ("ORANGE", "ORN")));
```

Method: fetchall( )

Signature

```
rows = cursor.fetchall( )
```

Synopsis

Fetches all remaining rows of a query result as a sequence of sequences.

Example

```
connection = MySQLdb.connect(host='carthage', user='test',
                             passwd='test', db='test');
cursor = connection.cursor( );
cursor.execute("SELECT * FROM TNAME");
for row in cursor.fetchall( ):
    # process row
```

fetchmany( )

Signature

rows = cursor.fetchmany([size])

Synopsis

Fetches the next set of rows of a result set as a sequence of sequences. If no more rows are available, this method returns an empty sequence.

If specified, the *size* parameter dictates how many rows should be fetched. The default value for this parameter is the cursor's *arraysize* value. If the *size* parameter is larger than the number of rows left, the resulting sequence will contain all remaining rows.

Example

```
connection = MySQLdb.connect(host='carthage', user='test',
                             passwd='test', db='test');
cursor = connection.cursor( );
cursor.execute("SELECT * FROM TNAME");
rows = cursor.fetchmany(5);
```

fetchone( )

Signature

row = cursor.fetchone( )

Synopsis

Fetches the next row of a result set returned by a query as a single sequence. This method will return None when no more results exist. It will throw an error if the SQL executed is not a query.

Example

```
connection = MySQLdb.connect(host='carthage', user='test',
                             passwd='test', db='test');
cursor = connection.cursor( );
cursor.execute("SELECT * FROM TNAME");
row = cursor.fetchone( );
print "Key: ", row[0];
print "Value: ", row[1];
```

insert_id( )*

Signature

id = cursor.insert_id( )

Synopsis

Returns the last inserted ID from the most recent INSERT on an AUTO_INCREMENT field.

Example

```
connection = MySQLdb.connect(host='carthage', user='test',
                             passwd='test', db='test');
cursor = connection.cursor();
cursor.execute("INSERT INTO TNAME (COL) VALUES (1)");
id = cursor.insert_id();
```

nextset( )

Signature

```
cursor.nextset( )
```

Synopsis

This method always returns None for MySQL.

setinputsizes( )

Signature

```
cursor.setinputsizes(sizes)
```

Synopsis

This method does nothing in MySQL.

setoutputsize( )

Signature

```
cursor.setoutputsize(size [,column])
```

Synopsis

This method does nothing in MySQL.

Index

Symbols

/* and */
    multiline comments in C, 280
    multiline comments in PHP scripts, 196
&& (AND logical operator), 324
* (asterisk)
    in Boolean mode searches, 54
    extended regular expression, 50
    multiplication operator, 46, 323
    naming tables in ON clause, 103
@ (at sign)
    function call prefix when using
        showerror(), 212
    identifying users to MySQL, 103
\ (backslash)
    escape character, 36
    escape sequences for MySQL, 278
    exporting tab delimited data, 302
& (bitwise AND operator), 323
<< (bitwise left-shift operator), 323
| (bitwise OR operator), 323
>> (bitwise right-shift operator), 323
[] (brackets), extended regular
        expression, 50
^ (caret), extended regular expression, 50
$ (dollar sign)
    extended regular expression, 50
    variable identifier in PHP, 196
"" (double quotes), for quoting
        identifiers, 279
= (equal sign)
    comparison operator, 47
    variable assignment operator in PHP, 197

== (double equals), variable equality test in
        PHP, 197
=== (triple equals), parameter equality test in
        PHP, 198
\\ escape sequence (MySQL), 278
\" escape sequence (MySQL), 278
\% escape sequence (MySQL), 278
\' escape sequence (MySQL), 278
_ escape sequence (MySQL), 278
>= (greater-than-or-equal-to comparison
        operator), 47, 323
<> (inequality operator), 47, 323
!= (inequality operator), 47, 323
< (left angle bracket)
    in Boolean mode searches, 54
    less-than comparison operator, 47, 323
<= (less-than-or-equal-to comparison
        operator), 47, 323
- (minus sign)
    in Boolean mode searches, 54
    subtraction operator, 46, 323
! (NOT logical operator), 324
<=> (null-safe operator), 48
// (one-line comments in PHP scripts), 196
|| (OR logical operator), 324
() parentheses
    in Boolean mode searches, 54
    overriding precedence rules, 48
% (percent)
    modulo of two values, 323
    pattern matching character, 49, 154
. (period), extended regular expression, 50
<?php (PHP begin tag), 194, 196
?> (PHP end tag), 194, 196

We'd like to hear your suggestions for improving our indexes. Send email to *index@oreilly.com*.

+ (plus sign)
    addition operator, 46, 323
    in Boolean mode searches, 54
(pound sign)
    comments in configuration files, 66
    one-line comments in C, 280
    one-line comments in PHP scripts, 196
> (right angle bracket)
    in Boolean mode searches, 54
    greater-than comparison operator, 47,
        323
; (semicolon)
    comments in configuration files, 66
    statement termination character in PHP
        scripts, 196
/ (slash) division operator, 47, 323
~ (tilde), in Boolean mode searches, 54
_ (underscore), pattern matching
        character, 49

Numbers

\0 escape sequence (MySQL), 235, 278
1NF (first normal form), 122
1-to-1 relationships, 127
    designing models for maintainable Perl
        programs, 165
    object/relational modeling, 146
1-to-M relationships, 128, 133
    designing models for maintainable Perl
        programs, 165
    wedding gift registry database, 203
2NF (second normal form), 126, 128
3NF (third normal form), 129

A

ABS() function, 325
absolute naming of database objects, 279
absolute(), 250
accessor methods, 166
ACOS() function, 325
action.php script, 217–220
add routine (aggregate UDF), 263, 264
ADDDATE() function, 325
addition operator (+), 46, 323
address book application, 145
administration tasks, 64–78
AGAINST keyword, 52–54
aggregate functions, 324
    UDFs (user-defined functions), 263–267
        example of, 265–267
aggregation relationship, 165

aliasing
    database objects, 279
    names in SQL statements, 42
ALL join type, 88
ALL keyword, 61
ALL PRIVILEGES privilege, 102
ALTER privilege, 100
ALTER TABLE statement, 33, 280–283
    ending transactions with, 56
--analyze option (isamchk/myisamchk
        utilities), 93
ANALYZE TABLE statement, 283
AND logical operator, 47, 324
ANSI SQL
    comments in, 280
    extended by MySQL, 7
    primary keys/foreign keys, 35
ANSI SQL2
    numeric data types supported by
        MySQL, 312
    specification for, 37
Apache: The Definitive Guide, 224
Apache web servers
    checking for PHP support, 200
    document root of, 194
    installation problems, 201
    resources for, 224
    securing include files, 213
apachectl script, 201
apilevel attribute (MySQLdb module), 394
AppConfig model, 159
application logic
    client/server architecture and, 138
    distributed architecture and, 139
    web architecture and, 141
application servers
    resource protection, 116
    user management issues, 115
applications
    architecture issues, 137–141
    client/server architecture and, 138
    connections and, 141
    distributed architecture and, 139
    object/relational modeling and, 144–146
    performance tuning for, 82–93
    security, 115–118
    support for, 8
    transaction management and, 142–144
    web architecture and, 140
architect role in MySQL installations, 98
architectures in database
        applications, 137–141

brackets ([]), extended regular
expression, 50
bridging technology for database access, 237
Brown, Doug, 23
browsers (see web browsers)
BSD systems, server startup/shutdown
for, 68
buffer overflows, security problems
with, 114
buffers, controlling size of, 93
Bunce, Tim, 147

C

C API (see MySQL, C API)
C commenting, 280
C++ programming, 225
Cache class, 169, 180
cacheMode property (twz JDBC driver), 242
cachePath property (twz JDBC driver), 243
Cache.pm module, 169
caching data in applications, 83
callproc() (MySQLdb module), 399
cardinality in relationships, 124
caret (^), extended regular expression, 50
case sensitivity
    MySQL extended regular expressions, 50
    SQL, 25, 277
CASE statement, 326
Caucho JDBC driver, 238
    configuration information for, 241
CEILING() function, 326
CGI module, Perl, 156–164
    MVC methodology, 157
    sample program, 158–164
CGI Programming with Perl, 157
CGI scripts and execution of arbitrary
    code, 115
CHAR BINARY data type, 33
CHAR data type, 30, 315, 364
    example of, 31
    storage space required by, 33
CHAR() function, 326
character data types, 31–33
CHARACTER SET option (SET
    statement), 305
character sets
    adding through configuration, 270–272
    creating custom character sets, 43
        complex, 272
        simple, 269–272
    editing array definitions, 270
    localized sorting and, 43

mysql_character_set_name() and, 367
    support for, 9
characterEncoding property (GNU JDBC
    driver), 242
CHARACTER_LENGTH() function, 326
CHAR_LENGTH() function, 326
CHARSETS_AVAILABLE list, 271
CHECK operation, 287
CHECKSUM option, 287
Christiansen, Tom, 164
class methods, 165
Class.forName(), 242
clean(), 214
cleaning up database applications, 142, 250
client applications and security issues, 118
client hostnames, specifying, 103
[client] section in configuration files, 66
client/server architecture
    database applications and, 138
    network security issues, 113–115
close() (MySQLdb module), 184, 396, 399
close_api() support function, 231
COALESCE() function, 326
Codd, Dr. E. F., 23, 122
columns
    creating physical databases, 131
    DESCRIBE statement and, 28
    ordering by, 43
    privileges that apply to, 102
    referencing, 278
    specifying as AUTO_INCREMENT, 38
    table creation and, 29
columns_priv table, 105
    primary key of, 110
    schema for, 110
command-line batch loads, 62
COMMENT option, 287
comments
    in configuration files, 66
    in PHP scripts, 196
    used in SQL, 280
COMMIT command, 56
commit() (MySQLdb module), 397
comparison operators, 47, 323
compiling queries, 86
compound variable types in PHP, 196
Comprehensive Perl Archive Network
    (CPAN), 152
compromising individual services and
    network security, 114
CONCAT() function, 326
CONCAT_WS() function, 326

debugRead property (twz JDBC driver), 243
debugWrite property (twz JDBC driver), 243
DECIMAL data type, 313, 364
DECODE() function, 329
DEFAULT attribute, 285
--default-character-set=CHARSET
        option, 43
--defaults-extra-file=filename command-line
        option, 65
degrees in relationships, 124
DEGREES() function, 329
deinit routine
    aggregate UDF, 265
    standard UDF, 255, 261
DELAY_KEY_WRITE option, 287
DELETE privilege, 101
    loading UDFs (user-defined
        functions), 269
DELETE statement, 39, 289
    EXPLAIN SELECT command and, 89–93
    issued by remove method (Model
        class), 166
delimiters and SELECT statement, 302
denormalizing databases, 82
DESC keyword, 43
    limiting query results, 46
Descartes, Alligator, 147
DESCRIBE statement, 28, 290
description attribute (MySQLdb
        module), 398
designing databases, 119–134
detecting table errors, 76
Deutsch, L. Peter, 6
developer role in MySQL installations, 98
development environment, 99
digital certificates, 116
direct compromise
    network security and, 114
    protecting application server against, 117
directory servers, storing users in, 115
dirty reads, 143
DISTINCT keyword, 301
distributed architecture and database
        applications, 139
division operator (/), 47, 323
document root of web servers, 194, 200
doGet(), 253
dollar sign ($)
    extended regular expression, 50
    variable identifier in PHP, 196
doPost(), 253
DOUBLE data type, 313, 364

double quotes (""), for quoting
        identifiers, 279
do...while loops in PHP, 198
downloading MySQL, 14
driver manager connectivity with JDBC
        API, 241–245
DriverManager class, 241–244
drivers, JDBC, 236, 241
    classifications of, 237
DROP DATABASE statement, 27, 291
    ending transactions with, 56
DROP FUNCTION statement, 291
DROP INDEX statement, 291
DROP privilege, 101
DROP statement, 282
DROP TABLE statement, 29, 292
    ending transactions with, 56
DSOs (dynamic shared objects) and PHP
        modules, 201
dumping databases, 74
dynamic database access, 251–253
dynamic shared objects (DSOs) and PHP
        modules, 201
dynamic SQL, processing, 253

E

echo statement (PHP), 196
ELT() function, 329
emigrator role in MySQL installations, 99
ENCODE() function, 329
encoding
    binary data types and, 33
    custom character sets and, 269
ENCRYPT() function, 59, 329
encryption
    as network security measure, 114
    in web database applications, 221
entities, 120
    first normal form, 122
    naming conventions for, 121
    relationships for, 124–126
        refining, 128
        types of, 127
    translating into tables, 131
    unique identifiers for, 123
ENUM data type, 33, 320, 364
environment variables
    configuring MySQL, 65
    $HTTP_ENV_VARS array and, 215
environments for migrating code, 99
eq_ref join type, 88

equal sign (=)
 comparison operator, 47
 variable assignment operator in PHP, 197
error handling
 in JDBC, 250
 managing connections, 142
 MySQL and PHP, 212
 MySQL C API, 228, 231–233
 Perl DBI module diagnostics, 152
 (see also mysql_errno(); mysql_error())
error logs, 70
error parameter (main routine), 260
escape character (\)
 exporting tab delimited data, 302
 INSERT statement and, 36
 MySQL escape sequences, 278
EscapeShellCmd(), 214
/etc/hostconfig file, 69
/etc/logrotate.d directory, 73
/etc/my.cnf file, 65
/etc/rc.d/init.d directory, 68
execute()
 bind variables and, 154
 cursors in Python DB-API and, 184
 MySQLdb module, 399
 processing dynamic SQL, 251, 253
 querying MySQL using Perl DBI, 149
executeBatch(), 190–192
executemany(), 185
 MySQLdb module, 400
executeQuery(), 248
executeUpdate(), 248
EXP() function, 329
EXPLAIN SELECT command, 86–93
EXPLAIN statement, 292
EXPORT_SET() function, 329
--extend-check option, 77
extended regular expressions, 50–52
extra column (EXPLAIN SELECT
 command), 89
EXTRACT() function, 330

F

failover and distributed application
 architecture, 140
fat and thin clients, 139
fetchall(), 185, 192
 MySQLdb module, 400
fetchmany(), 185
 MySQLdb module, 401
fetchone(), 185
 MySQLdb module, 401

fetchrow_arrayref(), 150
 vs. selectall_arrayref(), 155
field delimiters, removing, 302
field types in tables (MySQL C API), 364
FIELD() function, 330
FIELDS ENCLOSED BY keyword
 LOAD statement and, 297
 SELECT statement and, 302
FIELDS ESCAPED BY keyword, 298
FIELDS TERMINATED BY keyword, 297
FILE privilege, 62, 101
finally clause, closing database connections
 with, 251
FIND_IN_SET() function, 330
Fink for Mac OS X, adding PHP and MySQL
 support using, 200
firewalls and network security, 113
first normal form (1NF), 122
flags for fields in tables, 364
 mysql_field_flags() and, 350
FLOAT data type, 314, 364
FLOOR() function, 330
FLUSH statement, 293
 executed by RELOAD privilege, 101
flush-logs command, 73
for loops in PHP, 198
FOR UPDATE clause, 304
foreach statement in PHP, 198
FOREIGN KEY operation, 287
foreign keys, 35
 modeling relationships with, 132–134
 REFERENCES privilege and, 101
<form> environment, using, 195, 220–223
FORMAT() function, 330
formats in parameterized SQL, 186
Fred Fish debugging library, 369
FreeBSD systems
 compiling with gcc (GNU C
 compiler), 227
 server startup/shutdown, 68
FROM clause
 DELETE statement and, 40
 SELECT statement and, 41
FROM_DAYS() function, 330
FROM_UNIXTIME() function, 58, 330
full text searching, 52–55
FULLTEXT keyword, 52–55, 286
functions
 aggregate, 324
 date, 59
 general, 325–337
 SQL, 58–60, 324–337

N

\n escape sequence (MySQL), 278
naming and directory services, 239
native API drivers, 237
natural outer joins, 61
NCHAR data type, 317
net start/net stop commands, 21
networks
    JDBC drivers and network protocols, 237
    security for, 113–115
    topology and security issues, 113
new()
    mysql class, 178
    Publisher class, 168, 176
next(), 249
nextset() (MySQLdb module), 402
Niemeyer, Pat, 236
nonstandard syntaxes supported by
    MySQL, 37
normalizing databases, 82, 122–130
    first normal form, 122
    second normal form, 126, 128
    third normal form, 129
NOT IN operator, 49
NOT LIKE operator, 50
NOT logical operator, 47, 324
NOT NULL attribute, 29, 285
    declaring fields in indexes, 35
    IS_NOT_NULL() macro, 366
NOT REGEXP operator, 50
NOT RLIKE operator, 50
NOW() function, 59, 333
NULL attribute, 48, 286, 364
    mismatch between Java and MySQL, 250
    value for entity instances, 120
    value not returned into arrays in
        PHP, 210
null handlers and mysql_init(), 228
NULL keyword, specifying null literal, 278
NULLIF() function, 333
null-safe operator (<=>), 48
number literals (SQL), 278
NUMERIC data type, 314, 364
    IS_NUM() macro, 366
numeric data types, 31, 312–315
NuSphere, obtaining installation packages
    from, 200

O

object-oriented database management
    systems (OODBMS), 24

object-oriented programming
    creating maintainable Perl
        programs, 164–167
    object/relational modeling, 144–146
object-relational database management
    systems (ORDBMS), 24
objects
    instantiating, 145
    mysql_fetch_object() and, 349
OCT() function, 333
OCTET_LENGTH() function, 333
ODBC
    mysql_odbc_escape_string() and, 381
    mysql_odbc_remove_escape() and, 382
O'Dell, Devon, 224
ON clause (GRANT statement), 102–104
ON keyword, 61
one-and-only-one relationships, 124
--one-database mysql option, 75
one-or-many relationships, 124
one-to-many relationships, 128, 133
    designing models for maintainable Perl
        programs, 165
    wedding gift registry database, 203
one-to-one relationships, 127
    designing models for maintainable Perl
        programs, 165
    object/relational modeling, 146
OODBMS (object-oriented database
    management systems), 24
operating systems
    performance tuning for, 94
    security for, 111
operators, SQL, 46–52, 322–324
OPTIMIZE statement, 299
optimizing performance, 81–94
    using bind variables, 153–156
    slow query logs, 72
OPTIONALLY keyword, 63, 302
OR logical operator, 47, 324
    performing membership tests, 49
Oracle SQL, 24
Oracle vs. MySQL, 9
ORD() function, 334
ORDBMS (object-relational database
    management systems), 24
ORDER BY clause, 43, 304
ORDER BY RAND() clause, 43
Orion application server, 246
Orwant, Jon, 164
outer joins, 8, 60
ownership of binaries, setting up, 16, 19

ROW_FORMAT option, 288
rows
   adding to tables, 36, 247
   deleting, 39, 101
   fetching, 185, 209, 233, 373
   grouping, 44
   limiting query results, 46
   scrollable result sets and, 250
   sequence generation for primary keys, 37
rows column (EXPLAIN SELECT
         command), 89
RPAD() function, 335
RPM (RedHat Package Manager)
   adding PHP and MySQL support, 200
   installing MySQL using, 17
   mysql-log-rotate script, 73
   mysql.server script, 68
rpm utility, installing packages with, 17
RSLock property (twz JDBC driver), 243
RTRIM() function, 335

S

safe_mysqld command, 11, 16, 19, 67
   error logs and, 70
   log rotation and, 73
   starting MySQL
      on Mac OS X systems, 69
      on non-SVR4 Unix systems, 68
--safe-recover option, 77
scalability and distributed application
         architecture, 140
scalar variable types in PHP, 196
scrollable result sets, 249
searching on text elements, 52–55
second normal form (2NF), 126, 128
SECOND() function, 335
SEC_TO_TIME() function, 335
Secure Sockets Layer (SSL)
   data transfer between web browsers/web
         servers, 221
   in MySQL 4.0, 114
   mysql_ssl_cipher(), 390
   mysql_ssl_clear(), 390
   mysql_ssl_set(), 390
security, 95–118
   application security, 115–118
      client applications and, 118
   automatic variable initialization risks, 214
   database security, 95–110
      privilege management, 100–110
      user management, 96–100
   encrypting passwords, 221

include file problems, 213
system security, 111–115
   for hardware, 112
   for networks, 113–115
   for operating systems, 111
security libraries, 117
security tables, storing user privileges
         in, 105–110
SELECT INTO OUTFILE statement, 101
SELECT privilege, 101
SELECT statement, 40, 301–305
   aliasing and, 42
   EXPLAIN SELECT command and, 86–93
   functions in, 58
   using with INSERT statement, 296
   joining tables, 41
   limiting results, 45
   ordering/grouping results, 42–45
   sending queries using static methods, 166
   UNION clause and, 61
selectall_arrayref(), 155
SelectResource.properties file, 245
semicolon (;)
   comments in configuration files, 66
   statement termination character in PHP
         scripts, 196
sequences, generating, 37
SERIALIZABLE transaction isolation
         level, 144
server instances and configuration files, 65
server variables and $HTTP_SERVER_VARS
         array, 215
servers
   application
      resource protection, 116
      user management issues, 115
   backups, 73
   log files, 70–73
   performance tuning for, 93
   privileges that apply to, 102
   recovery
      from backups, 75
      from crashes, 76–78
   security issues for, 112
   starting
      binary distributions, 16
      source distributions, 19
      Windows distributions, 20–22
   startup/shutdown, 67–70
   in Windows binary distribution, 20
Services control panel, 21
session variables and $HTTP_SESSION_
         VARS array, 215

useradd utility
  binary distributions, 15
  source distributions, 18
user-defined functions (see UDFs)
useUnicode property (GNU JDBC
        driver), 242
/usr/backups directory, 75
/usr/lib directory, 268

V

value options, with SELECT statement, 323
VARCHAR BINARY data type, 33
VARCHAR data type, 30, 318, 364
  example of, 32
  storage space required by, 33
variable-length data type, 32
variables, automatic initialization of, 194
  security risks with, 214
VERSION() function, 337
versions of MySQL, installing, 13
View layer (MVC methodology), 157–159

W

Wall, Larry, 164
wasNull(), 250
web architecture and database
        applications, 140
web browsers
  cookies and, 216
  header() function and, 216, 220
  HTML <form> and, 195
  requesting scripts for PHP
        processing, 199
  retrieving data using, 194
  securing user data, 215
*Web Database Applications with PHP and
        MySQL*, 224
web servers, 138, 140
  document root of, 194, 200
  Perl CGI module and, 156–164
  (see also Apache web servers)
wedding gift registry database, 203–205
WEEK() function, 337
WEEKDAY() function, 337
Welling, Luke, 224
WHERE clause
  bind_where() and, 168, 173–175
  EXPLAIN SELECT command and, 89–92
  functions in, 58

Generic Where method and, 166
logical operators and, 47
make_where() and, 173–175
performance pros/cons of indexes, 85
phantom reads and, 143
Primary Key utility and, 167
SELECT statement and, 41, 303
UPDATE statement and, 39
vs. HAVING clause, 45
while loops in PHP, 198
Widenius, Michael "Monty", 5
wildcards
  determining user access rights, 106
  specifying host names with, 103
Williams, Hugh E., 224
Wilson, Torben, 224
Windows 2000 systems
  installing MySQL on, 21
  server startup/shutdown, 70
  shared libraries on, 268
Windows 9x systems
  installing MySQL on, 20
Windows NT systems
  installing MySQL on, 21
  server startup/shutdown, 70
  shared libraries on, 268
Windows systems
  configuration files on, 65
  error logs on, 70
  installing MySQL on, 20–22
  installing PHP on, 202
  shared libraries on, 268
winmysqladmin.exe utility, 21
WITH GRANT OPTION keyword, 102
write locks, 57

X

XML files, building with Python
        DB-API, 187–192

Y

YEAR data type, 320, 364
YEAR() function, 337

Z

\z escape sequence (MySQL), 278
Zmievski, Andrei, 224

About the Authors

George Reese has taken an unusual path into business software development. After earning a B.A. in philosophy from Bates College in Lewiston, Maine, George went off to Hollywood, where he worked on television shows such as *The People's Court* and ESPN's *Up Close*. The L.A. riots convinced him to return to Maine, where he finally became involved with software development and the Internet. George has since specialized in the development of Internet-oriented Java enterprise systems and the strategic role of technology in business processes. He is the author of *Database Programming with JDBC and Java* (O'Reilly) and the world's first JDBC driver, the mSQL-JDBC driver for mSQL. He currently lives in Minneapolis, Minnesota with his wife, Monique, and three cats, Misty, Gypsy, and Tia. He makes a living as the National Practice Director of Technology Strategy in J. Walter Thompson's digital branch in Minneapolis, Imaginet.

Randy Jay Yarger is the chief architect for Web Elite in Ann Arbor, Michigan. With over a decade of development experience, Randy spends most of his time designing cutting-edge solutions for business problems that, frankly, should have been solved before he was born. Randy lives in Ann Arbor with three cats, a dog, and lots of books.

Tim King has been working with computers since the early 1980s, when he programmed games on his Commodore 64 computer and founded a computer club in his high school. He earned a bachelor's degree in computer science from the University of Minnesota Institute of Technology in 1991. While there, he taught Unix and *vi* classes and was the leader of a ragtag group of *vi* devotees called the "VI Zombies." Presently, Tim is a software consultant in San Francisco, California, specializing in database and web technologies.

Hugh E. Williams is a senior lecturer in the School of Computer Science and IT at RMIT University in Melbourne, Australia, where he has taught since 1994. He currently teaches classes on file structures and database systems, web database applications, and research methods. His research interests include building better search engines, bioinformatics, and designing faster data structures. When not at work, Hugh likes to go running, watch Richmond play footy, and follow the test cricket. Hugh has a Ph.D. from RMIT University.

Colophon

Our look is the result of reader comments, our own experimentation, and feedback from distribution channels. Distinctive covers complement our distinctive approach to technical topics, breathing personality and life into potentially dry subjects.

The animal on the cover of *Managing and Using MySQL*, Second Edition, is a kingfisher. This type of bird can be found all over the world, including North America, Europe, Africa, and New Zealand, with the greatest numbers being found in southeast Asia. There are over 80 species of kingfishers, which range in size from five to eighteen inches and vary in color.

These typically long-billed birds pair for life and are considered to be very territorial. Their nests are long and tunnel-shaped, and are often found in exposed tree roots or water banks.

Most kingfishers live along the banks of rivers or lakes, as the primary staple of their diet is fish. To catch its prey, a kingfisher will perch on a branch above water, watch for a fish, hover for a moment, and then dive headfirst into the water, grabbing the fish in its beak, and heading back up to the surface. The process takes about a third of a second. The kingfisher's diet also includes spiders, insects, and small amphibians.

Linley Dolby was the production editor and copyeditor, and Matt Hutchinson was the proofreader, for *Managing and Using MySQL*, Second Edition. Sarah Sherman and Claire Cloutier provided quality control. Judy Hoer wrote the index. Phil Dangler and Sarah Sherman provided production assistance.

Edie Freedman designed the cover of this book. The cover image is a 19th-century engraving from Cuvier's Animals. Emma Colby produced the cover layout with QuarkXPress 4.1 using Adobe's ITC Garamond font.

David Futato designed the interior layout. Neil Walls converted the files from Microsoft Word to FrameMaker 5.5.6 using tools created by Mike Sierra. The text font is Linotype Birka; the heading font is Adobe Myriad Condensed; and the code font is LucasFont's TheSans Mono Condensed. The illustrations that appear in the book were produced by Robert Romano and Jessamyn Read using Macromedia Free-Hand 9 and Adobe Photoshop 6. The tip and warning icons were drawn by Christopher Bing. This colophon was written by Nicole Arigo.

Related Titles Available from O'Reilly

Open Source Database

High Performance MySQL

MySQL Cookbook

MySQL Pocket Reference

MySQL Reference Manual

Practical PostgreSQL

Web Database Apps with PHP and MySQL, *2nd Edition*

Keep in touch with O'Reilly

1. Download examples from our books

To find example files for a book, go to:

www.oreilly.com/catalog

select the book, and follow the "Examples" link.

2. Register your O'Reilly books

Register your book at *register.oreilly.com*

Why register your books?
Once you've registered your O'Reilly books you can:

- Win O'Reilly books, T-shirts or discount coupons in our monthly drawing.
- Get special offers available only to registered O'Reilly customers.
- Get catalogs announcing new books (US and UK only).
- Get email notification of new editions of the O'Reilly books you own.

3. Join our email lists

Sign up to get topic-specific email announcements of new books and conferences, special offers, and O'Reilly Network technology newsletters at:

elists.oreilly.com

It's easy to customize your free elists subscription so you'll get exactly the O'Reilly news you want.

4. Get the latest news, tips, and tools

www.oreilly.com

- "Top 100 Sites on the Web"—PC Magazine
- CIO Magazine's Web Business 50 Awards

Our web site contains a library of comprehensive product information (including book excerpts and tables of contents), downloadable software, background articles, interviews with technology leaders, links to relevant sites, book cover art, and more.

5. Work for O'Reilly

Check out our web site for current employment opportunities:

jobs.oreilly.com

6. Contact us

O'Reilly & Associates
1005 Gravenstein Hwy North
Sebastopol, CA 95472 USA

TEL: 707-827-7000 or 800-998-9938
      (6am to 5pm PST)

FAX: 707-829-0104

order@oreilly.com
For answers to problems regarding your order or our products. To place a book order online, visit:

www.oreilly.com/order_new

catalog@oreilly.com
To request a copy of our latest catalog.

booktech@oreilly.com
For book content technical questions or corrections.

corporate@oreilly.com
For educational, library, government, and corporate sales.

proposals@oreilly.com
To submit new book proposals to our editors and product managers.

international@oreilly.com
For information about our international distributors or translation queries. For a list of our distributors outside of North America check out:

international.oreilly.com/distributors.html

adoption@oreilly.com
For information about academic use of O'Reilly books, visit:

academic.oreilly.com